Copyright and Information Privacy

Ai miei genitori, Oneglia ed Enzo e a mio fratello, Vittorio:
per tutti i 'grazie' che non ho detto

Copyright and Information Privacy

Conflicting Rights in Balance

Federica Giovanella

Faculty of Law, University of Trento, Italy

Cheltenham, UK • Northampton, MA, USA

Published by
Edward Elgar Publishing Limited
The Lypiatts
15 Lansdown Road
Cheltenham
Glos GL50 2JA
UK

Edward Elgar Publishing, Inc.
William Pratt House
9 Dewey Court
Northampton
Massachusetts 01060
USA

A catalogue record for this book
is available from the British Library

Library of Congress Control Number: 2017947093

This book is available electronically in the **Elgar**online
Law subject collection
DOI 10.4337/9781785369360

ISBN 978 1 78536 935 3 (cased)
ISBN 978 1 78536 936 0 (eBook)

Typeset by Columns Design XML Ltd, Reading
Printed and bound in Great Britain by TJ International Ltd, Padstow

Contents

Acknowledgements

I have been staring at my laptop for ages, trying to find the best words with which to start these acknowledgements. But, of course, I have not been able to find anything meaningful, or even sufficient, to express what publishing this book means for me.

When Professor Roberto Caso first introduced me to the issue of the conflict between copyright and privacy, I was not sure whether I wanted to work on such a topic and what exactly I could write on it. In fact, the issue has proved to be not only highly topical, but also a very thorny, intricate question that has succeeded in holding my attention and keeping me busy for many years. Although I have worked on other subjects – and will, I hope, do so in the future too – the issue of 'balancing rights' will always constitute my initiation into research. I want to wholeheartedly thank Roberto for his help and his guidance, but most of all for encouraging me to follow the path of academic research (even though it may ultimately lead me to despair).

Many people have helped me in different ways throughout this work. I would first like to thank my family: my parents – Enzo and Oneglia – and my brother Vittorio, to whom this book is dedicated. No words can describe all they have done for me.

I have also been lucky enough to meet some very precious fellow researchers during my work at the University of Trento. Above all I want to thank Marta Tomasi and Lucia Busatta for their constant presence, patience and help. In other words: for their friendship. A big thank you goes also to Rossana Ducato, Serena Tomasi and Paolo Guarda, and to the members of the 'LawTech group'.

This work has benefited from the feedback of experienced scholars: to David Lametti, Giuseppe Bellantuono and Giorgio Resta I send my gratitude. I would also like to thank the anonymous referees for Edward Elgar, who made many insightful comments, and have helped me to write a better book. And thank you, too, to Edward Elgar Publishing, and John-Paul McDonald and David Fairclough, for their professionalism and understanding.

A warm thank you goes also to Rachel Murphy, whose careful proofreading of my English was indispensable to make this book totally understandable (this page included).

The completion of this book would have not been possible without the generosity of the Max Planck Institut für Innovation und Wettbewerb in Munich, which awarded me a scholarship in 2015, allowing me to take advantage of its premises and immense library. The research periods I spent at the Centre for Intellectual Property Policy at McGill University in Montreal were also invaluable for my work.

While I now have that typical sense of relief that follows the accomplishment of a project, I still distinctly remember the feeling of inadequacy that has dogged me all through the years that it has taken me to finish this book. On every single day of that – pretty long – journey I was supported unconditionally by my husband. No page of this book would have been written if he had not been there; he is the only person who has done more than I to bring this book into existence. Matteo, this book is mainly yours! (Well ... all views and errors remain my own).

Trento, 1 April 2017

Introduction

RATIONALE, METHOD AND SCOPE OF THE RESEARCH

Justice holding a set of scales in her hand is the classic representation of the idea that rights have to be balanced against one another. The scales evoke the idea of weighing opposite factors to reach a fair, stable solution. In legal terms – and in this book – balancing is the procedure by which courts take conflicting rights and their intrinsic weight into consideration in order to estimate which are the 'heavier' and must therefore prevail over the other(s).[1] This method of judging has gradually been endorsed – first by scholars and then by courts – as a way to adjudicate in an increasing number of decisions. Although the very idea of 'balancing' is by no means easily accepted or defined by legal scholars, it is now established practice and here to stay.

The aim of this book is to offer a humble contribution to the study of the balancing that the courts engage in; I intend to demonstrate how the decisions of judges are affected by what I call the 'conceptions' of the colliding rights. By 'conception' I mean the essence of the idea that a legal system has about that right. In order to understand the conception of a given right, one must look at the entire system of norms and policies introduced to enhance or to limit that same right. The conception of a right is 'strong' when that right is safeguarded through tools that are peculiar to it, such as – for instance – specific remedies or tribunals, or if it is protected by an independent authority. The conception of a right describes (and is described by) the level of its protection: the more a right is protected, the stronger the conception of that right is. And vice versa.

I use a case study in my attempt to shed light on the ways in which judges balance conflicting rights. The book focuses in particular on the conflict between copyright and information privacy. In recent decades

---

[1] Giorgio Pino, *Diritti e interpretazione. Il ragionamento giuridico nello Stato costituzionale* (Il Mulino 2010) 173. A critique of this metaphor can be found in Patrick M McFadden, 'The Balancing Test' [1988] Boston College Law Review 585, 628–632.

technological advances have caused these two rights to collide more and more frequently. The research illustrated in this book is centred around a selection of lawsuits in which copyright holders tried to enforce their rights against Internet users suspected of illegal file-sharing. A common feature of these cases is that users were usually only partially identifiable through their Internet Protocol (IP) addresses; their real identities were only known to the ISPs (Internet Service Providers) who were providing their Internet connections. The copyright holders therefore asked the ISPs to disclose the users' real identities. Some ISPs refused to collaborate, forcing copyright holders to sue them in order to obtain a judicial provision obliging the disclosure of users' data. A vibrant conflict between users' data protection and copyright holders' enforceable rights arose.

The conflicts analysed share two peculiarities. First, in each of the countries in my study, although in different fashions, the colliding rights are considered to be equally ranked and both are constitutionally protected. Second, judges are allowed some leeway in deciding which right should prevail: the norms do not clearly state whether or not one right must necessarily be dominant.

The cases analysed have another common trait: they were all decided by national 'lower courts', meaning by courts other than Supreme Courts or Constitutional Courts. To date, most of the research done on balancing relates to Supreme Courts; I have chosen instead to concentrate on 'lower courts', which also, on occasion, find themselves confronting the issue of balancing rights.

From a methodological point of view, this book is built on a case study in which judicial decisions are analysed in detail in order to understand the influence of conceptions of copyright and informational privacy on courts' decisions. The judgments examined were given in three different countries, the US, Canada and Italy. These jurisdictions were chosen for several reasons. Since the US is one of the biggest, most powerful countries in the world, its understanding of privacy and copyright has been influencing the rest of the world for at least a century. Europe's influence has also been considerable. Within the EU, the book focuses particularly on Italy, taking it as an example of the effects of Europeanization on both copyright and privacy regulations.[2]

My analyses of the Italian decisions also take into account the European cases on the same issues. However, the European level can

---

[2]   As will be demonstrated throughout the book, Italy has implemented most EU Directives on copyright and privacy almost verbatim.

only be considered to a limited extent, given that this book is primarily a study on the decisions taken by 'lower courts', in order to demonstrate that the methods they apply are very similar to those applied by Supreme Courts when balancing conflicting rights in constitutional cases. Since the decisions of the EU Court of Justice are more properly grouped with those of Constitutional and Supreme Courts they cannot be placed squarely within the overall frame of this book. This is why my focus is on a single Member State (Italy).

The Canadian system serves as my *tertium comparationis*. Canada is in many ways a middle ground between the EU and the US as it has historically mixed elements from each. With regard to both copyright and privacy, it represents a different model, in which both the European and the American approaches are partly applied; Canada thus serves as a useful aid in the comparison between the US and the EU.

The research upon which this book is based demonstrates the extent to which judges are influenced by the conception of each right when faced with conflicts between them. While the conception of rights is not – and cannot be – the only approach taken by judges when reaching conclusions, it is undoubtedly an important factor that carries weight when courts are balancing conflicting rights.

The results proposed in this monograph can be extended to similar cases involving other colliding rights, and conceptual balancing can be seen as one of the many concurring causes of any one court judgment. It is, in the end, just a way of describing the act of balancing that judges are called upon to carry out. Conceptual balancing can be applied to judicial reasoning regardless of the country in which a court is operating. In fact, comparing the solutions adopted in different countries is the best way to reveal the process of conceptual balancing; it is only by understanding a particular legal system's conception of the rights involved in a case that conceptual balancing can be understood.

This book builds upon the existing literature in its comparison of the three legal systems. Although it does not presume to propose new methodologies, or new approaches to comparative law,[3] it attempts to make a useful contribution to the study of this approach to legal science.

---

[3] Countless articles and books have been written on comparative law and its methodologies. Consider Rodolfo Sacco, 'Legal Formants: A Dynamic Approach to Comparative Law' [1991] AJCL 1; and [1991] AJCL 343; Konrad Zweigert and Hein Kötz, *An Introduction to Comparative Law* (3rd edn, OUP 1998); Mathias Reimann and Reinhard Zimmermann (eds), *The Oxford Handbook of Comparative Law* (OUP 2006); Pier Giuseppe Monateri (ed), *Methods of*

The research contained in this book is, inevitably, limited by certain factors. First of all, a number of basic structural differences exist between the three legal systems analysed: many aspects of the creation and interpretation of law, and of the selection and organization of the judiciary, differ sharply between the three countries. Perhaps the most immediate, and obvious, differences are those between countries that belong to the common law family and countries that belong to the civil law family.[4] Following this classification, the approaches of the US and Canada probably have commonalities not shared with the Italian system. The creative role of judges, for instance, is much greater in common law countries. However, judges create law in any country.[5]

My research is not intended to question the role of judges or that of legislators. With regard to judges, I would not dream of opining on which right should prevail or by what means judges should resolve conflicts. As for legislators, the existence of ambiguous norms, and their interpretation, are ontological characteristics of all legal systems.[6] Ambiguity may actually be desirable, since it allows different situations to be encompassed by a single norm, as required in subsumption.

In other words, the study is not prescriptive; it is not looking for, nor does it propose, an optimal solution. Instead, it aims to shed some light on the way judges balance conflicting rights and, in particular, to highlight how the conception of rights may play a decisive role in judicial decisions.

The book contains five chapters, and Chapters 1 and 5 are conceptually linked to one another. Chapter 1 provides a literature review on the theme of 'balancing' and collocates the book in the field of comparative law

---

Comparative Law (Edward Elgar Publishing 2012); H Patrick Glenn, *Legal Traditions of the World* (OUP 2014).

[4] I am referring to the classification proposed by René David and John EC Brierley, *Major Legal Systems in the World Today* (3rd edn, Stevens and Sons 1985) 17ff. Zweigert and Kötz (n 3) 63ff give an overview of the different classifications proposed by the most prominent scholars in the field of comparative law. On the decline of the idea of 'families' in comparative law, consider H Patrick Glenn, 'Comparative Legal Families and Comparative Legal Traditions' in Reimann and Zimmermann (eds) (n 3) 422. More recently by the same author, Glenn, *Legal Traditions of the World* (n 3). See also Jaakko Husa, 'The Future of Legal Families' [2016] Oxford Handbooks Online: Law 1, <www.oxford handbooks.com/view/10.1093/oxfordhb/9780199935352.001.0001/oxfordhb-978 0199935352-e-26?print=pdf> accessed 10 February 2017.

[5] David and Brierley (n 4) 117ff.

[6] Giorgio Pino, 'Conflitto e bilanciamento tra diritti fondamentali. Una mappa dei problemi' [2016] Etica & Politica/Ethics & Politics 1, 17–18.

and, in particular, within studies on judicial decisions. The chapter then introduces the conflicting rights that will be analysed and defines the scope of the research; lastly, it presents the idea of 'conceptual balancing', key to the entire book. To illustrate the conceptions of copyright and information privacy, Chapters 2 and 3 focus on the main features of the regulation of copyright (Chapter 2) and privacy (Chapter 3) in each of the three systems. Chapter 4 analyses in detail the judicial decisions that constitute the case studies of the research. It examines the procedures applied and the reasoning of the judges in the cases decided in the three systems.

Drawing on the previous chapters, in Chapter 5 I illustrate the conception of copyright and privacy in the three systems, before setting out my conclusions and explaining how 'conceptual balancing' constitutes a new lens through which judicial decisions can be read.

1.   The thorny issue of balancing rights

1. THE THORNY ISSUE OF BALANCING RIGHTS: THEORIES AND APPROACHES

1.1   What Does 'Balancing Rights' Mean?

The role of the courts is generally considered to be the resolving of conflicts between rights, and this is indeed their predominant task: deciding which right – and which part – must prevail in each and any of the lawsuits they judge. However, lawsuits are not all alike and some seem to entail a different process, that of balancing rights.

As explained in the Introduction to this book, the idea of balancing goes back to the old times where Justice was depicted as holding a set of scales in her hands. Balancing is considered in this work as the method by which courts 'weigh' conflicting interests and rights in order to find a stable solution; a solution that requires judges to tell which of the rights is the heaviest.[1]

Balancing is central not only to law, but also to life in general. It mirrors what happens in – particularly democratic – societies.[2] Balancing has been studied in detail by numerous legal scholars from different perspectives, such as philosophy and constitutional law, mainly with regard to Constitutional Courts.[3] More precisely, scholars have consistently focused on how constitutional courts weigh conflicting rights when

---

[1]   Giorgio Pino, *Diritti e interpretazione. Il ragionamento giuridico nello Stato costituzionale* (Il Mulino 2010) 173. For a critique consider Patrick M McFadden, 'The Balancing Test' [1988] Boston College Law Review 585, 628–632.

[2]   Aharon Barak, *Proportionality. Constitutional Rights and Their Limitations* (CUP 2012) 345–346.

[3]   The term 'Constitutional Courts' is here applied to courts that have the power to decide on the constitutionality of statutes and laws. Hence, it includes not only the Italian Constitutional Court but both the American and the Canadian Supreme Courts as well. It also includes the European Court of Justice, which can strike down the laws of Member States' if they collide with EU laws and principles.

they need to decide on the legitimacy of a norm the constitutionality of which has been questioned.

This section provides an overview of the main theories concerning the balancing of rights; it is not intended as an exhaustive illustration of all the existing theories and approaches,[4] but rather as the presentation of a bird's-eye view of the most influential and recent of these theories; its aims are twofold. First, to demonstrate that the vast majority of scholars have paid only scant attention to the fact that lower courts also balance conflicting rights, often in a similar way to that followed by constitutional courts.[5] Second, to create a basis for an understanding of the subsequent sections (and chapters), in which the conflict between privacy and copyright will be explained in detail, taking some case studies as examples.

The task of balancing rights belongs both to courts and to the legislator. In setting norms, the legislative power determines what right should prevail in the specific cases where the norm is applicable; the choices made by legislators thus constitute a balance made 'in advance', which is generally applicable to all the possible lawsuits in which the norm will be applied by courts. For their part, the courts also balance rights; however, this does not mean that they become substitutes for the legislative branch.[6]

The cases in which courts balance rights have been grouped by scholars into two main classes, according to whether the rights conflict 'directly' or collide 'indirectly'.[7] Rights conflict directly when they collide in the absence of a pre-existing 'rule of conflict'; the conflict is indirect when it has already been regulated by law, so that it is possible

---

[4] For a deeper understanding of the phenomenon of balancing I shall make reference to the books and articles cited throughout this section.

[5] For instance, Emilio Betti considered the issue of the resolution of conflicts of interest as a key role of any judge: Emilio Betti, *Interpretazione della legge e degli atti giuridici* (Giuffrè 1949) 18.

[6] '[I]n balancing, courts necessarily become legislators and administrators': Alec Stone Sweet, *The Judicial Construction of Europe* (OUP 2004) 11. Criticism from this point of view comes from T Alexander Aleinikoff, 'Constitutional Law in the Age of Balancing' [1987] Yale Law Journal 943, 984ff; Melvine B Nimmer, 'The Right to Speak From *Times* to *Time*: First Amendment Theory applied to Libel and Misapplied to Privacy' [1968] California Law Review 935, 947: 'definitional balancing ... may be criticized as a form of judicial lawmaking, and as such a usurpation of the legislative function'.

[7] Pino, *Diritti e interpretazione* (n 1) 202–203.

to consider this balancing as a 'second order', or 'meta-balancing',[8] i.e. further balancing, subsequent to that of the legislator.

In the first class of cases two rights enter into direct conflict with one another. In the second class, a right is limited by means of a norm that includes the rules of the conflict; the adoption of that norm is justified as a way of protecting another conflicting right. This means that the first right will need to be balanced not only with the conflicting right, but also with other 'justifications' that support the rule governing the conflict. The clashing rights, in these cases, are therefore not on the same level, since the legislator has already stated that one should cede to the other.[9]

Another possible classification of the conflict between rights considers four situations, which can be either intra- or inter-rights conflicts, involving either total or partial clashes. Intra-rights conflicts are cases where two aspects of the same right, or two scenarios involving that right, clash; inter-rights conflicts are situations where two different rights collide. Clashes can be total or partial: in a total conflict, when one of the two rights prevails, the other must succumb totally. In a partial conflict, on the other hand, a case-by-case approach is still possible, and neither of the two rights must necessarily be totally disregarded.[10]

As the cases analysed here involve informational privacy versus copyright, the conflict is clearly inter-rights; it is also partial, as 'case-by-case regulation' is possible.

The concept and theory of balancing have existed for more than a century. In fact, while courts – especially the US Supreme Court and its German counterpart the Bundesverfassungsgericht – started to rely on the idea and the mechanism of balancing in the mid-twentieth century, scholars had already begun to develop theories of balancing and weighing interests in the early years of the century.[11] The work of legal

---

8   Ibid 202.
9   This explanation is that of Pino, ibid 203.
10   Lorenzo Zucca, 'Conflicts of Fundamental Rights as Constitutional Dilemmas' in Eva Brems (ed), *Conflicts between Fundamental Rights* (Intersentia 2008) 19, 26–27. Riccardo Guastini, 'Teoria e ideologia dell'interpretazione costituzionale' [2006] Giurisprudenza costituzionale 743, 774–775 introduces a similar classification.
11   Barak, *Proportionality* (n 2) 178ff (consider also the graph at 182 that summarizes how proportionality migrated from Germany to other countries); Jacco Bomhoff, *Balancing Constitutional Rights. The Origin and Meaning of Postwar Legal Discourse* (CUP 2013) 31ff; Vincent Luizzi, 'Balancing of Interests in Courts' [1980] Jurimetrics 373, 374–376, 380–381; Aleinikoff (n 6) 955–963; McFadden (n 1) 603–611; Alberto Vespaziani, *Interpretazioni del bilanciamento dei diritti fondamentali* (Cedam 2002); Alec Stone Sweet and Jud

scholars is also thought to be one of the factors prompting the superior courts to consider, and begin to adopt, this new approach.[12]

In order to enable an understanding of balancing, a primary distinction is habitually made between *rules* and *principles*. This distinction is usually attributed to Ronald Dworkin[13] but probably pre-dates him.[14] The theorization, which is all but undisputed,[15] is based on a number of diverse features exhibited by rules and principles. In particular, principles are held to be norms of very high importance on which the entire legal system is based, and which are characterized by vagueness, indeterminacy and high generality; they proclaim the values and state the goals that legislators should pursue. Rules, in contrast, are considered to be linked to specific cases, indicating precise conduct to be followed; they could allow, forbid or oblige a subject to engage in a specific conduct.[16] Conflicts between rules might be resolved with the classical tool of 'subsumption'[17] and/or with the usual criteria of *lex posteriori derogat priori* and *lex specialis derogat legi generali*.[18] While rules could *only* be applicable to cases, and could not be weighed, principles would instead

---

Mathews, 'Proportionality Balancing and Global Constitutionalism' [2008] Columbia Journal of Transnational Law 72, 98ff.

[12] Aleinikoff (n 6) 952ff recognized three main causes of the US Supreme Court's adoption of the balancing approach: a political, a judicial and an academic imperative.

[13] Consider his seminal work: Ronald Dworkin, *Taking Rights Seriously* (Duckworth 1977).

[14] Robert Alexy, *A Theory of Constitutional Rights* (Julian Rivers tr, OUP 2002) 45ff.

[15] Dworkin (n 13) 24ff. See also, with a slightly different approach, Robert Alexy, 'The Construction of Constitutional Rights' [2010] Law & Ethics of Human Rights 21, and more generally, Alexy, *A Theory of Constitutional Rights* (n 14) 57ff; Roberto Bin, *Diritti e argomenti. Il bilanciamento degli interessi nella giurisprudenza costituzionali* (Giuffrè 1992) 9–18. Against the classification of 'rights as principles': Bernhard Schlink, 'Proportionality (1)' in Michel Rosenfeld and András Sajó (eds), *The Oxford Handbook of Comparative Constitutional Law* (OUP 2012) 725, 730.

[16] Pino, *Diritti e interpretazione* (n 1) 52–53; Alexy, *A Theory of Constitutional Rights* (n 14) 45ff and 86 ff. See also Barak, *Proportionality* (n 2) 86–89. Norms can sometimes assume the role of principles or of rules, according to Luigi Mengoni, *Ermeneutica e dogmatica giuridica* (Giuffrè 1996) 131–133.

[17] Robert Alexy, 'Constitutional Rights, Balancing, and Rationality' [2003] Ratio Juris 131, 133–134; Alexy, 'The Construction' (n 15) 21.

[18] Aharon Barak, 'Proportionality (2)' in Rosenfeld and Sajó (n 15) 738, 740; Robert Alexy, 'On Balancing and Subsumption. A Structural Comparison' [2003] Ratio Juris 433, 433–435.

need to be weighed in order to ascertain which was the heavier, i.e. the more important.[19] Indeed, 'rules are applicable in an all-or-nothing fashion',[20] meaning that they can be either applied or not applied (there is no room for fudging); while principles need to be weighed, to be measured. While principles have the dimension of 'weight' or 'importance', which means that when they clash they have to be weighed one against the other, rules do not.[21]

This sharp distinction between the two categories has been contested by many scholars, who claim that although there may be differences, norms cannot be easily divided into one of the two categories. Distinctions are more blurred than they appear at first sight.[22] Some scholars also hold that the same norm could be interpreted as a principle or as a rule, according to which specific argumentative mechanism (such as 'balancing') the court wanted to apply.[23]

The final aim of distinguishing between rules and principles is to create an axiological hierarchy among them, in which the former have to conform to, and not contrast with, the latter.[24] Balancing is itself an argumentative technique that allows for the establishment of an axiological hierarchy between two norms, where one of the two is considered to prevail over the other, without necessarily invalidating it.[25] Balancing allows the prevalence of one right over another to be decided in one particular case: it is not possible to state the prevalence of a given right in advance and/or 'once and for all'.[26]

---

[19]   Pino, *Diritti e interpretazione* (n 1) 52–53.

[20]   Dworkin (n 13) 24.

[21]   Ibid 26.

[22]   Pino, *Diritti e interpretazione* (n 1) 53–56, 72–76.

[23]   Ibid 72–76; Bin (n 15) 11–13; Guastini (n 10) 768. An Italian scholar proposes an additional classification that differentiates between constitutional principles and constitutional values: while principles are the normative formalization of cultural, ethical and moral values, values themselves would result in 'void concepts' if they were not incorporated into norms. Cf. Gino Scaccia, 'Il bilanciamento degli interessi come tecnica di controllo costituzionale' [1998] Giurisprudenza Costituzionale 3953, 3956.

[24]   In the words of Pino, *Diritti e interpretazione* (n 1) 73.

[25]   Ibid 178.

[26]   Bin (n 15) 33–42; Alexy, *A Theory of Constitutional Rights* (n 14) 96ff; Scaccia (n 23) 3964. There are nonetheless rights which are always given higher importance: Giorgio Pino, 'Conflitto e bilanciamento tra diritti fondamentali. Una mappa dei problemi' [2016] Etica & Politica/Ethics & Politics 1, 14; the same can be said with regard to freedom of speech in the American system. See

Balancing consists in finding an equilibrated solution between the two sides of a set of scales, protecting both rights, trying not to sacrifice one in favour of the other; the solution adopted should be the one that allows one of the rights to be applied with the least sacrifice of the other.[27] I have been using the term 'rights' to indicate two conflicting claims brought before a court. In many cases, scholars and courts have used the term 'interests',[28] understood as interests that obtain some normative acknowledgement. However, I believe that the term 'rights' is more straightforward and does not involve any substantive change.[29] More particularly, the rights that enter into conflict and need to be balanced usually have the same hierarchical value; they may be, for instance, constitutionally entrenched rights.[30] This is also true for the conflicting rights involved in the cases analysed here: as will be demonstrated in Chapters 2 and 3, both copyright and privacy are said to enjoy constitutional protection in each of the three systems examined, although in a different fashion.[31]

Clearly, not all constitutional rights have the same strength and importance: some can be considered 'superior' and should therefore prevail when they clash with other constitutional rights.[32]

I hope that, as we examine the cases below, the fact that a specific right can be considered prevalent in a given case, and not prevalent in another, even when the same rights are conflicting, will emerge clearly. This variance may depend on the different patterns of a given right.

---

below in this section on the difference between 'ad hoc' and 'definitional' balancing.

[27] Pino, *Diritti e interpretazione* (n 1) 183. See also Robert Alexy's theory below Section 1.2.

[28] 'Interests' were considered by Roscoe Pound, 'A Theory of Social Interests' [1943] Harvard Law Review 1. See also Theodore M Benditt, 'Law and the Balancing of Interests' [1975] Social Theory and Practice 321. Consider also the distinction made by Scaccia (n 23) 3954–3957.

[29] In this sense I share the view of Pino, *Diritti e interpretazione* (n 1) 185.

[30] Ibid 186. Scaccia (n 23) 3957. This view clearly entails the prominence of the Constitution and of constitutionality rights over other rights and norms. This is something that I take for granted here, as a common principle of the current legal systems of the three countries analysed.

[31] See specifically Chapter 2, Section 2 and Chapter 3, Section 2.

[32] Gustavo Ghidini, *Profili evolutivi del diritto industriale* (Giuffrè 2015) 62. See also Barak, 'Proportionality (2)' (n 18) 752ff. The author recalls the classification of rights made in American constitutional law, which distinguishes between fundamental rights, equality and other rights. See also Section 3 of this chapter on the First Amendment of the American Constitution.

Freedom of speech is a constitutional right in all three of the systems analysed; however, different kinds of speech exist and different 'freedoms of speech' are treated accordingly. This is the difference between 'abstract rights' and 'concrete rights', where every abstract right includes many different concrete rights, the latter being characterized by a higher specificity than the former.[33] The difference between abstract and concrete rights is also reflected in (and mirrors) the distinction drawn by some scholars between two main categories of balancing: 'ad hoc balancing' and 'definitional balancing'.[34] The former refers to cases where balancing is achieved on a 'case-by-case' basis, while the latter implies a more general and universal balancing. Ad hoc balancing results in a decision which is only valid and true for the specific case at issue. The same 'balancing rule' cannot be applied to other subsequent cases; in fact, given that each case presents its own peculiarities, there are no identical cases in which the same rule can be applied. This does not mean that there are no rules governing ad hoc balancing; rather that the exceptions and idiosyncrasies characterizing each case will lead the interpreter to different solutions for different cases. The axiological hierarchy is therefore 'movable',[35] i.e. it is applicable only to the specific case under scrutiny. Ad hoc balancing has been harshly criticized because it allegedly 'undermine[s] the development of stable, knowable principles of law'.[36] It also supposedly allows judges to be influenced by 'strong popular feelings'.[37]

We have a different scenario when courts apply 'definitional balancing'. Here courts identify a specific rule that could also be applicable to

---

[33]   Pino, *Diritti e interpretazione* (n 1) 184.

[34]   While 'ad hoc balancing' had been recognized by previous scholars, the distinction between it and 'definitional balancing' was first made by Nimmer (n 6) 938–945. See also Aleinikoff (n 6) 597–598, who calls 'ad hoc balancing' and 'definitional balancing' respectively 'result-balancing' and 'rule-balancing'. Consider also the difference between a 'basic balancing rule' – akin to an ad hoc balancing – and a 'specific balancing rule': Barak, *Proportionality* (n 2) 367–369.

[35]   Pino, *Diritti e interpretazione* (n 1) 189. This definition was first introduced by Guastini (n 10) 776. According to Guastini this means leaving discretion to courts.

[36]   Aleinikoff (n 6) 948.

[37]   Nimmer (n 6) 940 and 944. On the influence of society and culture on judges, when balancing conflicting rights, see Federica Giovanella, 'Effects of Culture on Judicial Decisions. Personal Data Protection vs. Copyright Enforcement' in Roberto Caso and Federica Giovanella (eds), *Balancing Copyright Law in the Digital Age. Comparative Perspectives* (Springer Verlag 2015) 65.

future cases.[38] This rule would be applicable whenever balancing involved the same rights. Hence, while definitional balancing rules are normally both explicit and stable, ad hoc balancing rules are implicit and prone to error.

To determine whether balancing has been made 'ad hoc' or with a 'definitional meaning', one should look at the way that courts – other than the one that made the balance – go on to apply the rule. When other judges tend to apply it in subsequent cases with neither modification nor objections, that balancing rule is definitional; when the contrary occurs, the balancing was ad hoc.[39]

The concept of 'principled balancing' is very similar to that of 'definitional balancing'; it was introduced by Aharon Barak, according to whom the rules of balancing 'would be formulated at a level of abstraction below that of the basic rule but above that of concrete balancing'.[40] Barak's principled balancing would differ from 'definitional balancing', for the former 'is based on a balance struck within the framework of a right of a given scope'.[41]

Balancing can more easily be defended from criticism when it is based on tests or other 'specific guides'.[42] Although, as mentioned, 'case-by-case' balancing has been criticized by many, it is also said to be a better way to solve conflicts than is definitional balancing. In fact, even though an ad hoc approach obviously decreases the foreseeability of any single decision, the judgment will nonetheless correspond better to the need for justice in that particular case.[43]

The distinction between ad hoc and definitional balancing may, in fact, merely be apparent: it may always be possible to find differences and peculiarities in each case, rendering former rules inapplicable and new ones desirable, and thus leading perforce to 'ad hoc balancing'.[44] In fact, whenever a court balances rights, it should consider the peculiarities of the case before it. As a consequence, definitional balancing, which can in

---

[38] Nimmer (n 6) 944; McFadden (n 1) 600–601.
[39] Pino, *Diritti e interpretazione* (n 1) 202.
[40] Barak, 'Proportionality (2)' (n 18) 747; Aharon Barak, 'Proportionality and Principled Balancing' [2010] Law & Ethics of Human Rights 1, 12ff.
[41] Barak, 'Proportionality and Principled Balancing' (n 40) 14.
[42] Luizzi (n 11) 394.
[43] Scaccia (n 23) 3995. Consider also the words of Stone Sweet (n 6) 11: '[b]alancing standards hold sway precisely where the law is (a) most indeterminate and (b) most in danger of being constructed in a partisan way'.
[44] Pino, *Diritti e interpretazione* (n 1) 191; Aleinikoff (n 6) 979–980; McFadden (n 1) 635; Bin (n 15) 149.

theory improve the certainty of decisions, would in fact reduce their coherence.[45] Some authors hold that balancing can never be a 'once and for all' solution: each balancing is connected to the circumstances of the case, and the hierarchical classification arising from that balancing is concrete and flexible.[46]

Regardless of whether there really are two distinct 'balancing methods', or they are just two sides of the same coin, or even two poles between which a wide variety of other methods are ranged,[47] it remains the case that when a rule is adopted by a superior court, this rule constitutes a precedent that will be – to a greater or lesser extent, depending on numerous factors[48] – applied in subsequent cases not just by the court that set the rule, but also by lower courts. Clearly, when a court does not explicate the standard it has applied, i.e. when – in Aleinikoff's words – 'the balancing takes place inside a black box',[49] the reliability of its balancing is more open to question and the replicability of the decision as a rule decreases dramatically. The same would be true for predictability, with the consequence that like cases would not be treated alike.[50]

Another possible distinction has been made between constitutional balancing and interpretative balancing. The first is meant to determine the constitutionality of a law, while the second is used to determine the aims and scope of the interpreted law.[51]

Conflicts in which courts have to weigh clashing rights are also divided into 'concrete conflicts' and 'abstract conflicts'. The latter can be solved through textual interpretation as the conflict remains at a conceptual level and does not have to be grounded in an actual case. The former

---

[45]   Aleinikoff (n 6) 979.

[46]   Scaccia (n 23) 3965 and 3967. The author maintains that 'definitional' or 'categorical balancing' would not be balancing in the proper sense, but rather an interpretation technique. The author also holds that the Italian Constitutional Court approach differs from that of the US Supreme Court, as the former's decisions have general and future validity, while the latter's would not. Ibid, 3967–3968.

[47]   Pino, *Diritti e interpretazione* (n 1) 193.

[48]   This is clearly different in common law vs. civil law systems, but it also depends on other factors such as, for instance, the need for equal treatment of equal situations or the need for coherence within the entire legal system. Ibid 192.

[49]   Aleinikoff (n 6) 976.

[50]   McFadden (n 1) 645–650. The author maintains that balancing 'requires a tolerance for *general* or *system* unpredictability' (at 650, emphasis in original).

[51]   Barak, *Proportionality* (n 2) 347.

are cases where in applying norms to an actual case, the interpreter realizes that two norms lead to two different, and incompatible, consequences. Hence, while abstract conflicts descend from the same structure of normative language, concrete ones depend on what happens in real life.[52]

Balancing has not only been criticized in its 'internal' composition and functioning,[53] but also in its 'external' implications. Aleinikoff offers a thorough critique of all facets of balancing.[54] There are, of course, also opposing voices, according to whom balancing is a technique that encourages courts to better motivate their judgments, thus increasing the transparency of decisions.[55]

More generally, the legitimacy of the balancing done by courts, as opposed to that of legislators, has been questioned. Proportionality is considered the domain of legislators, while preserving the boundaries of proportionality is the domain of the courts.[56] Whereas the legislature might be the better forum within which to balance interests, due to its participatory nature,[57] the courts could theoretically improve the balancing already done by the legislator, as they are more aware of the social context and of the impact of the interpretation of the Constitution. However, it has been argued that balancing is not the best instrument for 'the check and validating functions of constitutional law'[58] and that courts can also take social context into account while adopting approaches other than that of balancing.[59] Some maintain that judicial balancing could ultimately undermine the democratic standard as it demonstrates distrust in the functioning of Parliament.[60] This concern, however, should be viewed in the light of the relationship between courts and the legislative branch: whenever the former take into account the

---

[52] Guastini (n 10) 773–774.

[53] Aleinikoff (n 6) 972–983.

[54] Ibid, in particular 984ff.

[55] Vicki C Jackson, 'Constitutional Law in an Age of Proportionality' [2015] Yale Law Journal 3094, 3143.

[56] Barak, 'Proportionality (2)' (n 18) 748.

[57] McFadden (n 1) 641–642.

[58] Aleinikoff (n 6) 984–995.

[59] Ibid (n 6) 1001–1002; Nimmer (n 6) 940.

[60] Schlink (n 15) 735–736. *Contra*: Barak, 'Proportionality (2)' (n 18) 749–751; Robert Alexy, 'Balancing, Constitutional Review, and Representation' [2005] International Journal of Constitutional Law 572, 578–581.

latter's will and aims, and respect them,[61] the above objection becomes meaningless.

Aleinikoff's critique also included the idea that balancing had become 'mechanical jurisprudence', no longer able to persuade,[62] and rigid and formulaic.[63] This assessment is probably more appropriate to what has been called 'definitional balancing', than to 'case-by-case' balancing.

Many other critiques have been presented, some of which concern the opportunity for judges to be discretional.[64] While some authors dislike judges' discretion,[65] others consider it normal that they should make law (as when applying the method of balancing), although in a different manner to that used by legislators.[66]

1.2 Theories of, and Approaches to, 'Rights Balancing'

The practice of balancing is described by scholars either as a rational activity or as a solely intuitive process. The latter approach holds balancing to be a highly subjective activity, heavily coloured by the personal beliefs and opinions of the individual judge approaching the case[67] and inevitably an ideologically driven operation.

Although it is undeniable that judges bring their personal feelings and perceptions to each decision they make,[68] it is also the case that to consider all that judges do to be ideologically driven and subjective would undermine the basis of the modern judiciary, and be tantamount to

---

[61] Aharon Barak is critical of the way some courts 'submit' themselves to the legislative branch: Barak, 'Proportionality (2)' (n 18) 748.

[62] Aleinikoff (n 6) 983.

[63] Ibid 1005.

[64] See *contra*: Mengoni (n 16) 125. See also the explanations offered by Alexy, *A Theory of Constitutional Rights* (n 14) 394ff.

[65] Dworkin (n 13) 81ff. On judicial discretion: see Ibid, 69–71.

[66] Stone Sweet and Mathews (n 11) 87. Consider also Richard A Posner, *Reflections on Judging* (Harvard University Press 2013), especially 108–126.

[67] McFadden (n 1) 643ff. The author believes that this leaves space for inconsistency. According to Jacco Bomhoff, 'Rights, Balancing & Proportionality' [2010] Law & Ethics of Human Rights 109, 132–138, balancing discourse in Germany and in the US has been subject to different kinds of criticisms.

[68] 'Balancing is unavoidably subjective and political' according to Schlink (n 15) 726. '[S]ubjective appraisals of the judges ... will necessarily appear in balancing or in any alternative procedure': Carlos Bernal Pulido, 'The Rationality of Balancing' [2006] Archives for Philosophy of Law and Social Philosophy 195, 197–198.

saying that no objective criteria for assessing the admissibility of judicial decisions exist.[69]

An opposite approach is taken by the scholars who describe balancing as a rational process. Barak, for instance, holds that balancing could be rational since it is based on 'the social importance of realizing one principle and avoiding limitation of another principle'. Allowing judges some discretion does not entail a lack of rationality.[70]

The most prominent of the scholars supporting a rational view of 'balancing' is Robert Alexy, who proposes an extremely analytic and procedural method of balancing in his influential work, *A Theory of Constitutional Rights*.[71]

As a German scholar, Alexy mainly draws his theory – based on the assumption that principles differ from rules[72] – from the Bundesverfassungsgericht's decisions, which are based on the application of the 'principle of proportionality' to cases of conflicting constitutional principles.[73]

Proportionality itself is typically divided into three phases or subprinciples: suitability, necessity, and proportionality in its narrow sense.[74] This is the approach adopted in Robert Alexy's seminal works.[75]

Whether or not a measure limitative of a fundamental right is suitable for realizing the aims for which it was enacted determines its suitability.

---

[69] Pino, *Diritti e interpretazione* (n 1) 194. See also Dworkin (n 13) 81ff. *Contra*: Bernal Pulido (n 68) 205ff; Jackson (n 55) 3159 holds that 'there is good reason to think that, in some discrete areas, U.S. constitutional law could benefit from greater use of both the principle and the *structured* doctrine of proportionality' (emphasis added). See ibid 3166ff.

[70] Barak, 'Proportionality (2)' (n 18) 750.

[71] Alexy, *A Theory of Constitutional Rights* (n 14); see also Alexy's other papers cited in this chapter.

[72] In this respect, Alexy's view originates from Dworkin's, although it does differ from it: Vespaziani (n 11) 93 and 95ff; Kai Möller, 'Balancing and the Structure of Constitutional Rights' [2007] International Journal of Constitutional Law 453, 454–455.

[73] This is the so-called 'Verhältnismäßigkeitgrundsatz': Alexy, 'Constitutional Rights' (n 17) 135ff.

[74] 'Proportionality in the narrow sense' is also known as 'balancing in the strict sense' according to Stone Sweet and Mathews (n 11) 75.

[75] Alexy, 'Balancing' (n 60) 572; *A Theory of Constitutional Rights* (n 14) 66ff.

If the limitative measure cannot achieve the aims for which it was implemented, it can be considered illegitimate at this very first stage.[76]

Once its suitability has been ascertained, a measure's necessity must be evaluated. This means understanding whether the measure adopted is less invasive of citizens' rights than any of the possible alternatives – all of which are appropriate to achieve the aim of the legislator. When a given measure is suitable to achieve the (legitimate) intended aim and is also a necessary measure, the third step, proportionality in its narrow sense, must be assessed. This final step is in fact the actual activity of balancing: its goal is to determine whether the sacrifice imposed on the fundamental right by the adopted measure is balanced, taking into account the degree of satisfaction of the public interest realized by the measure itself.[77]

Alexy's whole theory is based on the concept of 'Pareto-optimality'. In economics, a Pareto-optimal point of equilibrium is one where the position of a part can be improved without detriment to any other. In Alexy's analysis, Pareto-optimality applies both to suitability and to necessity. With regard to sustainability, a Pareto-optimal approach would consider a means that obstructs the realization of one principle without promoting another to be non-suitable.[78] When two means are equally suited to promoting the same interest, the necessity principle requires that the one that interferes less with the opposite principle should be preferred.[79]

The most innovative idea in Alexy's theory is probably the so-called 'Law of Balancing', which states: 'The greater the degree of non-satisfaction of, or detriment to, one principle, the greater the importance of satisfying the other.'[80] This law can also be divided into three steps: first, one should understand the degree to which the first principle is not satisfied; second, the importance of satisfying the opposite principle

---

[76]   Pino, *Diritti e interpretazione* (n 1) 206. This step implies also checking whether the aim at which the measure is directed is legitimate in itself.

[77]   Ibid 207.

[78]   Alexy, 'Constitutional Rights' (n 17) 135. Criticism of the idea of optimization of rights can be found in Möller (n 72) 459–462.

[79]   Alexy, 'Constitutional Rights' (n 17) 135: such an approach requires that no third principle enters into play. For a critique, see Pino, *Diritti e interpretazione* (n 1) 196–199.

[80]   Alexy, *A Theory of Constitutional Rights* (n 14) 102ff. In similar terms: Barak, 'Proportionality and Principled Balancing' (n 40) 11.

should be established; lastly, it should be decided whether the importance of satisfying the second principle justifies the detriment to the first one.[81]

The interference with the first principle is proportionate when, in the absence of such interference, another constitutionally protected right would undergo equivalent, or major, interference.[82]

Intensity of interference and degrees of importance are evaluated following a 'triadic scale' on which the three illustrated steps are considered 'light', 'moderate' or 'serious'; the scale can also be developed to a 'double-triadic' model, allowing more nuances to be taken into account.[83] The establishment of such a triadic scale should overcome the difficulties linked to incommensurability.[84]

In Alexy's view, intensity of interference is the first value to be considered, since the conflicting rights are of equal weight in the abstract. If this were not the case – if the two rights did not have the same weight in the abstract – no balancing would be needed. The importance of satisfying the second principle is a function of the interference with the first principle: the possible effects that omitting to interfere with the first principle might have on the second must be considered.[85] The triadic scale would allow a weight to be assigned to the principles in the concrete case. Weight, represented as numbers, is then processed using a mathematical formula, which should enable precise balancing.[86] To improve balancing, Alexy suggests an additional 'second Law of Balancing': 'The more heavily an interference with a constitutional right weighs, the greater must be the certainty of its underlying premises.'[87] The picture becomes more complicated when a third (or more) right(s) enter(s) into it.[88]

Alexy's approach undoubtedly has a number of advantages, such as the precision of the balancing process involved, and the ease with which the operations entailed in one particular case can be replicated in subsequent cases. However, it is probably not as feasible as Alexy imagined it to be.

---

81 Alexy, 'Constitutional Rights' (n 17) 136.
82 Ibid 38.
83 Alexy, 'On Balancing and Subsumption' (n 18) 440–445 passim.
84 Ibid 442.
85 Ibid 440–441.
86 Ibid 442–446. Even though he did not refer to Alexy's theory, Scaccia (n 23) 3958 holds that balancing can never be boiled down to a logical-mathematical operation.
87 Alexy, 'On Balancing and Subsumption' (n 18) 446; Id, *A Theory of Constitutional Rights* (n 14) 418–419. The author himself renames the two Laws, calling them 'Substantive Law of Balancing' and 'Epistemic Law of Balancing'.
88 Alexy, 'On Balancing and Subsumption' (n 18) 448.

Determining the weight of each right and the degree of interference the conflicting rights experience is no easy task.[89] Moreover, the attribution of a given weight to a specific right seems to be made 'in a vacuum', while, as other scholars have observed, the weight of each right can only be determined in relation to the opposite, conflicting right.[90]

A number of criticisms have been made of both the idea of the three-step proportionality test and the way in which Alexy's formula further rationalizes this procedure.[91] Improvements to the formula have also been suggested.[92]

Some scholars do not even accept the basic division of proportionality into three steps.[93] All the proposed approaches have proportionality *stricto sensu* as their final stage; however, while some authors maintain that this last step is in itself the balancing process,[94] others consider it to be only a part of that process.[95] Others hold that the first of the three steps already entails a balancing activity, or that the procedure is over-simplified, as a single measure may often be pursuing different goals simultaneously.[96] If this were the case, Alexy's approach should not

---

[89]   Ricardo A Guibourg, 'On Alexy's Weighing Formula' in Jan-Reinard Sieckmann (ed), *Legal Reasoning: the Methods of Balancing* (Franz Steiner Verlag 2010) 145, 154–157.

[90]   Pino, *Diritti e interpretazione* (n 1) 197.

[91]   Scaccia (n 23) 3977–3978, who is critical of any type of economic approach to balancing; Pino, *Diritti e interpretazione* (n 1) 196–199 and Pino, 'Conflitto e bilanciamento' (n 26) 34–36; Bernardo Bolaños, 'Balancing and Legal Decision Theory' in Sieckmann (ed) (n 89) 63, 71–72; Jan-Reimand Sieckmann, 'Balancing, Optimisation, and Alexy's "Weight Formula"', in Sieckmann (n 89) 101. For an overview of the many different objections raised to Alexy's theory and, more generally, to the balancing of principles: Alexy, 'The Construction' (n 15) 24–26; Luizzi (n 11) 386–400. For an overview of other objections and an answer to them, as well as for some possible solutions to reduce the risks linked to balancing, ibid 401–403.

[92]   Bernal Pulido (n 68) 205–209.

[93]   Schlink (n 15) 722–725, who considers categorically prohibited means, legitimacy of the end, fitness or suitability, and balancing. Barak, 'Proportionality (2)' (n 18) 742–747, who recognizes 'proper purpose, rational connection, necessity, and proportionality in the narrow sense'.

[94]   Barak, 'Proportionality and Principled Balancing' (n 40) 7.

[95]   Balancing is seen by scholars both as a framework for proportionality analysis and as the last step of the proportionality test. See Schlink (15) 719, and cited references.

[96]   Pino, *Diritti e interpretazione* (n 1) 208–209.

be a model of reasoning for courts, but rather a mechanism for understanding what factors should be evaluated in order to reach a proportionate solution.[97]

A different approach is adopted by Aharon Barak, who takes into account not only the degree of limitation of the right, as Alexy does, but also the importance of the purpose and the magnitude of the constitutional right itself. Specifically, Barak's vision includes the social importance of rights: the social importance of the benefit obtained by realizing the purpose of a particular law, and the social importance of avoiding the limitation of the constitutional right in question.[98]

Another possible approach is described by some Italian authors, who, with reference to the balancing applied by the Italian Constitutional Court, propose the following three-step interpretation process: the interpreter should first identify the values compromised by the statute the constitutionality of which is under scrutiny; second, the weight of those rights in the specific case should be evaluated; third, it should be understood what public interest does the statute intend to serve by sacrificing the constitutionally protected values in play.[99]

The Italian scholar Roberto Bin, who studied numerous Constitutional Court decisions, identified some specific steps that the Court takes in making its judgments, the first of which is to draw what Bin calls the 'topography of the conflict': investigating whether the area protected by one right does in fact overlap with the area protected by the other one, and what residual area – other than the overlapping one – is left to both rights.[100] Bin considered such an approach to be akin to the US Supreme Court's definitional balancing.[101]

This preliminary activity should make it possible to define if and how a right actually undergoes a restriction, and also whether such a restriction is absolutely impairing for that right, or only limits it partially. The first step of the Court would therefore be to understand whether the interest protected by the constitutionally challenged law could justify the compression of the constitutional right.[102]

Proportionality itself is being applied not only by the Bundesverfassungsgericht, but also by an increasing number of other Supreme Courts,

---

[97]   Ibid 209.
[98]   Barak, 'Proportionality (2)' (n 18) 745–746.
[99]   Scaccia (n 23) 3972–3973; see also Bin (n 15) 62ff.
[100]   Ibid 62–63.
[101]   Ibid 65–68. Critiques of Bin's work can be found in Vespaziani (n 11) 127.
[102]   Bin (n 15) 70–72.

including the Court of Justice of the European Union (CJEU). The proportionality principle was invoked by the CJEU in the seminal case *Promusicae*, for example, as will be illustrated when discussing the case studies.[103] Proportionality is rarely explicitly mentioned by Constitutions or charters, but its existence is said to be grounded in the ontological construction of human rights and public interest.[104]

Proportionality and balancing are closely intertwined: they both look at the limitation of a specific right or principle. In addition, proportionality can be seen as one step within a wider balancing process.[105]

The Italian Constitutional Court does not apply the proportionality principle; however, it has elaborated a 'reasonableness criterion', which can be equated to proportionality.[106] The Court has elaborated certain criteria for balancing the conflicting interests in cases where a statute is challenged because of its unconstitutionality. These criteria include the ideas of 'tempering opposite interests', 'least invasive means' and 'co-essential limits'.[107] When the first criterion is applied, neither of the two conflicting rights is totally sacrificed. The 'least invasive means' criterion requires that fundamental rights are invaded as little as possible in the realizing of another constitutionally relevant interest.[108] The third criterion provides that a fundamental right cannot be compressed unless this is done to protect other fundamental constitutional values, and applying only non-excessive and strictly necessary means.[109]

Although it has theorized and applied these rules, the Italian Constitutional Court has never classified rights. In fact, even though courts 'are loath to build *intra*-constitutional hierarchies of norms'[110] and decide on a case-by-case analysis, some do nonetheless consistently apply specific tests or criteria. However, the Italian Court has never proposed consistent

---

[103]   Case 275/06 *Productores de Música de España v. Telefónica de España SAU* [2008] ECR I-00271, on which see Chapter 4, Section 5.1.
[104]   Barak, 'Proportionality (2)' (n 18) 741–742.
[105]   Pino, *Diritti e interpretazione* (n 1) 205.
[106]   Scaccia (n 23) 3975.
[107]   Translation is mine from the Italian: 'contemperamento', 'minimo mezzo', 'coessenzialità del limite': Scaccia (n 23) 3973–3985.
[108]   Bin (n 15) 81ff.
[109]   Scaccia (n 23) 3992.
[110]   Stone Sweet and Mathews (n 11) 87 (emphasis in original).

balancing tests or criteria,[111] unlike the Supreme Courts of both the US and Canada, which have developed tests to be applied in specific cases.[112]

The Canadian Supreme Court famously applies the so-called 'Oakes test', which originated in *R. v. Oakes*.[113] The test, which has been developed in subsequent decisions, involves Section 1 of the Canadian Charter of Human Rights and Freedoms.[114] This section states that the Charter 'guarantees the rights and freedoms set out in it subject only to such reasonable limits prescribed by law as can be demonstrably justified in a free and democratic society'. While the burden of proving the infringement of a right is borne by the challenger, the Court has to investigate the scope of the allegedly violated right. The judges need to understand whether the government acted legally and for reasons that are 'pressing and substantial in a free and democratic society'. If this is not the case, the procedure ends. If, however, the government proves that its action is justifiable, the Court proceeds with a three-step test: it assesses first whether the means chosen are rationally related to the legitimate object; second, whether they impair the protected rights to the minimum extent possible; third, whether the government's aims justify the harm to the right protected by the Charter. This final step is known as 'proportionality as such'.[115]

---

[111] Scaccia (n 23) 3963.

[112] See, for instance, the test developed by Justice Harlan in *Katz v. United States*, 389 U.S. 347 (1967), 361, on which see Chapter 3, Section 2.

[113] *R. v. Oakes* [1986] 1 S.C.R. 103, for a critique of which see: Sujit Choudhry, 'So What Is the Real Legacy of Oakes? Two Decades of Proportionality Analysis under the Canadian Charter's Section 1' [2006] South Carolina Law Review 501. For a comparison between the approaches taken by the US and Canada, see Jackson (n 55); for a comparison between the Canadian and the German approaches, see Dieter Grimm, 'Proportionality in Canadian and German Constitutional Jurisprudence' [2007] University of Toronto Law Journal 383. See also Stone Sweet and Mathews (n 11) 113ff.

[114] Canadian Charter of Rights and Freedoms, Part I of the Constitution Act, 1982, being Schedule B to the Canada Act, 1982, c. 11 (U.K.). The Charter is a Bill of Rights included in the Constitution Act of 1982, through which Canada obtained full political autonomy from the United Kingdom. The rights contained in the Charter are considered constitutional rights; hence they can override any state or federal law that clashes with them.

[115] For more details: Jackson (n 55) 3111–3113. The author reports that generally the Canadian Supreme Court finds laws unconstitutional under the 'minimally impairing' requirement (Ibid 3117). The entire procedure is actually based on a four-step test: Choudhry (n 113) 505.

While the approach adopted by the Canadian Supreme Court is quite similar to the German one, that followed by American judges seems to be different. Many scholars have examined the method applied in the American system where, to quote the title of Aleinikoff's article, 'constitutional law [has been] in the age of balancing' for many years.[116] The US Supreme Court applies balancing tests to many different areas of the law, including the Eighth Amendment, related to excessive bail, excessive fines, or cruel and unusual punishment;[117] the Fourth Amendment on the right of people to be secure against search and seizure;[118] and, of course, the First Amendment on freedom of speech.[119]

Even though balancing is ubiquitous in American case law, applicable tests, standards or rules vary according to the rights at stake.[120] For instance, as in First Amendment cases, the Court has often applied a test including 'the seriousness of the speech-related harm the provision will likely cause, the nature and importance of the provision's countervailing objectives, the extent to which the provision will tend to achieve those objectives, and whether there are other, less restrictive ways of doing so'.[121] The Court essentially assesses 'the need for a sufficiently important or "compelling" government purpose; the rational connection required between the means chosen and the end; and the "minimal impairment" inquiry into whether there are less restrictive means towards the same goal'.[122] These steps do constitute, in essence, a test of proportionality.[123]

It must be stressed that differences in approach can also be the result of differences in the function, tools and aims of the courts. While the US Supreme Court can dictate what the solution should be in a concrete case, the Italian Corte costituzionale gives general prescriptions; from this point of view, its decisions can very often be assimilated to 'definitional balancing' ones.[124]

---

[116]   Aleinikoff (n 6).

[117]   Jackson (n 55) 3104.

[118]   See for instance the famous case *Katzs* (n 112) or more recently *Kyllo v. United States*, 533 U.S. 27 (2001) and *U.S. v. Jones*, 132 S. Ct. 945 (2012).

[119]   On which consider the seminal article by Nimmer (n 6).

[120]   'From this identification of balancing techniques, it becomes clear that the number of models is many and that the term, "balancing of interests," refers to no single method of judicial decision making': Luizzi (n 11) 386.

[121]   *United States v. Alvarez*, 132 S. Ct. 2537 (2012), 2551.

[122]   Jackson (n 55) 3099.

[123]   *Alvarez* (n 121), 2551.

[124]   Bin (n 15) 125–126.

Vincent Luizzi has categorized US Supreme Court decisions into two main groups: the first includes 'models where judges follow specific guides' and 'models where rules guide the balance';[125] the second comprises decisions that do not explicitly follow any specific rule or guide. The first group of the first category comprises those decisions in which one of the interests at stake has been nominated as 'compelling' or 'substantial' and therefore has prevailed over the other. The second group of the first category comprises judgments that have followed an explicit rule, test or standard. Tests themselves constitute a part of the balancing process.[126] This is consistent with the approach adopted by the courts in resolving the conflict between information privacy and copyright in the lawsuits taken here as case studies. Cases resolved on the basis of a test may also be classified as 'definitional balancing' according to the reported definition.

The decisions grouped in the second category, in contrast, do not take a substantial or compelling right as the starting point for their balancing; instead they identify the 'paramount' interest solely on the basis of their balancing of the particulars of each case.[127] In Luizzi's view, this is genuine balancing, while when courts first search for the prevailing interest, no true balancing can actually take place.[128] In his seminal article on 'the age of balancing', Aleinikoff takes a different view. In his opinion, both cases where the US Supreme Court decides that one interest outweighs the other, and those in which the Court more properly strikes a balance, can be considered as 'balancing'.[129]

The absence of consensus on the exact nature of balancing, and how it should be accomplished, mirrors the evolution of the state of the law: a transition from procedural rules and deductions to the balancing of principles and values. The latter approach is the expression of the contemporary constitutional legal order.[130]

In the next section I will first illustrate the kind of conflict the courts resolved in the case studies considered here and then propose a hypothesis for what I call 'conceptual balancing'. Both the conflict under discussion and how the courts in each of the three countries resolved (or have attempted to resolve) it will be examined. It will emerge that in Canada and the US courts apply a specific test when deciding whether

---

125 Luizzi (n 11) 377–386.
126 Ibid 378–383.
127 Ibid 383–385.
128 Ibid 388–389.
129 Aleinikoff (n 6) 946.
130 Vespaziani (n 11) 129.

information privacy should be overridden to allow copyright enforcement, while a different approach is adopted by Italian judges. This is
consistent with the approaches of the three countries' Supreme Courts, as
we have seen above.

2. THE CONFLICT

Neither this chapter – nor this book as a whole – aims to define balancing
or how it should be carried out; the intention is to compare the ways in
which the lower courts of the three countries in question actually apply
this methodology. This comparison is made through case studies involving two rights which are usually considered to be fundamental: copyright
and (information) privacy, as illustrated in detail in the present section.

The cases examined in this book are examples of one of the most
recent steps taken by the music industry, and the entertainment industry
more generally, to stop what is usually known as 'copyright piracy'.
Broadly speaking, copyright piracy consists in the reproduction and
diffusion of copyrighted material without the consent of the copyright
holder.

Copyright piracy has now existed for decades, but has only become a
worldwide phenomenon with the spread of the Internet. Tape cassettes,
and then CDs, were commonly copied among friends. Pirate copies of
both types of medium were quite easily accessible on the 'parallel
market' but their existence and circulation were largely tolerated by
copyright holders.

With the advent of the Internet and then of MP3 files, sharing songs
around the globe became easy, cheap and fast; significantly, this file
compression format resulted in much smaller files than previous data
formats.[131] This led the recording industry to adopt a number of different
strategies in an attempt to combat online piracy.

---

[131] MP3 – full name MPEG audio level 3 – is 'a way of encoding digital
audio data into a compressed data format that is approximately one twelfth the
size of the original without perceptible loss of quality ... Because MP3 files are
compact and easy to copy, they are relatively quick to download and very easy to
distribute – which is causing problems for the original artists who are trying to
protect their copyright material', *Entry: MP3* in Simon MH Collin, *Dictionary of
Computing* (Peter Collin Publishing 2004).

Going back to the years in which analogue copying was a novelty, a quick reference to the seminal case *Sony v. Universal*[132] should be made. Although I will analyse this decision in greater detail in Chapter 4, a particular aspect of the case is relevant here, an aspect, indeed, which is usually overlooked – the fact that in *Sony v. Universal* privacy concerns were also raised.

As is well known, Sony was sued for contributory infringement of copyright laws for manufacturing and selling the Betamax, a video-recorder which could be used by individuals to record television programmes on video tapes in order to watch them at a more convenient time; the practice was known as 'time-shifting'. The plaintiffs were Universal City Studios and Walt Disney, the producers and copyright owners of many of the television programmes and popular shows airing when Betamax was released. In their opinion, since consumers used Betamax to record copyrighted works, the defendants were liable for copyright infringement under the US Copyright Act. The lawsuit was focused on vicarious liability and contributory infringement, to which I shall return in Chapter 4.

Even though the most famous decision in this case is that of the US Supreme Court, the District Court for the Central District of California made a remark of relevance to the core of my present analysis. Ferguson J recognized that taking copyright enforcement to the level requested by the plaintiffs would mean entering private homes. Private behaviour, such as home-recording, would be very difficult to control. In the legislative process leading up to the 1976 revisions to the Copyright Act, in fact, the Copyright Office was concerned 'about invasion of the individual's privacy in his home'. At the same time, the District Court understood that

> Of course, not all activity is made legal by virtue of occurring in a private home. Congress can constitutionally legislate against some activity which may occur in the home, but doing so necessarily requires caution. Here, legislative history shows that, on balance, Congress did not find that protection of copyright holders' rights over reproduction of their works was worth the privacy and enforcement problems which restraint of home-use recording would create.[133]

---

[132] *Universal City Studios, Inc. v. Sony Corp. of America*, 480 F. Supp. 429 (C.D. Cal. 1979); *Universal City Studios, Inc. v. Sony Corp. of America*, 659 F.2d 963 (9th Cir. 1981), *Sony Corp. of America v. Universal City Studios*, 464 U.S. 417 (1984). Dozens of comments have been written on this case, see Chapter 4 for bibliography.

[133] *Sony Betamax District court* (n 132) 445–446 *passim*. On this issue see Sonia K Katyal, 'Privacy v. Piracy' [2004] Yale J. Law & Tech. 222, 309ff.

According to Judge Ferguson, in this case it was Congress which had struck the balance between consumer privacy and copyright enforcement.

The case highlights how, in order to enforce copyright, intrusion into the privacy sphere of the alleged infringers is necessary. This is closely analogous both to the cases analysed in this book and to the conflict on which my research focuses. More recently, this onerous task appears to have been shifted to the courts, which are finding it difficult to cope with, as will be demonstrated throughout this work.

Sony Betamax – a case in which, in order to limit copyright infringement, copyright holders sued a subject (Sony) for being 'indirectly liable' – is undoubtedly one of the most famous cases of copyright enforcement in the 'analogue era'. However, this has been only one of a number of strategies adopted by the entertainment industry in their efforts to stop the infringing activities of final users.[134]

Twenty years after the Sony case, the Recording Industry Association of America (RIAA),[135] which represents the interests of the US recording industry and the holders of music copyright, started a number of lawsuits aimed at enforcing copyright against users allegedly liable for online piracy. The same strategy was followed in subsequent years by other copyright holders' associations, both within and outside the US.[136]

The starting point of these lawsuits, regardless of whether they took place in Europe, Canada or the US, was the same. Copyright holders had reason to believe that their works were being illicitly distributed through peer-to-peer file-sharing networks.

In order to pursue their strategy – i.e. the enforcement of copyright against final users – copyright holders need to discover the real identities hidden behind computers; users are usually only identifiable through their pseudonymous or Internet Protocol (IP) addresses.[137] Copyright holders rely on service companies, who collect data on peer-to-peer

---

[134]   See Chapter 4, Section 1 for further details.

[135]   'The Recording Industry Association of America (RIAA) is the trade organization that supports and promotes the creative and financial vitality of the major music companies. Its members are the music labels that comprise the most vibrant record industry in the world. RIAA members create, manufacture and/or distribute approximately 85% of all legitimate recorded music produced and sold in the United States', see RIAA's website <www.riaa.com/aboutus.php> accessed 10 February 2017. According to Robert P Merges, Peter S Menell and Mark A Lemley, *Intellectual Property in the New Technological Age* (5th edn, Aspen 2010) 682, the RIAA represents more than 500 companies related to the creation, manufacturing and distribution of sound recording.

[136]   For a detailed description of these cases, see Chapter 4.

[137]   For a definition, see below in this section.

traffic. Using a variety of methods, these service companies can crawl the network and find and collect the IP addresses of users, which they give to the copyright holders who then require the collaboration of the Internet Service Providers (ISPs), who are in unique possession of users' real identities. More precisely, copyright holders need the cooperation of so-called 'access providers', the companies supplying users with an Internet connection. Providers retain Internet traffic information for either legal or accounting reasons. Each IP is associated with a specific contract to supply a connection to the Internet. Therefore, ISPs can match IP addresses with their customers' contract information and discover users' real identities. This is why copyright holders need the ISPs to collaborate. However, some ISPs refused to cooperate, thus forcing copyright holders to turn to the courts to try to obtain orders to oblige providers to release user identities.

Although the tools used by plaintiffs vary according to the legal system in which they are operating,[138] they can all be considered to be discovery tools.[139] The ultimate goal of these devices is to provide the plaintiff with the information necessary for a lawsuit: information in the possession of a subject other than the defendants.

In the US system two different tools exist. The first is provided by § 512(m) the Digital Millennium Copyright Act (DMCA),[140] while the second is the so-called 'John Doe' process, based on the Federal Rule of Civil Procedure n. 45. The latter is equivalent to the device applied in the Canadian context, which relies on Rules 233 and 238 of the Federal Court Rules. In Italy the rule applied is that of art. 156*bis* of Legge 22 April 1941, n. 633, regulating *diritto d'autore* (copyright).

When asked to reveal their customers' information, providers raised concerns about user privacy and personal data protection. These concerns are at the heart of the conflict I wish to investigate in this book.

On one side we have the copyright holders, who are trying to enforce their rights, in compliance with the right to an effective remedy. On the other side stand the users whose activities have been traced and whose data have been collected without consent.

To give a better picture of my analysis of the conflict, further details are required. The clash of rights studied in this book is based on two

---

[138] See Chapter 2, Section 6 for a detailed explanation.

[139] The Italian system does not explicitly provide any of these tools. Nonetheless, an analysis of the tools provided for the enforcement of copyright reveals the similarities between these and the discovery tools existing in common law countries.

[140] An Act of October 28, 1998, Pub. L. 105–304, 112 Stat. 2860.

premises. First: to a greater or lesser extent the US, Canada and Italy all have regulations that hold file-sharing to be a copyright-infringing activity. One of the first objections that is often made to these lawsuits is that copyright has not actually been infringed by the users. For the purposes of my argument, I shall assume that copyright violation did, in fact, occur.[141] The second assumption is that all three countries protect privacy, both physical and informational. It is well known that the approach taken by the US differs considerably from that of the EU, and, in turn, of Italy. The Canadian experience is very close to the European.

In the cases examined here, the plaintiffs were associations of copyright holders, and not copyright holders themselves. This means that the enforced rights were clearly and solely economic.[142] There is reason to believe that this aspect was actually considered by some courts in their decisions, as will be demonstrated throughout this book. It is crucial to note, however, that if the uniquely economic nature of the rights had been more thoroughly considered, different decisions might have been reached. Indeed, if one considers copyright to be an 'economic' right and privacy to be a 'personality' right, the two should not be assigned equal value.[143]

With regard to privacy and personal data protection, it should first be noted that the service companies collected user data with neither the consent, nor even the knowledge, of the people concerned. The collected data were mainly IP addresses and traffic information, which leads to an initial question: are IP addresses personal data?

---

[141]   I shall nonetheless explain in Chapter 2 when and where the violation was actually present.

[142]   A different situation would be one where the rights enforced were 'moral rights'. Moral rights are recognized by the Berne Convention at art. 6*bis*. However, signatory states have implemented this provision differently. As is well known, European copyright also recognizes a 'moral right' of authors, which is a personality right that cannot be waived. The US does not recognize a moral right for any work of authorship; instead it has introduced specific provisions for some rights (for instance the Visual Artists Rights Act (VARA), Pub. L. 101–650, 104 Stat. 5132, December 1, 1990). Italian Legge 633/41 includes moral rights in arts. 20, 21, 24, 142 and 143. A similar situation exists in Canada, as the famous Supreme Court decision in *Théberge* clearly stated (*Théberge v. Galerie d'Art du Petit Champlain Inc* [2002] 2 S.C.R. 336). Moral rights in Canada are provided by the Copyright Act, S. 14.1, S. 14.2, S. 17.1, and S. 17.2.

[143]   Cf. Tar Roma, Ord. 26.09.2014, no. 10020, according to which the Italian Constitution puts fundamental rights and economic liberties on two different levels, so that, in case of conflict, the latter should be sacrificed.

To answer this question properly, I must first define what I mean by privacy in the context of this book. Unlike copyright, which is a legal concept, '[t]he term "privacy" is an umbrella term, referring to a wide and disparate group of related things. The use of such a broad term is helpful in some contexts yet quite unhelpful in others.'[144]

Since its first appearance in Warren and Brandeis' article,[145] scholars have been trying to give a precise definition of the 'right to privacy'.[146] It has been significantly claimed that 'privacy is so hopelessly diffuse as to be virtually indistinguishable from the related concepts of liberty, autonomy and freedom'.[147] So many different attempts to define privacy have been made that it is pointless to even try to summarize them here,[148] instead I would prefer just to quote an existing definition that should be kept in mind while reading this book. Privacy can be thought of 'as the ability of an individual to exercise control over how his/her personal information is collected, used or disclosed by third parties'.[149] This definition is very close to the one regarding the 'protection of personal data', which is at the core of my research. Indeed, the collection and use of an individual's personal information can have a great impact on their privacy; this puts privacy at the heart of personal data protection[150] and is very probably why the two concepts often overlap. I welcome this

---

[144] Daniel J Solove, 'A Taxonomy of Privacy' [2006] University of Pennsylvania Law Review 477, 485.

[145] Samuel D Warren and Louis Brandeis, 'The Right to Privacy' [1890] 4 Harvard Law Review 193.

[146] See the ironic words of Helen Nissenbaum, *Privacy in Context. Technology, Policy, and the Integrity of Social Life* (Stanford University Press 2010) 2–3. For useful insights, see Daniel J Solove, *Understanding Privacy* (Harvard University Press 2008) 1–39.

[147] Colin J Bennett, *Regulating Privacy. Data Protection and Public Policy in Europe and the United States* (Cornell University Press 1992) 26.

[148] For a summary and brief explanation of the 'leading definitions' of privacy, see Colin H H McNairn and Alexander K Scott, *Privacy Law in Canada* (Butterworths 2001) 4ff; see also Peter Burns, 'The Law and Privacy: The Canadian Experience' [1976] Reveu du Barreau Canadien/Canadian Bar Review 1, 4–12. Flaherty lists a number of information-related interests protected by the right to privacy: see David H Flaherty, *Protecting Privacy in Surveillance Societies* (North Carolina University Press 1992) 8, table 1.

[149] Mark S Hayes, 'The Impact of Privacy on Intellectual Property in Canada' [2006] Intellectual Property Journal 67, 68.

[150] Margaret Ann Wilkinson, 'Battleground Between New and Old Orders: Control Conflicts Between Copyright and Personal Data Protection' in Ysolde Gendreau (ed), *An Emerging Intellectual Property Paradigm: Perspectives from Canada* (Edward Elgar Publishing 2008) 227, 244–246, *sic passim*.

overlap, which is often proposed by laws, as well as by judges.[151] The term 'information privacy', which can be seen as a *crasis* of the two concepts of physical privacy and personal data protection, also testifies to this overlap.[152]

Another interesting definition which could be applied in this work was given by the Australian Privacy Commissioner: '[i]nformation privacy concerns the handling of "personal information", that is, information about a particular person or information that can be used to identify a particular person'.[153] The definition is also very close to Alan Westin's, that information privacy is 'the claim of individuals, groups or institutions to determine for themselves when, how and to what extent information about them is communicated to others'.[154] The manner in which personal information is spread can represent an individual's way of being, and is thus related to their personal identity.[155]

This work does not necessarily need to rely on a specific definition of privacy. It is, however, important that we share a general understanding of the concept, particularly with respect to information. For the sake of clarity, I will adopt the definition given above – and which best fits my present purpose – that privacy is 'the ability of an individual to exercise control over how his/her personal information is collected, used or disclosed by third parties'.[156] The terms privacy/information privacy/ personal data protection will be used interchangeably, although I am conscious that there are, or may in some circumstances be, differences between them. These differences are sometimes the result of the differences in the conception and perception of this right.[157] As will be seen

---

[151] Juliane Kokott and Christoph Sobotta, 'The Distinction Between Privacy and Data Protection in the Jurisprudence of the CJEU and the ECtHR' [2013] International Data Privacy Law 222.

[152] See Lee A Bygrave, 'Privacy and Data Protection in an International Perspective' [2010] Scandinavian Studies in Law 165, 168–171.

[153] 'What Is Information Privacy And Why Do We Need To Protect It?' in Australian Privacy Commissioner, *Information Privacy in Australia: A National Scheme for Fair Information Practices in the Private Sector*, August 1997 <http://www2.austlii.edu.au/itlaw/national_scheme/national-PART.html> accessed 12 August 2017.

[154] Cf. Alan F Westin, *Privacy and Freedom* (Atheneum 1967) 7.

[155] Giovanni Buttarelli, *Banche dati e tutela della riservatezza. La privacy nella società dell'informazione* (Giuffrè 1997) 95.

[156] Hayes (n 149) 68.

[157] Lee A Bygrave, 'International Agreements to Protect Personal Data' in James B Rule and Graham Greenleaf (eds), *Global Privacy Protection: The First Generation* (Edward Elgar Publishing 2008) 15, 15–17.

later, the US usually uses the term 'privacy', while the current European and Canadian frameworks revolve around the concept of 'personal data'.

Having clarified how the term 'information privacy' will be used in this work, I will now turn to IP addresses. In order to establish whether or not IP addresses fit into the definition of personal data, we must define them. So, an IP address is a number assigned to a device connected to a network that applies what is called 'Internet Protocol' communication. The number works both as an interface identification and as a locating address. Possession of a user's IP address enables detection of where the device with that number is; the IP address identifies the exact location of a given node on the Internet. At the consumer/user level, IP addresses are assigned by the access provider according to a specific method. IP addresses can be assigned either dynamically or statically. Dynamic assignation – the most common – means that each time a device connects to the network, the ISP assigns it a new number. Each ISP usually has a given number of IP addresses that it can assign to its customers and it may therefore suit an ISP, when one device disconnects from the system, to reassign its dynamic IP address to another device. Static IP numbers, in contrast, retain the same configuration, with the address being assigned 'once and for all'.[158]

Tracking and registering IP numbers enables whoever is carrying out the operation to know when users are doing what. So if, for example, I like to stream certain movies at night, tracking my IP will reveal what I am watching and at what time. This may be information that I am happy for others to have. It may, however, be information that I want to keep very secret. In either case, it is information about me. From this point of view, an IP constitutes 'personal data' and its tracking and recording by third parties is therefore a 'processing' of personal data.

IP addresses have been considered personal data by courts and by privacy authorities, although this depends on the legislation in place and, in particular, on how exactly 'personal data' is defined. For instance, the Assistant Privacy Commissioner of Canada held that IP addresses were personal information since they could be combined with the records of ISPs to identify users. The Canadian Personal Information Protection and Electronic Documents Act (PIPEDA), in fact, defines personal information as 'information about an identifiable individual' (Section 2(1)). Since an IP number can be associated to a specific person, it should be

---

[158] See *Entry: Internet Address* in Collin (n 131).

considered to be personal data.[159] The same interpretation was given by the Article 29 Data Protection Working Party,[160] according to which 'IP addresses attributed to Internet users are personal data and are protected by EU Directives 95/46 and 97/66'.[161] Indeed, the definition of personal data according to European Directive 95/46 comprises 'any information relating to an identified or *identifiable* natural person'.[162]

The European Data Protection Supervisor also considers IP addresses to be personal data under Directive 95/46. The Supervisor stated that, since 'an IP address serves as an identification number which allows finding out the name of the subscriber to whom such IP address has been assigned', 'it is only possible to conclude that IP addresses and the information about the activities linked to such addresses constitutes

---

[159] See PIPEDA Case Summaries n. 25/2001 – *A Broadcaster Accused of Collecting Personal Information via Web Site* <www.priv.gc.ca/en/opc-actions-and-decisions/investigations/investigations-into-businesses/2001/pipeda-2001-025/> accessed 10 February 2017; n. 2005/315 – *Web-centred company's safeguards and handling of access request and privacy complaint questioned* <www.priv.gc.ca/en/opc-actions-and-decisions/investigations/investigations-into-businesses/2005/pipeda-2005-315/> accessed 10 February 2017; n. 2005/319 – *ISP's anti-spam measures questioned* <www.priv.gc.ca/en/opc-actions-and-decisions/investigations/investigations-into-businesses/2005/pipeda-2005-319/> accessed 10 February 2017: 'an IP address can be considered personal information if it can be associated with an identifiable individual ... For the purposes of this complaint, which involved the sending of e-mail by the complainant, the Assistant Commissioner accepted that the originating IP address identified the complainant and was therefore his personal information, as per section 2' of PIPEDA.

[160] Art. 29 Working Party is so called because it was introduced by art. 29 of Directive 95/46/EC of the European Parliament and of the Council of 24 October 1995 on the protection of individuals with regard to the processing of personal data and on the free movement of such data. See Chapter 3, Section 3.2 for more information.

[161] Opinion 2/2002 on the use of unique identifiers in telecommunication terminal equipment: the example of IPv6, adopted 30 May 2002, at 3 <http://ec.europa.eu/justice/data-protection/article-29/documentation/opinion-recommendation/files/2002/wp58_en.pdf>. Consider also Opinion 4/2007 on the concept of personal data, adopted 20 June 2007, at 16 <http://ec.europa.eu/justice/data-protection/article-29/documentation/opinion-recommendation/files/2007/wp136_en.pdf> and Opinion 1/2008 on data protection issues related to search engines, adopted 4 April 2008, at 8 <http://ec.europa.eu/justice/data-protection/article-29/documentation/opinion-recommendation/files/2008/wp148_en.pdf> all accessed 10 February 2017.

[162] Emphasis added.

personal data'.[163] The CJEU has also considered IP addresses to be personal information.[164]

Inevitably, opinions on the qualification of IP numbers as personal data vary, among both academics and courts. Some academics, for instance, hold that an IP address does not identify a person, because it only reveals the device from which specific content comes. Therefore, the IP number itself cannot lead to the identification of a person: only the subsequent matching of that IP number with the personal information held by the ISP allows the identity of the user to be established. This would mean, in turn, that IP addresses were only 'partial' personal data.[165]

A recent decision by the CJEU provides another example of this interpretative ambiguity. In 2014 the Bundesgerichtshof (Federal Court of Justice of Germany) filed a reference for a preliminary ruling in order to establish whether an IP addresses could be considered personal data per se when only a third person has further information that would enable the user to be identified. The opinion of the Advocate General in the case was that 'a dynamic IP address ... constitutes ... "personal data", to the extent that an Internet service provider has other additional data which, when linked to the dynamic IP address, facilitates identification of the user'.[166] The Court itself reached a very similar conclusion, stating that IP addresses are personal data when the provider has additional information and the legal means with which to identify the subject.[167]

In addition to the above, it is important to be aware that IP addresses can give misleading information, especially in contexts such as the one here considered. As mentioned, dynamic IP numbers can be assigned to different people at different times. A subject may be sued because her IP number is linked to an infringing activity, even though she had nothing to

---

[163] EDPS Opinion, 22 February 2010, OJ 2010/C 147/1, Opinion of the European Data Protection Supervisor on the current negotiations by the EU of an Anti-Counterfeiting Trade Agreement (ACTA).

[164] See the CJEU's decision in Case C-70/10 *Scarlet Extended SA v. SABAM* [2011] ECR I-11959, para 26.

[165] Pieremilio Sammarco, 'Alla ricerca del giusto equilibrio da parte della Corte di Giustizia UE nel confronto tra diritti fondamentali nei casi di impiego di sistemi tecnici di filtraggio' [2012] Diritto dell'informazione e dell'informatica 297. For a very similar approach, see also Fanny Coudert and Evi Werkers, 'In the Aftermath of the Promusicae Case: How to Strike the Balance?' [2008] International Journal of Law and Information Technology 50, 57ff, spec. 60.

[166] Case C-582/14 *Patrick Breyer v. Bundesrepublik Deutschland* [2016] ECLI:EU:C:2016:339, Opinion of AG Campus Sanchez-Bordona, para 106.

[167] Case C-582/14 *Patrick Breyer v. Bundesrepublik Deutschland* [2016] ECLI:EU:C:2016:77914, paras 49 and 65.

do with the actual infringement. Furthermore, and most importantly, an IP address only identifies the machine that is linked to it, and not the person behind the screen when the infringing activity occurred. Some courts have raised these concerns, in cases such as the ones we are examining here.[168]

Based on these premises, IP numbers can be considered personal information. The nature of the conflict should now be obvious, and likewise the task that judges were (and are) obliged to carry out, that of balancing the conflict between copyright and informational privacy.

While the US, Canadian and Italian systems differ significantly in many ways, judges in all three jurisdictions have found themselves struggling to understand which right should prevail. As I will go on to discuss, this is partly due to the ambiguity of the above-mentioned provisions. It is also connected to the fact that the preservation of one of the rights is impossible without detriment to the other: if copyright is to be enforced, users' personal data must be disclosed and vice versa: the preservation of users' personal information means that copyright cannot be enforced.

It is true that the theories mentioned in the previous section always deal with fundamental or constitutional rights, which copyright and information privacy are not necessarily considered to be. However, the US, Canada and Italy all consider privacy (including informational privacy), to be a constitutional right. Even though none of the countries specifically mentions privacy in its fundamental Charter, they have all developed consistent case law that now permits the inclusion of privacy within constitutionally recognized rights.[169] In addition, some international and supranational charters, such as the European Convention on Human Rights (art. 8) and the European Charter of Fundamental Rights and Freedoms (arts. 7 and 8), consider privacy to be a fundamental right. Moreover, privacy is mentioned among the rights protected by art. 12 of the Universal Declaration of Human Rights.

The characterization of copyright as a constitutional, fundamental right is more questionable. None of the three systems explicitly includes copyright in its Constitution. Nonetheless, intellectual property (hence,

---

[168] '[T]his Court's concerns about the conduct of this litigation going forward, particularly in light of the serious questions about plaintiffs' ability to properly identify defendants based solely upon their IP addresses', *Malibu Media, LLC v. John Doe*, CV 12-1147 (JS) (GRB) 5 <http://beckermanlegal.com/Lawyer_Copyright_Internet_Law/inrebittorrent_120731Order.pdf> accessed 10 February 2017.

[169] See Chapter 3, Section 2.

copyright) is commonly traced back to the right to property, which is usually recognized as both a constitutional and a fundamental right.[170] Furthermore, copyright (intellectual property) is mentioned in art. 17 of the European Charter of Fundamental Rights and Freedoms. And so, although there is no unanimous consensus on the qualification of either right as 'fundamental' or even 'constitutional', for the purpose of this book we can accept that they have both been treated as such.

Both copyright and privacy originated, and continue to exist, as 'rights in balance'. As we will see in the next chapter, copyright regulation always contains certain limits to the copyright holder's rights. From its inception, copyright has provided a means for balancing the interests of author and public. Modern copyright legislation is the result of a checks-and-balances process in which the different rights of different stakeholders need to be preserved. A variety of measures, such as the choice of copyrightable works, the duration of copyright, and the exceptions and limitations applicable, (should) enable this balance to be achieved.

The same argument applies to privacy. The right to privacy has always been conceived as a limit to the freedom of speech; the notion of privacy arose as a counterbalance to the invasive thrust of journalism made possible by the introduction of new technologies.[171] This characteristic of the right to privacy persists, as the fact that privacy is more and more often juxtaposed with surveillance and national security demonstrates. The whole history of privacy and personal data protection is built on the concept of balancing[172] and so it is no surprise that information privacy has also collided with copyright enforcement.

The need to find equilibrium is an intrinsic part of modern society. On the one hand lie individual interests; on the other, public and/or collective ones. In democratic societies, the task of striking a correct balance is usually delegated to lawmakers and, in a second phase, to interpreters.

This book is an attempt to further investigate the role of interpreters – judges, in this instance – in the difficult task of rights balancing.

---

[170] See Chapter 2, Section 2.

[171] Here I am again referring to Warren and Brandeis (n 145). See also the book by M Tunick, *Balancing Privacy and Free Speech. Unwanted Attention in the Age of Social Media* (Routledge 2015). See also the words of the 'Soraya Case' by the Italian Corte di Cassazione: Cass. civ., 27.5.1975, n. 2129 in *Foro it.*, 1976, I, 2895.

[172] See Chapter 3, Section 2.

3. A DIFFERENT HYPOTHESIS: CONCEPTUAL BALANCING?

Balancing – in all forms – is now a fact; it originated a century ago in the minds of academics, was later taken up by courts, and is currently widespread in a number of different areas of law. It is therefore here to stay.

Although now extensively adopted as judicial practice,[173] balancing does not have the same meaning in all jurisdictions. On the contrary, in spite of what seems to be a 'common language', approaches may differ greatly.[174] However, many scholars believe that the approaches being taken on either side of the Atlantic are becoming increasingly more alike.[175] That said, even if the approaches taken were one day to become identical, the courts' decisions would not necessarily follow suit. Balancing depends on so many different factors that it will probably never have identical procedures, or results, in any two or more countries.

As indicated above, balancing has mainly been adopted by Supreme and Constitutional Courts when they have had to decide on a statute's constitutionality. In this section, and throughout the entire book, I shall maintain and demonstrate that balancing has, in fact, been applied by all kinds of judge, whenever they have found themselves in certain situations. The aim of the 'lower courts' – courts other than the Supreme or Constitutional – in engaging in balancing is different from that of the 'higher courts'. This is especially true when a Supreme Court engages in a 'judicial review', i.e. decides on the constitutionality of a particular norm. Such decisions clearly have a much greater effect than any lower court judgment and can hypothetically influence an indefinite number of lawsuits. This is the case of the Italian Corte costituzionale, which only decides on the constitutionality of norms: it has no power as a Supreme Court in lawsuits between private parties; this latter power is attributed to the Corte di cassazione. Hence, a decision adopted by the Italian Constitutional Court might not be the 'final word' in a lawsuit in which a particular constitutional challenge has arisen. The role and power of the

---

[173]   Stone Sweet and Mathews (n 11) 74.

[174]   Jacco Bomhoff, 'Balancing, the Global and the Local: Judicial Balancing as a Problematic Topic in Comparative (Constitutional) Law' [2008] Hastings International & Comparative Law Review 555, 560ff.

[175]   Barak, 'Proportionality (2)' (n 18) 754. See also the work of Stone Sweet and Mathews (n 11).

Corte costituzionale is thus absolutely different from those of all the other Italian courts.[176]

Leaving the Italian case aside, however, an obvious remark can be made: lower courts need to balance rights in order to achieve concrete ends – to allow the plaintiff to win and the defendant to lose, or vice versa.

The interpretation of constitutional rights provides lower courts with possible solutions in cases where norms do not supply incontrovertible directives.[177] Balancing thus becomes the tool by which judges reach a concrete decision; the instrument that allows them to overcome a stalemate,[178] going beyond 'the limitations of "law" in dealing with difficult cases'.[179] Balancing is the method which, as I shall later explain, not only enables the actual norm to be applied, but also, crucially, draws attention to the whole concept of conflicting rights.

But when do lower courts actually need to balance conflicting rights?

Even though lower courts may want to – and do – apply the tool of balancing in a number of different circumstances, my understanding is that they find themselves obliged to balance conflicting rights when the following two factors come into play simultaneously: the colliding rights are considered to be of the same 'rank' – i.e. constitutional or fundamental rights – within the legal system in which the judge is operating;[180] and the norms which have precipitated the conflict provide no clear indication of how it might be resolved.[181]

With regard to the first requirement, the previous section illustrated how both copyright and privacy (including information privacy) can be traced back to countries' Constitutions. Indeed, in all three of the systems under consideration the interpretations of the courts, including the Supreme Courts, testify to the relevance and importance of both rights,

---

[176] Bin (n 15) 120ff.

[177] Gino Scaccia, 'Il bilanciamento degli interessi in materia di proprietà intellettuale' [2005] AIDA – Annali Italiani Diritto D'Autore 198, 198. The use of constitutional rights by lower courts to reach solutions in the case before them is a result of the 'constitutionalization' of private law: Pino, 'Conflitto e bilanciamento' (n 26) 7–9.

[178] *Contra*: Zucca (n 10) 27.

[179] Bomhoff, 'Balancing, the Global and the Local' (n 174) 582.

[180] It should be noted, however, that the way that conflicts arise depends on the way rights are interpreted: Zucca (n 10) 27.

[181] Meaning when 'the issue to be decided … seems to be subsumable at the same time into two or more norms' and there is 'no precise and unambiguous rule to be applied' to the case: Pino, 'Conflitto e bilanciamento' (n 26) 2 [my translation].

and their fundamental, constitutional nature. This interpretation is also the result of the 'constitutionalization' of both rights at a supranational level, especially in the European context.

The analysis conducted in the next two chapters clearly demonstrates that the trend towards acknowledging both copyright and privacy as fundamental rights started many decades ago and is still ongoing. This, however, does not mean that one of the two rights cannot be accorded greater importance than the other within the system as a whole. Indeed – and this point lies at the heart of the book, and will be returned to later – this has been the basis of all of the decisions taken by judges when they have found themselves facing the conflict between privacy and copyright.

The second requirement, as stated above, refers to norms which create conflicts which they then leave open. For instance, a norm can easily solve a conflict if it includes a phrase such as 'notwithstanding the provision ...', clearly asserting that the protection of a right has to be safeguarded, even to the detriment of another/others. Conflicts can also be avoided by including specific exceptions within the norm itself.[182]

As will emerge from the case studies, the fact that the norms lacked clarity led judges into an impasse that could be – and in fact was – resolved only by weighing the interests at stake.[183] In cases where each litigant's legal interest is legitimate, but the court must nonetheless take a decision,[184] balancing becomes a necessity: it represents an empirical process through which judges can resolve a matter which would otherwise be irresolvable. The ambiguity resulting from the lack of a prevalent right – which may sometimes be intended by lawmakers, to give judges some leeway – means that judges have the opportunity, indeed the duty, to read the particular case in the light of the entire conception of each conflicting right.

Regardless of the methodological approach to balancing, which may differ from system to system, and even within a given system, judges who find themselves having to decide which right should prevail tend to consider what I have called the 'conception' of the conflicting rights. By 'conception' of a given right I mean the attitude of a legal system to that right. Conception emerges out of the organic whole of laws and policies

---

[182]   Pino, 'Conflitto e bilanciamento' (n 26) 16.
[183]   Ansgar Ohly, 'European Fundamental Rights and Intellectual Property' in Ansgar Ohly and Justine Pila (eds), *The Europeanization of Intellectual Property Law* (OUP 2013) 145, 156.
[184]   Stone Sweet (n 6) 11.

relating to a specific institution. It is both the essence of all regulations on a right and also the key to a systematic reading of the laws affecting that right.

This idea may not be immediately obvious; it should, however, be clarified by the analyses of copyright and (information) privacy found in Chapters 2 and 3 respectively. To begin with, the following example may prove helpful: Freedom of speech is generally recognized as a value of huge significance in the American system; even when it conflicts with other fundamental and constitutional rights it often prevails.[185] In my analysis of 'conception' this would mean that the 'conception' of freedom of speech in the US is particularly strong: the right pervades the entire legal system.

Although clearly not all rights or freedoms enjoy such a privileged position, some are regularly given pre-eminence over others. Essentially, the pre-eminence of a right is the product of a systematic interpretation of all the rules that govern it. The pre-eminence and strength of one right, and the inferiority or weakness of another, testify to the conception that a given system allocates to each right.

In some instances, a right is given predominance over others as a matter of law, this occurs (as already mentioned) when a law clearly states that one right must be preserved to the detriment of another. Another instance is when judges decide that one right should prevail over another: in such cases pre-eminence is not conferred by one specific regulation but is the by-product of a system of law, which, taken as a whole, portrays one right or freedom as more important than others.

This means that a situation in which two rights collide can always be resolved by looking at the system in its entirety, which entails looking at the systematic structure of the two rights. A further implication is that interpretation has to begin by examining the constitutional dimension of a right and carefully considering the way in which that right is regulated by the legal system. The conception of a given right is the sum of a number of indicators that can be gathered from any regulatory tool that involves and affects that right. A right's conception can be deduced by

---

[185] Paul Bernal, 'The EU, the US and Right to be Forgotten' in Serge Gutwirth, Ronald Leenes and Paul de Hert (eds), *Reloading Data Protection. Multidisciplinary Insights and Contemporary Challenges* (Springer Verlag 2014) 61, 69–70; Stone Sweet and Mathews (n 11) 164. This was called 'a rule of priority' by Zucca (n 10) 36–37. See, more generally, Frederick Schauer, 'The Exceptional First Amendment' in Michael Ignatieff (ed), *American Exceptionalism and Human Rights* (Princeton University Press 2005) 29.

analysing a wide range of legal tools, including the Constitution and its interpretation by courts, and governmental acts, at both national and local level. The conception of a right can also be derived by examining the framing and wording of laws and regulatory tools in general. As already mentioned, a simple statement that a particular right shall prevail demonstrates that a certain degree of importance is attached to that right: if only one right is mentioned, then it is clearly considered to be highly relevant or, at least, of higher relevance than the other rights involved.

Another signal of the value placed on a right is the way in which it is regulated: if lawmakers assume the burden of regulating most – or even any – aspects of the situations in which a right is at stake, that right is clearly considered to be of particular prominence in the system concerned. A virtuous circle then develops: the more a right is regulated, the greater the importance attached to and acquired by it becomes. Judges place ever higher value on the right and its importance consequently increases, and so on. Obviously, the opposite is also true: a right which is considered of lesser importance than others may be marginalized.

This is the process by which judicial reasoning is influenced by the conception of a given right, especially when the norms to be applied are not clear, as in the cases analysed in this book. Chapters 2 and 3 contain my analysis of the relevant legislation, revealing specific pictures for the two conflicting rights in each of the three countries. The decisions adopted by the courts of each country reflect – in the majority of cases – the conception of copyright and information privacy held by that country's legal system. I shall therefore maintain that when two rights have to be balanced against one another, the entire conception of each right weighs either in favour of or against it; the conception of the two rights is the ground for judicial rulings.

As I will demonstrate in Chapter 3, privacy is more highly valued in the Euro-Italian and Canadian contexts than it is in the American, where it is regarded as just one among many rights. Therefore, even though the approach taken by the three jurisdictions to copyright is similar (and has been getting closer), only in the US does the enforcement of copyright usually prevail over information privacy. I understand these outcomes as the result of the different conceptions of privacy and copyright in the three countries: this is what I call conceptual balancing.

Conceptual balancing can be summarized as follows: when two constitutional rights collide and there are no clear rules by which to define the dispute, courts approach the conflict by balancing the two rights. The solution is reached by considering the conception of both rights, i.e. their regulatory structure. Prevalence is given to the right to which the legal system as a whole attaches more importance.

While normally balancing is a technique applied by Supreme and Constitutional Courts, my aim is to show that, in fact, the 'lower courts' also apply the balancing method.

Of course, judges may be influenced by a number of factors, when weighing conflicting rights, and balancing can, on occasion, become a door through which cultural values enter into judicial decisions.[186] In fact, the entire conception of a right may be – and usually is – a by-product of the cultural understanding of that right. Policies may endorse and enhance the socio-cultural context in which they develop; policies, in turn, are embodied in judicial decisions.[187]

The interpretation of any right depends on the circumstances of the case in question, as well as on when and where the decision is taken. As mentioned earlier, balancing is influenced by a number of factors inherent within each legal system: the solution applied in one country may never be applied in another. Societal and cultural values are key factors in this regard, heavily influencing the cultural model and expectations of justice within the society in which the decision is delivered.[188] It has also been argued that balancing can have either an 'elementary form' or a 'sophisticated version': the latter also weighs societal interests beyond the actual conflict at stake.[189]

Many of the factors that impact upon judicial decision making are very hard to detect, just as 'gravity' is, when tangible objects are weighed on a set of scales.[190] From this perspective, balancing should neither be considered as a scientific method of weighing, nor as the description of such a method; rather, it is a metaphor for a multi-factorial decision, a decision taken by considering elements that go beyond simple logic or hermeneutical analysis of the text of the law.[191]

While there is a lot of scepticism about the very concept of balancing,[192] it may, in fact, be the only method by which all the values at stake in today's societies can be taken into account. Balancing should be

---

[186] Social perception is also key in accepting a specific decision and its rationale; this is especially true with respect to constitutional review: Alexy, 'Balancing' (n 60) 579–580.

[187] I have argued this more thoroughly elsewhere: Giovanella (n 37).

[188] Scaccia (n 23) 3964; Barak, 'Proportionality and Principled Balancing' (n 40) 7–10.

[189] McFadden (n 1) 586.

[190] Luizzi (n 11) 388–390.

[191] Scaccia (n 23) 3986.

[192] In addition to the works already cited, see Xavier Groussot, 'Rock the KaZaA: Another Clash of Fundamental Rights' [2008] Common Market Law Review 1745, 1761.

conceived of as a way of putting every factor in its just position. This is especially true when balancing is applied by 'lower courts', as in the cases here analysed. Technological development may allow new types of copyright infringement and privacy violation but balancing should be seen as a tool that enables judges to make proper decisions on the basis of each actual case.

As a final remark, I would like to point out once again that this work is based on case studies and thus only examines a limited range of lawsuits, namely those involving copyright and information privacy. Nonetheless, the methodology employed, as well as the overall idea of 'conceptual balancing', can be applied in any case where two (or more) rights collide. The analysis conducted in this book can serve as an example of a wider problem and may be considered a prototype, or an emblematic example, of clashes between two rights. Conceptual balancing should be seen as a new categorization of a not-so-new approach to judicial reasoning. My analysis is not intended to prescribe any particular role for the judges involved, and even less to explain how they should decide cases. It is just another, humble, contribution to the analysis of judicial reasoning.

2. Copyright and file-sharing regulation in the US, Canada and Italy

1. COMPARING NATIONAL LEGAL FRAMEWORKS FOR COPYRIGHT AND FILE-SHARING

The current chapter is devoted to the exploration of the legal frameworks for copyright in the US, Canada and Italy. The frameworks show some common points and some differences, which will be outlined through the analysis of specific aspects of copyright legislation. It can already be anticipated that, somehow, US and Italian frameworks are closer to each other than they are to the Canadian framework. This difference, which used to be more obvious in the past, has lessened due to recent Canadian reforms. Nevertheless, the analysis will demonstrate that the US and Italy offer higher protection for copyright than Canada does. This conclusion can be drawn if considering copyright regulations in their entirety.

Starting from the international level, the US, Canada and Italy are all part of the most important Treaties governing copyright, namely the Berne Convention for the Protection of Literary and Artistic Works[1] and the World Intellectual Property Organization (WIPO) Treaties of 1996.[2]

---

[1] The Berne Convention was the first and most important of the multilateral copyright agreements. It replaced the agreements existing prior to 1886. See Sam Ricketson, *The Berne Convention of the Protection of Literary and Artistic Works: 1886–1986* (Longman 1987) 39ff. On the Berne Convention in general, see also Sam Ricketson and Jane Ginsburg, *The Berne Convention for the Protection of Literary and Artistic Works: 1886–1986* (OUP 2006). On international copyright law: Silke von Lewinski, *International Copyright Law and Policy* (OUP 2008); Paul Goldstein and P Bernt Hugenholtz, *International Copyright. Principles, Law, and Practice* (OUP 2013); Daniel J Gervais (ed), *International Intellectual Property. A Handbook of Contemporary Research* (Edward Elgar Publishing 2015).

[2] For a detailed analysis of the WIPO Treaties, see Mihály Ficsor, *The Law of Copyright and the Internet: the 1996 WIPO Treaties, Their Interpretation, and Implementation* (OUP 2002); Jörg Reinbothe and Silke von Lewinski, *The WIPO Treaties on Copyright. A Commentary on the WCT, the WPPT, and the BTAP* (OUP 2015).

Regarding the former, Italy was one of the signatory states in 1886.[3] Canada joined the Treaty in 1928,[4] while the US only entered the Convention in 1988,[5] mostly due to the need for an in-depth modification of its copyright legislation in the event of accession to the Convention. Other international agreements followed the Berne Convention: these Treaties were mainly linked to neighbouring rights.[6]

More recent important treaties include the WIPO Copyright Treaty (WCT) and the WIPO Performances and Phonograms Treaty (WPPT) adopted in 1996. At the core of these Treaties was the concern for the impact of digital technologies on copyright and related rights. The Treaties also introduced enforcement measures of various kinds.[7]

The US enacted the most important provisions of the WIPO Treaties as early as 1998, with the Digital Millennium Copyright Act (DMCA).[8] Italy's implementation is a derivation of EU Directive 2001/29/EC on the harmonisation of certain aspects of copyright and related rights in the

---

[3]   Ratified and executed in Italy with Legge 20.6.1978, no. 399.

[4]   On 10 April 1928 Canada declared the continued application of the Treaty, which had been ratified by the UK when Canada was a British territory.

[5]   Berne Convention Implementation Act of 1988, An Act to amend title 17, United States Code, to implement the Berne Convention for the Protection of Literary and Artistic Works, as revised in Paris on July 24, 1971, and for other purposes.

[6]   For instance, Rome Convention for the Protection of Performers, Producers of Phonograms, and Broadcasting Organizations of 1961; Geneva Convention for the Protection of Producers of Phonograms Against Unauthorized Duplication of Their Phonograms of 1971; Brussels Convention Relating to the Distribution of Programme-Carrying Signals Transmitted by Satellite of 1974; and the Agreement on Trade-Related Aspects of Intellectual Property Rights (TRIPS) of 1994. See also the recent WIPO Beijing Treaty on Audiovisual Performances of 2012, not yet in force. For an in-depth analysis, see references cited at nn 1 and 2. On the TRIPs agreement: Daniel J Gervais, *The TRIPS Agreement. Drafting History and Analysis* (Sweet & Maxwell 2012).

[7]   On enforcement provisions, see Ficsor (n 2) 579ff.

[8]   An Act passed on October 28, 1998, Pub. Law No. 105-304, 112 Stat. 2860. On this regulation see David Nimmer, 'Appreciating Legislative History: The Sweet and Sour Spots of the DMCA's Commentary' [2002] Cardozo Law Review 917; Id, *Copyright: Sacred Test, Technology, and the DMCA* (Kluwer Law International, 2003); Christine Wildpaner, *The U.S. Digital Millennium Copyright Act. A Challenge for Fair Use in the Digital Age*, Vienna (Medien und Recht, 2004) 49ff; Brandon Brown, 'Fortifying the Safe Harbors: Reevaluating the DMCA in a Web 2.0 World' [2008] Berkeley Technology Law Journal 437 <http://scholarship.law.berkeley.edu/btlj/vol23/iss1/18/> accessed 15 February 2017.

information society,[9] through decreto legislativo 9.4.2003, no. 68. The Canadian path to the implementation of the WIPO Treaties was much longer and more arduous: the WIPO Treaties were not implemented until 2012, with the Copyright Modernization Act.[10] Even though the current legal frameworks of the three countries are similar, the fact that Canada took so much longer than the US and Italy to implement the WIPO Treaties demonstrates the extent to which its approach differs from that of the other two countries.

To give a more robust account of these differences, this chapter will start with a concise explanation of the legal framework for copyright in the three countries and will go on to analyse certain important aspects of copyright regulation. In particular, the focus is on four cardinal aspects: first, the constitutional protection of copyright (Section 2.2); second, copyright protection for musical works, with a particular reference to its exceptions and limitations, and the regulation of file-sharing activities (Sections 2.3, 2.4 and 25); third, specific enforcement provisions (Section 2.6); and fourth, the liability of online intermediaries (Section 2.7).

These aspects were chosen as a testing ground to highlight the differences and similarities between the three systems:[11] the investigation reveals that, in spite of the existence of international Treaties, national implementation and interpretation are still key to the shaping of copyright in these countries. Canada, for example, still takes a softer, looser approach than that of the US and Italy, in more ways than one.

---

[9] Directive 2001/29/EC of the European Parliament and of the Council of 22 May 2001 on the harmonisation of certain aspects of copyright and related rights in the information society (InfoSoc Directive) [2001] OJ L 167/10. Recitals 15 and 19 of Directive 2001/29 explain that the Directive represents the implementation of WIPO Treaties. For a comment on this Directive, see Michael Walter and Silke Von Lewinski, 'Information Society Directive' in Michael Walter and Silke Von Lewinski (eds), *European Copyright Law* (OUP, 2010), 921; Christophe Geiger, Franciska Schönherr, Irini Stamatoudi and Paul Torremans, 'The Information Society Directive' in Irini Stamatoudi and Paul Torremans (eds), *EU Copyright Law* (Edward Elgar Publishing 2014) 395.

[10] Previous Bills had tried to implement the Treaty: Bill C-11, An Act to amend the Copyright Act, 1st Sess., 41st Canadian Parliament, 2011. Previous attempts include: Bill C-60, An Act to amend the Copyright Act, 38th Canadian Parliament, 1st Session, 2005; Bill C-61, An Act to amend the Copyright Act, 39th Canadian Parliament, 2nd Session, 2008; Bill C-32, An Act to amend the Copyright Act, 40th Canadian Parliament, 3rd Session, 2010.

[11] The scope of the analysis is inherently limited. Copyright law is an extensive – increasingly broad – subject, which cannot be covered in its entirety in a few pages. The analysis therefore concentrates on some specific aspects, those most relevant to the cases examined in this book.

2. CONSTITUTIONAL PROVISIONS ON COPYRIGHT

The first clear difference between the three systems lies in the constitutional protection of copyright.

Only the US Constitution contains explicit copyright provision – the famous 'Copyright clause' or 'Progress clause'[12] – universally considered to be the source of copyright, and, more generally, intellectual property (IP), protection in the US. Clause 8, Section 8, Article 1 of the US Constitution notably states: 'The Congress shall have the power … [t]o promote the progress of science and useful arts, by securing for limited times to authors and inventors the exclusive right to their respective writings and discoveries'. This section is the benchmark against which all US laws on copyright have to be measured.[13]

The Copyright clause both provides the basis for the power of Congress to legislate in the field of IP and defines the grounds upon which such legislation should rest. In what might be considered a typically utilitarian manner,[14] Section 8 tries to balance the encouragement of intellectual creativity with the need to allow knowledge to

---

[12]   On the Copyright Clause see, particularly, Karl Fenning, 'The Origin of the Patent and Copyright Clause of the Constitution' [1929] Georgetown Law Journal 109; Ralph Oman, 'The Copyright Clause: "A Charter For A Living People"' [1987] University of Baltimore Law Review 99; Edward C Walterscheid, 'To Promote the Progress of Science and Useful Arts: The Background and Origin of the Intellectual Property Clause of the United States Constitution' [1994] Journal of Intellectual Property Law 1; L Ray Patterson, 'Understanding the Copyright Clause' [2000] Journal of the Copyright Society of USA 365; Edward C Walterscheid, *The Nature of the Intellectual Property Clause: A Study in Historical Perspective* (William S Hein & Co 2002); Dotan Oliar, 'Making Sense of the Intellectual Property Clause: Promotion of Progress as a Limitation on Congress's Intellectual Property Power' [2006] Georgetown Law Journal 1771.

[13]   It was very difficult to understand who could be considered an 'author' and what could be considered 'writings'. See Committee on Judiciary, Subcommittee on Patents, Trademarks and Copyright, 86th Cong., 1st Sess., Copyright Law Revision, 'Study No. 3, The Meaning of "Writings" in the Copyright Clause of the Constitution', 1956, 61ff <www.copyright.gov/history/studies/study3.pdf> accessed 15 February 2017.

[14]   Robert P Merges, Peter S Menell and Mark A Lemley, *Intellectual Property in the New Technological Age* (5th edn, Aspen 2010) 11ff. There are many theories – philosophical, social, economic, etc. – underpinning and/or justifying IP. Some clues are provided in Peter Drahos, *A Philosophy of Intellectual Property* (ANU Press 1996); Justin Hughes, 'The Philosophy of Intellectual Property' [1988] Georgetown Law Journal 287; William Fisher,

circulate freely in society. The US Supreme Court specified that the limits and purposes stated in Section 8 should be taken into account in evaluating the overall copyright regulation rather than each single legislative act.[15]

The existence of this clause demonstrates the will of the founding fathers to promote science and knowledge, while still protecting authors' rights. The clause was obviously carefully considered, but there was no debate about its adoption: it seems that the founding fathers never discussed *whether* or not to put such a clause into their Constitution.[16] At the time of the Constitution's enactment, the United States envisioned itself as a promised land for scientists, whose work it would protect, thereby encouraging their migration and thus improving US society.[17] The Constitutional provision was intended to both encourage the production of thinkers and scientists in the new federal state, and to harmonize federal and common law protection.[18]

Whatever the original idea underlying the clause, both courts and lawmakers have undoubtedly interpreted its words with considerable latitude. The existence of the Copyright clause has never been an obstacle to the extension of copyright protection, either with regard to the terms of

---

'Theories of Intellectual Property' in Stephen R Munzer (ed), *New Essays in the Legal and Political Theory of Property* (CUP 2001) 168; Peter S Menell, 'Intellectual Property: General Theories', in Boudewijn Bouckaert and Gerrit de Geest (eds), *Encyclopedia of Law & Economics*, vol 2 (Edward Elgar Publishing 2000) 129; William A Landes and Richard A Posner, *The Economic Structure of Intellectual Property Law* (Harvard University Press 2003). For copyright in particular, see L Ray Patterson and Stanley F Birch, 'A Unified Theory of Copyright' [2009] Houston Law Review 215 <www.houstonlawreview.org/archive/downloads/46-2_pdf/01_Patterson.pdf> accessed 15 February 2017.

[15] See *Eldred v. Ashcroft*, 573 U.S. 186 (2003): the decision dealt with the extension of copyright term through the so-called Copyright Term Extension Act (Pub. L. 105-298). For a critical view, see Edward C Walterscheid, 'Musings on the Copyright Power: A Critique of Eldred v. Ashcroft' [2004] Albany Law Journal of Science & Technology 309.

[16] See Walterscheid (n 12) 83. The same work also explains the introduction of this clause into the US Constitution, at 83ff; Craig Joyce and L Ray Patterson, 'Copyright in 1791: An Essay Concerning the Founders' View of the Copyright Power Granted to Congress in Article I, Section 8, Clause 8 of the US Constitution' [2003] Emory Law Journal 909; Oliar (n 12) 1789–1790.

[17] Irah Donner, 'The Copyright Clause of the U.S. Constitution: Why Did the Framers Include It With Unanimous Approval?' [1992] American Journal of Legal History 361, 362.

[18] Committee on Judiciary (n 13) *passim.*

protection or with regard to the subject matter of protection.[19] In the nineteenth century major amendments were introduced which continuously modified the original provisions of the Copyright Act.[20]

Neither the Italian nor the Canadian system has a clause similar to the US one. However, since Canada, like the US, is a federal state, Section 91(23) of the Constitution Act of 1867 explicitly gives the Parliament exclusive legislative authority on copyright.[21]

The similarities stop here. The Canadian Constitution baldly states that the Canadian states cannot legislate on copyright: the provision is absolutely cut and dry and leaves no space for creative interpretation. In contrast, as mentioned, the US Copyright clause provides fruitful ground from which to elaborate interpretations. Furthermore, while the US Supreme Court has declared that the Progress clause also empowers Congress to define the scope of these rights, the Canadian Supreme Court has held that Parliament is not allowed to define the scope of the jurisdiction recognized by the Constitution.[22]

The US Copyright clause, which is more elaborately worded, has been considered by some to be a grant of power to Congress, and, by others, a limitation on that power.[23] The peculiarity of the Progress clause is that it is the only constitutional concession of authority to Congress that simultaneously specifies the means through which Congress shall exercise that authority;[24] namely 'by securing for limited times to authors and inventors the exclusive right to their respective writings and discoveries'.

It has been asserted that if the founding fathers had wanted to grant limitless power to Congress, they simply would not have written the

---

[19]   Ibid 71ff.

[20]   Morris A Singer, 'The Failure of the PRO-IP Act in a Consumer-Empowered Era of Information Production' [2009] Suffolk University Law Review 185, 189, referring to *Sony Corp. of America v. Universal City Studios*, 464 U.S. 417 (1984), at 430; for a summary of this seminal case see Chapter 1.

[21]   The Constitution Act of 1867, formerly known as the British North America Act (BNA Act), forms a significant part of the Canadian Constitution. See P.W. Hogg, *Constitutional Law of Canada* (Carswell 2010) 1–7ff.

[22]   Jeremy De Beer, 'Copyrights, Federalism, and the Constitutionality of Canada's Private Copying Levy' [2004] McGill Law Journal 735, 744, referring to the US case *Eldred v. Ashcroft* (n 15) and to the Canadian case *Reference Re Same-Sex Marriage* [2004] 3 S.C.R. 698. See also David S Olson, 'A Legitimate Interest in Promoting the Progress of Science: Constitutional Constraints on Copyright Laws' [2011] Vanderbilt Law Review 185, 189.

[23]   *Graham v. John Deere Co.*, 383 U.S. 1 (1966). See Walterscheid (n 12) 153ff. Different interpretations of the aim of the clause exist: Oliar (n 12) 1810ff.

[24]   Walterscheid (n 12) 11.

preamble to the clause.[25] If this statement were correct, and given the unambiguous wording of the Canadian Copyright clause, the Canadian Parliament would have unlimited scope for legislation. This is not actually the case: as I shall demonstrate in the next few pages, Canada's legislation is more restrictive and more focused on authors' rights than US legislation.[26]

In the Italian system, legislative power over intellectual property rights (IPR) is exclusive to the state: art. 117 of the Constitution provides a list of subjects on which only the state can legislate and letter r) of art. 117 includes 'creative works'. This wording has been interpreted as including every kind of IPR.[27] Residual subjects are under the jurisdiction of the regions.

The Italian Constitution never explicitly mentions copyright, but the protection of IP can be traced back to different provisions, including those related to the protection and promotion of culture and scientific research (art. 9), or the freedom of arts and sciences and their teaching (art. 33),[28] or freedom of expression (art. 21). As well as these provisions, art. 3 protects people's equality; this includes the possibility to generate and publish creative works, which are considered to be avenues for the full development of the human personality.

These articles provide that the state has a duty to protect the creation and publication of works of authorship; they do not require the state to grant exclusive rights in creative works. Nonetheless, the constitutional protection accorded to science, art, and freedom of expression justifies

---

25   Olson (n 22) 189–190.

26   See De Beer (n 22) for a critique on the intervention of the Canadian Parliament outside the scope of the Copyright clause. The author states (at 762): 'Canada's copyrights clause does not give Parliament carte blanche to enact cultural, economic, technological, or regulatory policies under the auspices of the *Copyright Act.* Copyrights legislation must remain tightly linked to authors' cultural creativity.' Wanda Noel and Louis BZ Davis, 'Some Constitutional Consideration in Canadian Copyright Law Revision' [1981] Canadian Patent Reporter 17 expressed their opinion for a broader interpretation of Section 91(23) of the Constitution Act of 1867, in light of the possible introduction of neighbouring rights in Canadian copyright law.

27   Consider, for instance, the decision by the Italian Constitutional Court of 14.11.2008, no. 368, in Giur. cost. 2008, 6, 4380.

28   See Corte Cost., 6.4.1995, no. 108, in AIDA, 1995, 348.

the state's intervention, including through the implementation of exclusive rights.[29] The Italian Constitutional Court has held that the importance of the protection of intellectual works is a rationale for the implementation of a criminal protection of copyright law.[30]

Italy is also bound by the Charter of Fundamental Rights of the EU, which became legally binding with the Lisbon Treaty of 13 December 2007. Article 17 of the Charter contains a specific provision which states that '[i]ntellectual property shall be protected'. The provision, which makes no reference to the limited nature of IP, has been interpreted as an obligation for EU law to protect existing and future IP rights.[31] At the same time, the dry wording of the provision could be seen as a simple clarification of art. 17(1) regarding the right to property,[32] which states that IP is a form of property protected by EU law.[33] Interpreted thus, IPR could still be seen as limited.

---

[29] Luigi Carlo Ubertazzi, *Commentario breve alle leggi su proprietà intellettuale e concorrenza* (CEDAM 2016) 1455.

[30] See the decisions of Corte Cost., 13.4.1972, no. 65 <www.giurcost.org/decisioni/1972/0065s-72.html> and 17.4.1968, no. 25 <www.giurcost.org/decisioni/1968/0025s-68.html> both accessed 15 February 2017.

[31] Christophe Geiger, 'Intellectual Property Shall be Protected!? – Article 17 (2) of the Charter of Fundamental Rights of the European Union: a Mysterious Provision with an Unclear Scope' [2009] European Intellectual Property Review 113. The English version of the provision differs from those in other languages (German: 'Geistiges Eigentum wird geschütz'; French: 'La propriété est protégée'; Italian: 'La proprietà intellettuale è protetta'): all these versions say that 'IP is protected'. The use of 'shall' seems to evoke a duty to strengthen the protection, see ibid, 115.

[32] Art. 17(1) states: 'Everyone has the right to own, use, dispose of and bequeath his or her lawfully acquired possessions. No one may be deprived of his or her possessions, except in the public interest and in the cases and under the conditions provided for by law, subject to fair compensation being paid in good time for their loss. The use of property may be regulated by law in so far as is necessary for the general interest.'

[33] See Geiger (n 31) 116; Jonathan Griffiths, 'Criminal Liability for Intellectual Property Infringement in Europe – the Role of Fundamental Rights' in Christophe Geiger (ed), *Criminal Enforcement of Intellectual Property. A Handbook of Contemporary Research* (Edward Elgar Publishing 2012) 197; Jonathan Griffiths and Luke McDonagh, 'Fundamental Rights and European Intellectual Property Law – The Case of Art 17(2) of the EU Charter' in Christophe Geiger (ed), *Constructing European Intellectual Property Achievements and New Perspectives* (Edward Elgar Publishing 2013) 80. On balancing, and on copyright as property, see Caterina Sganga, 'EU Copyright Law Between Property and Fundamental Rights: A Proposal to Connect the Dots' in Roberto Caso and Federica Giovanella (eds), *Balancing Copyright Law in the Digital*

Although whether or not the EU is bound by the Charter has still not been firmly established,[34] the CJEU and the EU itself have already demonstrated their intent to respect this new fundamental right in various cases.[35]

While the US clause declares that IP rights are (somewhat) limited and that exclusive rights are the means through which to protect IP, art. 17(2) of the European Charter only proclaims that IP has to be protected. Even though it is clear that IP needs to be balanced with and limited by other rights, the European provision leaves even more possibilities open than does the US provision.

In general, copyright is today increasingly considered to be a property right. This has not always been the case; on the contrary, as recently as in 1948, art. 27 of the Universal Declaration of Human Rights categorized it as a 'cultural right', stating that 'Everyone has the right freely to participate in the cultural life of the community, to enjoy the arts and to share in scientific advancement and its benefits'; and 'Everyone has the

---

Age. Comparative Perspectives (Springer 2015) 1. Some scholars argue that the Italian Constitution also protects IPR as property: Ubertazzi, *Commentario* (n 29) 1456.

[34]   On 18 December 2014, the CJEU delivered an opinion related to the EU's accession to the European Convention on Human Rights (ECHR). The Court ruled that the Draft Accession Agreement (DAA) for the accession of the EU to the ECHR was not compatible with the EU Treaties. The Court had already expressed itself thus almost 20 years earlier, with Opinion n. 2/94 on 28 March 1996 <http://curia.europa.eu/juris/showPdf.jsf?text=&docid=99549&pageIndex=0&doclang=en&mode=lst&dir=&occ=first&part=1&cid=13221> accessed 15 February 2017. The 2014 opinion appears to be a step back, or at least a halt, in the coordination between the EU and both the European Charter and Court of Human Rights. For a brief comment, see Tobias Lock, 'Oops! We Did It Again – the CJEU's Opinion on EU Accession to the ECHR' (VerfBlog, 19 December 2014) <www.verfassungsblog.de/en/oops-das-gutachten-des-eugh-zum-emrk-beitritt-der-eu> accessed 15 February 2017; Jed Odermatt, 'A Giant Step Backwards? Opinion 2/13 on the EU's Accession to the European Convention On Human Rights', KU Leuven Working Paper No. 150 – February 2015 <https://ghum.kuleuven.be/ggs/wp150-odermatt.pdf> accessed 15 February 2017.

[35]   See, for example, Recital 32 of Directive 2004/48/EC of the European Parliament and of the Council of 29 April 2004 on the enforcement of intellectual property rights. Consider also the *Promusicae v. Telefonica* decision of 29 January 2008, on which see Chapter 4, Section 5.1.

right to the protection of the moral and material interests resulting from
any scientific, literary or artistic production of which he is the author'.[36]

It is unquestionable that globally IP protection has been levelled out,
through international Treaties, and the three systems under discussion
have been part of this process. On the other hand, the 'constitutionality'
of IP – and of copyright – is still under debate.[37]

3. PROTECTION OF WORKS, MUSICAL ONES IN PARTICULAR

The countries' different constitutional approaches are mirrored in their
different copyright regulations. This section briefly describes the legal
protection provided in the three countries for musical works and similar
products. Although most of the lawsuits analysed here involve the
copyright infringement of musical works, and some provisions apply
only to such works, the majority are equally applicable to cinematographic or electronic literary works, which are, like songs, subject to
file-sharing.

Copyright legislation in the US, Canada and Italy has been amended
many times in an attempt to update rules and protect copyright from the
threats posed by technological evolution. The current statutes protecting
copyright – of which the Canadian is the oldest – were enacted in the
twentieth century. As previously mentioned, all three countries have
signed the major relevant international Treaties: this has led to the
relative homogenization of their legal frameworks for copyright.

The US regulation used to be part of the common law on copyright, in
conjunction with statutes on specific issues. Although common law had

---

[36] A tight wording was adopted in art. 15(1)(b) and (c) of the International
Covenant on Economic, Social and Cultural Rights adopted on 16 December
1966 by the General Assembly of the UN.

[37] For a different 'constitutional approach' to IP, and especially to copyright,
see Roberto Mastroianni, *Diritto internazionale e diritto d'autore* (Giuffrè 1997)
21ff; Roberto Mastroianni, 'Proprietà intellettuale e costituzioni europee' [2005]
AIDA 11; Christophe Geiger, '"Constitutionalising" Intellectual Property Law?
The Influence of Fundamental Rights on Intellectual Property in the European
Union' [2006] International Review of Intellecual Property and Competition Law
371; Christophe Geiger, 'Copyright's Fundamental Rights Dimension at EU
Level' in Estelle Derclaye (ed), *Research Handbook on the Future of EU
Copyright* (Edward Elgar Publishing 2009) 27; Laurence R Helfer, 'The New
Innovation Frontier? Intellectual Property and the European Court of Human
Rights' [2008] Harvard International Law Journal 1.

been unequivocally replaced as early as 1834 in the famous *Wheaton v. Peters* case[38], a common law or state law copyright was still recognized and enforced in unpublished works until the enactment of the Copyright Act of 1976.[39] Since then, in the US, as in Canada, there has been no common law of copyright.

The Copyright Act – Title 17 of the US Code (U.S.C.) – has undergone frequent revisions and has been the subject of important judicial interpretations. The current Copyright Act was introduced in 1976,[40] after decades of work, to replace the previous Act of 1909,[41] considered too basic to cope with modern American society. The Act of 1976 expanded both the scope and the duration of copyright protection, and introduced a pre-emption provision in favour of federal institutions. According to 17 U.S.C. § 301(a), 'no person is entitled to any such right or equivalent right in any such work under the common law or statutes of any State'.[42]

The same approach is taken by Canada, where, as noted above, only federal lawmakers can legislate on copyright/*droit d'auteur* by virtue of Section 91(23) of the Constitution Act of 1867. The current Copyright Act was enacted in 1921 and is the sole copyright legislation applicable, even though it has been frequently and substantially amended since its appearance.[43] The Act states that no copyright or other rights should exist in Canada other than under the Copyright Act itself.

The Italian protection for *diritto d'autore* is provided by Legge 22.4.1941 no. 633. This statute includes almost all the provisions related to copyright; only a few provisions can be found in the 1942 Civil Code.[44] Italian law no. 633/1941 maintains its original structure, despite the numerous amendments introduced, often the result of EU interventions.[45] In fact, even though the 1957 Treaty establishing the European

---

[38] 33 U.S. (Pet. 8) 591 (1834).

[39] Sheldon W Halpern, Craig Allen Nard and Kenneth L Port, *Fundamentals of United States Intellectual Property Law: Copyright, Patent, Trademark* (Wolters Kluwer Law 2012) 2.

[40] Enacted on 19 October 1976, as Pub. L. No. 94-553, came into effect from the beginning of 1978.

[41] Enacted on 4 March 1909, as Pub. L. No. 60-349.

[42] See Halpern, Nard and Port (n 39) 2–3.

[43] Copyright Act, R.S.C., 1985, c. C-42. For an account of Canadian copyright reforms, see John S McKeown, *Fox on Canadian Law of Copyright and Industrial Designs* (3rd edn, Carswell 2000) 39ff.

[44] Arts. 2575–2583 of the Italian Civil Code.

[45] For example, effective modifications occurred with Legge 18.8.2000, no. 248, the so-called 'anti-piracy law'. To implement European Directive 98/71/EC on legal protection of designs, Legge 633/41 was modified by decreto legislativo

Economic Community did not directly consider copyright, art. 30 of that Treaty allowed restrictions to the free circulation of goods and services for the protection of industrial property.[46] This provision has been used as a picklock, allowing Europe to intervene, with increasing frequency, in this strategic economic sector.

The current US Copyright Act has rendered common law copyright, and the distinction between published and unpublished works, obsolete.[47] US copyright exists in all original creative expressions, as long as they are 'fixed in any tangible medium of expression, now known or later developed, from which they can be perceived, reproduced, or otherwise communicated, either directly or with the aid of a machine or device' (Section 102).[48] Therefore, the current requirement is for a work to be fixed in any tangible medium of expression.[49] Section 101 defines as being 'fixed in a tangible medium of expression' any work which is 'sufficiently permanent or stable to permit it to be perceived, reproduced, or otherwise communicated for a period of more than transitory duration'. The list of Section 102 is considered open, capable of covering upcoming works of authorship.

Under US law prior to 1978 an author had to fulfil certain requirements before acquiring copyright in a work, which had to be registered, deposited and accompanied with an appropriate notice in order to gain the protection of the federal law. If notice was not given, protection was lost and the work fell into the public domain. These formalities still exist,[50] as they do in Canada. Under the 1976 Act, these formalities are

---

2.2.2001, no. 95. It was also amended by decreto legislativo 9.4.2003, no. 68 (which enacted Directive 2001/29/EC, on the harmonisation of certain aspects of copyright and related rights in the information society). Of particular relevance are the innovations introduced by decreto legislativo 16.3.2006, no. 140, introducing European Directive 2004/48/EC on the enforcement of intellectual property rights.

[46]   As of 1 December 2009, when the Lisbon Treaty came into force, the title of the 'Treaty establishing the European Community' is replaced by 'Treaty on the Functioning of the European Union' (TFEU) and the numbering of the two Treaties has been changed. The current numbering of art. 30 is art. 36.

[47]   Halpern, Nard and Port (n 39) 32ff. These changes were also necessary to comply with the Berne Convention for the Protection of Literary and Artistic Works, 9 September 1886.

[48]   17 U.S.C. § 102(a).

[49]   The work should be perceived, reproduced or otherwise communicated from this medium, with or without the aid of a machine, cf. 17 U.S.C. § 102.

[50]   Mary LaFrance, *Copyright Law in a Nutshell* (1st edn, Thomson West 2008) 95–114.

no longer a condition affecting the existence of the right; however, deposit and registration affect the ability to enforce copyright and to obtain certain remedies.[51] In an action for infringement, registration allows the use of some procedural and remedial issues, which are not available for unregistered work.[52] Registration also influences the damages recoverable by the plaintiff,[53] a peculiarity of the US copyright regime.

Similar conditions apply to the registration of works in Canada. Currently, the Canadian Copyright Act states that no copyright or other rights should exist in Canada other than under the Copyright Act itself. Copyright is granted to a host of different works upon their creation.[54] Automatic protection of copyright is not affected by the possibility of registering the work. Registration is, in fact, unnecessary for the subsistence of copyright, but, as in the US, a certificate of registration constitutes evidence that copyright exists in that work and that the person

---

[51] Sheldon W Halpern, *Copyright Law. Protection of Original Expression* (2nd edn, Carolina Academic Press 2010) 430ff. Registration is, for example, a prerequisite for an action for infringement of a 'United States work', see 17 U.S.C. § 411. This requisite is limited to US works in order not to affect foreign authors, as required by the Berne Convention. See LaFrance (n 50) 287ff. In order to comply with the obligations of the Berne Convention and other Treaties, only US works are subject to registration, see Halpern, Nard and Port (n 39) 36–37. Through the PRO-IP Act (An Act of October 13, 2008, Pub. Law No. 110–403, 122 Stat. 4256 – intended to enhance remedies for violations of intellectual property laws, and for other purposes) Congress intentionally eliminated the requirement of registration for criminal cases, making it easier to obtain copyright infringement criminal enforcement. Before the PRO-IP Act, it was unclear whether the registration requirement also applied in criminal cases. See Michael M DuBose, 'Criminal Enforcement of Intellectual Property Laws in the Twenty-First Century' [2006] Columbia Journal of Law & Arts 481, 488–489.

[52] For example, if the work is registered within five years of its first publication, the certificate of registration is *prima facie* evidence of the validity of the copyright, as well as of the facts stated in the certificate, see 17 U.S.C. § 410(c). Furthermore, certain formalities continue to have a key role in determining the copyright status of works that were first published before February 1989, see LaFrance (n 50) 95.

[53] See 17 U.S.C. § 412: only if registration precedes the act of infringement or infringement began after first publication, although if the infringement has occurred before registration, the plaintiff can recover statutory damages and attorney fees.

[54] Copyright Act, Section 5(1).

registered is the owner of the rights. In other words, it is a piece of *prima facie* evidence of copyright ownership.[55]

A different approach is taken by Italian Legge 633/1941, which, unlike the previously existing Italian laws on copyright, does not contemplate a registration system of copyrightable works. There are currently three different registers, but a work does not have to be registered to obtain protection under Legge 633/41.[56] Nonetheless, registration can help to prove both the existence and the paternity of a work, as in Canada and the US.[57] Protection is accorded to works which are exteriorized: a work is protected when it 'comes into the world'; nonetheless, some rights can be enjoyed only when a work becomes public.[58] The commonalities in the three systems can all be traced back to the provisions of the Berne Convention, art. 5(2) of which states that copyright enjoyment and exercise shall not be subject to any formality.

The Italian legislation begins by declaring that protection is extended to all creative works, in literature, music, figurative arts, architecture, theatre and cinematography, regardless of their form or expression. In other words, there are two requirements for a work to be protected: its 'creative character' and its affiliation to 'literature, music, figurative arts, architecture, theatre, and cinematography'.[59] Article 2, Legge 633/41 contains a list of copyright-protected works, including musical compositions and works (with or without words), music dramas, and those music variations which constitute original works. This list is interpreted by the majority of scholars as an open catalogue, allowing the protection of new forms of expression.[60]

---

[55]   McKeown (n 43) 403ff; Elizabeth F Judge and Daniel J Gervais, *Intellectual Property: The Law in Canada* (2nd edn, Carswell 2011) 248–250.

[56]   The three registers are a general register for all kinds of creative works, except for cinematographic works and computer programs, which have their own registers. Italy abandoned its registration regime as long ago as 1914, with Legge 14.10.1914, no. 1114, ratifying the Berlin Act of 13 November 1908, revising the Berne Convention for the Protection of Literary and Artistic Works. See Ubertazzi, *Commentario* (n 29) 1496ff and 1916ff.

[57]   See art. 103, co. 5, Legge 633/41.

[58]   Ubertazzi, *Commentario* (n 29) 1494ff.

[59]   Art. 1, Legge 633/41. Nicolò Abriani, Gastone Cottino and Marco Ricolfi, *Diritto industriale* in *Trattato di diritto commerciale diretto da Cottino*, vol. 2 (Cedam 2001) 360.

[60]   Paolo Greco and Paolo Vercellone, *I diritti sulle opere dell'ingegno* (Utet 1974) 55; Andrea Sirotti Gaudenzi, *Il nuovo diritto d'autore* (1st edn, Maggioli 2012) 73; Ubertazzi, *Commentario* (n 29) 1471–1487. Parallel to Legge 633/41, the Italian Civil Code (c.c.) also contemplates a few articles concerning IP

The Canadian and American regulations also protect a wide variety of works. When the Canadian Copyright Act was enacted, it only applied to published manuscripts. Nowadays, it protects many different kinds of works, including music, architectural plans, computer programs and unpublished works. Moreover, it grants copyright to 'every original literary, dramatic, musical and artistic work' upon the creation of the work.[61] This wording is loose enough for its interpretation to enable evolving technologies to obtain copyright protection.[62]

In the US system, the list of rights provided by Section 106 is considered complete and exhaustive.[63] According to this section, the author of a copyrighted work has the exclusive right to any of the following actions:

1. to reproduce the copyrighted work in copies or phonorecords;
2. to prepare derivative works based upon the copyrighted work;
3. to distribute copies or phonorecords of the copyrighted work to the public by sale or other transfer of ownership, or by rental, lease or lending;
4. in the case of literary, musical, dramatic and choreographic works, pantomimes, and motion pictures and other audiovisual works, to perform the copyrighted work publicly;
5. in the case of literary, musical, dramatic and choreographic works, pantomimes, and pictorial, graphic or sculptural works, including the individual images of a motion picture or other audiovisual work, to display the copyrighted work publicly; and
6. in the case of sound recordings, to perform the copyrighted work publicly by means of a digital audio transmission.

The first three rights are applicable to all categories of copyrightable works, while the other three apply only to the works they mention. The

---

works. Among them, art. 2575 c.c. provides that intellectual creative works belonging to science, literature, music, the figurative arts, architecture, theatre and cinematography are subject to copyright, regardless of their way or form of expression. The wording of this article is essentially the same as that of art. 1, Legge no. 633/41. The Italian Civil Code, in fact, came after Legge 633/41; the Code was enacted with Regio Decreto 16.03.1942, no. 262. Art. 2575 c.c. is considered to be an open provision for the protection of works of intellectual creation, see Sirotti Gaudenzi, above, 69.

[61] Copyright Act, Section 5(1).

[62] David Vaver, *Intellectual Property Law. Copyright, Patent, Trademark* (2nd edn, Irwin Law 2011) 64.

[63] Halpern, Nard and Port (n 39) 54.

right to reproduce is clearly the basic copyright protection, and also comprises the making of 'phonorecords'.[64] There is a 'tangibility requirement' that applies both to copies and to phonorecords.[65] Under Section 101, copies are 'material objects, other than phonorecords, in which a work is fixed by any method now known or later developed, and from which the work can be perceived, reproduced, or otherwise communicated, either directly or with the aid of a machine or device'; phonorecords are 'material objects in which sounds, except those accompanying a motion picture or other audiovisual work, are fixed by any method now known or later developed, and from which the sounds can be perceived, reproduced, or otherwise communicated, either directly or with the aid of a machine or device'. The term 'phonorecords' 'includes the material object in which the sounds are first fixed': the Act does not take into account the nature of the copying device or the medium, or the method, used.[66] It emerges from this definition that the difference between copies and phonorecords is that a phonorecord is the tangible fixation of sounds, while a copy is any tangible fixation other than a phonorecord.[67]

The reproduction right is independent from the public distribution right: the former is breached as soon as a copy is made, regardless of whether that copy is distributed or not.[68] The Copyright Act does not contain a definition of 'distribution'. Nonetheless, Section 101 defines 'publication' as the 'distribution of copies or phonorecords of a work to the public by sale or other transfer of ownership, or by rental, lease, or lending'.

The right to make available was not needed in US copyright, because it was already covered by the distribution right, together with the reproduction right. This means that the right to distribute also covers the offer to distribute.[69]

---

64   Ibid 55; LaFrance (n 50) 159.
65   LaFrance (n 50) 160.
66   Halpern, Nard and Port (n 39) 55–56.
67   Therefore, 'an mp3 file of a sound recording is a phonorecord, while a DVD, or any other tangible embodiment of an audiovisual work, is a copy': LaFrance (n 50) 160.
68   LaFrance (n 50) 163. Italy adopts the same approach: Greco and Vercellone (n 60) 133; Abriani, Cottino and Ricolfi (n 59) 415; Ubertazzi, *Commentario* (n 29) 1537ff.
69   Michael Schlesinger, 'Legal Issues in Peer-to-peer File-sharing, Focusing on the Right to Make Available' in Alain Strowel (ed), *Peer-to-peer File-sharing and Secondary Liability in Copyright Law* (Edward Elgar Publishing 2009) 43, 47 and 64ff. See *Elektra Entertainment Group v. Barker*, 551 F.Supp.2d 234

Section 106(4) should be included in the consideration of copyright for musical works as it protects the right 'to perform the copyrighted work publicly'.[70] The key elements of this definition are the words 'perform' and 'publicly'. Under Section 101 'perform' equals to recite, render, play, dance or act a work, either directly or by means of any device or process. Any act which allows a copyrighted work to be perceived by a viewer or listener, or causes a work to be reproduced, is a performance.[71] Hence, a performance can be by a 'human' performer, such as a singer or orchestra, as well as by a music player. Furthermore, the Act states that a separate performance occurs when a copyrighted work is transmitted or re-transmitted.[72]

'Publicly' is again defined by Section 101 as performing or displaying a work in a place open to the public or where a substantial number of people gather, provided that those people are outside the 'normal' family circle and its close acquaintances.[73] Also considered a public performance is the transmission or communication of a performance or the display of a work in a public place – as just defined – by means of any device or process, regardless of whether the public receives the performance or display in that place and at that time, or in different places, and at different times.[74]

A transmission can also be a performance to the public. This is the case when people receive it simultaneously or sequentially, i.e. if a hotel shows a movie in individual rooms upon the request of its guests.[75]

(2008); *Motown Record v. Theresa DePietro*, Civ. No. 04-CV-2246 (Feb. 16, 2007); *Atlantic Recording v. Anderson*, No. H-063578, 2008 WL 2316551 (S.D. Tex. Mar. 12, 2008), but *contra* see *London-Sire Records v. Does* 1-4, D. Mass., No. 1:04-cv-12434 (2008).

[70] It is essential to distinguish between the rights in a sound recording and those in a musical composition. Sound recordings enjoy a different kind of public performance right, under § 106(6), see LaFrance (n 50) 177.

[71] Merges, Menell and Lemley (n 14) 572.

[72] Halpern, Nard and Port (n 39) 70–71.

[73] A performance could still be considered public, even if carried out in a private place, if in front of a 'substantial number' of people, and depending on the nature of the occasion and the relationships between the members of the audience. See LaFrance (n 50) 179–180; Halpern, Nard and Port (n 39) 71.

[74] As an example of public performance, consider a videocassette rental store showing rented videocassettes in small rooms. See *Columbia Pictures Industries, Inc. v. Redd Home, Inc.*, 749 F.2d 154 (3d Cir. 1984), especially 158–159.

[75] Halpern, Nard and Port (n 39) 71–72, referring to *Columbia Pictures Industries, Inc. v. Professional Real Estate Investors, Inc.*, 866 F.2d 278 (1989).

Streaming audio or video transmissions on the Internet can be a performance when it is possible for members of the public to receive them, even if these people are in different places, and receive the transmission at different times. Therefore, although streaming transmission cannot be considered a public distribution because it does not allow the copyrighted work to be downloaded,[76] it nevertheless constitutes a public performance.[77] On the other hand, the download of a song cannot constitute a performance since the user needs to take further steps to play the song after downloading it.[78]

Section 102 of the US Copyright Act covers 'musical works, including any accompanying words' and 'sound recordings' in the protected categories. Section 101 of the Copyright Act provides a number of definitions, such as 'sound recordings', which 'are works that result from the fixation of a series of musical, spoken, or other sounds, but not including the sounds accompanying a motion picture or other audiovisual work, regardless of the nature of the material objects, such as disks, tapes, or other phonorecords, in which they are embodied'. Sound recordings were not covered by copyright until 1972, when the Sound Recording Amendment provided for the protection of the performance of a work independent of the copyright in the work being performed.[79]

Sound recordings represent non-traditional items, which communicate works, but do not really constitute a work of authorship. These protected items do not fall within the Berne Convention, but under the Rome Convention for the Protection of Performers, Producers of Phonograms, and Broadcasting Organizations of 1961. Sound recordings are covered by what are usually referred to as 'neighbouring rights' or 'related rights' or *droits voisins*. These rights obtained protection quite recently in the

---

In this case, since the hotel rented videodiscs to its guests for playing on in-room equipment, it did not violate the transmit clause of the Copyright Act.

[76]   Actually there is software which allows this action.

[77]   LaFrance (n 50) 182.

[78]   *United States v. American Society of Composers, Authors and Publishers*, 627 F.3d 64 (2010), spec. 73.

[79]   Act of October 15, 1971, Pub. L. No. 92-140 modifying the Copyright Act of 1909. Oddly, this amendment was introduced 'to provide for the creation of a limited copyright in sound recordings for the purpose of protecting against unauthorized duplication and *piracy* of sound recording, and for other purposes' (emphasis added). The Act was consistent with the Geneva Convention for the Protection of Producers of Phonograms against Unauthorized Duplication of Their Phonograms, which came into force in the US in 1974.

US and Canada, while the Italian system has always offered some sort of protection to performers.[80]

The Copyright Act of 1976, in creating the sound recording copyright, did not include performance rights in the exclusive rights of the owner.[81] The above-mentioned exclusive right granted by Section 106(6) was introduced by the Digital Performance Right in Sound Recordings Act.[82] Since the section refers only to digital transmissions, this performance right does not apply to analogue transmissions such as those of radio broadcasting stations. In 1998 the DMCA expanded the scope of exclusive rights in sound recordings under Section 114, which now comprises Internet performance as well as some measures related to antipiracy provisions.[83] As a result, under Section 114 a sound recording copyright owner has the exclusive right to:

- duplicate the work in the form of phonorecords or copies that directly or indirectly recapture the actual sounds fixed in the recording;
- create derivative works in which the sounds fixed in the sound recording are rearranged, remixed, or otherwise altered in sequence or quality;
- publicly distribute copies of the sound recording;
- and publicly perform the recording 'by means of any digital audio transmission'.

Except for this last right, the author of a sound recording does not have any public performance right in the recording itself.[84]

A somewhat different approach is provided by the Canadian Copyright Act,[85] which defines 'musical work' as 'any work of music or musical composition, with or without words and includes any compilation

---

[80]   See art. 80ff Legge 633/1941.

[81]   See 17 U.S.C. § 114(a). For this reason, the US cannot adhere to the Rome Convention.

[82]   An Act of November 1, 1995, Pub. Law No. 104-39, 109 Stat. 336. See 17 U.S.C. § 114(d).

[83]   Halpern, Nard and Port (n 39) 84.

[84]   See 17 U.S.C. § 114(a). US lawmakers are, in any event, undertaking 'continuing legislative efforts' to broaden the performance right in sound recordings. See Halpern, Nard and Port (n 39) 30–31.

[85]   For a brief history of the protection of musical and dramatic works starting from the Statute of Anne, see McKeown (n 43) 188ff.

thereof'.[86] The sentence 'with or without words' was inserted with an amendment, which took effect after 1993, in order to include songs under this section's protection.[87] The earlier definition only applied to musical works in their printed or graphic form, but not to the acoustic presentation of the work.[88] Musical recordings are separately protected, under neighbouring rights, related to the performance, recording or broadcasting of a work. To strengthen the protection of these rights, a substantial change in the Act was made in 1997.[89] However, the forms of protection for *les droits voisins* are rather different from those for traditional works; their terms of protection, for example, are not the same.[90] Thus, there are various 'layers' of copyright protection in a larger musical work: the music as written, the lyrics, the lyrics and music together as the song, the sound recording, and, as we shall see, any performance and broadcasting rights associated with that 'song'.[91]

Neighbouring rights, which entered the Canadian system only after the Rome Convention of 1961, are divided into performers' rights, the rights of sound recording makers and the rights of broadcasters. Performance is 'any acoustic or visual representation of a work, performer's performance, sound recording or communication signal, including a representation made by means of any mechanical instrument, radio receiving set or television receiving set'.[92] Therefore, unlike in the US, this provision is also applicable to radio broadcasting.

Although the Act does not define a 'performer', it does describe the performer's three most important sole rights. When a work is not fixed in a tangible form, the performer has the right to communicate it to the public by telecommunication; to perform it in public, where it is

---

[86] Copyright Act, Section 2. The Act included cinematographic works as dramatic works, the latter include works 'expressed by any process analogous to cinematography, whether or not accompanied by a soundtrack'.

[87] The previous definition included 'any combination of melody and harmony, or either of them, printed, reduced to writing or otherwise graphically produced or reproduced', see David Vaver, *Copyright Law* (Irwin Law 2000) 47; McKeown (n 43) 188.

[88] McKeown (n 43) 465.

[89] The changes were first proposed by Bill C-32, An Act to amend the Copyright Act, S.C. 1997, c. 24, Section 6.

[90] Sunny Handa, *Copyright Law in Canada* (Butterworths 2002) 143.

[91] See the example given by Judge and Gervais (n 55) 251.

[92] For a definition of 'performer's performance' see Section 2 of the Copyright Act. The Copyright Modernization Act added a new Subsection to Section 15, which considers copyright of performers when it is performed within Canadian borders.

communicated to the public by telecommunication other than a communication signal; and to fix it in any material form. Whenever the work has already been fixed, the performer can reproduce any fixation that was made without the performer's authorization; where the performer authorized a fixation, reproduce any reproduction of that fixation, if the reproduction being reproduced was made for a purpose other than that for which the performer's authorization was given; and where a fixation was permitted as an exception to infringement or for private use, reproduce any reproduction of that fixation, if the reproduction being reproduced was made for a purpose other than one permitted under the exception to infringement or for private use. In any case, the performer has the right to rent out a sound recording of the performance and to authorize any of the above listed acts (Section 15(1)).[93]

The Canadian Copyright Act also provides specific protection for 'sound recordings', defined as recordings, fixed in any material form, consisting of sounds, whether or not of a performance of a work. Within the scope of the Act, soundtracks of a cinematographic work where it accompanies the cinematographic work are excluded from sound recordings.[94] Section 18 of the Act provides that the maker of a sound recording has a sole right related to the sound recording, or to any substantial part of it, to publish it for the first time, to reproduce it in any material form, and to rent it out. It also includes the right to authorize any of these actions.[95]

More generally, the Canadian Copyright Act, Section 3(1) defines what constitutes copyright in a work and provides a list of economic rights. Copyright is therefore 'the sole right to produce or reproduce the work or any substantial part thereof in any material form whatever, to perform the work or any substantial part thereof in public or, if the work is unpublished, to publish the work or any substantial part thereof'. Copyright includes other rights, i.e. the right to produce, reproduce, perform or publish a translation of the copyrighted work; or in the case of a literary work, the right to reproduce, adapt and publicly present it as a cinematographic work. In any case, the copyright owner has the right to authorize such acts.[96]

---

[93]   Copyright Act, Section 15(1)(a)–(c); see Handa (n 90) 182ff. These rights are limited by Section 15(2).

[94]   Copyright Act, Section 2. See also *Re: Sound v. Motion Picture Theatre Associations of Canada*, 2012 SCC 38, [2012] 2 S.C.R. 376.

[95]   Copyright Act, Section 18(1). There rights are conditional on the existence of certain factors listed in Section 18(2).

[96]   Copyright Act, Section 3(1)(a)–(i).

The right to publish is the right to decide whether to publish a work or not. It protects the intention of an author to remain unknown. This right clearly vanishes when the work is first published. A work cannot be said to have been published if the communication to the public occurred without the consent of the copyright owner.[97] The right to publish, also granted by the Italian legislation, is close to the right to produce, meaning the right to bring a work into existence.[98]

The right to reproduction is not defined by the Act but it has been interpreted as a synonym for the notion of copying.[99] Reproduction can affect either the entire work or any substantial part of it. The definition of 'substantial' reproduction requires that all the circumstances of the case be taken into account: factors such as the quality and quantity of the material taken, with quality taking precedence over quantity, the significance of the parts taken, the purpose for which the material was taken and the effects on sales of the plaintiff's work.[100]

In addition to the mentioned rights, a right to perform is granted. A performance has been defined as an act that causes the work to be heard or seen.[101] Subsection 3(1) only grants a copyright holder the sole right to perform a work when that performance is public.[102] For instance, the transmission of a musical work by electronic signals through telephone cables has been considered to be a public performance,[103] as the watching of a copyrighted work on cable television or the Internet could be, if the activity occurs in a public place.[104] This right differs from that granted to the performer under Section 15, and exists side by side with the right of reproduction.[105]

For the above reasons, a recorded musical work, such as a song, enjoys the protection of multiple sections. Hence, the copying of a song, for example through peer-to-peer file-sharing, could potentially infringe several aspects of copyright; the same holds true for cinematographic works.

---

[97] Copyright Act, Section 2.2(3).

[98] *Compo Co. v. Blue Crest Music Inc.*, [1980] 1 S.C.R. 357, para 32.

[99] Handa (n 90) 196, citing *Hanfstaengl v. Empire Palace* [1894] 2 Ch. 1.

[100] For an overview of the different indicators taken into account see McKeown (n 43) 424ff.

[101] *Canadian Admiral Corp. v. Rediffusion Inc.* [1954] Ex. C.R. 382, para 62.

[102] Copyright Act, section 3(1).

[103] *Associated Broadcasting Co. et al. v. Composers, Authors, and Publishers Association of Canada Ltd* [1954] 3 All ER 708, cited by Handa (n 90) 198.

[104] *Canadian Cable Television Assn. v. Canada (Copyright Board)*, 34 C.P.R. (3d) 521, para 30.

[105] McKeown (n 43) 190.

Subject to Section 23, copyright in a performer's performance exists for 50 years from the end of the calendar year in which the performance occurs. However, if the performance is fixed in a sound recording before the copyright expires, the copyright continues for another 50 years. However, if a sound recording in which the performance is fixed is published before the copyright expires, the copyright continues until either 70 years after the end of the calendar year in which the first such publication occurred, or 100 years from the end of the calendar year in which the first fixation of the performance in a sound recording occurred – whichever date is earlier.

The protection period provided by the Canadian Copyright Act was modified in 2015,[106] bringing it closer to the terms provided by the US and Italian systems. In the US the so-called 'Sonny Bono Copyright Term Extension Act' of 1998 extended the term of protection for most works to life plus 70 years.[107] In Italy, art. 25 Legge 633/41, last time modified in 1996, provides that the exclusive rights expire 70 years after the author's death.[108]

Italian regulation provides a similar protection to those existing in Canada and the US. As mentioned, art. 2 of Legge 633/41 lists the protected works, the authors of which enjoy the right to publish the work (art. 12); to reproduce it in many copies (art. 13); to transcribe the oral work (art. 14); to execute, represent or play in public (art. 15); to communicate (art. 16); to distribute (art. 17); to elaborate, translate and publish collective works (art. 18); to rent and to loan (art. 18*bis*).

---

[106] Modifications occurred through the 'Economic Action Plan 2015 Act, No. 1'; S.C. 2015, c. 36, 23 June 2015, An Act to implement certain provisions of the budget tabled in Parliament on 21 April 2015 and other measures.

[107] See Sonny Bono Copyright Term Extension Act, title 1 of Pub. Law No. 105-298, 112 Stat. 2827 (amending chapter 3, title 17, U.S.C., to extend the term of copyright protection for most works to life plus 70 years), enacted 27 October 1998. See § 302 'Duration of copyright' for works created after 1978. The starting point for the term can vary depending on the type of work, see Halpern, Nard and Port (n 39) 109; LaFrance (n 50) 115ff. See also Halpern (n 51) 434ff and the table reported in Merges, Menell and Lemley (n 14) 509. For a historical review of the modification of the period of protection see Halpern, Nard and Port (n 39) 105ff.

[108] Arts. 25ff, Legge 633/41 provide the criteria to calculate the duration of the rights and the point from which the duration starts to run. The duration period was modified by art. 1, Decreto legislativo luogotenenziale 20.7.1945, no. 440; by art. 1, Legge 19.12.1956, no. 1421; art. 1, Legge 27.12.1961, no. 1337; art. 17, Legge 6.2.1996, no. 52. According to art. 23, Legge 633/41 moral rights can be exercised without time limits.

Article 12 considers the right to publish a work for the first time, which enables the author to stop other persons from publishing her work.[109] To the extent of art. 12, any act of exploitation of the work is considered a publication, as long as it occurs in front of the general public. This right may be considered a source of the subsequent rights since it explains that the author has an exclusive right to exploit the work economically, through the exercise of the other rights. Article 13, which provides the exclusive right to reproduction, is at the core of Italian copyright legislation. It was modified somewhat in order to implement European Directive 2001/29/EC, this latter being a partial implementation of the WIPO Treaties of 1996.[110] The current wording describes the right to reproduction as the right to copy the work directly or indirectly, temporarily or permanently, totally or partially, in any way or form, including hand copy, print, lithography, recording, photography, cinematography, and any other technical means by which it could become possible to make a copy of the work.

Numerous amendments have updated the regulation of reproduction through digital technologies. Some scholars argue that although the previous wording allowed for an interpretation covering digital copying, these modifications undoubtedly clarify the applicability of the article to such copies, and the download of a song from the Internet is now considered to be an act of reproduction.[111]

As in the US, the right to reproduce is interpreted as independent from publication or distribution: it is infringed as soon as an unauthorized copy is made, regardless of whether the copy is later distributed or not.[112]

The right to execute, to perform or to play in public is protected under art. 15. This right concerns the execution, performance or playing, in whatever way, either free of charge or for payment, of any kind of work. The form of communication mainly related to music is execution as it comprises the communication of different types of works, in particular musical compositions, regardless of whether they contain a text or not, as long as there is no dramatic action.[113] Performance, on the other hand, is

---

[109]   Greco and Vercellone (n 60) 123–124.

[110]   Implemented by decreto legislativo 9.4.2003, no. 68. For an analysis of the previous text of art. 13, see Abriani, Cottino, Ricolfi (n 59) 414–421. See also Ubertazzi, *Commentario* (n 29) 1535–1536, and in particular, on the single types of reproduction see 1537ff.

[111]   Sirotti Gaudenzi (n 60) 94.

[112]   Greco and Vercellone (n 60) 133; Abriani, Cottino and Ricolfi (n 59) 415; Ubertazzi, *Commentario* (n 29) 1537.

[113]   Abriani, Cottino and Ricolfi (n 59) 436–437.

linked to staged representations, while play is the simple recounting of a literary work, without any dramatic action.[114]

When an execution, performance or playing occurs within the ordinary family circle, or at a boarding school, school or nursing home, it cannot be considered public, as long as it is not intended to make a profit. A qualitative criterion should be applied in deciding whether or not the execution has occurred within the family circle.[115]

For the purposes of this research, the most important exclusive authorial right is that to communicate, covered by art. 16. This provision includes the right to diffuse a work through means such as television, radio, telegraph, etc.[116] The current wording of the article is the product of many amendments, the most recent of which is the result of the implementation of European Directive 2001/29. Article 16 currently regulates the exclusive right to communicate a work to the public, through distance means, either wired or wireless. The article also comprises communication via satellite, cable rebroadcasting, and communication to the public with particular access conditions. Furthermore, the article includes what has been called 'interactive communication',[117] that is the making available of the work so that everyone can have access to it, where and when decided by the individual.[118] Thus, art. 16 includes all communications made when the public are not physically present, including file-sharing and streaming.[119] The second part of the article clarifies that this right does not exhaust itself with any of these kinds of communication, including the act of making available.[120]

---

[114] Sirotti Gaudenzi (n 60) 98. See also Greco and Vercellone (n 60) 135ff. It is often very difficult to distinguish between these activities, see the examples given in Abriani, Cottino and Ricolfi (n 59) 437. The Italian Corte di cassazione held that the author of a musical work not only possesses the exclusive right to execute, perform and reproduce her work, she also has the right to diffuse it through distance means such as radio or television, see Cass. pen., 18.10.1999, no. 12820, in *Cass. pen.*, 2001, 620.

[115] Greco and Vercellone (n 60) 138–139; Ubertazzi, *Commentario* (n 29) 1554–1555.

[116] For a comment on the previous formulation, see Greco and Vercellone (n 60) 141ff; Abriani, Cottino and Ricolfi (n 59) 440ff.

[117] Ubertazzi, *Commentario* (n 29) 1562ff.

[118] Art. 16*bis* supplies the definition to understand art. 16. Abriani, Cottino and Ricolfi (n 59) 445 claim that 'somehow, *diritto d'autore* is going from copyright to access right'.

[119] See Ubertazzi, *Commentario* (n 29) 1563.

[120] The right to make available was introduced by decreto legislativo 68/03, implementing Directive 2001/29.

The subsequent article considers the right to distribute the work with or without profit-making aims:[121] this is the right to commence the commercialization of a work, i.e. the exclusive right of the author to the economic exploitation of her creation. Article 17 was modified by decreto legislativo 68/03, which widened the applicability of the right. The current text considers the right to put the original work on the market or into circulation, or to make it available to the public in any way, with whatever means and for whatever use. It is this right that gives the author the power to prevent the transfer of ownership or of exploitation rights, including the making available of the work through, for instance, a loan.[122]

With regard to neighbouring rights, Italian copyright regulation has always offered a protection for performers.[123] The current wording of these articles is again the result of the implementation of European Directives. Currently, art. 72 states that the producer of a phonogram has the exclusive right to authorize the direct or indirect, temporary or permanent, reproduction of her phonograms, in whichever way or form, totally or partially, and through whatever duplication process. The phonogram producer also has the exclusive right to distribute her phonograms, to rent and loan them, and to make them available 'in such a way that members of the public may access them from a place and at a time individually chosen by them'.[124] Even though a material support is needed for the existence of a phonogram, its protection goes beyond the

---

[121]   In the past this right was related only to distribution intended to make a profit; see Abriani, Cottino and Ricolfi (n 59) 422; Greco and Vercellone (n 60) 150ff.

[122]   Abriani, Cottino and Ricolfi (n 59) 423. The article also contemplates the so-called 'exhaustion principle', when the author definitely decides to put her work on the market. See Greco and Vercellone (n 60) 151; Abriani, Cottino and Ricolfi (n 59) 423ff; Ubertazzi, *Commentario* (n 29) 1569ff. According to art. 17, the right to distribute the work does not exhaust itself within the European Community, unless the first act of sale or act of transfer is made either by the right holder or with her consent. This provision is not applicable when the work is made available such that everyone can have access to it from a place and at a time individually chosen by the user. In 2012 the CJEU delivered its well-known decision on the exhaustion principle of computer software licences in the Internet environment in Case C-128/11 *UsedSoft GmbH v. Oracle International Corp.*, 3 July 2012. See Giorgio Spedicato, 'Online Exhaustion and the Boundaries of Interpretation' in Caso and Giovanella (n 33) 27.

[123]   Under arts. 80ff. See Sirotti Gaudenzi (n 60) 431ff.

[124]   This is the text of art. 3 of Directive 2001/29 on the 'Right of communication to the public of works and right of making available'.

existence of any material support: the phonogram appears, in fact, to be considered as if it were an immaterial object. What is protected is neither the interpreted work nor the interpretation – both enjoy specific protection provisions – but the fixation or registration of sounds onto a specific material support.[125]

This right persists for 50 years from the moment at which the work is fixed; when publication is later than fixation, rights expire 70 years after the publication. This term of 70 years also applies to communications to the public, even when the work has not been previously published (art. 75). Articles 78*ter* and 79 also recognize these rights, for a period of 50 years, to the producers of films, and to broadcasting organizations, i.e. radio and television operators. Finally, art. 80 considers the same right for performers, including actors, singers, musicians, dancers and anybody who performs, sings, plays or tells or gives performances of works of authorship in any way, regardless of whether those works are under copyright or in the public domain.

4. FAIR USE; FAIR DEALING; EXCEPTIONS AND LIMITATIONS

We have reached a point at which the three systems provide complete protection for the entire world of creations. Nevertheless, some space for free use still exists in the three countries, as is required by key international treaties such as the Berne Convention, the TRIPs Agreement and the WIPO Treaties.[126]

With regard to free use, the approach adopted varies significantly from one system to another. I shall now give a very brief account of these approaches, in order to enable a better understanding of the subsequent section, in which some specific exceptions to copyright are considered.

US Copyright legislation provides a number of narrow limitations on the exclusive rights of the owner. These limitations are listed in Sections 108–122 and allow exemptions for some specific uses or subjects, such

---

[125] Paulo Auteri, Giorgio Floridia, Vito Maria Mangini, Gustavo Olivieri, Marco Ricolfi, Rosaria Romano and Paolo Spada, 'Diritti connessi al diritto d'autore' in Paolo Auteri and others, *Diritto industriale. Proprietà intellettuale e concorrenza* (Giappichelli 2016) 675, 678ff.

[126] Consider the 'Three-step test' of art. 9(2) of the Berne Convention, which provides an exception for reproduction of copyrighted works. See also art. 2*bis* and 10-10*bis* of the Convention. For the TRIPs Agreement, see art. 13, while for WCT and WPPT consider respectively art. 10 and art. 16.

as libraries, hotels, jukeboxes and so on. Section 107 of the 1976 Copyright Act codifies the so-called doctrine of 'fair use', which had been developed by the courts.[127] Its aim is to allow a necessary balance between the copyright owner's rights and the public interest. The fair use clause should permit a flexible interpretation, which is not allowed in the wording of limitations listed in Sections 108–122.[128] It has been effectively defined as a 'privilege in persons other than the owner of a copyright to use the copyrighted material in a reasonable manner without his consent, notwithstanding the monopoly granted to the owner'.[129]

Fair use doctrine has also famously been called 'the most troublesome in the whole law of copyright'.[130] Indeed, scholars and judges have thought deeply about this tricky 'equitable rule of reason'.[131] It is an open clause, a 'safety valve',[132] which allows courts to consider the use of a copyrighted material as licit when society would benefit more from its use than from the prevention of that use. Each case has its own particular facts to be considered: courts thus have to balance a variety of factors. The Supreme Court first applied the fair use doctrine in *Sony Corp. of America v. Universal City Studios*, a seminal case that also constitutes the basis for secondary liability for infringement in copyright.

Section 107 of the Copyright Act, in fact, provides a non-exhaustive list of factors that a court should consider,[133] as well as a number of purposes for which a use can be 'fair'. The first is 'the purpose and

---

[127] According to Halpern, Nard and Port (n 39) 117 and Merges, Menell and Lemley (n 14) 592, this concept originated in *Folsom v. Marsh*, 9 F. Cas. 342 (C.C.D. Mass. 1841). Fair use doctrine is at the centre of many contributions. For a brief overview of the fair use doctrine, see Halpern (n 51) 540ff; Robert P Merges and Jane G Ginsburg, *Foundations of Intellectual Property* (Foundation Press 2004) 387ff (a collection of some of the most interesting scholarly contributions on the issue of fair use). For a more detailed analysis: Leon E Seltzer, *Exemptions and Fair Use in Copyright: the Exclusive Rights Tensions in the 1976 Copyright Act* (Harvard University Press 1978); William F Patry, *The Fair Use Privilege in Copyright Law* (2nd edn, BNA Books 1995) and Id, *Patry on Fair Use* (West Publishing 2010).

[128] Halpern, Nard and Port (n 39) 91.

[129] Horace G Ball, *Law of Copyright and Literary Property* (Bender & Co. 1944) 260.

[130] See *Dellar v. Samuel Goldwyn, Inc.*, 104 F.2d 661, 662 (2d Cir. 1939).

[131] *Sony Corp. of America v. Universal City Studios*, 464 U.S. 417 (1984). The meaning and limits of fair use are still hotly debated. See Pierre N Leval, 'Toward a Fair Use Standard' [1990] Harvard Law Review 1105, 1105–1107.

[132] Halpern, Nard and Port (n 39) 91.

[133] The factors are very similar to those used by Justice Story in *Folsom v. Marsh*, 9 F. Cas. 342, 348ff (C.C.D. Mass. 1841).

character of the use, including whether such use is of a commercial nature or is for nonprofit educational purposes'. The *Sony Betamax* decision introduced a presumption: whenever a use was for profit, it was presumed to be unfair, while a non-commercial use would imply a presumption of fairness.[134] This interpretation was later abandoned and nowadays the simple fact that a use is not for profit does not qualify it as fair. Equally, a for-profit use may be considered entitled to a fair use exemption.[135]

The second factor is 'the nature of the copyrighted work'. Here the investigation focuses on the type of work, since some works are considered 'closer to the core of intended copyright protection than others'; for instance, copies of artistic works are rarely considered to be fair, while those of factual compilations are more easily granted exemption on such grounds.[136]

Third, 'the amount and substantiality of the portion used in relation to the copyrighted work as a whole' needs to be evaluated, in both qualitative and quantitative terms: the quantity of material taken may not be a sufficient indicator for the fairness or unfairness of use. The way in which the defendant transformed the taken part is also evaluated: the more transformative a use, the higher the probability it will qualify as fair.[137]

Lastly, 'the effect of the use upon the potential market for or value of the copyrighted work' is measured. This factor has been considered by some to be the most important of the four;[138] both existing and potential markets have to be taken into account, as does the market for derivative works.[139] The main point at issue is whether the defendant's use constitutes a substitute for the copyrighted work.[140] The way in which the fair use clause is built could, in theory, allow a number of uses as non-infringing. However, in neither of the cases analysed here, nor in others like them, has fair use ever exempted file-sharing activities, which – as explained later – are considered to be infringing behaviours.

---

[134] *Sony Betamax* (n 131) 449.
[135] *Campbell v. Acuff–Rose Music, Inc.*, 510 U.S. 569 (1994), 584, citing dissenting opinion by Justice Brennan in *Harper & Row Publishers, Inc. v. Nation Enterprises*, 471 U.S. 539 (1985), 592.
[136] *Campbell* (n 135) 586.
[137] *Campbell* (n 135) 587–588.
[138] *Harper* (n 135) 566.
[139] *Harper* (n 135) 568.
[140] Halpern, Nard and Port (n 39) 99–100.

Although often mentioned together with US fair use, Canadian fair dealing doctrine diverges in many ways from the US approach, most notably in its different wording.[141] While the US clause is open ended and based on a non-exclusive list of factors,[142] the Canadian clause is tightly worded and, until 2012, the Canadian Copyright Act contained exceptions only for research or private study (Section 29 of the Copyright Act),[143] criticism or review (Section 29.1) and news reporting (Section 29.2). There are also several exceptions for particular categories of users, such as libraries, museums and educational institutions (Sections 29.3ff).

The Copyright Modernization Act modified the wording of Section 29, which now states that '[f]air dealing for the purpose of research, private study, education, parody or satire does not infringe copyright', and introduced some new exceptions, including 'Non-commercial User-generated Content' (Section 29.21), 'Backup Copies' (Section 29.24) and 'Reproduction for Private Purposes' (Section 29.22), which can affect the legality of file-sharing. All in all, the 2012 amendments have greatly expanded the realm of fair dealing activities.

Like US fair use, fair dealing basically regulates the cases in which a person can use a copyrighted work without asking the right holder for permission as the use does not interfere with the copyright holder's rights.[144] When a use would anyway be non-infringing, fair dealing provisions are not necessary, but their role is fundamental in cases where a given use would otherwise be infringing.[145]

Fair dealing provisions do not provide a general defence, under which a dealing is automatically considered 'fair'; the fairness of a particular

---

141 See Giuseppina D'Agostino, 'Healing Fair Dealing? A Comparative Copyright Analysis of Canada's Fair Dealing to U.K. Fair Dealing and U.S. Fair Use' [2008] McGill Law Journal 309.

142 Carys J Craig, 'The Changing Face of Fair Dealing in Canadian Copyright Law: A Proposal for Legislative Reform' in Michael Geist (ed), *In the Public Interest: The Future of Canadian Copyright Law* (Irwin Law 2005) 437, 440; Vaver, *Intellectual Property Law* (n 62) 234; see ibid for an explanation of fair dealing (before the Copyright Modernization Act).

143 On this particular fair dealing provision, see the following decisions: *Alberta (Education) v. Canadian Copyright Licensing Agency (Access Copyright)*, 2 S.C.R 345 (2012); *Society of Composers, Authors and Music Publishers of Canada v. Bell Canada*, 2 S.C.R. 326 (2012) – considering that short preview clips streamed by online music retailers qualify as fair dealing for the purpose of research.

144 Handa (n 90) 288.

145 John S McKeown, *Canadian Intellectual Property Law and Strategy* (OUP 2010) 290.

use is determined by whether or not it was carried out for one of the purposes listed under Section 29.[146]

Several potential factors are involved in determining whether or not a dealing is fair: its purpose and character, the nature of the source work, the effect of the dealing on the potential market for the source work, and so on.[147]

Fair dealing had always been considered a rigid doctrine, implying the application of mechanical rules.[148] However, in 2004 both the Federal Court of Appeal and the Supreme Court rejected the classical strict construction of the doctrine and opened a somewhat different path for the application of this exemption.[149] In the case *CCH Canadian Ltd. v. Law Society of Upper Canada*,[150] the Supreme Court interpretation broadened the scope of this exception 'dramatically'.[151] The current approach is closer to the US fair use concept since the Supreme Court has introduced six criteria to determine fairness:

1.   The purpose of the dealing: for this to be fair it must be listed in Sections 29, 29.1 and 29.2 of the Copyright Act, which the Court stated should not be interpreted in a restrictive way.

---

[146]   Craig (n 142) 439.

[147]   Vaver, *Copyright Law* (n 87) 191; see also McKeown (n 43) 549ff.

One of the main Copyright Law reforms, made through the 1997 Act (An Act to amend the Copyright Act, S.C. 1997, c. 24), enacted a set of exceptions for non-profit libraries, archives, and museums (LAMs).

[148]   Craig (n 142) 443.

[149]   Ibid 438.

[150]   [2004] S.C.R. 339. The case was widely commented on, due to its innovative approach to some fundamental copyright issues. See William L Hayhurst, 'The Canadian Supreme Court on Copyright: CCH Canadian Ltd. v Law Society Of Upper Canada' [2004] Canadian Business Law Journal 134; Teresa Scassa, 'Recalibrating Copyright Law? A Comment on the Supreme Court of Canada's Decision in CCH Canadian Ltd. v. Law Society of Upper Canada' [2004] Canadian Journal of Law and Technology 89; Parveen Esmail, 'CCH Canadian Ltd v. Law Society of Upper Canada: Case Comment on a Landmark Copyright Case' [2005] Appeal 13; Daniel J Gervais, 'Canadian Copyright Law Post-CCH' [2004] Intellectual Property Journal 131. For comments on the decisions of the lower courts, see Denis S Marshall, 'First Impressions of a Troubling Case: Some Comments on CCH Canadian Limited v. The Law Society of Upper Canada' [2000] Canadian Law Libraries 19; Abraham Drassinower, 'CCH Canadian Limited v. The Law Society of Upper Canada: A Primer' [2003] 28 Canadian Law Libraries 201.

[151]   Esmail (n 150) 19.

2. The character of the dealing: in the judges' opinion, in assessing the character of a dealing, courts should examine the real context, for example giving relevance to the customs or practices within a particular industry.[152]

3. The amount of the dealing: this should be considered together with the importance of the work allegedly infringed. When the amount taken from a work is very small, the court should not even consider the issue of fair dealing, because the action does not constitute copyright infringement. At the same time, the use of the whole work does not per se constitute an infringement because an entire work may also be fairly dealt with.[153]

4. Alternatives to the dealing: when an alternative non-copyrighted version of the same work is available, this should be considered by the court. This will also help to determine whether or not the dealing was necessary to achieve the defendant's purpose.

5. The nature of the work: judges should consider whether or not the work has yet been published and, in the latter case, whether the work was obtained by the defendant confidentially.

6. The effect of the dealing on the work: if the reproduced work is a competitor to the original, this may suggest that the dealing is not fair. However, no case should be decided solely, or even mainly, on the basis of this factor.[154]

Canadian courts have more flexibility than their US counterparts since the former do not have to apply all these criteria in each case. Furthermore, some of them (numbers 1 and 6) are defined more loosely than the corresponding US criteria.[155] It was held that *CCH* transformed fair dealing 'from a limited exception to an integral part of the copyright system; from a controversial privilege to a recognized right; from an anomaly in an owner-oriented system to an instantiation of the public-owner balance'.[156] In *CCH* the Court went so far as to define fair dealing as a *user's right*: to maintain the proper balance between the rights of the

---

[152] *CCH Canadian Ltd* (n 150) para 55.
[153] The Court gives an example taken from Vaver, *Copyright Law* (n 87) 191: an art critic may need to reproduce an entire picture in order to explain her opinion on it.
[154] *CCH Canadian Ltd* (n 150) paras 53–60.
[155] Gervais, 'Canadian Copyright Law Post-CCH' (n 151) 159; Craig (n 142) 448.
[156] Craig (n 142) 461.

copyright holder and of users, courts must not interpret fair dealing restrictively.[157]

The Italian approach differs from those of both the US and Canada. Italian law on *diritto d'autore* provides 'exceptions and limitations' in its arts. 65–71*decies*.[158] These exceptions and limitations were modified with decreto legislativo 68/2003 and they substitute the 'free use' provisions that existed when Legge 633/1941 was enacted. Free uses were previously worded as limited and specific derogations from the copyright regime.[159] Most modifications of these provision are the result of EU interventions, particularly Directive 2001/29 on copyright in the information society, which introduced a list of exemptions to be adopted by the Member States. Italy has implemented them all, thus widening the scope of many exceptions.[160]

The provisions for exceptions and limitations are divided into three sections: the first relates to the reproduction of published works; the second concerns private reproduction for personal use; the third contains some provisions common to both.[161] As these provisions are considered to be 'exceptions', they are usually interpreted by scholars and courts in a restrictive manner, consistent with Italy's rules on legal interpretation.[162] Some scholars approach free use differently, considering copyright to be characterized by a number of intrinsic (or ontological) limits that allow it to be balanced against other rights and freedoms. The interpretation of free use therefore needs to be very carefully laid out, depending on the particular scope of each clause.[163]

---

[157]   *CCH Canadian Ltd* (n 150) para 48.

[158]   See Thomas Margoni, 'Eccezioni e limitazioni al diritto d'autore' [2011] Giurisprudenza Italiana 1959; Niccolò Abriani, 'Le utilizzazioni libere nella società dell'informazione: considerazioni generali' [2002] AIDA 98; Alberto Maria Gambino, 'Le utilizzazioni libere: cronaca, critica, parodia' [2002] AIDA 127.

[159]   Abriani, Cottino and Ricolfi (n 59) 460.

[160]   Sirotti Gaudenzi (n 60) 152. The author also provides a table comparing the previous and current versions of the article, providing exceptions and limitations (see pp. 155ff).

[161]   For a commentary, see Ubertazzi, *Commentario* (n 29) 1696ff.

[162]   It is a general rule of legal interpretation in Italian law that when a provision is an exception it has to be interpreted in a restrictive way. See art. 14 of the preliminary provisions of the Italian Civil Code. See Ubertazzi, *Commentario* (n 29) 1702–1703; Paolo Auteri, 'Il contenuto del diritto d'autore' in Auteri and others (n 125) 623, 657.

[163]   Abriani, Cottino and Ricolfi (n 59) 460–462.

Exceptions and limitations may protect either public or private interests. The former include limitation for education, criticism, scientific
research and library use. The latter include private copy exceptions, or
exceptions for the visually impaired. Very often private interest exceptions also (indirectly) protect a public scope.[164]

Some exceptions and limitations allow the free use of a copyrighted
work, others are subject to a fee. Exceptions and limitations vary widely:
some have a broader scope, some relate to very narrow – if not marginal
– hypotheses. Some exceptions apply to all kinds of works, while others
apply only to specific types.[165]

The Italian courts have ruled out the applicability of the exemptions
contained in arts. 65ff Legge 633/1941 to online use.[166]

Whether as open clauses or exceptional rules, limitations on copyright
are usages of a copyrighted work removed from the copyright holder's
control, even though copyright protection has not yet expired. They are
one of the tools with which an individual's interest in the protection of
exclusive works and a general interest in the use of the same works can
be balanced.

5. LEGAL FRAMEWORKS FOR FILE-SHARING ACTIVITIES

Generally speaking, and for the purpose of this investigation, 'file-
sharing' is understood as a system for distributing electronic information,
such as music or video files, through a network. In a peer-to-peer (P2P)
file-sharing system all participants have the same possibilities, which is
why participants are called 'peers'. Each peer's computer acts simultaneously as a client and as a server. File-sharing systems have changed a
lot since their first appearance. P2P systems have moved from a
centralized to a decentralized, and then a distributed, model. In a
decentralized system, some – bigger – nodes work as servers while others
do not; in the latter the nodes are absolutely equal and the hardware

---

164   Ibid.
165   Ubertazzi, *Commentario* (n 29) 1696ff.
166   Margoni (n 158) 1964.

infrastructure is equally distributed.[167] This distributed model is called a 'pure P2P system'.[168]

The spread of file-sharing dates back to the early days of the Internet and the creation of Napster.[169] The ease with which songs – and nowadays also movies and e-books – could be downloaded for free generated the fear that copyrighted works would cease to be remunerative. This feeling led to a wave of new legislative interventions, starting at the international level: the 1996 WIPO copyright treaties were clearly devised in response to the spread of file-sharing technologies.

Some countries, however, had already started tightening up their laws on copyright and introducing criminal sanctions, which have now been in force for decades.[170] The original version of the US Copyright Act of 1976 contained provisions punishing those who 'willfully and for purposes of commercial advantage or private financial gain' infringed copyright.[171] As early as 1982, Congress increased the criminal penalties

---

[167] See Alfred WS Loo, *Peer-to-peer Computing: Building Supercomputers with Web Technologies* (Springer Verlag 2007) 1ff.

[168] Ralf Steinmetz and Klaus Wehrle, *Peer-to-peer Systems and Applications* (Springer Verlag 2005) 10ff. For a brief history of P2P file-sharing software see ibid 18ff; see also Alain Strowel, 'Introduction: Peer-to-peer File-sharing and Secondary Liability in Copyright Law' in Strowel (n 69) 1ff.

[169] For an overview of the Napster (*A&M Record Inc. v. Napster, Inc.*, 239 F.3d 1004 (2001)) case, see Chapter 4. For an overview and a comparison of the legal frameworks for music transmission over the Internet, including an analysis of Canada, the US and Europe, see Daniel J Gervais, 'Transmissions of Music on the Internet: An Analysis of the Copyright Laws of Canada, France, Germany, Japan, the United Kingdom, and the United States' [2001] Vanderbilt Journal of Transnational Law 1363.

[170] Many scholars state that the increase in sanctions and the use of criminal provisions for copyright infringement are the effect of lobbying, following the so-called 'theory of rent-seeking': among others, see the economic analysis proposed by Lanier Saperstein, 'Copyrights, Criminal Sanctions and Economic Rents: Applying the Rent Seeking Model to the Criminal Law Formulation Process' [1997] Journal of Criminal Law and Criminology 1470. For an historical perspective of criminal enforcement of copyright, see David Lefranc, 'Historical Perspective on Criminal Enforcement' in Geiger (ed), *Criminal Enforcement* (n 33) 101, spec. 107–108 for musical works.

[171] Title 17 U.S.C. § 506(a). The US Congress first imposed criminal penalties in 1897 for the unauthorized performance or representation of dramatic and musical compositions. However, it was only in 1971 that criminal sanctions were also applied for the infringement of sound recordings. See Daniel J Gervais, 'Criminal Enforcement in the US and Canada' in Geiger (ed), *Criminal Enforcement* (n 33) 276; Irina D Manta, 'The Puzzle of Criminal Sanctions for Intellectual Property Infringement' [2011] Harvard Journal of Law & Technology

for the reproduction or distribution of sound recordings and other audiovisual works.[172] In 1992 the Copyright Felony Act came into force,[173] bringing felony penalties for all categories of copyright infringement and tightening up criminal sanctions.[174] The Act required that the infringement be for purposes of commercial advantage or private financial gain.

An important amendment to the US Copyright Act was made in 1997 with the promulgation of the No Electronic Theft Act (NET Act).[175] This Act was intended to increase the criminal provisions applied to copyright infringement. The NET Act constitutes just one of the numerous statutes through which the US has imposed criminal sanctions on copyright infringement.[176] The NET Act amended several sections of Title 17 and erased the requirement that the infringement be for commercial advantage or private financial gain.[177] It also modified and expanded the

---

469, 481ff. Manta's work interestingly compares the different approaches of copyright and trademark versus patent infringement, and gives an account of why criminal sanctions only exist for the two former violations.

[172]   Criminal penalties for the unauthorized reproduction or distribution of at least 65 copies of a motion picture, or at least 100 copies in the case of sound recordings, within a 180-day period, were increased to a maximum fine of $250,000, up to five years in prison, or both. Sharham A Shayesteh, 'High-Speed Chase on the Information Superhighway: The Evolution of Criminal Liability for Internet Piracy' [1999] Loyola of Los Angeles Law Review 183, 201. See 18 U.S.C. § 2318. See also Peter J Toren, *Intellectual Property and Computer Crimes* (Law Journal Press 2014) § 2.02[1].

[173]   An Act of October 28, 1992, Pub. Law No. 102-561, 106 Stat. 4233.

[174]   Shayesteh (n 172) 202.

[175]   An Act of December 16, 1997, Pub. Law No. 105-147, 111 Stat. 2678 – to amend the provisions of Titles 17 and 18, United States Code, to provide greater copyright protection by amending criminal copyright infringement provisions, and for other purposes.

[176]   Toren (n 172) §§ 2.01ff; Min A Yu, Ryan Lehrer and Withney Roland, 'Intellectual Property Crimes' [2008] American Criminal Law Review 665, spec. 685ff; Saperstein (n 170) 1474ff.

[177]   It seems that this Act is a response to the case *United States v. LaMacchia*, 871 F. Supp. 535 (1994), stating that infringers could not be prosecuted under the Copyright Act for electronic copyright infringement if they did not realize commercial advantage or private financial gain. See Shayesteh (n 172) 204; Benthon Martin and Jeremiah Newhall, 'Criminal Copyright Enforcement Against File Sharing Services' [2013] North Carolina Journal of Law & Technology 101, 109; Manta (n 171) 482–484. Before the enactment of the NET Act, another Bill had been introduced as a response to the *LaMacchia* case. This Bill was never enacted: the Criminal Copyright Improvement Act of 1995 – S. 1122, 104th Cong., 1st Sess (1995). See Toren (n 172) § 2.02[2].

definition of 'financial gain' contained in Section 101, which now comprises 'receipt, or expectation of receipt, of anything of value, including the receipt of other copyrighted works'. This modification allowed the prosecution of non-profit-infringement.[178] The Act modified Section 506 of Title 17 U.S.C., introducing criminal punishment for the reproduction or distribution of copyrighted work by 'electronic means'.[179] It attracted a lot of criticism,[180] although Congress had emphasized that the new statute would only punish those who had acted intentionally.[181]

Just two years later Congress passed the Digital Theft Deterrence and Copyright Damages Improvement Act.[182] The Act increased civil sanctions for copyright infringement and made it clear that a stricter approach would henceforth be adopted in the criminal prosecution of copyright.

In 2005 the Artist's Rights and Theft Prevention Act led to further amendments of the Copyright Act,[183] which now, in Section 506, criminally punishes 'the distribution of a work being prepared for commercial distribution, by making it available on a computer network accessible to members of the public, if such person knew or should have known that the work was intended for commercial distribution'.

The US has also enacted specific statutes to tackle file-sharing, and numerous Bills have been proposed to target individual file-sharers and/or file-sharing technologies and their producers.

---

[178] Martin and Newhall (n 177) 109–110.

[179] See Title 18 § 2319 titled 'Criminal infringement of a copyright'.

[180] See for example Shayesteh (n 172) 222ff; Andrew Grosso, 'Legally Speaking: the Promise and Problems of the No Electronic Theft Act' [2000] Communications of the ACM 23.

[181] See 143 Cong. Rec. H9883 (ed. Nov. 4, 1997) – Statement of Representative B. Frank <www.gpo.gov/fdsys/pkg/CREC-1997-11-04/pdf/CREC-1997-11-04-pt1-PgH9883.pdf> accessed 15 February 2017.

[182] An Act of December 9, 1999 – to amend statutory damages provisions of title 17, United States Code, Pub. Law No. 106-160, 113 Stat. 1774.

[183] The Act was part of a larger Act entitled Family Entertainment and Copyright Act of 2005 (An Act of April 27, 2005, to provide for the protection of intellectual property rights, and for other purposes; Pub. L. n. 109-9, Rep. n. 109-33). Just one year earlier Congress had passed the Anti-counterfeiting Amendments Act, which introduced new crimes, mainly related to counterfeiting and trafficking labels of protected works (An Act of December 23, 2004 to prevent and punish counterfeiting of copyrighted copies and phonorecords, and for other purposes; Pub. Law No. 108-482, 118 Stat. 3912).

One such Bill is the Inducing Infringement of Copyrights Act (INDUCE Act) of 2004:[184] the Act would have inserted an 'intentional inducement' of any violation of the exclusive rights of the copyright owner, punishing those who intentionally aid, abet, induce, counsel or procure this infringement. The 'intent' could be shown by 'acts from which a reasonable person would find intent to induce infringement based upon all relevant information about such acts then reasonably available to the actor, including whether the activity relies on infringement for its commercial viability'. The amendment explicitly stated that no modification would be brought to the doctrines of vicarious and contributory liability for copyright infringement. In the proposers' view, this amendment could have stopped, or at least reduced, illegal file-sharing.

The Bill was said to have been a consequence of the *Grokster* case as decided by the inferior courts,[185] which held that the providers of software enabling users to exchange copyrighted material were not liable for copyright infringement because they could not control users. This Bill, too, was strongly criticized for undermining innovation:[186] it intended to target P2P companies liable for inducing users to file-share, as decided later by the Supreme Court in the *Grokster* case.[187] Some argued that the Bill could overrule the famous *Sony Betamax* decision.[188] Although any eventual overruling would have depended on a court's interpretation of the wording, this very wording of the amendment could have been problematic, in particular the reference to the 'reasonable person standard'.[189]

---

[184] S. 2560, 108th Congress, 2d Session – A Bill to amend Chapter 5 of title 17, United States Code, relating to inducement of copyright infringement, and for other purposes <www.gpo.gov/fdsys/pkg/BILLS-108s2560is/pdf/BILLS-108s2560is.pdf> accessed 15 February 2017.

[185] *MGM Studios, Inc. v. Grokster, Ltd*, 259 F.Supp. 2d 1029 (C.D. Cal. 2003) and *MGM Studios, Inc. v. Grokster, Ltd*, 380 F.3d 1154 (9th Cir. 2004) on which see Chapter 4.

[186] Jason M Schultz, 'The False Origins of the Induce Act' [2005] Northern Kentucky Law Review 527; Michael Raucci, 'Congress Wants to Give the RIAA Control of Your IPod: How the INDUCE Act Chills Innovation and Abrogates *Sony*' [2005] John Marshall Review of Intellectual Property Law 534.

[187] *MGM Studios, Inc. v. Grokster, Ltd*, 545 U.S. 913 (2005), on which see Chapter 4.

[188] Schultz (n 186) 540ff.

[189] The broad wording of the Bill could have created a constitutional problem; see Raucci (n 186) 549.

In 2003 a Bill specifically targeting P2P was proposed, the 'Peer-to-peer Piracy Prevention Act'.[190] This Bill would have modified Section 514 of the Copyright Act to protect copyright owners from legal actions that could arise from 'blocking, diverting or otherwise impairing the unauthorized distribution, display, performance, or reproduction of his or her copyrighted work on a publicly accessible peer-to-peer ("P2P") file trading network'. It would have created a safe harbour, shielding copyright owners from liability for damage to users' computers, for example, linked to actions designed to prevent the unauthorized distribution of their works to the public through P2P technologies. Whenever a copyright holder wanted to stop the distribution of her works, she would have to notify the Attorney General of the method she wanted to apply and, upon request, also provide the rights and reasons behind her action.[191] Once again, the wording of the Bill would probably have entailed problems, due to the breadth and unclear wording of the safe harbour provision.[192] The Bill never became law.

In 2004 two other Bills were proposed: the Piracy Deterrence and Education Act and the Protecting Intellectual Rights Against Theft and Expropriation Act (PIRATE Act).[193] The PIRATE Act would have authorized the Justice Department (i.e. the Attorney General) to file civil lawsuits against infringers instead of limiting the possibility of initiating an action to copyright holders.[194] This Act was intended to be an amendment to the previous NET Act. In fact, even though the NET Act stated that the Justice Department could bring criminal charges against

---

[190] H.R. 5211, 107th Congress, 2d Session – A Bill to amend title 17, United States Code, to limit the liability of copyright owners for protecting their works on peer-to-peer networks <www.gpo.gov/fdsys/pkg/BILLS-107hr5211ih/pdf/BILLS-107hr5211ih.pdf> accessed 15 February 2017.

[191] H.R. 5211 (n 190) § 514(a)–(c).

[192] See James S Humphrey, 'Recent Development: Debating the Proposed Peer-to-Peer Piracy Prevention Act: Should Copyright Owners be Permitted to Disrupt Illegal File Trading Over Peer-to-Peer Networks?' [2003] North Carolina Journal of Law & Technology 375, 380ff.

[193] Respectively H.R. 4077, 108th Congress, 2d Session – An Act to enhance criminal enforcement of the copyright laws, to educate the public about the application of copyright law to the Internet, and for other purposes; and S. 2237, 108th Congress, 2d Session – An Act to amend chapter 5 of title 17, United States Code, to authorize civil copyright enforcement by the Attorney General, and for other purposes.

[194] See Fara Tabatabai, 'A Tale of Two Countries: Canada's Response to Peer-to-Peer Crisis and What It Means for the United States' [2005] 73 Fordham Law Review 2321, 2355.

infringers, certain technicalities, such as the high burden of proof required, had led to no criminal cases against file-sharers being filed in the first years after the Act came into force.[195] The PIRATE Act would have avoided these problems because the Department of Justice could have brought civil suits directly, with a lower burden of proof.[196] In the end, the Act was rejected by the House Committee on the Judiciary. Variations of the same Act have been proposed but none has yet been approved.[197]

The Piracy Deterrence and Education Act would have punished file-sharers who offered more than $1,000 of copyrighted materials 'for distribution to the public' with prison (up to three years) and with fines of up to $25,000. Furthermore, it would have lowered the burden of proof for criminal prosecution. The Bill was intended to finally enable the criminal punishment of individual file-sharers, who had, until then, been immune from criminal prosecution because they did not distribute copyrighted works for financial gain.[198] This Act did not become law either.

After these failed attempts, Congress finally enacted the Prioritizing Resources and Organization for Intellectual Property Act (PRO-IP Act) of 2008.[199] The Act has been called 'a culmination of all [the] historical, legislative, and executive developments of criminal IP law'.[200] The initial draft of the Bill had a provision that would have allowed the Attorney General to file civil actions on behalf of the allegedly damaged party.

---

[195] Declam McCullagh, '"Pirate Act" raises civil rights concerns' *CNET-News.com* (26 May 2004) <http://news.cnet.com/'Pirate-Act'-raises-civil-rights-concerns/2100-1027_3-5220480.html> accessed 15 February 2017, reporting that '[t]he Justice Department has indicated that it won't target peer-to-peer networks for two reasons: Imprisoning file-swapping teens on felony charges isn't the department's top priority, and it's always difficult to make criminal charges stick'.

[196] Tabatabai (n 194) 2356.

[197] See, for example, the Intellectual Property Enforcement Act of 2007 – A bill to amend titles 17 and 18, United States Code, and the Trademark Act of 1946 to strengthen and harmonize the protection of intellectual property, and for other purposes, 110th Congress, 1st Session, S. 2317.

[198] Tabatabai (n 194) 2357.

[199] An Act of October 13, 2008, Pub. Law No. 110-403, 122 Stat. 4256 – to enhance remedies for violations of intellectual property laws, and for other purposes.

[200] Grace Pyun, 'The 2008 Pro-IP Act: The Inadequacy of the Property Paradigm in Criminal Intellectual Property Law and Its Effect on Prosecutorial Boundaries' [2009] DePaul Journal of Art, Technology & Intellectual Property Law 355, 373.

This provision was later thought to be too severe and was cancelled. Nevertheless, the whole Congress felt it was necessary to prosecute infringers with criminal sanctions in order to discourage their unlawful behaviour.[201] Therefore, the Act expressly designated copyright infringement as a 'felony', replacing the milder term of 'offense'.[202] The Act also created an Intellectual Property Enforcement Coordinator (IPEC), appointed by the President, whose task is to oversee an interagency IP enforcement advisory committee to develop a 'joint strategic plan' for the enforcement of IP.[203] Unsurprisingly, this Act was also criticized: for failing to address the problem of the ever-increasing gap between the social perception of copyright and its legal consideration.[204] In other words, it did not take into account the social norms currently governing (digital) copyright infringement. The Act also seemed to have totally disregarded the need for a balance between copyright holders and copyright users.[205]

During 2011 two further Bills were introduced in the House of Representatives and in the Senate: the Stop Online Piracy Act (SOPA)[206] and the PROTECT IP Act (PIPA).[207] SOPA was designed to strengthen law enforcement agencies in the fight against the online trafficking of copyrighted materials and counterfeit goods. Among its provisions was the possibility for copyright owners to ask a court to order an Internet Service Provider (ISP) to block access to their website(s). It would also have expanded existing criminal laws to cover the streaming of copyrighted contents, and have allowed for the imposition of prison sentences. PIPA was similar to SOPA and was intended to give US government and

---

[201] Ibid 374.

[202] The Act also extends the provisions related to civil and criminal forfeiture.

[203] Singer (n 20) 199.

[204] Pyun (n 200) 209.

[205] Ibid 388: '[t]he ultimate purpose of IP law is to preserve the balance between public access and IP owner rights, and the PRO-IP Act demonstrates Congress's pro-IP industry policies'.

[206] A Bill to promote prosperity, creativity, entrepreneurship, and innovation by combating the theft of U.S. property, and for other purposes. 112th Congress, 1st Session, H. R. 3261 <www.gpo.gov/fdsys/pkg/BILLS-112hr3261ih/pdf/BILLS-112hr3261ih.pdf> accessed 20 February 2017.

[207] Full title: Preventing Real Online Threats to Economic Creativity and Theft of Intellectual Property Act, A Bill to prevent online threats to economic creativity and theft of intellectual property, and for other purposes, 112th Congress, 1st Session, S. 968 <www.gpo.gov/fdsys/pkg/BILLS-112s968is/pdf/BILLS-112s968is.pdf> accessed 15 February 2017.

copyright holders additional tools against online threats to copyrighted materials. This Bill was also designed to enhance enforcement, especially against websites operated and registered overseas.

Both Bills gave rise to widespread protests against what users called 'Internet censorship'.[208] This worldwide disapproval, supported by some voluntary website blackouts,[209] led the votes on the two Bills to be delayed indefinitely in both the Senate and the House.[210]

Other, similar, Bills are currently pending before the US House or Senate.[211]

The US Copyright Act provides a specific exemption for the non-commercial use of digital or analogue copies of musical recordings.[212] The source of this norm was the introduction of digital audio taping technology (DAT), which enabled users to obtain high fidelity copies on tape (as they would later be able to do on CD). The recording industry, which feared this new technology, protested strongly against the diffusion of DAT. As a result, the Audio Home Recording Act (AHRA) added Chapter 10 – 'Digital Audio Recording Devices and Media' to Title 17 of the U.S.C.[213] This Act was intended to prevent the wholesale copying of a work and it imposes a royalty obligation on manufacturers or importers of equipment used for digital audio; these royalties are then distributed among recording companies, publishers and composers.[214] This was the first time that the American government imposed 'technological design

---

[208] See for example Jaikumar Vijayan, 'Protests against SOPA, PIPA go viral. Google, Wikipedia, Reddit, BoingBoing plan unprecedented Internet "strike" Wednesday' *Networkedworld.com* (17 January 2012) <www.networkworld.com/article/2184877/data-center/protests-against-sopa–pipa-go-viral.html> accessed 20 February 2017.

[209] I am referring in particular to Wikipedia: Jon Mitchell, 'Wikipedia: So How Do You Like Censorship?' *readwriteweb.com*, (19 January 2012) <http://readwrite.com/2012/01/19/wikipedia_so_how_do_you_like_censorship-2/> accessed 15 February 2017.

[210] Dave Copeland, 'SOPA, PIPA Votes Indefinitely Delayed', *readwriteweb.com* (20 January 2012) <http://readwrite.com/2012/01/19/sopa_pipa_votes_indefinitely_delayed/> accessed 20 February 2017.

[211] Consider, for example, Online Protection and Enforcement of Digital Trade Act (OPEN Act) – 112th Congress – Introduced in Senate no. 2029. A Bill to amend the Tariff Act of 1930 to deter unfair imports that infringe United States intellectual property rights, and for other purposes. The Bill is considered an alternative to SOPA and PIPA.

[212] 17 U.S.C. § 1008.

[213] Halpern, Nard and Port (n 39) 60. AHRA, an Act of October 28, 1992, Pub. Law No. 102-563, 106 Stat. 4237.

[214] 17 U.S.C. §§ 1001ff.

constraints on the manufacture of copying recording media'.[215] As recording technology improved, this provision became obsolete, and the courts held that neither computer hard disks nor MP3 players are 'digital audio recording devices'. This led to the interpretation that the manufacturer of an MP3 player which can record from a hard drive is not subject to either the above-mentioned restrictions or royalties.[216] The Ninth Circuit used the same argumentation to claim that the non-commercial downloading of copyrighted music from the Internet onto a computer hard drive is not immunized by Section 1008.[217]

Parallel to the right to distribute is the right to publish. The definition of 'publication' includes simply 'offer[ing] to distribute' copyrighted material for further distribution, public performance or public display. This has led to conflicting court decisions on whether public distribution takes place when files are 'made available' on the Internet, but there is no proof that a copy has been made or even that the material has been distributed. Most courts have claimed that downloadable Internet transmissions are indeed a form of public distribution, given that people receiving a downloadable transmission can save a non-transitory copy. This raises the additional issue of whether distribution occurs when the recipient actually downloads the files or at the moment when the material is made available.[218]

Some amendments have been recommended: the inclusion of 'transmission' within 'distribution', and the redefinition of 'publication' to include 'transmission', so that a transmitter who diffuses a copyrighted work is thus infringing these rights. Congress did not welcome this proposal, although some courts did. In fact, in the famous *Napster* case, the Ninth Circuit Court held that Internet transmission of a sound recording is an act infringing the 'distribution right' of the sound recording and of the copyrighted music it contains.[219] There have also been opposing opinions, holding that a defendant cannot be considered

---

[215] Merges, Menell and Lemley (n 14) 668. The system allowed users to make copies directly from a CD but not from digital copies made using this technology; the aim was to limit 'second-generation' copies.

[216] *RIAA v. Diamond Multimedia System, Inc.*, 180 F.3d 1072 (9th Cir. 1999), 1081. For a brief overview of the case see Chapter 4.

[217] *Napster* (n 169) 1024. See Chapter 4 for a summary of the decision.

[218] LaFrance (n 50) 173–177 *sic passim*.

[219] *Napster* (n 169) 1013 stating: '[w]e agree that plaintiffs have shown that Napster users infringe at least two of the copyright holders' exclusive rights: the rights of reproduction, § 106(1) and distribution, § 106(3)'.

liable for public distribution if no copy of the work is actually found on the defendant's system.[220]

Under the current legal framework, the duplication of an MP3 file on a computer or other electronic recording devices is considered to be a copy. Copying occurs when files are uploaded from a computer to a server and when they are shared among computers, adding the material to the hard disk of the recipient's PC while retaining a copy in the sender's computer hard disk.[221]

Courts have interpreted as copyright violations both the upload of a file onto the Internet – since it amounts to distributing the file – and the download of a file from the web, because it amounts to copying.[222] The sending of a file to an anonymous recipient has also been held to infringe copyright, since it is clearly not a personal use.[223]

In a more recent criminal case, the Court doubted that simply '[m]aking a work available' could 'establish distribution for copyright purposes under 17 U.S.C. Section 106(3)'. Making a file available does not necessarily mean that someone actually downloads the file.[224] A different conclusion was reached in a previous case, where the Court stated that '[l]isting unauthorized copies of sound recordings using an online file-sharing system constitutes an offer to distribute those works, thereby violating a copyright owner's exclusive right of distribution'.[225]

This different interpretation may result from the fact that US copyright legislation does not yet entail a specific 'right to make available'. Some authors and copyright owners' advocacy groups have asked for an amendment of the Copyright Act to include the right to make available,

---

[220] *Perfect 10, Inc. v. Amazon.com, Inc.*, 508 F.3d 1146 (9th Cir. 2007), 1162.

[221] It remains unclear whether a temporary copy on the random access memory (RAM) of a computer could be an infringement, since § 101 asks 'for a period of more than transitory duration'. The majority of courts have held that temporary storage on RAM *is* a fixation; nevertheless, one court suggested that there is no fixation when transmission is automatic and transitory, as in the case of transmission through the facilities of an ISP (see *CoStar Group, Inc. v. LoopNet, Inc.*, 373 F3d 544 (4th Cir. 2004) at 551); see LaFrance (n 50) 161–162.

[222] *Marobie-Fl. v. National Association of Fire Equipment Distributors*, 983 F. Supp. 1167 (1997), 1172; *In re Aimster Copyright Litig.*, 334 F.3d 643 (2003), 645.

[223] See *A & M Records, Inc. v. Napster, Inc.*, 114 F. Supp. 2d 896 (2000), 912.

[224] *Capitol Records, Inc. v. Thomas*, 579 F. Supp. 2d 1210 (2008), 1217.

[225] *Warner Bros. Records, Inc. v. Payne*, 2006 U.S. Dist. LEXIS 65765 (2006), 8, citing *Napster* (n 169) 1014.

pursuant to the WCT. Other scholars consider that the introduction of this right would be redundant, because the behaviours that it entails – including file-sharing activities – are already covered by existing provisions, such as the right to reproduce, to public display or to public performance.[226]

Finally, mechanical copies of musical works – other than works of music drama – can be made and distributed without the consent of the copyright owner, if a person pays a compulsory licence fee for 'making and distributing phonorecords'.[227] This is only possible if the primary purpose of the copying is to distribute the phonorecords to the public for private use.[228] In 1995, through the Digital Performance Right in Sound Recordings Act,[229] the licence was extended to digital audio delivery of non-dramatic musical work. This licence only covers the distribution of 'phonorecords', not any other kind of reproduction of a copyrighted work.[230]

The Italian legislation is not clear on whether file-sharing activities constitute copyright infringement or not. Legge 633/41 provides some exceptions and limitations to the right to reproduction; and art. 71*sexies* to art. 71*octies* provide a framework for private reproduction for personal use.[231] Art. 71*sexies* allows the private reproduction of phonograms and videograms on any kind of support, made by a person for an exclusively private use, as long as there are no direct or indirect marketing aims, and no purposes of profit-making.[232] No other copyrighted works enjoy this

---

[226] Among them, the leading scholar Peter S Menell, 'In Search of Copyright's Lost Ark: Interpreting the Right to Distribute in the Internet Age' [2011] Journal of Copyright Society USA 1. For a critique: Andrew P Bridges, 'Comment of the Right of Making Available Before the United State Copyright Office', Docket No. 2014-2 <www.copyright.gov/docs/making_available/comments/docket2014_2/Andrew_Bridges.pdf> accessed 20 February 2017; Rick Sanders, 'Will Professor Nimmer's Change of Heart on File-sharing Matter?' [2013] Vanderbilt Journal of Entertainment and Technology Law 857.

[227] For an account of the actual functioning of the licences, see Halpern, Nard and Port (n 39) 61ff.

[228] 17 U.S.C. § 115.

[229] An Act of November 1, 1995, Pub. Law No. 104-39, 109 Stat. 336. See 17 U.S.C. § 114 (d).

[230] Halpern, Nard and Port (n 39) 61–62.

[231] This section was added to Legge 633/41 through art. 9, decreto legislativo 68/03. See arts. 65ff Legge 633/41.

[232] See art. 71*sexies*, co. 1, Legge 633/41. See Greco and Vercellone (n 60) 167ff for the original regulation of reproduction for private use. For a deeper analysis, see Ubertazzi, *Commentario* (n 29) 1747ff.

copyright limitation, which concerns only phonograms and videograms. Reproduction is licit only if carried out by the legitimate buyer of the copyrighted work, and not by third parties. The entire system of private copies is based on royalties and levies paid by consumers when buying devices which enable the recording of videos or songs. Remunerations are then redistributed among copyright holders,[233] as in the US.

In the 1990s lawmakers introduced some amendments to Legge 633/41 designed to punish the sharing of copyrighted works.[234] Articles 171, 171*ter* and 174*bis* of Legge 633/41 contain the provisions related to the protection of copyright on the web. The provisions contain criminal sanctions, which have been harshly criticized by scholars.[235]

Article 171*ter* was read as the first attempt to punish file-sharing activities. The article has been subject to a number of amendments, mainly focused on establishing the 'aim' of the infringer's conduct.[236] The article wording was (and still is) quite controversial in its co. 2 letter *abis*). This criminal provision punishes the infringer with imprisonment from one to four years, and also imposes a maximum fine of 15,500 euros. The punishable conduct consists in entirely or partially communicating a copyrighted work to the public, by introducing it into telecommunication networks, whatever the connection used. This conduct shall be in violation of the right to communicate to the public (art. 16)

---

[233]   See art. 71*septies–71octies*, Legge 633/41; Ubertazzi, *Commentario* (n 29) 1747–1759.

[234]   See Greco and Vercellone (n 60) 62ff. The authors, who wrote their book in 1974, interestingly considered the problems for the protection of music connected to the use of computers.

[235]   Carlo Blengino, 'La tutela penale del copyright digitale: un'onda confusa e asincrona' in Antonella Ardizzone Lorenzo Benussi, Carlo Blengino, Andrea Glorioso, Giovanni Battista Ramello, Giancarlo Ruffo, Massimo Travostino, *Copyright digitale. L'impatto delle nuove tecnologie tra economia e diritto* (Giappichelli 2009) 69. For an analysis of the criminal laws protecting copyright in Italy, see Augusto Colucci and Fulvio Fiore, *La tutela penale nel diritto d'autore* (Giappichelli, 1996); David Terracina, *La tutela penale del diritto d'autore e dei diritti connessi* (Giappichelli 2006); Mario Morra, *I reati in materia di diritto d'autore* (Giuffrè 2008); for a comparison of the Italian and American systems, see Roberto Flor, *Tutela penale ed autotutela tecnologica dei diritti d'autore nell'epoca di Internet. Un'indagine comparata in prospettiva europea ed internazionale* (CEDAM 2010).

[236]   The article was introduced by decreto legislativo 16.11.1994, no. 658, later modified by: Legge 18.8.2000, no. 248; decreto legislativo 9.4.2003, no. 68; Legge 21.5.2004, no. 128 (consolidated version of 'Urbani decree'); and Legge 31.3.2005, no. 43.

and have profit-making aims. If the conduct is of very little importance, the judge can lessen the punishment.

As noted above, the article has been subject to numerous modifications. The initial wording asked for the existence of a 'profit-making aim' (*a fini di lucro* in the Italian text). Later on, this aim was substituted with that of 'gaining a benefit' (*per trarne profitto*), but was then modified again, returning to the original version. The main difference between the two forms concerned the possibility of punishing the single user. In fact, the word *lucro* (meaning profit) is usually linked to commercial activities, as the profit made by a company. According to some interpretations, the word *profitto* should also be applied to small gains, such as the savings made by users who copy instead of buying a CD. This particular wording has led to inconsistent rulings by the Italian Supreme court (Corte di cassazione).[237]

In addition to art. 171*ter*, art. 171, co. 1, letter a*bis*) imposes a fine of between 50 and 2,050 euros on persons who make a copyright work completely or partially available to the public, through the input of the work into a telecommunication network, without having the right to do so, regardless of the aim or form used. This provision undoubtedly refers to peer-to-peer, but it only considers the introduction of the copyrighted work onto the web and not the consequent sharing and diffusion.[238] Moreover, art. 174*bis* prescribes that, in conjunction with criminal punishment, those who violate art. 171, co. 1, letter a*bis*) also be punished with a fine of up to double the market price of the violated work:[239] this sanction is applied in relation to each item that has been duplicated.

---

[237] See for example Cass. pen., 9.1.2007, no. 149, in *Dir. Internet*, n. 3/2007, 257. On this issue, see Astolfo Di Amato, 'Musica on-line e tutela penale' [2007] Dir. Internet 329; David Terracina, 'Lucro e profitto nella giurisprudenza della Corte di Cassazione in materia di violazione del diritto d'autore e dei diritti connessi' [2007] Dir. Internet 259.

[238] Ubertazzi, *Commentario* (n 29) 2155. For an explanation of the relationship between this provision and the one introduced by art. 171*ter*, co. 2, letter a*bis*), see ibid 1958. The main difference is that art. 171, co. 1, letter a*bis*) punished 'making available', while the other provision concentrates on 'communication to the public' (see again ibid 1968). For an explanation of the coordination between these criminal provisions see Flor (n 235) 163ff.

[239] When the price cannot easily be determined, the violation is punished with a monetary sanction of between 103 and 1,032 euros.

Another rule has been interpreted by scholars as a provision punishing illegal download:[240] art. 174*ter* punishes with a monetary fine, and with the forfeiture of the material concerned, those who make illegal use either via ether or cable, or duplicate, reproduce, totally or partially, by whatever process, works or materials which are protected by copyright. The punishment for this conduct cannot concur with that in arts. 171 and 171*ter*.

With regard to actual cases, it seems that until now Italian courts have dealt mainly with disputes involving Internet websites or intermediaries who enabled the exchange or downloading of files,[241] rather than final users.

The Canadian landscape differs greatly from the US and Italy: in Canada the illegality of the file-sharing of musical works seems to be disputed, with doubts being mainly related to Section 80 of the Copyright Act, which provides for a copyright exemption.

Section 80(1) of the Copyright Act provides a specific exception to infringement related to sound recordings, the so-called 'private copying' exception, according to which reproducing all, or a substantial part, of a musical work onto an 'audio recording medium', such as an audio cassette tape, for the private use of the person who makes the copy, does not constitute infringement. The provision, however, has some limitations: it does not apply to subjects who copy music with the aim of selling, renting out, distributing, communicating to the public by telecommunication, or performing the work in public.[242]

Some scholars question the applicability of Section 80 to P2P activities, for many reasons. First, they doubt that a computer can be considered to be an audio recording medium ordinarily used for the reproduction of sound recordings, necessary to provide a platform for the exception. Although making a file available for P2P users was not considered a communication to the public until the amendments of 2012, it would nevertheless count as the distribution of a work. Therefore, when copies are made for subsequent distribution, Section 80 cannot be applied because of the wording of the section itself, which qualifies the copy made for distribution as 'non private'.[243]

---

[240] Stefano Ricci and Giuseppe Vaciago, 'Sistemi peer to peer: rilevanza penale delle condotte in violazione dei diritti d'autore e diritti connessi' [2008] Dir. Internet 280.

[241] For an overview of criminal cases, see Flor (n 235) 329ff.

[242] Copyright Act, Section 80(1) – *Where no infringement of copyright* – and Section 80(2) – *Limitations*.

[243] See Judge and Gervais (n 55) 179ff.

It is important to stress that Section 80 only applies to musical works or sound recordings; it is not applicable to other works, such as movies or e-books. This section was added in 1997 as a response to the ceaseless complaints of the music industry about the alleged decline in record sales due to the unauthorized home copying of sound recordings.[244] In order to compensate copyright holders for the losses they might incur as a result of the introduction of this section, the Act introduced a levy to be paid to a collecting body by the manufacturers and importers of blank audio recording media.[245] The levy revenues are divided between authors, performers and record makers.[246] Levies are filed by collective societies with the Copyright Board of Canada.[247]

Section 80(1) has proven to be very important for file-sharers in Canada; the interpretation of this section, in conjunction with other factors, has led to the conclusion that the file-sharing of music files in Canada is not illegal, or at least that the illegality of music file-sharing is questionable. This interpretation is supported by three significant decisions: *BMG Canada Inc. v. John Doe* by the Federal

---

[244] Vaver, *Copyright Law* (n 87) 223.

[245] For an overview of the Canadian collective societies, see Daniel J Gervais, 'A Uniquely Canadian Institution: the Copyright Board of Canada' in Ysolde Gendreau (ed), *An Emerging Intellectual Property Paradigm: Perspectives from Canada* (Edward Elgar Publishing 2008) 199ff. One of these collective societies is the Society of Composers, Authors and Music Publishers of Canada (SOCAN).

[246] See the Copyright Board's decision *Private Copying*, 18 December 1999 <www.cb-cda.gc.ca/decisions/1999/19991217-c-b.pdf> accessed 20 February 2017. See also Copyright Act, Section 84. Some commentators claim that levies would still be the best solution to P2P: see, for example, Neil W Netanel, 'Impose a Noncommercial Use Levy to Allow Free Peer-to-Peer File-sharing' [2003] Harvard Journal of Law & Technology 1.

[247] Copyright Act, Section 81(1)ff. The Copyright Board of Canada, established in 1936 under the name of the Copyright Appeal Board, is an economic regulatory body, whose primary function is to consider the statements of fees and royalties that performing rights societies propose to charge. The Board is also entitled to supervise agreements between users and licensing bodies. Furthermore, it has jurisdiction over the above matters as an independent administrative tribunal. Decisions made by the Copyright Board do not have a statutory right of appeal. In fact, applications for judicial review must be made before the Federal Court of Appeal (see Handa (n 90) 355). The activities and responsibilities of the Board are regulated by the Copyright Act, Section 66(1)ff. For details see McKeown (n 43) 692; Handa (n 91) 141; Gervais, 'A Uniquely Canadian Institution' (n 245). For the procedure involved in introducing a new tariff, see ibid 210–211.

Court,[248] *CCH v. Law Society of Upper Canada* by the Supreme Court,[249] and the *Private Copying 2003–2004* decision by the Copyright Board.[250]

In December 2003 the Copyright Board, attempting to resolve certain issues related to the exemption for private copying, stated:

> The [*private copying*] regime does not address the source of the material copied. There is no requirement ... that the source copy be a non-infringing copy. Hence, it is not relevant whether the source of the track is a pre-owned recording, a borrowed CD, or a track downloaded from the Internet.

Then it added that

> [a]lthough the source of the copy does not matter, the destination does ... Section 80 creates an exemption that applies as long as two conditions are met: the copy must be for the private use of the person making it, and it must be made onto an audio recording medium, as defined in Section 79.[251]

Taking this position, the Board stated that the downloader – at least – could not be considered an infringer.

In the same decision, the Copyright Board also clarified that a work is considered to have been 'transmitted' even when it has been fragmented into many packages since the file can later be reconstituted. This is true as long as the transmission is made by telecommunication as defined by Section 2 of the Copyright Act and is public. This decision, which was taken some years before the amendments introduced in 2012 through the Copyright Act, stated that making available did not amount to communication. Communication would only occur when the work was requested by another user.[252]

In *BMG*, relying in part on the Copyright Board reasoning mentioned above, the Federal Court held that 'downloading a song for personal use does not amount to infringement'.[253] Referring to the *CCH* decision, the

---

[248] *BMG Canada Inc. v. John Doe* [2004] 3 F.C.R. 241. See Chapter 4 for a detailed analysis.

[249] *CCH Canadian Ltd.* (n 150).

[250] *Private Copying 2003–2004*, 12 December 2003 <www.cb-cda.gc.ca/decisions/2003/20031212-c-b.pdf> accessed 20 February 2017.

[251] Ibid 20. Section 79 supplies a definition of the Part of the Copyright Act related to Private Copying.

[252] See SOCAN Statement of Royalties, Public Performance of Musical Works 1996, 1997, 1998 (Tariff 22, Internet) (Re) 1 C.P.R. (4th) 417, at §§ 103ff.

[253] *BMG* Federal Court (n 248) para 25. However, the Federal Court of Appeal in *BMG Canada Inc. v. John Doe* [2005] F.C.J. No. 858 expressly declined to confirm these words, contained in von Finckestein J's decision.

Federal Court claimed that there had not been any distribution or authorized reproduction of sound recordings. *CCH*, indeed, stated that a secondary liability infringer must 'authorize' the illegal activity of the primary infringer. Given the fact that a file-sharer puts files in her computer that can be downloaded by her peers without her knowledge, or even permission,[254] there was no evidence that the alleged infringer had distributed or authorized the reproduction of sound recordings. The Court saw no difference between the *CCH* case, in which a library put a photocopy machine in a room full of copyrighted material, and the *BMG* case, in which users placed a *personal copy* of songs on a shared directory in their computers, linked to a P2P. Furthermore, this did not count as distribution since there was no positive act by the owner of the shared directory.[255] Although the Federal Court of Appeal was not of like mind and clarified that it was premature to reach a conclusion with regard to the legality of P2P file-sharing,[256] authors and commentators believe that this was a win for P2P legality in Canada.[257]

CCH reasoning on secondary liability certainly applies to ISPs and P2P software producers.[258] However, it may not be applicable to users, as the Court in *BMG* wished. Even if it is true that P2P users have no duty to supervise their peers, it cannot easily be argued that their role is completely passive:[259] according to some scholars, at the moment in which a P2P user puts a sound recording in her shared folder, her copy for private use has been distributed and/or communicated.[260] Although 'distribution' is not an exclusive right of the copyright holder in the Canadian system, if a copy has been made for distribution, it is not covered by Section 80(1) since it is not for 'private use'. Furthermore,

---

[254]   Some P2P systems place a user's downloaded songs in a shared folder by default, and this passive sharing does not seem enough to count as an 'authorization' to copyright infringement. See Tabatabai (n 194) 2347.

[255]   *BMG* Federal Court (n 248) paras 26–28, *sic passim.*

[256]   *BMG* Appeal (n 253) paras 46ff.

[257]   See, for example, Tabatabai (n 194) 2343ff.

[258]   Judge and Gervais (n 55) 184.

[259]   P2P users normally act both as uploaders and downloaders, simultaneously. See Gregory R Hagen and Nyall Engfield, 'Canadian Copyright Reform: P2P Sharing, Making Available and the Three-Step Test' [2006] University of Ottawa Law and Technology Journal 477, 485 fn 34 <www.uoltj.ca/articles/vol3.2/2006.3.2.uoltj.Hagen.477-516.pdf> accessed 20 February 2017.

[260]   Judge and Gervais (n 55) 184; see also Gervais, 'Canadian Copyright Law Post-CCH' (n 150) 150ff.

unless the software operates automatically, when placing a song in the shared folder a user infringes the right to 'authorize'.

Besides, Section 80(1) considers the act of copying 'onto an *audio recording medium*'; some scholars argue that a personal computer is not a 'medium' within the meaning of Section 80(1). In fact, an audio recording medium is regarded as one that is 'ordinarily used' (Section 79) by individuals to record music and on which consumers pay the already mentioned levy. The section does not cover media that are considered not to be ordinarily used to record music; for example, consumers do not pay the levy on DVDs, but nor are they allowed to use the 'private copying' exception. Hence, in such a case the person would be infringing copyright, unless she had the rights holder's permission to copy their work.[261] The categorization of a medium as 'ordinarily used' for the recording of music is quite problematic. Some think that this definition should be considered dynamically: the provision should apply not only to those media ordinarily used for that purpose at the time of the enactment, but also to those which become ordinarily employed over time.[262] This is the approach taken by the Copyright Board.[263] Others propose a case-by-case approach in which the 'ordinary use' of a product, such us a computer's hard disk, is to be considered an empirical question, and not an *a priori* matter of law.[264]

The very concept of 'medium' is also under question. The Copyright Board claimed in one of its decisions that it was important to take into consideration the kind of device in which the recording medium was incorporated. This meant that a hard disk would be a medium under Section 79 if embedded in an MP3 player, but not in a personal computer.[265] So, this reading of Section 79 could lead to the conclusion that whenever a consumer downloads directly onto her computer hard

---

[261]   Judge and Gervais (n 55) 260. But see *Private Copying 2003–2004* (n 250) 21: '[i]t would indeed seem illogical that the scope of the exemption could depend on the rights-holders' unilateral choice to propose or not a tariff. For instance, simply because the Board has not been asked to certify a tariff on hard disks in personal computers, it does not follow that private copies made onto such media infringe copyright. Moreover, to argue that a private copy on a particular kind of medium is legal only if a levy was paid on that particular unit would be to add a condition that is not currently included in Section 80.'

[262]   Judge and Gervais (n 55) 261.

[263]   *Private Copying 2003–2004* (n 250) 43. But see Judge and Gervais (n 55) 262.

[264]   Hagen and Engfield (n 259) 488.

[265]   *Private Copying 2003–2004* (n 250) 44.

disk, the exception provided by Section 80(1) does not apply.[266] The Federal Court of Appeal, in reversing the Copyright Board's decision, ruled that the Board had erred in its decision and that the type of device was not to be taken into account. The Federal Court also acknowledged that the Board had interpreted Section 79 in that sense, in order to include MP3 players in the list of media to which the levy should apply.[267]

If anything, in the Court's view, in *BMG* the file-sharers' act would have been a 'making available' of the copies of the songs. At the time of the *BMG* decision, Canada had not yet implemented the WIPO Treaties, which contain the right to make available. Article 8 of the WCT states that

> authors of literary and artistic works shall enjoy the exclusive right of authorizing any communication to the public of their works, by wire or wireless means, including the *making available to the public* of their works in such a way that members of the public may access these works from a place and at a time individually chosen by them.[268]

After the introduction of the Copyright Modernization Act of 2012, the private copy regime partially changed. This Act introduced a new exception called 'Reproduction for Private Purposes' under Section 29.22 of the Copyright Act. Thus, it does not now constitute infringement to reproduce a work (entirely or substantially) if:

a. the copy of the work or other subject matter from which the reproduction is made is not an infringing copy;
b. the individual legally obtained the copy of the work or other subject matter from which the reproduction is made, other than by borrowing it or renting it, and owns or is authorized to use the medium or device on which it is reproduced;
c. the individual, in order to make the reproduction, did not circumvent ... a technological protection measure, ... or cause one to be circumvented;
d. the individual does not give the reproduction away; and
e. the reproduction is used only for the individual's private purposes.

---

[266] Judge and Gervais (n 55) 185 and 265.

[267] *Canadian Private Copying Collective v. Canadian Storage Media Alliance* [2005] 2 F.C.R. 654, paras 151–157.

[268] A similar right is also recognized for fixed performances and phonographs by the WIPO Performances and Phonogram Treaty; see art. 10 'Right of Making Available of Fixed Performances' and art. 14 'Right of Making Available of Phonograms'.

The new section describes a 'medium or device' as a 'digital memory in which a work or subject-matter may be stored for the purpose of allowing the telecommunication of the work or other subject-matter through the Internet or other digital network'. Furthermore, subsection 3 states that when the reproduction deals with a musical work or a sound recording, this new section does not apply if the reproduction is made onto an audio recording medium as defined in Section 79. This last statement is consistent with the above-described pre-2012 legal scene, and the reference to an 'audio recording medium' clarifies neither the newly introduced provisions nor the existing ones.

In addition to these provisions, the 2012 amendments specified that 'making a work available' amounted to communication. Before the introduction of the Copyright Modernization Act, Canadian courts had interpreted the activity of making a copyrighted work available as not infringing copyright because it was not explicitly mentioned in the text among the sole rights of an author.[269] Just before the modifications of 2012, the Supreme Court of Canada interpreted the Copyright Act as encompassing only three rights: reproduction, performance and publication.[270] Furthermore, the Supreme Court held that the transmission of a copy of a musical work to members of the public is not a communication to the public within the meaning of Section 3(1)(f), merely constituting a reproduction.[271] The Supreme Court also stated that streaming – as a transmission to a single individual – is not communication to the public; however, on-demand transmission of music streams made available by online music services does constitute communications 'to the public',

---

[269] *Society of Composers, Authors & Music Publishers of Canada (SOCAN) v. Canadian Association of Internet Providers*, 2 S.C.R. 427 (2004).

[270] Jeremy De Beer and Mira Burri, 'Transatlantic Copyright Comparisons: Making Available via Hyperlinks in the European Union and Canada' [2014] EIPR 95, 98, referring to the so-called 'Copyright pentalogy', on which see Michael Geist (ed), *The Copyright Pentalogy: How the Supreme Court of Canada Shook the Foundations of Canadian Copyright Law* (University of Ottawa Press 2013).

[271] *Entertainment Software Association and Entertainment Software Association of Canada (ESA) v. Society of Composers, Authors and Music Publishers of Canada (SOCAN)* [2012] 2 S.C.R. 231. The case focused on the transmission of musical works contained in a video game through an Internet download in order to decide whether this could be considered a communication to the public.

because the content is available for anyone who wants to access it at different times and places.[272]

The 'right to make available' is now also considered an author's right in sound recordings by the Canadian Copyright Act, under Section 18(1.1). The Copyright Modernization Act added a clause to the definition of 'communication to the public by telecommunication', clarifying that this also includes 'making available' (Section 2.4(1.1)). Yet is seems that making a work available amounts to either communication or reproduction, depending on the subsequent use that someone else makes of the work.[273]

Canada's approach to criminal sanctions is less strict than that of either the US or Italy. Sections 42 and 43 of the Canadian Copyright Act provide criminal sanctions for a number of different behaviours, but these criminal provisions 'are very rarely used'.[274] In addition to the provisions in the Copyright Act, since 2007 the 'Unauthorized recording of a movie' and the 'Unauthorized recording for purpose of sale' have been subject to criminal sanction under the Canadian Criminal Code.[275] Despite the infrequent application of these provisions, the tightening of sanctions has also affected Canadian copyright: while until 1988 the maximum penalty was $200,[276] in some cases copyright infringement can now lead to imprisonment.[277] Furthermore, the 2012 amendment extended criminal sanctions to new hypotheses.[278] Punishable conduct now includes making for sale or rental an infringing copy of a copyrighted work; selling or renting or offering for sale an infringing copy; distributing infringing

---

[272] See *Rogers Communications Inc. v. Society of Composers, Authors and Music Publishers of Canada*, 2 S.C.R. 283 (2012), which at para 54 cited Vaver, *Intellectual Property Law* (n 62) 173.

[273] De Beer and Burri (n 270) 99.

[274] Judge and Gervais (n 55) 241. On the infrequent application of criminal provisions in Canada, see also Cal Becker, 'Criminal Enforcement of Intellectual Property Rights' [2003] Canadian Intellectual Property Review 183; Gervais, 'Criminal Enforcement' (n 171) 271.

[275] Criminal Code, RSC 1985, S. 432. The reference is explicitly made to the Copyright Act.

[276] Gervais, 'Criminal Enforcement' (n 171) 272.

[277] Greg Hagen, Cameron Hutchison, David Lametti, Graham Reynolds, Teresa Scassa and Margaret Ann Wilkinson, *Canadian Intellectual Property Law. Cases and Materials* (Emond Publishing 2013) 242–243.

[278] See Copyright Modernization Act, Section 48, amending Copyright Act, Section 42.

copies either for the purpose of trade or 'to such an extent as to affect prejudicially the owner of the copyright'.[279]

In the case of *R. v. JPM*, the accused was condemned for sharing computer programs through a bulletin board.[280] Since software is clearly protected under the Copyright Act as a literary work, the author had the exclusive right to communicate it to the public. The accused had placed copies of the program on the bulletin board so that other users could copy them and he also provided software that helped other users to obtain the infringed copies. This behaviour was considered to be punishable under Section 42(1)(c). Apart from this example, no cases of copyright infringement through file-sharing have yet been punished under criminal law.

Under the Canadian system, as in Italy and the US, the alleged infringer must have acted wilfully to be criminally punishable.[281]

The criminal approach to copyright infringement is also reflected in international agreements. Article 61 of the TRIPs Agreement required signatory states to implement criminal procedures and penalties for 'copyright piracy on a commercial scale'. The 'Proposal for a Directive of the European Parliament and of the Council on criminal measures aimed at ensuring the enforcement of intellectual property rights' took a similar approach:[282] its art. 3 would have obliged Member States to ensure that intentional infringements on a commercial scale were treated as criminal offences. Although the European Commission withdrew the proposal,[283] its drafting testifies to an increasingly widespread recourse to criminal sanctions for the enforcement of copyright.[284]

---

[279] See Canadian Copyright Act, Section 42.

[280] *R. v. JPM* [1996] 150 N.S.R. (2d) 143. For some cases of criminal infringement of copyright in Canada see Gervais, 'Criminal Enforcement' (n 171) 272–275.

[281] Toren (n 172) §§ 2.04[3]ff; Handa (n 91) 270; Flor (n 235) 159ff, *passim*.

[282] COM/2006/0168 final.

[283] Text withdrawn by the Commission on 18 September 2010: OJ C 252, 18 September 2010, 9.

[284] The introduction of criminal sanctions was also prescribed by the Anti-Counterfeiting Trade Agreement (ACTA) between the EU and its Member States, Australia, Canada, Japan, the Republic of Korea, the United Mexican States, the Kingdom of Morocco, New Zealand, the Republic of Singapore, the Swiss Confederation and the United States of America at <http://register.consilium.europa.eu/pdf/en/11/st12/st12196.en11.pdf> accessed 20 February 2017. The agreement, which was signed by the EU and many of its Member States in 2011, was rejected by the EU Parliament on 4 July 2012 due to subsequent worldwide protests. On ACTA, see – among dozens of contributions

6. SPECIFIC ENFORCEMENT PROVISIONS

Having described the general structure of copyright regulation in the three systems, the following sections examine two further aspects of each regulation, beginning with its specific provisions for copyright enforcement. The very fact of their existence in the US and Italy, but not in Canada, is further evidence of the different approaches taken by the three systems.

The final section examines ISP liability. Although the regulation of intermediaries' liability is not 'copyright regulation', the two spheres are closely intertwined, as can be seen from the case studies. Analysing the two aspects together can therefore afford us both a clearer, broader picture of the regulations of the three countries, and a sharper understanding of the case studies.

'The law of remedies says something, by implication, about the nature and strength of IP rights.'[285] However, an investigation of all the remedies available for enforcing copyright law is far beyond the scope of this work, which will only illustrate those applied in the cases here analysed.[286] Each system has an array of tools at its disposal, among which injunctions have recently been playing a significant role.[287]

– Pedro Roffe and Xavier Seuba (eds), *The ACTA and the Plurilateral Enforcement Agenda: Genesis and Aftermath* (CUP 2014); Duncan Matthews and Petra Žikovská, 'The Rise and Fall of the Anti-Counterfeiting Trade Agreement (ACTA): Lessons for the European Union' [2013] IIC 626. With reference to ACTA's criminal provisions, see specifically Christophe Geiger, 'The Anti-Counterfeiting Trade Agreement and Criminal Enforcement of Intellectual Property: What Consequences for the European Union?' in Jan Rosen (ed), *IP Rights at the Crossroads of Trade* (Edward Elgar Publishing 2012) 167.

[285] Vaver, *Intellectual Property Law* (n 62) 616.

[286] A more thorough and complete explanation of some enforcement tools will be provided in the analysis of the real cases. For an account of the other remedies provided for copyright infringement, see the references cited in this section.

[287] Jiarui Liu, 'Copyright Injunctions after eBay: An Empirical Study' [2012] Lewis & Clark Law Review 215; Martin Husovec, 'Injunctions against Innocent Third Parties: The Case of Website Blocking' [2013] JIPITEC 116 <www.jipitec.eu/issues/jipitec-4-2-2013/3745/husovec.pdf> accessed 20 February 2017; Christina Angelopoulos, 'Are Blocking Injunctions against ISPs Allowed in Europe? Copyright Enforcement in the Post-Telekabel EU Legal Landscape' [2014] Journal of Intellectual Property Law & Practice 812; Eleonora Rosati, '2015: The Year of Blocking Injunctions?' [2015] Journal of Intellectual Property Law & Practice 147.

The enforcement tools applied in the case studies included in this book were introduced in the US through the DMCA, Section 512, which was the outcome of long negotiations between copyright owners and ISPs.[288] As will be shown later in the chapter, copyright holders have, from the start, tried to pressurize ISPs into collaborating in the enforcement of copyright. Meanwhile, ISPs want their business to be profitable; they want to enjoy freedom of entrepreneurship; and they want to be shielded from liability. These tensions already existed when the DMCA was enacted, prompting Congress to opt for a sort of trade-off: service providers could receive liability protection in exchange for assisting copyright owners in identifying infringers.[289]

In order to encourage this cooperation, in conjunction with specific 'safe harbour' provisions,[290] Section 512(h) introduced a *subpoena duces tecum*. A subpoena is a discovery tool that emanates from a court and orders a person (other than the parties) to attend a trial and give testimony, or to produce a document, or other information.[291] Section 512 contemplates a *subpoena duces tecum*, meaning a judicial process by which the court, at the request of a party, orders a third person to produce papers, documents or other tangible items of evidence at a trial.[292] Section 512 states that '[a] copyright owner or a person authorized to act on the owner's behalf may request the clerk of any United States district court to issue a subpoena to a service provider for identification of an alleged infringer'. This rule has proven to be of crucial importance in more than one lawsuit between copyright holders and ISPs, as we will see later.

---

[288]   According to *In re Charter Communications, Inc., Subpoena Enforcement Matter*, 393 F.3d 771, 773 (8th Cir., 2005).

[289]   See *In re Verizon Internet Services*, 240 F. Supp. 2d 24 (D.D.C. 2003), 37.

[290]   An explanation of ISP liability in the US follows later.

[291]   Fed. R. Civ. P. 45(a). See Richard D Freer, *Civil Procedure* (Wolters Kluwer 2009) 367ff; see Entry: *Subpoena* in Henry C Black, *Black's Law Dictionary* (5th edn, West Publishing 1979) 1279.

[292]   Entry: *Subpoena duces tecum* in Black (n 291) 1279. Nowadays one can achieve the production of documents from a non-party directly with a subpoena. This was once possible only through a *subpoena duces tecum*, which required the non-party to attend the trial and to bring the required documents. The non-party then had to swear, and was asked if she had brought the documents. When she had identified the documents, her deposition was complete and the party could inspect the documents. The procedure is now easier, since the party can merely serve the non-party with a subpoena for production of the materials. There is no longer any need to go through the process of noticing her deposition. See Freer (n 291) 374–375.

Through the DMCA subpoena, copyright holders can obtain information on unknown users who are allegedly infringing their rights.

Technically, as prescribed by Section 512(h)(2) of the DMCA, the request for the subpoena shall be accompanied by:

a. a copy of a specific notification, described in Subsection (c)(3)(A);
b. the proposed subpoena;
c. a sworn declaration to the effect that the purpose for which the subpoena is sought is to obtain the identity of an alleged infringer and that such information will only be used for the purpose of protecting copyrights.

The process seems to rely on speed: if the request submitted by the copyright owner satisfies certain requirements, 'the clerk shall *expeditiously* issue and sign the proposed subpoena and return it to the requester for delivery to the service provider'.[293] 'Upon receipt of the issued subpoena, ... the service provider shall *expeditiously* disclose to the copyright owner or person authorized by the copyright owner the information required by the subpoena ...'.[294]

The interpretation of this section by the courts has led to divergent outcomes in the cases between ISPs and copyright holders. In fact, some issues have been raised on the constitutionality of the DMCA subpoena under the 'overbreadth doctrine'.[295] This doctrine is a typical case of constitutional 'facial challenge' in the US, i.e. a constitutional challenge that aims to obtain a declaration of the 'facial invalidity' of a law in its entirety. Facial invalidity is in contrast to 'as-applied' invalidity, which denotes the constitutional invalidity of a specific interpretation of a statute. In the latter case, a judicial determination of unconstitutionality does not render the law itself completely invalid, only making that particular application inoperative.[296]

---

[293] 17 U.S.C. § 512(h)(4), emphasis added.
[294] 17 U.S.C. § 512(h)(5), emphasis added.
[295] The overbreadth doctrine has been widely studied. See, for example: Note, 'The First Amendment Overbreadth Doctrine' [1970] Harvard Law Review 844; David S Bogen, 'First Amendment Ancillary Doctrines' [1978] Maryland Law Review 679, spec. 705ff; Henry P Monaghan, 'Overbreadth' [1981] Supreme Court Review 1. The overbreadth doctrine seems to originate in *Thornhill v. Alabama*, 310 U.S. 88 (1940), see Laurence H Tribe, *American Constitutional Law* (Foundation Press 1978) 710ff; Kathleen M Sullivan and Gerald Gunther, *First Amendment Law* (3rd edn, Foundation Press 2007) 340ff.
[296] Note (n 295) 844–845; Bogen (n 295) 705. See more generally the latter article for insights on how constitutional challenges work.

Overbreadth doctrine challenges the validity of the law itself by arguing that, being too broad, it is unconstitutional on its face.[297] This particular doctrine is usually applied with reference to the First Amendment, which, as is well known, protects free speech. An overbroad law is one that, in limiting unprotected speech, also hampers protected speech. The overbreadth doctrine has regard to the precision of law and the tailoring of its effects to the desired legislative goals. A law limiting free speech may be clear on its face, but indiscriminately reaches both protected and unprotected expressions. Protected expression could be chilled or suppressed by such an over-reaching law.[298] In such a case, the challenged statute is declared not to be applicable in any circumstance.[299]

The constitutionality of the DMCA subpoena has also been challenged on the grounds of another parameter, namely the province of powers. In particular, Section 512(h) may violate Article III of the Constitution 'because it authorizes federal courts to issue binding process in the absence of a pending case or controversy'.[300] Article III of the US Constitution refers to the judicial branch;[301] it divides the judicial power into a Supreme Court and other inferior courts, which must function within the specified jurisdictional boundaries of the same article. Section 2 of the article specifies the subject matter of the federal courts, using the words 'cases' and 'controversies'. This affirmative grant of power has also been read as encompassing a negative limitation: judicial power does not extend beyond cases and controversies.[302] As explained later in this book, despite constitutional challenges, DMCA subpoenas have been considered valid by some courts as a clerk's issuing of a subpoena has been interpreted not as the exercise of judicial power, but rather as a 'ministerial duty', without any discretion.[303]

The application of this specific tool to the cases between copyright holders and ISPs was not always successful. Without going into detail

---

[297]   Jerome Barron and C Thomas Dienes, *Constitutional Law in a Nutshell* (4th edn, West Publishing 2005) 382; Tribe (n 295) 1022ff.

[298]   Ibid 383.

[299]   Calvin R Massey, *American Constitutional Law: Powers and Liberties* (Aspen Publishing 2001) 1043. In a case that I go on to examine in depth, the ISP Verizon tried to quash a subpoena (partly) on the grounds of the overbreadth doctrine. See below *In re Verizon Internet Services*, 257 F. Supp. 2d 244 (D.D.C. 2003).

[300]   *In re Verizon Internet Services* (n 299) 247.

[301]   See Barron and Dienes (n 297) 18ff.

[302]   Kathleen M Sullivan and Gerald Gunther, *Constitutional* Law (16th edn, Aspen Publishing 2007) 31.

[303]   *In re Verizon Internet Services* (n 299) 249.

here, we can note that one of the possible interpretations of the DMCA subpoena leads to its inapplicability to 'mere conduit' providers: online intermediaries that just provide users with an Internet connection, or in some way transmit users' information, but do not act on it.[304]

The DMCA subpoena's inapplicability to these cases led US copyright owners to consider a different tool, the so-called 'John Doe' proceeding. This tool, which has proved successful in the US, is not specifically tailored for IP issues and procedures, but is a procedural tool that can be applied in any civil lawsuit following the rules of civil procedure and has been widely used especially in Internet cases of defamation.[305] A 'John Doe' action consists of an '*ex parte* discovery'. In an *ex parte* proceeding, one of the parties is neither present nor represented, not having been notified of its existence.[306] Through this proceeding, a party (the copyright holder, in the cases here considered) can obtain an 'immediate discovery' that authorizes them to serve a third party (the ISP) with a subpoena for the production of specific documents or information (the user identities behind dynamic IP addresses). The proceeding starts by suing a fictional person: John or Jane Doe. The plaintiff then asks for a subpoena to compel the ISPs to supply the final users' information linked to the received IP numbers. Once this information has been obtained, the plaintiff can amend the complaint, replacing 'Doe' with the alleged infringer's real name.[307]

John Doe proceedings are being applied with increasing frequency for defamation, copyright, and other IPR infringements. Since the Federal Rules of Civil Procedure are unclear about anonymous defendants, courts have reached different decisions, based on different interpretations, on whether defendants' interests in anonymity should be overridden by

---

[304]   Ibid 255.

[305]   Erik P Lewis, 'Unmasking "Anon12345": Applying an Appropriate Standard When Private Citizens Seek the Identity of Anonymous Internet Defamation Defendants' [2009] University of Illinois Law Review 947; Ryan M Martin, 'Freezing the Net: Rejecting a One-Size-Fits-All Standard For Unmasking Anonymous Internet Speakers in Defamation Lawsuits' [2007] 75 University of Cincinnati Law Review 1217.

[306]   Entry: *Ex parte* in Black (n 291) 517. For a brief history of the development and use of 'Does', see Carol M Rice, 'Meet John Doe: It Is Time For Federal Civil Procedure to Recognize John Doe Parties' [1996] University of Pittsburgh Law Review 883, spec. 889ff.

[307]   See Robert G Larson and Paul A Godfread, 'Bringing John Doe to Court: Procedural Issues in Unmasking Anonymous Internet Defendants' [2009] William Mitchell Law Review 328, spec. 337ff.

disclosing their identities.[308] While I shall go into more detail in an analysis of the case studies in Chapter 4, it may now be useful to recall the common standards applied to all 'Doe proceedings', regardless of the cause of action.

First, 'good faith', initially developed in a case of defamation.[309] The Circuit Court of Virginia ruled that an ISP should be ordered to disclose a subscriber's identity only

> (1) when the court is satisfied by the pleadings or evidence supplied to that court (2) that the party requesting the subpoena has a legitimate, good faith basis to contend that it may be the victim of conduct actionable in the jurisdiction where suit was filed and (3) the subpoenaed identity information is centrally needed to advance that claim.[310]

A second standard is based on the 'prima facie case', as applied by the District Court of Northern California in the *Seescandy.com* case[311] concerning a trademark infringement on the web. The Court introduced a balancing test based on four limiting principles: first, the plaintiff should identify the unknown party with sufficient specificity; second, she should demonstrate efforts in locating the defendant; third, the plaintiff should satisfy the Court that the suit could withstand a motion to dismiss; fourth and last, the plaintiff should file a request for discovery with justifications for the request, naming a limited number of persons or

---

[308]   Ibid 337; see also, more in general, Rice (n 306).

[309]   *In re Subpoena Duces Tecum to Am. Online, Inc.*, 52 Va. Cir. 26 (Va. Cir. Ct. 2000). For an account of the tests applied by courts, see: Larson and Godfread (n 307) 351ff; Victoria Smith Ekstrand, 'Unmasking Jane and John Doe: Online Anonymity and the First Amendment' [2003] Communication Law & Policy 405, spec. 417ff; Nathaniel Gleicher, 'John Doe Subpoenas: Toward a Consistent Legal Standard' [2008] 118 Yale Law Journal 320, 338ff; Susanna Moore, 'The Challenge of Internet Anonymity: Protecting John Doe on the Internet' [2009] John Marshall Journal Computer & Information Law 469, spec. 472ff; Lyrissa Barnett Lidsky, 'Anonymity in Cyberspace: What Can We Learn from John Doe?' [2009] Boston College Law Review 1373, 1376; Clay Calvert, Kayla Gutierrez, Karla D. Kennedy and Kara Carnley Murrhee, 'David Doe v. Goliath, Inc.: Judicial Ferment in 2009 for Business Plaintiffs Seeking the Identities of Anonymous Online Speakers' [2009] John Marshall Law Review 1; Jonathan D Jones, 'Cybersmears and John Doe: How Far Should First Amendment Protection of Anonymous Internet Speakers Extend?' [2009] First Amendment Law Review 421; Matthew Mazzotta, 'Balancing Act: Finding Consensus on Standards for Unmasking Anonymous Internet Speakers' [2010] Boston College Law Review 833, 866ff.

[310]   *In re Subpoena Duces Tecum to Am. Online* (n 309) 37.

[311]   *Columbia Ins. Co. v. Seescandy.com*, 185 F.R.D. 573 (N.D. Cal. 1999).

entities on whom the discovery might be served, and showing likelihood of success of that request in identifying the defendant.[312]

A very close test was applied in a subsequent case of copyright infringement against file-sharing. In *Sony Music Entertainment, Inc. v. Does 1-40*,[313] the District Court of Southern New York, inspired by the previous decisions of other courts,[314] developed a sort of 'balancing test' to decide whether a subpoena seeking the disclosure of user identities should be quashed or not. The test is of particular relevance to my investigation since it is based on users' privacy interests: in both this and some other – mainly defamation – cases, the courts have focused on the relation between the ISP and the user. Defendant-users may have an expectation of privacy related to their identity[315] but this depends on the terms of the service agreement they have with their provider.

The test applied is based on five requirements:

1. concrete showing of a prima facie claim of actionable harm;
2. specificity of the discovery request;
3. absence of alternative means of obtaining the subpoenaed information;
4. central need for the subpoenaed information to advance the claim;
5. the party's expectation of privacy.[316]

The eventual outcomes of the applications of these tests are analysed in the case studies in Chapter 4. Here, I examine with particular care the approach taken by the courts, which require plaintiffs, or their cause of action, to follow certain prescribed steps.

As far as my analysis is concerned, it is also worth stressing that, even though the procedure followed by the American courts in deciding Doe cases is very similar to that of the Canadian courts, they come to diametrically opposed conclusions. Canada has no equivalent instrument to Section 515(h) of the DMCA and Canadian copyright holders have

---

[312] *Seescandy* (n 311) 578–581.

[313] *Sony Music Entertainment, Inc. v. Does 1-40*, 326 F. Supp. 2d 556 (S.D.N.Y. 2004). Followed by *London-Sire Records, INC., et al. v. DOE 1 et al.*, 542 F. Supp. 2d 153, 158 (S.D.N.Y. 2009).

[314] *Seescandy* (n 311); *America Online, Inc. v. Anonymous Publicly Traded Company*, 261 Va. 350 (2001); *Dendrite Int'l, Inc. v. Doe*, 342 N.J. Super. 134 (2001); *Recording Indus. Ass'n of America, Inc. v. Verizon Internet Servs., Inc.*, 359 U.S. App. D.C. 85 (2003). See *Sony Music Entertainment* (n 313) 565.

[315] The concept of 'expectation of privacy' arose from the seminal case *Katz v. United States*, 389 U.S. 347 (1967), briefly analysed in Chapter 3, Section 2.

[316] *Sony Music Entertainment* (n 313) 564–565.

therefore always had to rely on 'John Doe' proceedings, depending on Rules 233 and 238 of the Federal Court Rules to obtain users' personal data.[317] Just as in the US, these rules are part of the so-called discovery phase of the process, in which each party can access all the documents of possible relevance to their claim or defence that are in the possession of the other party, or, as in this case, of a non-party.[318]

According to Rule 233(1), examination can be ordered 'if the document is relevant and its production could be compelled at trial'. In Canada discovery is usually limited to parties to the proceeding; however, in exceptional cases and in the instance of a motion such as those proposed by the copyright holders, the court can order the production of documents in the possession, control or power of a person who is not a party. This only happens when it would be unfair to require the moving party to proceed to trial without obtaining the discovery of the document. In order to evaluate the fairness of such an action, different criteria have been considered: normally, however, the threshold for perceived unfairness is high, so as to limit the number of cases in which such disclosure will be compelled.[319]

Rule 238 refers to the examination of non-parties. As with Rule 233, it is generally believed that only in exceptional circumstances can a non-party be asked to supply information for a case. There are, however, occasions when information critical to the preparation of a party's case is available only to a non-party; rules providing for tests to ascertain the possibility of examining a non-party have therefore been conceived. These tests generally require the requesting party to demonstrate the existence of certain conditions. In order to decide whether leave to examine should be granted, courts normally balance the interest of the party seeking the examination with the interest of the party subject to the possible examination.[320] Rule 238(3) determines when a court may grant leave:

if it is satisfied that

(a) the person may have information on an issue in the action;
(b) the party has been unable to obtain the information informally from the person or from another source by any other reasonable means;

---

[317] *Federal Court Rules*, 1998, S.O.R./98-106 [FCR].
[318] Documentary discovery involves two steps: disclosure and production. Examination for discovery then enables parties to ask questions of representatives of the other party. Janet Walker and Lorne Sossin, *Civil Litigation* (Irwin Publishing 2010) 167–170.
[319] Ibid 179.
[320] Ibid 186.

(c) it would be unfair not to allow the party an opportunity to question the person before trial; and

(d) the questioning will not cause undue delay, inconvenience or expense to the person or to the other parties.

As we shall see, how both these rules were interpreted has proved crucial in a number of cases regarding the enforcement of IPR.

In conjunction with the rules of civil procedure already described, the Canadian cases also considered certain procedural rules coming from British case law, such as the 'Norwich orders'. A 'Norwich order' is an equitable relief that requires an innocent person who has become involved in the wrongful activity of a third party against a moving party to provide any information necessary for the moving party to pursue a claim against the tortfeasor. The innocent person is subject to an equitable duty to help the victim of the third person's wrongdoing.[321] The *Norwich* principle gives courts the power to order disclosure before proceedings have started, and against a non-party.[322]

The order originates in *Norwich*,[323] a case decided in the United Kingdom pertaining to a patent infringement involving illegal imports. Norwich Pharmacal, an American corporation, owned a patent for which Smith Kline and French Laboratories Ltd were the subsidiary and licensee. The claimants had a strong belief that a patented product had been imported illicitly but did not know who the illegal importers were, and therefore had no one to sue for patent violation. So they decided to sue the Customs and Excise Commissioners, on the grounds that the importers had to fill in a form of entry – which included the name of the importers, as well as other information on the goods – and the Commissioners were therefore in possession of documents which could identify the infringers and provide evidence related to the importation of the

---

[321] Linda S Abrams and Kevin P McGuinnes, *Canadian Civil Procedure Law* (2nd edn, Lexis Nexis 2010) 1089 1090; Melody Yiu, 'A New Prescription for Disclosure: Reformulating the Rule for Norwich Order' [2007] University of Toronto Faculty Law Review 41, 44ff.

[322] UK Civil Procedure Rule 31.17, which provides the possibility of obtaining information from a non-party, and Rule 31.18, which preserves the court's pre-civil procedure rules powers to order disclosure before proceedings have started, as in the case of a Norwich Pharmacal order; see Dijendra Basu, 'Obtaining Disclosure from Non-parties' [2005] Journal of Personal Injury 198, 200.

[323] *Norwich Pharmacal Co. v. Commissioners of Customs and Exercise* [1974] AC 133 (HL).

material infringing Norwich's patent. Since this information was confidential, the claimants sought an order for disclosure of the names and addresses of the infringers, basing their claim on the 'equitable right to file a Bill for discovery'.

Norwich had begun by actually suing the Commissioners for patent infringement, either as principals or as parties, hoping thus to oblige the defendants to reveal the importers' identities. But the Court of Appeal concluded that the claimant had no reasonable cause of action and consequently no right of discovery.[324]

The House of Lords had a different perspective: no disclosure should be ordered since this would infringe the 'mere witness' rule. According to this rule, information may not be obtained by discovery from a person if this person could be compellable 'either to give oral testimony as a witness or on a *subpoena duces tecum* – unless there was a separate cause of action against the person from whom the information was sought which could be relied upon'.[325]

The House of Lords pointed out that this rule could not be applied in a case where, without the requested information, the trial of the wrongdoer would never take place. Besides, the appellants were only seeking the names of the alleged infringers from the Commissioners and not the discovery of documents. Given that no trial could be started unless the infringers were identified, the House of Lords granted the order. However, the Lords specified that this relief would have not been available against every bystander: the Commissioners were in a special position, since the infringing goods were under their control. The Commissioners had therefore been innocently mixed up in the importers' tort, but nevertheless 'without certain action on their part the infringements could never have been committed'.[326] The core principle of *Norwich Pharmacal*, in fact, states that:

> If through no fault of his own a person gets mixed up in the tortious acts of others so as to facilitate their wrong-doing he may incur no personal liability

---

[324]   Kevin LaRoche and Guy J Pratte, 'The Norwich Pharmacal Principle and Its Utility in Intellectual Property Litigation' [2001] 18 Canadian Intellectual Property Review 117, 119.

[325]   The rationale of this rule is that the testimony would be available by other means, either in an action already in progress or in an action that could be brought. See Charles Hollander, 'Norwich Pharmacal Takes Wings' [2009] Civil Justice Quarterly 458. The purpose of the mere witness rule is not to prevent, but only to postpone, the recovery of the data sought. See *Norwich Pharmacal* (n 323) 174.

[326]   *Norwich Pharmacal* (n 323) 174.

but he comes under a duty to assist the person who has been wronged by giving him full information and disclosing the identity of the wrong-doers.[327]

The fact that the person had become involved involuntarily, or in the course of her duty, was irrelevant – the disclosure was available as long as an individual had a connection with the wrongdoing (other than being a mere spectator) and was in possession of documents relating to the wrongful action.[328]

Furthermore, Lord Reid pointed out that the disclosure needed to be weighed against public policy considerations, which might prevent it. In this case, however, he accorded the disclosure on the grounds that the information was not confidential and its disclosure did not constitute a potential hindrance to the Commissioners' conduct of their duty. As for the possibility that the disclosure could be prejudicial to those whose identities would be disclosed, Lord Reid considered that in the particular case the possibility that those individuals were innocent was 'remote'.[329]

Other Lords expressed their concern about this interpretation and the consequent application of the bill of discovery. Lord Cross, in particular, set out the criteria that a court might follow in ordering discovery. These requirements, which are also applied by the Canadian courts, were, in the opinion of Lord Cross, indispensable, because the proposed application of the equitable disclosure could have been the 'thin edge of the wedge', opening up the possibility of 'fishing requests' by plaintiffs who wanted to collect evidence for further cases.[330]

In several Canadian provinces the rules of civil procedure have for many years contained provisions that permit discovery before a proceeding starts. This may be one of the reasons why the Norwich order has not

---

[327] *Norwich Pharmacal* (n 323) 175.

[328] Paul Cox, 'Evolution or Revolution? Norwich Pharmacal Orders over the Last 20 Years' [2004] Trademark World 40, 41.

[329] *Norwich Pharmacal* (n 323) 176.

[330] *Norwich Pharmacal* (n 323) 199. '*Norwich Pharmacal* does not give claimants a general licence to fish for information that will do no more than potentially assist them to identify a claim or a defendant', see John O'Hare and Kevin Browne, *Civil Litigation* (14th edn, Sweet & Maxwell 2009) 506 for further explanation of the functioning of the order; Adrian Zuckerman, *Zuckerman on Civil Procedure* (1st edn, Sweet & Maxwell 2006) 578ff. The *Norwich* order is also used in the UK for the purpose of enforcing copyright against file-sharing in cases such as those analysed in this work, see Tom O'Flynn, 'File-sharing: An Holistic Approach to the Problem' [2006] Entertainment Law Review 218, 218; LaRoche and Pratte (n 324) 122–123.

often been applied in the Canadian system.[331] The first Canadian case to adopt this approach was *Glaxo Wellcome*[332] and the case is, in fact, very similar to *Norwich*. The Federal Court listed four criteria, revised versions of the English requirements:

1.   The plaintiff must show a bona fide claim. This provision is intended to avoid frivolous actions for bills of discovery.
2.   The plaintiff must share some relationship with the defendants. This is 'an alternative formulation of the principle that a bill of discovery may not be issued against a mere witness or disinterested bystander'.[333]
3.   The person to whom the request is made must be the only practical source of information available.
4.   The public interest against disclosure must be considered by the court before ordering the disclosure. As Lord Reid specified in *Norwich*, the court should weigh the requirements of justice for the appellants against the respondent's argument for non-disclosure.[334]

These orders usually deal with confidentiality, which means that the requested information usually originates in a professional environment.[335] Confidentiality arises from an implicit or explicit agreement between two parties; however, in the lawsuits analysed here, the information was 'personal' and, in fact, the privacy at stake can be said to relate simply to the 'intrinsic sensitivity' of certain matters.[336]

---

[331]   Yiu (n 321) 43.

[332]   *Glaxo Wellcome PLC v. Minister of National Revenue* [1998] 4 F.C. 439.

[333]   Ibid para 24.

[334]   Ibid paras 22–30. Yiu (n 321) 74 argues that Norwich orders should be limited to their initial scope of finding wrongdoers and should not become a means of pre-proceeding discovery. This, in turn, would mean that the plaintiff's claim should be well grounded, although not necessarily as high as a *prima facie* standard.

[335]   A court shall then apply the so-called 'Wigmore test', a case-by-case analysis, named after the scholar who proposed this test, see John H Wigmore, *Evidence in Trials at Common Law*, vol 8 (Wolters Kluwer 1961) 527. See Chapter 4 for a deeper analysis.

[336]   For a critical approach to how confidentiality, privacy and data protection have been confused in recent years see Margaret A Wilkinson, 'Battleground Between New and Old Orders: Control Conflicts Between Copyright and Personal Data Protection' in Gendreau (n 245) 227, 252ff.

The US and Canadian approaches described above, despite certain differences, nevertheless originate in a shared conception of civil procedure. It is therefore not surprising that the Italian approach differs from both North American approaches to a much greater extent than they do from one another.

In fact, although the tools illustrated below have been perceived by some as the introduction of 'common law discovery' into the Italian system,[337] this is actually far from being the case.

The instruments expressly providing for the enforcement of *diritto d'autore* are described by arts. 156 and 156*bis* of Legge 633/41. Both provisions were introduced by decreto legislativo 16.3.2006, no. 140, implementing the so-called 'IPR Enforcement Directive', i.e. Directive 2004/48/EC.[338] The Directive, which was a response to the increasing threats posed by new technologies to IP, did no more than introduce new procedural tools for the enforcement of IPR. The Directive was also a response to the requirements of the TRIPs Agreement.[339]

Article 156 offers a tool to the copyright holder who fears the violation of her exploitation right, or who wants to prevent the perpetuation or repetition of a violation which has already been committed. The right holder can ask the judge to ascertain the violation and to enjoin the

---

[337] 'Peppermint case', Trib. Rome, 17.3.2008, in Giur. It., n. 7/2008, 1738 – see Chapter 4. See also Ubertazzi, *Commentario* (n 29) 2074.

[338] Directive 2004/48/EC of the European Parliament and of the Council of 29 April 2004 on the enforcement of intellectual property rights, OJ L 195, 2.6.2004, 16. For a comment on the implementation of the Directive in the Italian system see Luca Nivarra, 'L'enforcement dei diritti di proprietà intellettuale dopo la Direttiva 2004/48/CE' [2005] Rivista di Diritto Industriale, I, 33. For a comment on the Directive: Jörg Reinbothe, 'The EU Enforcement Directive 2004/48/EC as a Tool for Copyright Enforcement' in Irina A Stamatoudi, *Copyright Enforcement and the Internet* (Kluwer 2010) 3; Michael Walter and Dominik Gobel, 'Enforcement Directive' in Walter and Von Lewinski (eds) (n 9) 1193; Irini A Stamatoudi, 'The Enforcement Directive' in Stamatoudi and Torremans (eds) (n 9) 528.

[339] Under the enforcement provisions of the TRIPs Agreement, art. 43 concerns 'Evidence' and art. 44 'Injunctions'. According to Leonardo Benvenuto, 'Il Sistema della discovery e del diritto di "informazione" nel codice della proprietà industriale' [2007] Rivista di Diritto Industriale, II, 108, 110, these provisions are the result of a compromise between the discovery tools of common law systems and the principles related to evidence of civil law systems.

prosecution of either the author of the infringement or the intermediary whose services were used to perpetrate it.[340]

Article 156*bis* is unquestionably the most important provision for the cases here analysed. The interpretation of this rule is still debated: as mentioned, some scholars claim that art. 156*bis* introduced the common law institution of 'discovery' into the Italian system. Others, however, interpret it as merely an enlargement – for the sole purpose of copyright protection – of tools which are already available within the Italian Code of Civil Procedure.[341]

Article 156*bis* states that when a party (a) gives convincing evidence, from which it can be inferred that its claims are sound, and (b) the same party has detected documents, evidence or information held by the counterparty, which could confirm this convincing evidence, it can ask the judge to order the exhibition or disclosure of the information from the counterparty. The party can also ask the judge to order the counterparty to hand over evidence that would identify the individuals involved in the production and distribution of the goods or services which constitute the violation of the copyright. The same article also prescribes that when a judge applies one of these provisions, she should adopt suitable measures to ensure the protection of confidential information, taking into account the counterparty's observations as well (art. 156*bis*, co. 3).

Article 156*bis* should not be considered a way of obtaining information through an 'explorative' process: it should only be applied when the plaintiff has already shown sufficient proof of the infringement.[342]

Some scholars and courts have claimed that art. 156*bis* provides a 'precautionary measure', intended to prevent the right holder's situation from deteriorating over time, and her rights from undergoing an irreparable prejudice. They typically provide for injunctions which enjoin the counterparty from a particular action, or oblige a particular behaviour. Such actions have some peculiar characteristics. First, they must be instrumental in a subsequent ordinary lawsuit. This means that they are usually temporary and cannot therefore lead to a definite resolution, since the latter would require an ordinary lawsuit. These lawsuits are concise, meaning that judicial measures are taken on the basis of elements of proof

---

[340] For an account see Andrea Sirotti Gaudenzi (ed), *Proprietà intellettuale e diritto della concorrenza. La tutela dei diritti di privativa*, vol 2 (Utet 2010) 142ff; Ubertazzi, *Commentario* (n 29) 2055ff.

[341] See Sirotti Gaudenzi (n 340) 148.

[342] Ubertazzi, *Commentario* (n 29) 2073.

given by the claimant: there is no investigation for evidence. Nevertheless, some of them can also continue to have effects indefinitely.[343]

An injunction can be ordered by a judge when the two main requirements for such action exist: *periculum in mora* (the risk of an imminent and irreparable damage) and *fumus boni iuris* (the presumption of sufficient legal basis to grant the requested measure,[344] based on foreknowledge of the result of the entire lawsuit[345]). Some authors claim that *periculum in mora* is *in re ipsa* in the case of violation of economic copyrights. This would mean that, since the damage is certain to worsen during the period of the lawsuit, there is no need to prove this deterioration. However, some judges have held that this is not the case and that the existence of a danger has to be proven by the claimant in order to obtain the requested injunction.[346]

Decreto legislativo 140/2006 also introduced art. 156*ter*, which provides the plaintiff's 'right of information'. This rule allows a court, if asked, to order the provision of information on the origin and distribution networks of the goods or services which infringe an IPR from any person who:

(1) was found in possession of the infringing goods on a commercial scale or was found to be using the infringing services on a commercial scale; or
(2) was found to be providing on a commercial scale services used in infringing activities; or
(3) was indicated by subjects referred to under numbers (1) and (2) as being involved in the production, manufacture or distribution of the goods or the provision of the services.[347]

---

[343] See Crisanto Mandrioli, *Corso di diritto processuale civile. Editio minor*, vol. III (9th edn, Giappichelli 2011) 240; Claudio Consolo, *Spiegazioni di diritto processuale civile. Le tutele: di merito, sommarie ed esecutive* (Giappichelli 2010) 269–270.

[344] Mandrioli (n 343) 238.

[345] Consolo (n 343) 271. Each precautionary measure has its own characteristics, see ibid 272.

[346] See Sirotti Gaudenzi (n 60) 368. The author refers to Trib. Napoli (ord.), 4.2.2005, in Dir. Ind., 2005, 637; in the same line also Trib. Napoli, 21.5.2004, in Riv. Dir. Farmaceutico, 2005, 267.

[347] Here I mainly use the words of EU Dir. 2004/48, since the Italian implementation is very close to the original text.

The information usually relates to the names and addresses of people producing, distributing or in any way possessing infringing products or services, as well as information on the quantities of infringing goods.

The order can also be directed to people who are not part of the process, as long as they are involved in the illicit activity.[348]

The Italian system is therefore inherently different from those of the US and Canada. Although art. 156*bis* resembles a discovery tool, its applicability to each concrete case is not decided by the results of a test for the existence of certain requirements. Moreover, even though a corresponding provision exists for other IP rights,[349] there are no similar tools for addressing the infringement of other kinds of rights, and the instruments which do exist are not as strong as those for IPR.[350]

The Canadian and US tools bear a much closer resemblance to each other, especially with regard to 'John Doe' proceedings. On the other hand, Italy and the US offer an enforcement tool specifically designed for the enforcement of copyright, which Canada does not have. In fact, the 'John Doe' proceeding is a general tool, used in many different anonymity cases, including those of defamation; the tool provided by art. 156*bis* of the Italian Code of Civil Procedure and the DMCA *subpoena* can only be applied in copyright cases.

This divergence may be another indicator of the fact that the US and Italy have adopted a more protective approach than Canada has.[351]

---

[348] Ubertazzi, *Commentario* (n 29) 2080ff. Practically, information is obtained through the examination of the subjects under numbers (1)–(3).

[349] I am referring to arts. 121ff. of the Italian Code of Industrial Property (decreto legislativo 10.02.2005, no. 30). A similar provision has existed for IPR other than copyright since 1996, when Italy implemented some of the TRIPs Agreement provisions through decreto legislativo 19 marzo 1996, no. 198. See Ubertazzi, *Commentario* (n 29) 646ff; Andrea Giussani, 'L'attuazione dell'accordo TRIPs e l'esibizione dei documenti' [2000] AIDA 256; Luigi Paolo Comoglio, 'Istruzione e discovery nei giudizi in materia di proprietà industriale' [2000] AIDA 270.

[350] See, for example, art. 210 (*actio ad exhibendum*) of the Italian Code of Civil Procedure. On the topic of anonymity and unmasking anonymous users, see Giorgio Resta, 'Anonimato, responsabilità e identificazione: prospettive di diritto comparato' [2014] Dir. Inf. 171 and the works cited by the author.

[351] This section was intended as an introductory tool to understand the different perspectives from which the three countries allow copyright enforcement. A deeper understanding will be gained through the analysis of the actual cases.

7. THE LIABILITY OF ONLINE INTERMEDIARIES FOR COPYRIGHT INFRINGEMENT

The liability of online intermediaries is certainly among the thorniest issues related to copyright infringement on the Internet. Their key position in the Internet environment has put them at the centre of important cases and laws, and is also why their liability regime is constantly under scrutiny, both from the courts and from scholars.[352]

Providers have always played a critical role in the battle against file-sharing. In the case studies analysed here, without the collaboration of the ISPs copyright holders would have been unable to obtain the information they needed to sue final users. ISPs have also sometimes been sued directly by copyright holders, especially in the first years of the spread of the Internet. Obviously, ISP liability touches on more than just copyright infringement. Indeed, many cases have arisen concerning the infringement of other rights, including other IPRs. Nevertheless, ISP liability regimes with regard to copyright infringement may serve as an index for the way a particular country deals with digital copyright generally.

The liability of intermediaries for copyright infringement can either be a 'secondary liability' or a 'third-party liability'. In the first case, a person is held liable for concurring in, helping, or being responsible for, the wrongful action of someone else. This was the notion upon which the very famous cases of *Sony Betamax* and *Grokster* were based.[353] To have a secondary liability, a primary infringer must exist.[354]

If no specific regulatory scheme had been introduced, the development of secondary liability might have turned ISPs into scapegoats for any case of copyright infringement. Actually, even before introducing a specific regulatory scheme, all three countries had developed case law to

---

[352]   See the case study done by the Berkman Center for Internet & Society of Harvard University: Urs Gasser and Wolfgang Schulz, 'Governance of Online Intermediaries: Observations from a Series of National Case Studies' (2015) The Berkman Center for Internet & Society Research Publication Series 15/5 <https://papers.ssrn.com/sol3/papers.cfm?abstract_id=2566364> accessed 20 February 2017.

[353]   *Sony Betamax* (n 131); *MGM Studios, Inc. v. Grokster, Ltd* (n 185) and (n 187).

[354]   See Chapter 4 for a short explanation of the doctrine behind secondary liability for copyright infringement. For both an overview of secondary liability and for a hypothetical tertiary liability regime, see Benjamin H Glatstein, 'Tertiary Copyright Liability' [2004] University of Chicago Law Review 1605.

deal with this issue. As often happens with new technologies, courts applied the reasoning developed for the (old) analogic world to the (new) digital world.[355] Specific regulations followed; the US was the first to implement a statutory regime for ISP liability, while Canada was the last, only adopting specific legislation in 2012.

In 1996 US Congress passed the Communications Decency Act (CDA), as part of the Telecommunication Act,[356] and two years later the Online Copyright Infringement Liability Limitation Act (OCILLA) – part of the DMCA – was implemented.[357] Among other provisions, Section

---

[355]   See, for example, the description in Loftus E Becker Jr, 'The Liability of Computer Bulletin Board Operators for Defamation Posted by Others' [1989] Connecticut Law Review 203, spec. 213ff. See also Note, 'Computer Bulletin Board Operator Liability for User Misuse' [1985] Fordham Law Review 439; Note 'Computer Bulletin Boards and Defamation: Who Should Be Liable? Under What Standard?' [1987] Journal of Law and Technology 121. See also the case *Stratton Oakmont v. Prodigy Servs. Co.*, 23 Media L. Rep. 1794 (1995), which considers the ISP to be a publisher and therefore strictly liable for the defamatory content posted by a third party on the bulletin board. For the Italian system: Massimo Franzoni, 'La responsabilità del provider' [1997] AIDA 248; Vincenzo Zeno-Zencovich, 'La pretesa estensione alla telematica del regime della stampa: note critiche' [1998] Dir. Informazione e informatica 15; Sara Alvanini, 'La responsabilità dei service provider' [2010] Dir. industriale 329. Consider the decisions by Trib. Macerata, (ord.) 2.12.1998, in Riv. Dir. Ind., 1999, 35, and by Trib. Napoli, 9.8.1997, in Riv. Dir. Ind., 1999, II, 38, in which the tribunal held that 'the Internet, as an international system of interrelation between big and small telematics networks, [was] comparable to the press'.

[356]   Pub. Law No. 104-104, 110 Stat. 56. An Act to promote competition and reduce regulation in order to secure lower prices and higher quality services for American telecommunications consumers and encourage the rapid deployment of new telecommunications technologies, enacted on February 8, 1996. On the origin of CDA see Robert Cannon, 'The Legislative History of Senator Exon's Communications Decency Act: Regulating Barbarians on the Information Super-highway' [1996] Federal Communications Law Journal 51. On the functioning of both regulations and for a comparison, see Jonathan Band and Matthew Schruers, 'Safe Harbors Against The Liability Hurricane: The Communications Decency Act and The Digital Millennium Copyright Act' [2002] Cardozo Arts & Entertainment Law Journal 295; Adam Holland, Chris Bavitz, Jeff Hermes, Andy Sellars, Ryan Budish, Michael Lambert and Nick Decoster, 'Online Inter-mediaries Case Studies Series: Intermediary Liability in the United States' (2015), The Global Network of Internet & Society Research Centers <https://publixphere.net/i/noc/page/OI_Case_Study_Intermediary_Liability_in_the_United_States> accessed 20 February 2017.

[357]   17 U.S.C. § 512; see Steven E Halpern, 'New Protections for Internet Service Providers: An Analysis of "The Online Copyright Infringement Liability

230 of the CDA specifically addresses the issue of civil liability for ISPs, stating that '[n]o provider or user of an interactive computer service shall be treated as the publisher or speaker of any information provided by another information content provider'.[358]

OCILLA only deals instead with online copyrighted content. In enacting the DMCA, Congress clearly needed to contemplate different interests, including those of copyright owners and ISPs: the first title of the Act thus safeguards the interests of the former, while the second title provides liability limitations for the latter.[359] According to its legislative history, the whole section was 'intended to preserve incentives for online service providers and copyright owners to cooperate and detect and address copyright infringements that occur in the digital networked environment'.[360]

OCILLA constitutes paragraph 512 of the Copyright Act and defines the so-called 'safe harbour provisions', which limit the liability of OSPs for the infringing activity of their users.[361] More precisely, the Act provides safe harbours from monetary damages for ISPs under some given circumstances. Monetary damages include damages, costs, attorneys' fees and any other monetary payment. In addition, ISPs are not subject to injunctions or other equitable reliefs[362] but they can still be

---

Limitation Act'" [1999] Seton Hall Legislative Journal 359; see also the other works cited in this paragraph.

[358] The Act was enacted to regulate pornographic material on the Internet. In 1997 the US Supreme Court landmark case *Reno v. ACLU*, 521 U.S. 844, struck down the anti-indecency provisions of the Act, in defence of First Amendment freedom of speech. Nevertheless, § 230 was not touched by the Supreme Court sentence. See Sue A Mota, 'Neither Dead nor Forgotten: The Past, Present, and Future of the Communications Decency Act in Light of Reno v. ACLU' [1998] Computer Law Review & Technology Journal 1; David K Djavaherian, 'Reno v. ACLU' [1998] Berkeley Technology Law Journal 371; Kim L Rappaport, 'In the Wake of Reno v. ACLU: The Continued Struggle in Western Constitutional Democracies with Internet Censorship and Freedom of Speech Online' [1998] American University International Law Review 765.

[359] As 'deep pocket' subjects, ISPs have been targeted far and wide by copyright holders in copyright infringement cases, starting from 1993 – see *Playboy Enterprises, Inc. v. Frena*, 839 F. Supp. 1552 (MD Fla. 1993); the cases described in this section just provide some examples.

[360] 144 Cong. Rec. S11890 (ed. Oct., 8, 1998) – Statement of senator Leahy <www.gpoaccess.gov/crecord/98crpgs.html> accessed 20 February 2017.

[361] See 17 U.S.C. § 512(a)(1), (b)(1), (c)(1), (d)(1); see Halpern (n 357) 387ff; LaFrance (n 50) 348ff.

[362] There are, however, some limits to these liability restrictions, see LaFrance (n 50) 359–361.

subject to the specific injunctions described in § 512(j). Failure to qualify for any of these safe harbours does not affect other possible defences and ISPs could therefore still be found not liable for other reasons.[363]

The conditions for satisfying safe harbours differ according to the particular function of the provider concerned. Four main activities are listed in Section 512(a)–512(d); each section provides for a different level of protection against liability, depending on the particular activity carried out by the provider.[364] The activities are classified as follows:[365]

1.   Transmission: the ISP only acts as a data conduit, transmitting information from one point on a network to another, following someone else's request. This limitation covers the transmission or routing of, or the provision of connections for, information, as well as the automatic creation of intermediate and transient copies in the operation of a network.
2.   System caching: the provider retains copies, for a limited period, of material made available online by a network user, and then transmitted to another subscriber at the direction of the former. In this way the intermediary can fulfil other requests for the same material by just transmitting the retained copy, instead of retrieving the material directly from the original source.
3.   Storing of material: the provider hosts material or other information repositories on her system, where material is stored at the user's direction.
4.   Providing information-location tools: this occurs when the intermediary supplies users with a reference or a link to a site containing requested material. Search engines seem to be part of this category.

The safe harbours of Sections 512(b), (c) and (d) require providers to be unaware of the infringing activity and to promptly remove or disable access to infringing material, upon receiving a notice of claimed infringement. This is usually referred to as the 'notice and take down' procedure. To be effective, the notice must meet the following requirements, detailed

---

[363]   Ibid 349.

[364]   Carolyn Andrepont, 'Digital Millennium Copyright Act: Copyright Protection for the Digital Age' [1999] DePaul-LCA Journal of Art & Entertainment Law 397, 412ff.

[365]   For the following explanation I rely on the U.S. Copyright Office, 'Summary of The Digital Millennium Copyright Act of 1998', 1998, 8ff. <www.copyright.gov/legislation/dmca.pdf> accessed 20 February 2017.

in Section 512(c)(3). It must be a written communication including: the signature (either physical or electronic) of the copyright holder or an authorized person; identification of the allegedly infringed copyrighted work; identification of the material allegedly infringing the copyrighted work; information sufficient to allow the provider to contact the complaining party; a statement that the complainant has a good faith belief that the use of the material is not authorized by the owner or by law; a statement that the notification is accurate and the complaining party is authorized to act on behalf of the copyright holder. If lacking one or more requirements, the notice will not be effective and therefore will not be taken into account when determining whether or not the provider was aware of the infringing circumstances.[366] To take advantage of the safe harbours an intermediary must implement a policy providing for the termination of repeat infringements and must inform its users about this termination.[367]

Furthermore, to obtain safe harbour protection by § 512(c) or § 512(d), there is another requirement: if the provider has the right and the ability to control the infringing activity, it shall not receive a financial benefit directly attributable to that activity.[368]

Knowledge under § 512(c) and (d), 'awareness of facts or circumstances from which the infringing activity is apparent', is usually investigated under a 'red flag' test. This test has both a subjective and an objective part: the subjective part is the provider's awareness of the facts or circumstances; the objective test analyses whether the infringement would have been apparent to a reasonable person with that awareness.[369] The way in which providers deal with content is thus key to their liability, or lack of it: 'if there is no content curation, there is no liability'.[370]

The safe harbour discipline is closely connected to the copyright enforcement provisions previously illustrated – the 'subpoena to identify infringer' is, indeed, one of the § 512 provisions.

To preserve the freedom of Internet providers, at least in part, § 512(m) states that ISPs are not requested to monitor or take positive actions to search for infringing material.[371]

---

[366] § 512(c)(3)(B).
[367] § 512(i).
[368] §§ 512(c)(1)(B) and 512(d)(2).
[369] Band and Schruers (n 356) 306.
[370] Gasser and Schulz (n 352) 6.
[371] Ironically, the title of § 512(m) is: 'Protection of privacy'.

European Directive 2000/31/EC, dealing with 'certain legal aspects of information society services, in particular electronic commerce', includes a very similar rule, in art. 15.[372] This Directive was implemented in the Italian system through decreto legislativo 9.4.2003 no. 70, which reproduces the provisions of the Directive verbatim:[373] arts. 12–15 of the Directive are mirrored in arts. 14–17 of the Italian decree.[374]

The main innovation of the Directive, which legislates on electronic commerce in general, is in its treatment of ISP liability regulation. The Directive states when and how an ISP can be considered liable for a violation committed by itself or by a third party, based on the particular role of that provider in the virtual world.

The three main activities considered are 'mere conduit', 'caching' and 'hosting'. As in the DMCA,[375] the more an ISP is involved in the online

---

[372] Directive 2000/31/EC of the European Parliament and of the Council of 8 June 2000 on certain legal aspects of information society services, in particular electronic commerce, in the Internal Market (Directive on electronic commerce), OJ L 178, 17.7.2000, 1. See Rosa Julià-Barceló and Kamiel J Koelman, 'Intermediary Liability: Intermediary Liability in the E-Commerce Directive: So Far so Good, but It's not Enough' [2000] Computer Law & Security Review 231; Pablo Baistrocchi, 'Liability of Intermediary Service Providers in the EU Directive on Electronic Commerce' [2002] Santa Clara Computer & High Technology Law Review 111; Thibault Verbiest, Gerald Spindler, Giovanni Maria Riccio and Aurélie Van der Perre, 'Study on the Liability of Internet Intermediaries' (2007) <http://ec.europa.eu/internal_market/e-commerce/docs/study/liability/final_report_en.pdf> accessed 20 February 2017.

[373] This verbatim transposition has been criticized: Giovanni Maria Riccio, 'La responsabilità degli Internet providers nel d.lgs. n. 70/03' [2003] Danno e Resp. 1157, 1158ff; Giorgio Spedicato, 'Postille in tema di responsabilità extracontrattuale del provider alla luce del recente Decreto Legislativo n. 70/2003' [2003] Ciberspazio e diritto 155, 155–156. For a thorough analysis of the Italian regulation of ISP liability, see Giovanni Maria Riccio, *La responsabilità civile degli Internet providers* (Giappichelli 2002); Teresa Pasquino, *Servizi telematici e criteri di responsabilità* (Giuffrè 2003); Marialuisa Gambini, *Le responsabilità dell'Internet service provider* (ESI 2006); Marcello De Cata, *La responsabilità civile dell'Internet service provider* (Giuffrè 2010).

[374] I just describe the Italian context here, as a typical example of the EU model, and only occasionally refer to the European level.

[375] Some scholars think that the EU Directive was also inspired by the DMCA. See Riccio, *La responsabilità degli Internet providers* (n 373), *passim*; Leonardo Bugiolacchi, 'La responsabilità dell'host provider alla luce del d.lgs. n. 70/2003: esegesi di una disciplina "dimezzata"' [2005] Resp. civ. prev. 188, *passim*.

user's activity, the higher the probability that it will be held liable, and the more difficult it is to prove its innocence in relation to the illicit action.

Article 12 of the Directive, implemented by art. 14, decreto legislativo 70/03, considers the activity of a 'mere conduit' to be 'the transmission in a communication network of information provided by a recipient of the service, or the provision of access to a communication network'. In this case, the national legislation implementing the Directive has to 'ensure that the service provider is not liable for the information transmitted, on condition that the provider: (a) does not initiate the transmission; (b) does not select the receiver of the transmission; and (c) does not select or modify the information contained in the transmission'.

Article 13 of Directive 2000/31, transposed in art. 15 of decreto legislativo 70/03, describes the function of 'caching providers' as 'the transmission in a communication network of information provided by a recipient of the service'. Member States had to implement a regulation which ensured that the ISP was not liable for the automatic, intermediate and temporary storage of data, as long as this action was performed for the sole purpose of improving the efficiency of the information's transmission to other recipients of the service, when requested. This exemption from liability can be obtained under the condition that

> a) the provider does not modify the information; b) the provider complies with conditions on access to the information; c) the provider complies with rules regarding the updating of the information, specified in a manner widely recognised and used by industry; d) the provider does not interfere with the lawful use of technology, widely recognised and used by industry, to obtain data on the use of the information; and e) the provider acts expeditiously to remove or to disable access to the information it has stored upon obtaining actual knowledge of the fact that the information at the initial source of the transmission has been removed from the network, or access to it has been disabled, or that a court or an administrative authority has ordered such removal or disablement.

The activity of 'hosting' is defined by art. 14 of Directive 2000/31 and by art. 16 of the Italian decree implementing the Directive. Hosting 'consists of the storage of information provided by a recipient of the service'. To protect intermediaries providing this service, Member States had to implement a regulation which preserves the service provider from liability for information stored at the request of a customer, as long as

> a) the provider does not have actual knowledge of illegal activity or information and, as regards claims for damages, is not aware of facts or circumstances from which the illegal activity or information is apparent;

or (b) the provider, upon obtaining such knowledge or awareness, acts expeditiously to remove or to disable access to the information.[376]

The second part of the provision ensures that this rule does not apply when the customer is acting under the authority or under the control of the intermediary.

The liability system also includes the above-mentioned provision in art. 15 of the Directive (art. 17, decreto legislativo 70/03), which introduces the absence of a general obligation to monitor, with the obvious aim of avoiding the infamous 'chilling effect'. The Directive was careful to ensure that national legislation would not impose a general obligation on intermediaries to monitor the data they store or transmit, let alone a general obligation to actively seek out illegal conduct.[377] The same article nevertheless provides that Member States may establish either: (a) an obligation for ISPs to inform the competent public authorities of the existence of allegedly illegal behaviours undertaken, or information provided, by customers; or (b) an obligation to communicate, if requested by competent authorities, information enabling the identification of recipients of their service, with whom they have storage agreements.

Art. 17, decreto legislativo 70/03 provides in its third part for a particular provision which is not considered by art 15 of Directive 2000/31. The Italian provision introduces another form of liability for the

---

[376] Although the Italian implementation of Directive 2000/31 was a sort of copy and paste, art. 16, decreto legislativo 70/03 differs from art. 14 of the Directive. In fact, letter e) of art. 14 exempts the provider from liability, as long as it 'acts expeditiously to remove or to disable access to the information'. The Italian version requires, instead, a further element, since this expeditious removal should be done 'upon the request of competent authorities'. Italian scholars have interpreted the provision introduced by art. 16, decreto legislativo 70/03 in different ways. Some claim that the hosting provider should be considered liable only when both conditions a) and b) are met; for example: Bugiolacchi (n 375) 198ff; Spedicato (n 373) 160–161. Others authors maintain that letters a) and b) apply to criminal and civil proceedings respectively, given the different types of knowledge required by the two branches of law before a person can be considered liable; see for instance Riccio, *La responsabilità degli Internet providers* (n 373) 1162. Lastly, other scholars consider the two conditions as being alternatives; see Giuseppe Cassano and Iacopo P Cimino, 'Il nuovo regime di responsabilità dei providers: verso la creazione di un novello "censore telematico"' [2004] I Contratti 88, 91ff.

[377] Before the adoption and implementation of the EU Directive, Italian courts held an ISP liable in tort due to a failure of a duty to supervise: Trib. Cuneo, (ord.) 23.8.1997, in AIDA, 1997, 500.

provider: the ISP will be liable in tort when, if requested by the administrative or judicial authority, it does not promptly act to stop access to illegal content. It will also be liable when, despite knowledge of the illicit or prejudicial nature of the content to which the provider itself gives access, it does not inform the competent authorities.[378]

This rule is not a direct implementation of an explicit provision of the Directive. It derives from recital n. 48, according to which the Directive does not affect national legislators' possibility to require ISPs hosting information provided by recipients of their services to apply a duty of care, which could reasonably be expected from the said ISPs, in order to detect and prevent certain illegal conduct.

The Italian courts' interpretations of all these provisions has been inconsistent: some courts tend to exclude certain ISP activities from the application of decreto legislativo 70/03; others do not.[379]

European, and therefore Italian, regulation for intermediaries' liability applies to all kinds of conduct. Hence, it applies both to defamation and to copyright infringement, unlike in the US, where the two issues are regulated by two different Acts.[380]

The European Directive did not explicitly ask for a 'notice and take down' regime. Article 21 required re-examination of the Directive three years after enactment, particularly with regard to the need for 'notice and take down' procedures and any eventual liability following the taking down of allegedly infringing content. No notification system has yet been adopted at the European level, although some Member States have implemented their own systems.[381]

---

[378] For an analysis of the problems in interpreting this article, and its relation to those previously summarized, see Gambini (n 373) 302ff.

[379] Consider the decision of the Tribunal of Milan, 9.9.2011, in Riv. dir. ind., 2011, 375, which was recently reversed by Corte d'Appello of Milan, 7.1.2015, in Resp. Civ. Prev., 2015, 1245 on the qualification of 'Yahoo! Video' as a hosting provider, and on the applicability of decreto legislativo 70/03.

[380] Most of the contributions cited here include a comparative analysis of US and EU approaches; see, for a deeper analysis: Rosa Julià-Barceló, 'On-line Intermediary Liability Issues: Comparing E.U. and U.S. Legal Frameworks' [2000] European Intellectual Property Review 105; Miquel Peguera, 'The DMCA Safe Harbors and Their European Counterparts: A Comparative Analysis of Some Common Problems' [2009] Columbia Journal of Law & the Arts 481.

[381] Commission of the European Community, First Report on the Application of Directive 2000/31/EC of the European Parliament and of the Council of 8 June 2000 on the Directive on Electronic Commerce, COM(2003) 702 final, Brussels, 21.11.2003, 14ff. In the report 'A clean and open Internet: Public consultation on procedures for notifying and acting on illegal content hosted by

The recently implemented regulation of the Italian 'Authority for Communications' (Autorità per le Garanzie nelle Comunicazioni – or AGCom) is a move in this direction;[382] the regulation, as well as further implementing decreto legislativo 70/2003, provides a new enforcement tool, activated through an application from the copyright holder.[383] Upon receipt of such an application, the AGCom sends a communication to the copyright holder and the ISP(s) involved, as well as – when possible – to the uploader of the infringing content and to the website manager. The communication also informs alleged infringers that they can either comply with the request of the copyright holder or present their counter-argument. If the Authority finds that there is an infringing activity, it orders the ISP(s) involved to stop the said activity. This procedure cannot

---

online intermediaries' (at <http://ec.europa.eu/internal_market/consultations/docs/2010/e-commerce/summary_report_en.pdf> last accessed 28 July 2017) criticism emerges on the lack of uniformity among Member States for 'notice and take down' procedures. See also a proposal for a specific 'notice and action' procedure in Commission Communication to the European Parliament, the Council, the Economic and Social Committee and the Committee of Regions, a coherent framework for building trust in the Digital Single Market for e-commerce and online services, 11.01.2012, 39ff, at <http://ec.europa.eu/internal_market/e-commerce/docs/communication2012/SEC2011_1641_en.pdf> last accessed 28 July 2017. On this topic, see Aleksandra Kuczerawy, 'Intermediary Liability & Freedom of Expression: Recent Developments in the EU Notice & Action Initiative' [2015] Computer Law & Security Review 46.

[382]   Regolamento in materia di tutela del diritto d'autore sulle reti di comunicazione elettronica e procedure attuative ai sensi del decreto legislativo 9 aprile 2003, n. 70 [Regulation on the enforcement of copyright in e-communications' networks, and on the implementation procedures according to decreto legislativo 09.04.2003, no. 70], adopted by the Italian Communications Authority, with resolution n. 680/13/CONS. On the source of AGCom's power in the field of copyright see Sara Alvanini and Alessandro Cassinelli, 'I (possibili) nuovi poteri di AGCom in material di diritto d'autore nel settore dei media' [2011] Dir. Industriale 543, spec. 546ff. See more generally Luigi Carlo Ubertazzi (ed), *Il regolamento Agcom sul diritto d'autore* (Giappichelli 2014); Andrea Stazi, 'Il regolamento di cui alla delibera n. 680/13/CONS dell'AGCcom per la tutela del diritto d'autore in rete' [2014] Riv. Dir. Industriale 142. The current wording of the regulation is the result of public consultations on the previous texts, on which see Giuseppe Colangelo, 'Comunicazioni elettroniche, contenuti digitali e diritto d'autore: commento al Regolamento AGCOM' [2011] Mercato concorrenza regole 576, spec. 586ff.

[383]   Art. 5 states that the procedure contained in the resolution does not interfere with eventual 'notice and take down' practices adopted by providers.

be initiated, or must be suspended, if the same parties have brought, or bring, the same issue before a judicial authority.[384]

This regulation has attracted a great deal of criticism.[385] Some scholars believe that it does not supply the necessary guarantees to protect freedom of speech and information: the regulation was actually challenged before the Italian Constitutional Court on these grounds[386] but the Court's answer was not entirely clear on this point.[387]

While the Italian system is slowly moving closer to the US model, Canada has developed its own approach to the issue of ISP liability. Until the amendments of 2012, Canada did not have any specific statutory provision to regulate ISP liability, which was a matter of case law only.

Secondary liability in the Canadian context emerges from Section 3 and Section 27 of the Copyright Act. As explained above, Section 3 provides that the copyright owner has certain rights, including the right to authorize any such right. Section 27 states that it is an infringement of copyright to do anything that the Act itself reserves only to the owner,

---

[384] See art. 6-8, resolution n. 680/13/CONS.

[385] The AGCom promoted some public consultations before the final approval of the regulation. See the reports developed by the NEXA Center for Internet & Society: Marco Ricolfi and others, 'Osservazioni del Centro NEXA for Internet & Società sulle proposte di intervento di cui all'allegato b) alla delibera n. 668/10/cons del 17 dicembre 2010 "Lineamenti di provvedimento concernente l'esercizio delle competenze dell'autorità nell'attività di tutela del diritto d'autore sulle reti di comunicazione elettronica"' (2011) <http://nexa. polito.it/nexafiles/Nexa-Consultazione%20AGCOM%20definitivo-marzo2011.pdf>; Id, 'Osservazioni del Centro NEXA for Internet & Society sullo schema di regolamento in materia di tutela del diritto d'autore sulle reti di comunicazione elettronica di cui all'allegato A) alla delibera n. 398/11/cons del 6 luglio 2011' (2011) <http://nexa.polito.it/nexafiles/Nexa_consultazione_398-11.pdf>; Id, 'Osservazioni del Centro Nexa for Internet & Society sullo schema di regolamento di cui all'allegato A) alla delibera n. 452/13/CONS del 25 luglio 2013' (2013) <http://nexa.polito.it/nexacenterfiles/nexa_consultazione_agcom_452_13. pdf> all accessed 20 February 2017.

[386] See the news item: Arturo Di Corinto, 'Diritti d'autore, deciderà la Corte Costituzionale', *Repubblica.it* (20 October 2014) <www.repubblica.it/economia/ affari-e-finanza/2014/10/20/news/diritti_dautore_decider_la_corte_costituzionale-98539164/> accessed 20 February 2017. Constitutional issues have already been highlighted by Marco Orofino, 'L'intervento regolamentare dell'AGCOM in materia di diritto d'autore: profili di criticità formale e sostanziale' in Franco Pizzetti (ed), *Il caso del diritto d'autore* (Giappichelli 2013) 123, 141ff.

[387] At the end of 2015, the Constitutional Court rejected the claim on procedural grounds and therefore it did not really address the constitutionality questions, which currently remain unanswered. See Corte Cost., 3.12.2015, n. 247, in Foro it., 2016, I, 405.

without the owner's consent. In the *CCH* case, the Canadian Supreme Court has interpreted Section 27 as including the 'right to authorize'. The decision, which – as seen – is a cornerstone in defining fair dealing doctrine, also ruled on secondary liability.

CCH is a publishing company that provides services for professionals in the area of law. The Law Society of Upper Canada maintains and runs a library in Toronto, with one of the largest collections of legal material in Canada. The library provides a 'request-based photocopy' service for Law Society members, the judiciary and other authorized people. Through this photocopy service legal materials were reproduced by the library staff and delivered directly or via mail. CCH sued the Law Society, claiming a violation of the copyright on its publications.

The case reached the Supreme Court. With regard to secondary liability, the question was whether the Law Society had breached copyright either by providing the custom photocopy service by which the publisher's works were reproduced and sent to patrons upon request, or by maintaining the self-service photocopiers, and copies of the works, in the library. Justice McLachlin, delivering the Court's decision, asked herself (a) if the Great Library authorized copyright infringement by maintaining self-service photocopiers and copies of the publishers' works for its patrons' use; and (b) if CCH had consented to have its works reproduced by the Great Library.[388]

In answering the first question it was important to understand whether or not there was a primary infringer. In fact, as in the US and Italy, a secondary infringer can only exist if the activity carried out by a first person is infringing.[389] As already mentioned, under Section 27(1) of the Copyright Act, it is an infringement for anyone to do anything that would be allowed only to the owner, including authorizing the exercise of her rights. The Court investigated whether the Great Library had authorized copyright infringement by maintaining the self-service photocopy machines. The main point here was to understand what was meant by 'authorize'. According to McLachlin CJ, the word had to be strictly interpreted, according to its 'strongest dictionary meaning, namely, "[g]ive approval to; sanction, permit; favour, encourage"'.[390] In the Judge's view this did not mean that merely authorizing the use of equipment that could be used to infringe copyright would always mean infringing copyright. According to the Supreme Court's interpretation,

388   *CCH Canadian Ltd* (n 150) para 4.
389   Vaver, *Intellectual Property Law* (n 62) 190.
390   *CCH Canadian Ltd* (n 150) para 38.

judges should presume that in authorizing an activity, a person does so only in so far as it is in respect of the law.[391] This presumption could be overridden by showing that there is a certain relation or degree of control between the authorizer and the infringer.

The Supreme Court stated that even if the users had infringed copyright, the Law Society lacked sufficient control over its users for it to be concluded that the Society approved the alleged infringement. There is no master–servant or employer–employee relationship between the Law Society and the Great Library patrons, and so there can be no exercise of control.[392] Given these premises, McLachlin CJ concluded that there had been no authorization by the Society[393] and therefore no secondary liability.

Contrary to the US Supreme Court position over the last 30 years,[394] the Canadian Supreme Court explicitly excluded that an analogy could be made between 'master–servant' or 'employer–employee' relationship and copyright liability.[395]

In the same year, the Canadian Supreme Court tested its reasoning for Internet intermediaries, in *Society of Composers, Authors & Music Publishers of Canada (SOCAN) v. Canadian Association of Internet Providers (CAIP)*.[396] SOCAN represented the Canadian composers and artists whose music had been downloaded from the web. The plaintiffs wanted to impose royalties on ISPs because, in their view, the latter's activities constituted infringement of copyright owners' right to communicate and to authorize such communication.

The Supreme Court refuted the SOCAN claims on the basis of the *CCH* interpretation of 'authorization': an ISP's knowledge that someone can use its technology to infringe copyright does not necessarily suffice to constitute authorization, which, on the contrary, must be an approval or encouragement, as decided in *CCH*. If authorization were broadly interpreted, this would put ISPs in the difficult position of having to ascertain whether or not a specific content was infringing.[397] The activity

---

[391] Citing *Muzak Corp. v. Composers, Authors and Publishers Association of Canada, Ltd.* [1953] 2 S.C.R. 182, 193.
[392] These are two typical hypotheses of third-party liability.
[393] *CCH Canadian Ltd* (n 150) paras 39–45.
[394] See the cases cited in Chapter 4.
[395] *CCH Canadian Ltd* (n 150) para 44.
[396] n 270.
[397] *SOCAN v. CAIP* (n 269) para 127.

of ISPs in communicating (even infringing) copyright works was therefore considered 'neutral'.[398] Neutrality would cease if the ISP noticed the
existence of infringing material on its system and failed to take remedies,
such as asking the customer through a 'take down notice' to remove the
infringing content. If the host server provider does not take the appropriate steps, then it can be considered as authorizing the infringing
activity.[399] This should be inferred from the facts of each case.[400]

In addition to the above, the Court applied a statutory defence for
communication to the public by telecommunications: the so-called 'common carrier exception'. Section 2.4(1)(b) of the Canadian Copyright Act
provides that:

> For the purposes of communication to the public by telecommunication, a
> person whose only act in respect of the communication of a work or other
> subject-matter to the public consists of providing the means of telecommuni-
> cation necessary for another person to so communicate the work or other
> subject-matter does not communicate that work or other subject-matter to the
> public.

Therefore, if a person only provides the means through which a communication is made, then that person is not herself communicating, and
therefore is not violating, the copyrighted work. This provision could also
be applied to ISPs, when they operate merely as a conduit for the
transmission of information. Hyperlinking would fall outside this exception[401] but when a provider only offers ancillary services, it is covered by
the provision of Section 2.4(1)(b). An ISP's possible knowledge that
someone could use its facilities to infringe copyright does not entail
liability.[402] However, this provision applies only to liability for communication to the public by telecommunication, while there is no similar
provision for the act of reproducing works.[403]

---

[398]   Ibid, *passim*.
[399]   With regard to this issue, the Supreme Court referred to the Canadian
Association of ISPs' Code of Conduct. See *SOCAN v. CAIP* (n 269) para 110.
[400]   Ibid para 127.
[401]   On the delicate, topical issue of hyperlinking liability see De Beer and
Burri (n 270); Mira Burri, 'Permission to Link: Making Available via Hyperlinks
in the European Union after Svensson' [2014] JIPITEC 245 <www.jipitec.eu/
issues/jipitec-5-3-2014/4098> accessed 20 February 2017.
[402]   *SOCAN v. CAIP* (n 269) paras 32–33. The Court (para 96) compared ISPs
to the owners of telephone wires and cited a previous Supreme Court decision:
Electric Despatch Co. v. Bell Telephone Co., 20 S.C.R. 83 (1891).
[403]   Teresa Scassa and Michael Deturbide, *Electronic Commerce and Internet
Law in Canada* (2nd edn, CCH 2012) 428.

In the same decision, the Supreme Court also expressed a wish for a 'notice and take down' regime such as that of the EU (*sic!*) or the US.[404] Remember that until the Parliament enacted the Copyright Modernization Act in 2012, Canada had no statutes regulating this intricate issue. Furthermore, although Canada currently has specific legislation, this relates only to copyright matters. In other cases, such as defamation, SOCAN and CCH rules still apply.

The Canadian regulation, included in the Copyright Act, considers three kinds of provider, similar to the categories listed by the European (and Italian) legislation. The structure of the provision, however, is somewhat different.

The regime introduced by the Copyright Modernization Act opens with the provision of Section 31.1(1), which focuses on access providers and states:

> A person who, in providing services related to the operation of the Internet or another digital network, provides any means for the telecommunication or the reproduction of a work or other subject-matter through the Internet or that other network does not, solely by reason of providing those means, infringe copyright in that work or other subject-matter.

The provision is wider than both those introduced by the US DMCA and by the EU Directive. In fact, it applies to 'services related to the operation of the Internet or another digital network', therefore including services that cannot strictly be considered ISPs, such as P2P intermediaries. This provision is considered to be an 'explicitly broader common carrier exemption' than the one in Section 2.4(1)(b).[405]

Sections 31.1(2) and 31.1(4) introduced liability limitations for caching providers and for hosting intermediaries, respectively.

A caching provider is not liable for the act of caching or carrying out any similar act in relation to a work, if: it does not modify the copyrighted content, other than for technical reasons; it ensures that its activities are compliant with industry practice; it does not interfere with the use of technology that is lawful and consistent with the same practices in order to obtain data on the use of the work.

A hosting provider is understood as 'a person who, for the purpose of allowing the telecommunication of a work or other subject-matter

---

[404] *SOCAN v. CAIP* (n 269) para 127.

[405] Gregory R Hagen, '"Modernizing" ISP Copyright Liability' in Michael Geist (ed), *From 'Radical Extremism' to 'Balanced Copyright'. Canadian Copyright and the Digital Agenda* (Irwin 2010) 361, 377.

through the Internet or another digital network, provides digital memory in which another person stores the work or other subject-matter'. The hosting provider cannot be considered liable by virtue of its activities unless it knows of a court decision or a decision from another competent jurisdiction ruling that the host provider's storage of a work or other subject matter amounts to an infringement of copyright.

A closing provision, applicable to all kinds of provider, states that liability limitation does not apply to an act that constitutes copyright infringement under Subsection 27(2.3), known as the 'enabling provision'. According to this provision, it is an infringement of copyright to provide a service primarily for the purpose of enabling acts of copyright infringement if an actual infringement occurs by means of the use of that service. This last provision is designed to punish those who provide P2P technologies in order to exchange copyright-protected content.[406] Unlike in the US and Europe, Canadian provisions do not precisely state that ISPs are exempted from liability but that certain ISP activities do not constitute copyright infringement.

Furthermore, the Canadian system does not contemplate an extra-judicial remedy like the DMCA 'notice and take down', which obliges hosting providers to remove infringing material: an ISP is liable only when it knows of an order from a court or other judicial authority. However, the Canadian Copyright Act includes a so-called 'notice and notice' regime in Sections 41.25, 41.26 and 41.27(3), which came into force in 2015.

The 'notice and notice' system applies to all types of provider and requires them to forward the notices of copyright infringement they receive from copyright owners to their users who have uploaded the allegedly infringing content. The procedure starts with a notice of claimed infringement sent by the copyright owner to either an access provider, a content provider or a hosting provider (respectively Sections 41.25(1)(a), (b) and (c)). Section 41.25(2) describes the content and the form of the notice, which shall identify the work allegedly infringed and specify the infringement claimed.[407]

---

[406] The provision does not apply to 'off-line' devices (see ibid 380) and therefore differs from the secondary liability regimes of the US (namely, contributory and vicarious liability; inducement of infringement), on which see Chapter 4. Section 27(2.4) provides a non-exhaustive list of factors that courts can take into account to determine whether there has been copyright infringement under Section 27(2.3).

[407] The note shall be in written form and shall: (a) state the claimant's name and address and any other particulars prescribed by regulation that enable

The provider shall then 'as soon as feasible forward the notice electronically to the person to whom the electronic location identified by the location data specified in the notice belongs' and inform the claimant. Furthermore, the provider shall retain records that allow the identification of the alleged infringer.[408] If the provider does not comply with this regime, it is liable only for statutory damages, which are limited in amount by Section 41.26(3).[409] The approach is thus different from those of Italy or the US, where if an ISP does not comply with the requirements of decreto legislativo 70/03 and the DMCA respectively, it loses its safe harbour protection.

Another difference marks the Canadian and European approaches: in the latter, no specific provision refers to search engines and this has led to different decisions, at both European and Italian levels.[410] The Canadian Copyright Act includes a specific regime under Section 41.27, which largely treats search engines like other providers. A specific provision, namely Section 41.27(3), limits the period of immunity to 30 days; this has been criticized as a de facto 'notice and take down' regime.[411]

The Canadian statutory regulation of ISP liability is the newest of the three regimes under consideration. Before its implementation, Canadian ISPs had been applying a self-imposed code of conduct[412] and a 'notice

---

communication with the claimant; (b) identify the work or other subject-matter to which the claimed infringement relates; (c) state the claimant's interest or right with respect to the copyright in the work or other subject-matter; (d) specify the location data for the electronic location to which the claimed infringement relates; (e) specify the infringement that is claimed; (f) specify the date and time of the commission of the claimed infringement; and (g) contain any other information that may be prescribed by regulation.

[408] Section 41.26(1)(b) also prescribes for how long the provider shall retain this information. Moreover, Section 41.26(c) provides that the Minister in charge may fix a maximum fee that providers can charge for performing their duty under Section 41.26(1).

[409] Not less than $5,000 and not more than $10,000.

[410] For the EU, see Joined Cases C-236, 237 and 238/08 *Google France SARL and Google Inc. v. Louis Vuitton Malletier SA* [2010] ECR I-02417. For Italy, see Trib. Roma, 22.3.2011, in Dir. informatica 2011, 532 as well as Trib. Milano, 9.9.2011 (n 380) reversed by App Milano, 7.1.2015 (n 380).

[411] See Sheryl N Hamilton, 'Made in Canada: A Unique Approach to Internet Service Provider Liability and Copyright Infringement' in Geist (n 142) 285, 308.

[412] Canadian Association of Internet Providers 'Code of Conduct' <www.cata.ca/Communities/caip/codeofconduct/CodeConduct.html> accessed 20 February 2017.

and notice' system agreed with the Canadian Cable Television Association and the Canadian Recording Industry Association (CRIA). Under this regime, CRIA members could notify an ISP by e-mail about an infringement, providing a precise claim and the location of the material. The ISP would then deliver a notice to the subscriber, advising her of the CRIA information and encouraging her to contact CRIA to resolve the issue. The ISP would then confirm to CRIA that the information had been passed on to the subscriber (alleged infringer). If the subscriber did not remove the content, the CRIA could seek the remedies provided by the Copyright Act.[413]

The regime introduced by the Copyright Modernization Act is largely based on this procedure. The codification of the 'notice and notice' system should be seen as advantageous because it brings certainty and includes all copyrighted material, while the self-adopted regime was only for music.[414]

The regulation of ISP liability is currently a highly topical area of Internet regulation. One of the most critical issues is the courts' continuous struggle to frame the specific functions of the ISPs.[415] And even once these functions have been ascertained, other important questions and hurdles remain, making it very difficult to achieve a satisfactory balance between rights enforcement, freedom of speech and the ISPs' business freedoms.

This chapter has outlined the approaches taken by the US, the EU and Canada in the hope that this will further increase our understanding of how the three areas differ in their dealing with the issue of copyright. In fact, as will be examined in greater depth later in this book, ISPs have had a key role in copyright enforcement ever since they first appeared.[416]

---

[413] See Hamilton (n 411) 296. The author refers to one of the previous attempts to amend the Copyright Act, namely Bill C-60, An Act to Amend the Copyright Act, 1st Sess., 38th Parl., 2005. The legislative text is nonetheless the same.

[414] Hamilton (n 411) 296.

[415] See Gasser and Schulz (n 352) *passim*. See also the remarks of Niva Elkin-Koren, 'After Twenty Years: Revisiting Copyright Liability of Online Intermediaries' in Susy Frankel and Daniel J Gervais (eds), *The Evolution and Equilibrium of Copyright in the Digital Age* (CUP 2014) 29.

[416] See Strowel (ed), *Peer-to-peer File-sharing and Secondary Liability in Copyright Law* (n 69).

3. Personal data protection legislation

1. COMPARING THE LEGAL FRAMEWORKS FOR PRIVACY AND PERSONAL DATA PROTECTION

Privacy rights today are both extensively and inevitably shaped by technology; among these technologies, the Internet is probably the most influential. Surprisingly, in our globalized, interconnected world, there are no international agreements protecting privacy. There are, in fact, no agreements comparable to those on copyright which we have analysed and, so far, there has been no international pressure to increase protection of privacy and personal data per se.[1]

In relation to privacy rights, only two texts have had any real impact at the international level: the Universal Declaration of Human Rights and the Guidelines of the Organisation for Economic Co-operation and Development (OECD).[2] However, in Europe, both the European Convention on Human Rights and the European Charter of Fundamental Rights protect privacy.

Article 12 of the 1950 Universal Declaration states: 'No one shall be subjected to arbitrary interference with his privacy, family, home or correspondence, nor to attacks upon his honour and reputation. Everyone has the right to the protection of the law against such interference or

---

[1] Colin J Bennett, *The Privacy Advocates: Resisting the Spread of Surveillance* (MIT Press 2008) 199.

[2] In 2004 the Asia-Pacific Economic Cooperation (APEC) Privacy Framework was endorsed by the APEC countries, which include the US. Given the Framework's non-binding nature, and the fact that the protection it envisions is not of a high level, the text has attracted some criticism. See, for instance, Graham Greenleaf, 'APEC's Privacy Framework: A New Low Standard' [2005] Privacy Law and Policy Reporter 121; Id, 'Five Years of the APEC Privacy Framework: Failure or Promise?' [2009] Computer Law & Security Report 28. More generally, on privacy at the international level, see Lee A Bygrave, 'International Agreements to Protect Personal Data' in James B Rule and Graham Greenleaf (eds), *Global Privacy Protection: The First Generation* (Edward Elgar Publishing 2008) 15 and Id, *Privacy and Data Protection in an International Perspective* (OUP 2014) 180ff.

attacks.' This clearly represents the first acknowledgement, and protection at an international level, of the right to privacy.[3]

Around 30 years later, the OECD Guidelines were developed; these Guidelines have undoubtedly influenced the development of privacy regulation worldwide[4] since they constitute the only multilateral Treaty dealing directly with personal data protection.[5] Although the OECD Guidelines are not binding, many of the signatory countries have incorporated them into their privacy laws.[6] A short account of the contents of this OECD document will later be provided, given the significant influence it has had on regulation in the three countries analysed.

In 1990 the United Nations adopted 'Guidelines for the regulation of computerized personal data files'.[7] The Guidelines are non-binding but are intended as a tool to influence national legislation or other international organizations' approaches to personal data.[8]

The fact that no supranational agreements are in place makes it much more difficult to harmonize different national regulations, including,

---

[3] Art. 17 of the International Covenant on Civil and Political Rights also provides a definition very close to the one previously mentioned: 'No one shall be subjected to arbitrary or unlawful interference with his privacy, family, home or correspondence, nor to unlawful attacks on his honour and reputation.'

[4] According to Daniel J Solove and Mark Rotenberg, *Information Privacy Law* (Aspen Publishers 2003) 713, the EU Data Protection Directive 95/46/EC (Directive 95/46/EC of the European Parliament and of the Council of 24 October 1995 on the protection of individuals with regard to the processing of personal data and on the free movement of such data [1995] OJ L 281/31) – on which see below – was also very influential globally. The OECD Guidelines related to the handling of personal data can be found at <www.oecd.org/ document/18/0,3746,en_2649_34255_1815186_1_1_1_1,00.html> accessed 25 February 2017. I shall later illustrate how these principles, and the European privacy law, have influenced Canadian privacy protection. In fact, while developing its Guidelines, the OECD worked closely with the Council of Europe, which was already drafting its own Convention on Privacy: the two texts/documents are indeed very similar. In 2013 the Guidelines were revised but, since the privacy regulations here analysed are based on the first (1980) version, I shall refer only to it. For the updated version see the cited website.

[5] Bygrave (n 2) 19.

[6] See Solove and Rotenberg (n 4) 714; Barbara McIsaac, Rick Shields and Kris Klein, *The Law of Privacy in Canada* (Carswell 2011) 5-2ff.

[7] General Assembly, 68th plenary meeting, 14 December 1990, 45/95. Guidelines for the regulation of computerized personal data files <www.un.org/ documents/ga/res/45/a45r095.htm> accessed 25 February 2017.

[8] Carlo Focarelli, *La privacy* (Il Mulino 2015) 113–114.

naturally, those of the US, Canada and Italy; even though the three countries apply the same basic principles of protection to privacy rights, their actual regulations differ greatly – most notably those of Italy and the US.

These differences have most probably grown out of the pan-national struggle to clearly define the right to privacy itself. As explained earlier,[9] scholars and courts have been trying for decades to craft a definition of privacy. More and more often, the concept of – and the right to – privacy overlaps with that of 'personal data protection', also known as 'information(al) privacy'.

In this work, too, the above-mentioned notions will frequently overlap. My understanding of privacy/personal data protection corresponds to the following definition: 'the ability of an individual to exercise control over how his/her personal information is collected, used or disclosed by third parties'.[10]

As we will see in Section 2, privacy was originally conceived of in physical terms, while information privacy is mainly linked to the diffusion of computers and other digital devices. Nowadays, threats to informational privacy are undoubtedly of greatest concern since personal data protection is a precondition of physical privacy.

A prominent Italian scholar has offered an interesting classification of these changes regarding the concept of privacy. Dividing the private sphere into four areas, he proposed a shift, first, from the 'right to be let alone' to the right to control one's own information; second, from privacy to the right to informational self-determination; third, from privacy to non-discrimination; fourth and last, from secrecy to control.[11] The way in which personal information circulates can mirror an individual's way of being, thereby affecting perception of his/her personal identity.[12]

---

⁹ See Chapter 1, Section 2.

¹⁰ Mark S Hayes, 'The Impact of Privacy on Intellectual Property in Canada' [2006] Intellectual Property Journal 67, 68. For a summary and brief explanation of the 'leading definitions' of privacy, see Colin HH McNairn and Alexander K Scott, *Privacy Law in Canada* (Butterworths 2001) 4ff; John DR Craig, 'Invasion of Privacy and Charter Values: The Common-Law Tort Awakens' [1997] McGill Law Journal 355, 378–379. See also the interesting classification provided by Rachel L Finn, David Wright and Michael Friedewald, 'Seven Types of Privacy' in Serge Gurthwirth, Ronald Leenes, Paul de Hert, Yves Poullet (eds), *European Data Protection: Coming of Age* (Springer Verlag 2013) 3, spec. 7ff.

¹¹ See Stefano Rodotà, *Repertorio di fine secolo* (Laterza 1999) 209–210.

¹² Giovanni Buttarelli, *Banche dati e tutela della riservatezza. La privacy nella società dell'informazione* (Giuffrè 1997) 95.

Bearing the above in mind, and taking into account the contents of Chapter 1, I shall now turn to a more detailed description of privacy regulation in the US, Italian and Canadian systems.

The next section describes the constitutional protection of privacy in each of the countries observed; a short analysis of the legal framework of privacy and data protection follows. The last two sections are devoted to an examination of two particular institutions of privacy regulation. The first, data subject consent, has also been widely analysed by scholars in disciplines other than law. The issue of consent is central to an understanding of the philosophy that underlies the regulation of informational privacy. Enabling data subjects to exert their will with regard to the disclosure of their information is a form of empowerment which demonstrates that – at least in theory – uncontrolled circulation of data cannot be accepted. This shows, in turn, that the state attaches great importance to personal data and the necessity for subject consent.[13]

I will also examine the data protection authorities, whose role in the defence of privacy and personal data in at least two of the three countries in this study (Canada and Italy) has been pivotal. The very different structure of the US authority is perhaps another indicator of the differences between the three systems, as will emerge during the course of this chapter.

2. THE HISTORY AND CONSTITUTIONAL DIMENSION OF PRIVACY AND PERSONAL DATA

This analysis – like that of the different copyright frameworks – starts with an overview of the protection and warranties granted by the Constitution of each country. It is worth noting to begin with that no explicit mention of the right to privacy is made in any of the three Constitutions. However, in each system, both the courts and scholars have made extraordinary efforts to trace the right to privacy back to the Constitution. This process began in the early twentieth century and has culminated in somewhat different achievements in the three countries. Evolving interpretations have focused more on privacy than on personal

---

[13]   The actual efficacy of 'consent' will later be – briefly – questioned. For further details, see the bibliography cited below in Section 4.

data protection although recently the latter has also obtained unanimous recognition as a constitutional right.[14]

The analysis starts with the US, generally considered the 'cradle of privacy'. Just as every classical treatise on US copyright starts by mentioning Clause 8 of the Constitution, serious discussions of US privacy start by citing the seminal article by Warren and Brandeis 'The Right to Privacy'.[15] The piece is probably 'the most important article ever written about privacy'.[16]

The origins of this influential paper have been analysed in depth, by many scholars. One of the most plausible analyses focuses on the introduction of a new technology: Warren and Brandeis were worried that 'yellow journalism' would become increasingly intrusive with the invention of the portable camera, which took instant pictures, thus allowing photographers to capture images quickly and easily in public places, with the result that newspaper editors could start using photographs exclusively, finally abandoning drawings.[17] Samuel Warren may well have written the article because of the intrusion of journalists into his private life. Warren was a rich and powerful Boston attorney, in practice with

---

[14] For an overview of privacy as a constitutional right, see Manuel José Cepeda Espinosa, 'Privacy' in Michel Rosenfeld and András Sajó (eds), *The Oxford Handbook of Comparative Constitutional Law* (OUP 2012) 966.

[15] Samuel D Warren and Louis Brandeis, 'The Right to Privacy' [1890] Harvard Law Review 193, spec. 198ff, wherein the authors draw a parallel between individual privacy and the protection of ideas and thoughts or of works of art (eventually combining privacy and copyright). My account of the history and framework of the right to privacy will necessarily be brief, given the scope of this work. For a thorough analysis of the issue and further bibliography, see, among others, Solove and Rotenberg (n 4) 2003; John T Soma and Stephen D Rynerson, *Privacy Law in a Nutshell* (1st edn, West Publishing 2008); Daniel J Solove and Paul M Schwartz, *Privacy, Information, and Technology* (Aspen Publishers 2009) 10; Daniel J Solove and Paul M Schwartz, *Information Privacy Law* (5th edn, Wolters Kluwer 2015). See also Alan F Westin, *Privacy and Freedom* (Atheneum 1967), spec. 330ff. For an in-depth analysis of the historical development of privacy in the US, see Frederick S Lane, *American Privacy. The 400-Year History of Our Most Contested Right* (Beacon Press 2010).

[16] Solove and Schwartz, *Information Privacy Law* (n 15) 10. The authors report that in the Supreme Court case *Kyllo v. United States*, 533 U.S. 27 (2001), Warren and Brandeis' article was cited by the majority, by the judges who concurred in the opinion, and even by those who dissented.

[17] Warren and Brandeis (n 15) 195–196; Solove and Schwartz, *Information Privacy Law* (n 15) 11; Westin (n 15) 338 and 344ff. For various explanations of the origins of Warren and Brandeis' article, see Solove and Schwartz, *Information Privacy Law* (n 15) 11–12.

Brandeis (who eventually became a Supreme Court Justice), and married to the daughter of a well-known senator from Delaware. Many authors claim that Warren's impetus for writing the article came from his displeasure at newspaper coverage of his social life.[18]

Whatever the article's origins, its authors referred to privacy as 'the right to be let alone',[19] recommending the introduction of an action in tort and an injunction as remedies for its protection. The article suggested that the existing common law could not protect privacy and that new laws could, and ought to, intervene to do so. The courts did not hesitate: by the early twentieth century they had already started to recognize a number of privacy torts, intended to fill the gaps that the two authors had identified, and some states passed laws introducing tort actions to protect privacy.[20] This led to an increase in judicial decisions, which inspired a seminal article by William Prosser later discussed in this chapter.[21]

Although the US Constitution never specifically mentions privacy, courts and scholars have extrapolated its protection from a number of different constitutional provisions;[22] the many different approaches to privacy to which it has given rise, however, may be grouped under two

---

[18] Solove and Schwartz, *Privacy, Information and Technology* (n 15) 12; William L Prosser, 'Privacy' [1960] California Law Review 383, 383. For an analysis of how the increasing use of technology heightened first fear of intrusion, and then awareness of the need for privacy, see Westin (n 15) 298ff. Warren and Brandeis said that privacy was a modern citizen's right, necessitated by modern society (Warren and Brandeis (n 15) 196). Westin disagrees, basing his argument on history: Westin (n 15) 337.

[19] Warren and Brandeis (n 15) 195.

[20] Solove and Schwartz, *Privacy, Information and Technology* (n 15) 25–26 cite some cases, including *Roberson v. Rochester Folding Box Co.*, 64 N.E. 442 (N.Y. 1902). As a consequence of this decision, which asked for the intervention of the legislative body, New York state introduced a privacy tort action by statute. See also *Pavesich v. New England Life Insurance Co.*, 50 S.E. 68 (Ga. 1905), which, according to Solove and Schwartz, made Georgia the first state to recognize a common law tort action for privacy invasion. Both these previously mentioned cases involved the publication of the plaintiff's images without consent.

[21] Prosser (n 18).

[22] Although the federal Constitution does not mention privacy, some states have provided for the protection of this right in their own Constitutions. For instance, the California Constitution states: '[a]ll people are by nature free and independent and have inalienable rights. Among these are enjoying and defending life and liberty, acquiring, possessing, and protecting property, and pursuing and obtaining safety, happiness, and *privacy*' (art. I, § 1; emphasis added). Other examples are art. I, § 22 of the Alaska Constitution, and art. I, § 23 of the Florida

main umbrellas: individual privacy or autonomy on the one hand, and data privacy or control of information on the other.[23]

In general, the constitutional protection of privacy can be traced back to either the First or the Fourth Amendment.[24] It is important to stress that these constitutional rights apply only against government actions: they do not protect or cover privacy issues between private parties. Moreover, these rights rarely oblige the government to act, merely serving to restrain it from acting in certain ways.

The First Amendment states: 'Congress shall make no law respecting an establishment of religion, or prohibiting the free exercise thereof; or abridging the freedom of speech, or of the press; or the right of the people peaceably to assemble, and to petition the government for a redress of grievances.' Under this Amendment, people have a primordial right to speak anonymously.[25] The same Amendment can protect against compulsory disclosure of certain information, such as the names and addresses of the members of an organization, or the names of organizations to which – for example – public teachers belong.[26]

The First Amendment mainly protects privacy as a right to self-determination, whereas the Fourth Amendment, which requires that people 'be secure in their persons, houses, papers, and effects, against unreasonable searches or seizure', has played a more prominent role. Ironically, an important dissenting opinion on the applicability of the Fourth Amendment was delivered by the same Justice Brandeis who,

---

Constitution. See Soma and Rynerson (n 15) 170ff for state Constitutions and statutes on privacy.

[23] Soma and Rynerson (n 15) 57ff.

[24] The Third and Fifth Amendments have sometimes also been considered to protect privacy: the Third Amendment holds: 'No soldier shall, in time of peace be quartered in any house, without the consent of the owner, nor in time of war, but in a manner to be prescribed by law.' The Fifth Amendment protects people against compulsory divulgation of information about themselves, through the 'privilege against self-incrimination': 'No person ... shall be compelled in any criminal case to be a witness against himself ...'. See Fred H Cate, *Privacy in the Information Age* (Brookings Institution Press 1997) 50ff.

[25] See the famous case *McIntyre v. Ohio Elections Commission*, 514 U.S. 334, 357 (1995), in which the Supreme Court held that an Ohio law prohibiting anonymous political literature was unconstitutional.

[26] Solove and Schwartz, *Privacy, Information, and Technology* (n 15) 33, cite *NAACP v. Alabama*, 357 U.S. 449 (1958) with respect to the disclosure of the personal data of members of organizations and *Shelton v. Tucker*, 364 U.S. 479 (1960) regarding a law which required state teachers to reveal which organizations they belonged to.

almost 30 years earlier, had published the above-mentioned seminal article in the *Harvard Law Review*. The Supreme Court decision – *Olmstead v. United States* – was on the use of wiretapping, which the majority held could not be considered an invasion of privacy since there was no physical trespass to the home. Olmstead was a bootlegger who had been convicted of violating federal Prohibition laws and whose conviction was based on evidence obtained through telephone wiretapping. Olmstead claimed that wiretapping was a violation of the Fourth or the Fifth Amendment, since they protected not only property, but also the individual, in his liberty and private life. After having lost in front of both the federal trial judge and the appellate court, Olmstead went to the Supreme Court, which held that neither the Fourth nor the Fifth Amendment provided protection against wiretapping, since it involved no physical trespass.

In his dissenting opinion, Justice Brandeis stressed the existence of that 'right to be let alone', which had appeared in the 1890 article he wrote with Warren. Justice Brandeis claimed that the scope of the Amendment extended well beyond protection against physical intrusion and that happiness, the pursuit of which everyone is entitled to, was also to be found in immaterial things. He argued that the Amendments conferred the right to be let alone, which was 'the most comprehensive of rights and the right most valued by civilized men'.[27]

Justice Brandeis' interpretation, despite being a dissenting opinion, was later very influential in cases involving the application of the Fourth Amendment. In fact, in another seminal case – *Katz v. United States* – the US Supreme Court held that the Fourth Amendment 'protects people, not places'.[28]

The case was about the legality of an FBI device which, attached to the outside of a telephone booth, monitored conversations about gambling operations. The plaintiff Katz argued that, contrary to the government opinion, the telephone booth was a constitutionally protected area. The Court held that physical trespass was not required for the Fourth Amendment to come into play since the Amendment protects people and not places: the telephone bug constituted a violation of privacy and a search and seizure under the Fourth Amendment.

In this seminal decision Justice Harlan delivered a concurring opinion, which set the standard for the 'reasonable expectation of privacy'. This test enables a better understanding of when the Fourth Amendment

---

[27] *Olmstead v. United States*, 277 U.S. 438 (1928), 478.
[28] *Katz v. United States*, 389 U.S. 347 (1967).

applies; it consists of two steps: first, a person must have exhibited an actual subjective expectation of privacy and, second, the expectation has to be one that society is prepared to recognize as reasonable.[29]

In the 1965 landmark case of *Griswold v. Connecticut*, the US Supreme Court determined that an individual has a constitutional right to privacy.[30] The case was initiated against a Connecticut statute that prohibited the prescription and use of contraceptives. Two doctors had opened a birth control clinic in New Haven, Connecticut. Shortly after the clinic was opened, they were both arrested, tried, found guilty and, finally, fined. The decision eventually reached the Supreme Court, which held that the Connecticut statute was a violation of marital privacy. This privacy right was to be found in many fundamental Constitution laws, which created penumbras of privacy, derived from a broad interpretation of the Bill of Rights. As a result, the Connecticut statute was considered unconstitutional.

The privacy right set out in this case was close to that advocated by Warren and Brandeis[31] and it cleared the way for other important decisions related to decisional privacy and autonomy.[32]

Some years later the Supreme Court extended the right to privacy to the informational sphere, recognizing 'the individual interest in avoiding disclosure of personal matters'.[33] This case involved New York Statutes which required that information related to drug prescriptions be reported and stored. Physicians were obliged to report certain information which

---

[29]   Ibid 361. As usually happens with 'reasonable standards', many problems emerged in this case, since '*Katz* itself provides no clear indication how the lower courts are to draw th[e] line', see Richard G Wilkins, 'Defining the "Reasonable Expectation of Privacy": An Emerging Tripartite Analysis' [1987] Vanderbilt Law Review 1077, 1089. See also Gerald G Ashdown, 'Legitimate Expectation of Privacy' [1981] Vanderbilt Law Review 1289, A. Libeu, 'What Is a Reasonable Expectation of Privacy?' [1985] Western State University Law Review 849; Solove and Schwartz, *Privacy, Information and Technology* (n 15) 99ff.

[30]   *Griswold v. Connecticut*, 381 U.S. 479 (1965).

[31]   Westin (n 15) 355. See the words of Justice Black in *Griswold* (n 30) 510.

[32]   See, for example, the famous *Roe v. Wade*, 410 U.S. 113 (1973). In this case the Supreme Court struck down a Texas law on abortion. To reach this conclusion the Court analysed the right to privacy and found that the Fourteenth Amendment due process clause was to be considered an expression of personal liberty, a right to privacy. Furthermore it stated that 'the Ninth Amendment's reservation of rights to the people, is broad enough to encompass a woman's decision whether or not to terminate her pregnancy'; see ibid 153.

[33]   *Whalen v. Roe*, 429 U.S. 589 (1977), 599.

was then kept by the State Department. A group of patients, several doctors and two medical associations challenged the statute. The Supreme Court, for the first time, recognized a right to information privacy on the basis of two individual interests: one in avoiding disclosure of personal matters and another in independence in making certain important decisions.[34]

Subsequent to these cases, the right to privacy has enjoyed consistent constitutional coverage although the form this protection has taken has differed from that found in Italy or Canada.[35]

In the Canadian system, constitutional protection is granted by the Canadian Charter of Rights and Freedoms although its text does not directly contemplate privacy.[36] In 1987 the Canadian House of Commons' Justice Committee suggested, in vain, that serious consideration should be given to the idea of creating a constitutional right to privacy.[37] These attempts to introduce a constitutional right to privacy failed; nowadays privacy is usually traced back to Sections 7 and 8 of the Charter.

Section 7, titled 'Life, liberty and security of person', states that '[e]veryone has the right to life, liberty and security of the person and the right not to be deprived thereof except in accordance with the principles of fundamental justice'. There has been a growing consensus, including in the Supreme Court's jurisprudence, that Section 7 may be a source of constitutional protection for privacy. In the leading case *R. v.*

---

[34]   Nevertheless, the Supreme Court held that the New York statute needed to remain valid and that the prescription of certain drugs had to be recorded since the statute did not really constitute a threat to individual interests or to the US Constitution. In the words of Sonia K Katyal, 'Privacy v. Piracy' [2004] Yale Journal of Law & Technology 222, 240–241 'the unanswered question the Court left open in *Whalen* – that is, whether there is a constitutionally protected right to informational privacy – is the very question that informs the relationship between intellectual property and privacy in the digital age'.

[35]   See, for example, the cases *Kyllo* (n 16) applying the Fourth Amendment; *U.S. v. Jones*, 132 S. Ct. 945 (2012); *Torrey Dale Grady v. North Carolina*, 135 S. Ct. 1368 (2015).

[36]   For a complete overview of the Canadian legislation for privacy and data protection, see McIsaac, Shields and Klein (n 6); McNairn and Scott (n 10); Michael Power, *The Law of Privacy* (LexisNexis 2013) as well as the other references cited in this chapter.

[37]   David H Flaherty, 'On the Utility of Constitutional Rights to Privacy and Data Protection' [1991] Case Western Reserve Law Review 831, 843. The author discusses the feasibility and utility of introducing a right to privacy in the Canadian Constitution and expresses some doubts on the matter. See especially 849ff.

O'Connor,[38] for instance, the party accused of sexual assault wanted access to the complainant's medical records. It was a case of 'third-party discovery', and the Court had to weigh the complainant's interest in the records against the right of the accused to obtain full information. The first step was to ascertain whether or not the complainant had a privacy interest in those records. The judges all agreed that the Charter gives constitutional protection to the right to privacy but the clearest judgment was that of L'Heureux-Dubé J. She held that therapeutic records implied a reasonable expectation of privacy and thus required the protection of Section 7.[39] Later on, other decisions expressly supported this view.[40]

In the more recent case of *R. v. Mills*, however, the judges concluded that privacy had to be traced back to Section 8, rather than Section 7.[41] Section 8, titled 'Search or seizure', can be equated to the American Fourth Amendment since it states: 'Everyone has the right to be secure against unreasonable search or seizure.' Although the case was very close to *R. v. O'Connor*, namely in the production of complainants' private records in sexual assault proceedings, the Court in *Mills* held that an order to produce records would be a search or seizure matter and therefore covered by Section 8.[42] This different approach was explained as follows: 'courts will protect the privacy right under the rubric of Section 8 wherever a search or seizure occurs. However, if there is no search or seizure made by the government, then Section 7 may serve as the source of constitutional protection of the right to privacy'.[43] Hence, privacy is rooted in two different aspects of the Charter of Rights and Freedoms, either of which can be invoked, depending on the type of intrusion privacy has suffered.

Three different 'zones' of privacy have been recognized in case law:

1. territorial, such as the privacy a person should enjoy in her home;
2. personal or corporeal, related to the human body and physical personality;
3. informational, protecting intimate information about people.[44]

---

[38] [1995] 4 S.C.R. 411.
[39] Ibid para 119.
[40] For instance: *M. (A.) v. Ryan* [1997] 1 S.C.R. 157, especially at para 80.
[41] *R. v. Mills* [1999] 3 S.C.R. 668.
[42] Ibid para 62.
[43] McIsaac, Shields and Klein (n 6) 2-9.
[44] *Ruby v. Canada* (Attorney General) [2000] 3 F.C. 589 (C.A.), para 166.
But first see *R. v. Dyment* [1988] 2 S.C.R. 417, para 30, citing *Privacy and*

Clearly, the ability to control the dissemination of personal information is considered part of the right to privacy.[45]

Furthermore, according to the courts' interpretation, two indicators must be applied in understanding the extent of a person's right to privacy: (a) the degree to which an individual's liberty or security is threatened by the state's intrusion into their private affairs, and (b) the extent of the individual's reasonable expectation of privacy.[46] The latter issue mainly concerns Section 8, which has been interpreted as protecting people and not places.[47]

According to the case law, courts should consider a case-by-case analysis when assessing the requirement of a reasonable expectation of privacy.[48] The need for privacy may vary according to circumstances; therefore, any investigation into whether a reasonable expectation of privacy exists has to be 'factually' driven,[49] i.e., objective and subjective elements must be taken into account.[50] Courts must understand the privacy component of a specific right or freedom. Once it has been determined that a privacy element exists, judges can decide whether the limits imposed on privacy are reasonable or not.[51]

The concept of a 'reasonable expectation of privacy' has also been applied to computer surveillance and other technology-related cases. In the 2012 Supreme Court case *R. v. Cole*,[52] a teacher charged with

---

Computers (Ottawa, 1972), a report of the Task Force established by the Department of Communications and the Department of Justice of Canada.

[45] *Ruby v. Canada* (n 44) para. 169.

[46] Ibid para 168. See: Power (n 36) 240ff; McNairn and Scott (n 10) 18ff; McIsaac, Shields and Klein (n 6) 2-17ff.

[47] *Hunter v. Southam Inc.* [1984] 2 S.C.R. 145, para 23, whereby the Canadian Supreme Court referred to the US Supreme Court seminal case *Katz* (n 28). Since *Hunter v. Southam Inc.* was a criminal law decision, the requirements and thresholds applied are not necessarily the same used in civil lawsuits: see McIsaac, Shields and Klein (n 6) 2-17.

[48] In *R. v. Edwards* [1996] 1 S.C.R 128, para 45, the Supreme Court listed a number of factors which should be taken into consideration in assessing an expectation of privacy.

[49] See, for example, *R. v. Colarusso* [1994] 1 S.C.R. 20, para 19 and *R. v. Wong* [1990] 3 S.C.R. 36, para 47.

[50] For an example of the questions to be asked in order to understand whether an expectation of privacy is reasonable, see *R. v. Tessling* [2004] 3 S.C.R. 432, paras 32ff.

[51] Flaherty (n 37) 845.

[52] *R. v. Cole* [2012] 3 S.C.R. 34. The case relied heavily on a previous Supreme Court case: *R. v. Morelli* [2010] 1 S.C.R. 253.

possession of child pornography questioned the legitimacy of the evidence gathered because it was obtained in violation of his rights, infringing, specifically, Section 8 of the Charter. The evidence had been found on Cole's work laptop, which had been searched without a warrant. The accused held that he had a reasonable expectation of privacy in the laptop's content. The case eventually reached the Supreme Court, which considered that the man did indeed have a reasonable expectation of privacy in the laptop. While the expectation was lower than in the case of a home computer, it was still reasonable and could be subject to state intrusion only under a reasonable law. Therefore, the Supreme Court decided that the evidence had been obtained illicitly.

As this brief overview demonstrates, the concept of privacy has received a great deal of attention in Canada and the right has been traced back to the Charter of Rights and Freedoms by both scholars and courts, even though the Charter never explicitly mentions physical privacy, let alone information privacy. There is no predetermined solution for privacy cases, and a case-by-case analysis with a balancing test is usually applied,[53] emphasizing the importance of this right.

It should be remembered, however, that the Charter only applies to Crown actions – governments and other state actors – and therefore, although it has an important role, it cannot serve to protect citizens in their exchange of personal information in the private sector.[54]

In Italy the Supreme Court (Corte di Cassazione) played a fundamental role in the creation of the right to privacy. The Cassazione has, in fact, shaped a coherent system of protection for privacy, drawing principles directly from the Constitution.[55]

The Cassazione's first decision in its evolution of privacy protection was taken in 1956[56] and concerned the diffusion of information about the

---

[53]   See Chapter 4 for some examples of the tests applied.

[54]   Stephanie Perrin, Heather Black, David H. Flaherty and T. Murray Rankin, *The Personal Information Protection and Electronic Documents Act: An Annotated Guide* (Irwin Law 2001) 7.

[55]   See Massimiliano Atelli, 'Riservatezza (diritto alla). III) Diritto Costituzionale', *Enciclopedia Giuridica Treccani*, vol. XXVII (1995) 2ff. For an explanation of the history of privacy in the Italian system, both in scholarly works and in case law, and for further bibliographical references, see Sergio Niger, *Le nuove dimensioni della privacy: dal diritto alla riservatezza alla protezione dei dati personali* (Cedam 2006) 37ff. For a brief overview of the many constitutional provisions relating to privacy, see Buttarelli (n 12) 81–90. For an in-depth analysis of Italian privacy and data protection regulations, see the various references cited in this chapter.

[56]   Cass. civ., 22.12.1956, no. 4487 in Foro it., 1957, I, 423.

private life of a famous person, the tenor, Enrico Caruso. It involved two films which depicted the life of the artist and showed some difficult episodes in his life, including his attempted suicide.[57] Caruso's heirs thought that the films damaged the tenor's privacy and they sued the production company for compensation.[58] The Corte di Cassazione, however, held that the Italian system did not recognize a right to privacy. There were only other 'rights of personality',[59] which were recognized and protected on an individual basis. Communication to the public of information about the lives of other people was allowed, especially in those cases where the information had itself been legitimately obtained.

In 1963 a similar case arose.[60] A book was published on the life of Claretta Petacci, Benito Mussolini's mistress. Petacci's heirs sued the author of the book since they felt that he had revealed information that violated her privacy and damaged her reputation. The Court of Appeal of Milan recognized the existence of a right to privacy, understood as the power to exclude any interference from outside a person's intimate, or

---

[57] See Giovanni Pascuzzi and Federica Giovanella, 'Dal diritto alla riservatezza alla computer privacy' in Giovanni Pascuzzi (ed), *Il diritto dell'era digitale* (Il Mulino 2016) 43, 43–44. See also Gianluca Gardini, *Le regole dell'informazione. Principi giuridici, strumenti, casi* (Mondadori 2009) 216ff.

[58] Before reaching the Supreme Court, the case was decided by Trib. Rome, 14.9.1953 (in Foro it., 1954, I, 115) and by the Corte d'Appello of Rome (17.5.1955, in Foro it., 1956, I, 793). Both courts awarded non-pecuniary damages for the plaintiffs for a violation of honour and reputation. Only the Tribunal, however, recognized the existence of a right to privacy.

[59] Rights of personality ('diritti della personalità') are a category of inalienable rights, which cannot be waived; they are defined as fundamental rights and freedoms, but are not confined to this category, which has long been debated by scholars, who do not agree on whether the right to personality is a single right or multiple. Among the numerous contributions, see Pietro Rescigno, 'Personalità (diritti della)', *Enciclopedia Giuridica Treccani*, vol. XXIII (1990); Vincenzo Zeno-Zencovich, 'Personalità (diritti della)', *Digesto discipline privatistiche, Sezione civile*, vol. XIII (1995) 430. The concept of 'personality rights' or 'rights of personhood' has no common law equivalent, see Giorgio Resta, 'Personnalité, Persönlichkeit, Personality. Comparative Perspectives on the Protection of Identity in Private Law' [2014] European Journal of Comparative Law & Governance 215. Privacy and personal data protection are considered to be 'personality rights' and this is why sometimes the data subject's consent is not enough for the processing of data; see Stefano Rodotà, 'Persona, riservatezza, identità. Prime note sistematiche sulla protezione dei dati personali' [1997] Riv. critica diritto privato 599.

[60] Cass. civ., 20.4.1963, no. 990, in Giust. civ., 1963, I, 1280 and in Foro it., 1963, I, 1298.

family, sphere.[61] The Cassazione held that there was no right to privacy
in the specific case, but that, nevertheless, the author had violated
Petacci's 'absolute right to personality': her right to the self-
determination of the individual. The protection of this right, which has
erga omnes validity, was a limit to the publication of news pertaining to
private lives unless the nature of either the activity carried out by the
person or the communicated facts were of public interest.

Since then, lower courts have started to recognize the existence of a
right to privacy and its need for protection. However, the Corte di
Cassazione did not actually affirm the existence of such a right until
1975.[62] The context was somewhat similar to Mr Warren's situation
almost 100 years before. Soraya Esfandiari had been the Empress of
Persia but she was disowned by her husband and exiled to Italy. A
photographer with a zoom lens took pictures of her while she was
engaged in intimate behaviour with a man, within the walls of her house.
The pictures were later published in a tabloid newspaper. The former
Empress sued the tabloid, claiming that the publication violated her right
to privacy.

The Supreme Court held that the Italian system acknowledged a right
to privacy. This ruling was based on a number of different provisions,
from different branches of the law. For example, the judges considered
the provisions related to the protection of the integrity of the body (art. 5
Civil Code), of the name (arts. 6–9 Civil Code) and of the personal image
(art. 10 Civil Code). The judges also considered some rules related to
anonymity and unpublished works (arts. 21 and 24, Legge 633/41) and to
the protection of domicile and correspondence (arts. 614 and 616 of the
Criminal Code).

The Supreme Court also extrapolated some important principles
directly from the Constitution. Article 2 recognizes and grants inviolable
human rights and acknowledges the protection of human personality,
both as an individual and as part of a social group, within which an
individual's personality can develop. The Court held that privacy was to
be included within these rights. Article 3 concerns the equal social
dignity of people: the Court held that in order to enjoy such dignity
people need to have their own space for autonomy and must not to be
subject to undue interference. In this regard art. 13, which also deals with
the sanctity of personal freedom, was taken into consideration: it was to

---

[61] See Gardini (n 57) 217, citing the verdict of the Court of Appeal of Milan
of 26.8.1960, in Foro it., 1955, I, 386.
[62] Cass. civ., 27.5.1975, n. 2129 in Foro it., 1976, I, 2895.

be interpreted as having a wider scope than mere physical freedom. The Court also considered art. 14, which concerns the protection of the domicile against inspections, searches and seizures, and art. 15, which provides for the protection of freedom and secrecy of correspondence.[63]

Based on these legal principles, the Supreme Court stated that the right to privacy – *diritto alla riservatezza* – safeguards strictly personal and family situations or events, which, even if they take place outside one's domicile, do not generate a socially valuable interest. These moments shall be protected from interference that is not justified by a public interest, even if that interference is legitimate and does not violate honour, reputation or decency. The Court also held that this right did not need a precise definition: such a definition would make the concept less flexible and thus less easily adapted to changing times.

This decision by the Supreme Court proved to be a cornerstone of the definition of the right to privacy and its protection. Many other important cases have since been decided. Among them, a judgment from 1985 is worth mentioning.[64] Even though this case was not primarily focused on privacy, it is considered to have been very important in shaping the concepts of privacy and of personality rights as a category.[65]

Professor Umberto Veronesi, a famous Italian oncologist, who had spent his life researching cancer, gave an interview to a newspaper on the cancer risk associated with cigarette smoking. During the interview, which was published in 1978, Dr Veronesi claimed that, although new – lighter and less harmful – cigarettes had been developed, they did not eliminate the danger of cancer. A few days after the interview was published, an advertisement for an Austrian brand of cigarettes appeared in another newspaper, with a slogan which misrepresented Dr Veronesi as having held that this type of cigarettes reduced the risk of cancer by almost 50 per cent. Since this sentence was damaging to Dr Veronesi's reputation, he sued the cigarette producer and the editor of the news-paper, asking for compensation. The Supreme Court granted Veronesi's request and held that the Italian system recognizes a right to 'personal identity': the right of a person to impede misrepresentations of her own personal intellectual, political, social, religious, scientific, ideological or professional beliefs or belongings. In other words, the right of a person to

---

[63]   These are the most relevant provisions cited by the Corte di Cassazione, which also referred to other articles.

[64]   Cass. civ., 22.6.1985, n. 3769, in Foro it., 1985, I, 2211.

[65]   See Roberto Pardolesi, 'Dalla riservatezza alla protezione dei dati per-sonali: una storia di evoluzione e discontinuità' in Roberto Pardolesi (ed), *Diritto alla riservatezza e circolazione dei dati personali* (Giuffrè 2003) 23.

have their 'real' identity represented, as this identity is recognized by society. This right can be traced back to art. 2 of the Constitution.

As previously mentioned, this right is not part of the right to privacy; nevertheless, its definition throws light on the depth and range of the right to privacy in Italy. Furthermore, it provides some cues for a comparison of the Italian and American contexts. In the US the right to privacy encompasses many different meanings and protects a large variety of situations, which fall outside the realm of privacy in the Italian system.

The path followed by the Italian courts, and the Corte di Cassazione in particular, led to a clear recognition of the need for the protection of a right to privacy that corresponded closely to the definition of the 'right to be let alone', formulated by Warren and Brandeis at the end of the nineteenth century. Hence, it was still far from a 'right to have control of one's own personal data'.[66] The definition provided by the Italian Supreme Court was somewhat static and did not consider the developing technologies and business models which required an increasing use of information. The 'right to be let alone' was no longer adequate: attention needed to shift to more 'dynamic profiles' and, in particular, to those usually linked to information privacy, namely the control of personal information.[67] However, steps were only taken in this direction in the late 1990s, thanks to the intervention of European legislation.

The Italian system is, naturally, influenced by the European Charter of Fundamental Rights, briefly described at the beginning of this chapter. The Charter addresses the institutions, agencies and offices of the EU and its Member States; it is not binding on private parties. Nonetheless, in order to fulfil the obligations stipulated in the Charter, Member States may be obliged to implement specific regulations and measures to protect the private lives of their citizens.[68]

In the wake of the developments described so far, and despite the fact that none of the three countries has an explicit reference to privacy in their Constitution, the courts in each system have evolved a constitutional protection for the right to privacy. As a result, the three countries present similar constitutional frameworks. However, this is arguably the only characteristic that the three approaches share.

---

[66] Pascuzzi and Giovanella (n 57) 45.

[67] Buttarelli (n 12) 101. For a summary of developments in privacy in Italy, see Rodotà (n 11) 216–217.

[68] Juliane Kokott and Christoph Sobotta, 'The Distinction Between Privacy and Data Protection in the Jurisprudence of the CJEU and the ECtHR' [2013] *International Data Privacy Law* 222, 225–226.

3. OVERVIEW OF THE LEGAL FRAMEWORKS

As illustrated above, the OECD *Guidelines on the Protection of Privacy and Transborder Flows of Personal Data* set out eight key principles with the aim of protecting privacy and personal information. The principles were envisioned as being either a tool for the harmonization of national privacy legislation or as a basis for future legislation in those countries that had not yet implemented specific laws. In particular, they were to be 'regarded as minimum standards which [were] capable of being supplemented by additional measures for the protection of privacy and individual liberty'. The Guidelines 'apply to personal data, whether in the public or private sectors, which, because of the manner in which they are processed, or because of their nature or the context in which they are used, pose a danger to privacy and individual liberties'.[69] Since many OECD countries had either already implemented, or were in the process of implementing, their own legislation, the Organisation was worried about possible disparities in national legislation, which might hamper the free flow of personal data across borders, negatively affecting economies.

Since the US, Canada and Italy are all in the OECD, the Guidelines naturally influenced the crafting of their privacy laws: all three frameworks comply with the principles included in the Guidelines, although their forms differ. The first principle is that of 'collection limitation', according to which the collection of personal data should be limited, and obtained only by lawful means, with the consent of the data subject, *where appropriate*. The second principle is that of 'data quality': collected data should be accurate, complete and up to date, and, crucially, relevant to a specific purpose, which, according to the third principle, should be settled at the beginning of the processing ('purpose specification' principle). This principle is linked to the fourth, which prescribes that data ought to be used only for the specified, limited purposes for which they were gathered ('use limitation' principle). The fifth principle, 'security', prescribes that data collection and storage be performed to reasonably prevent loss, theft or modification of records. At the same time there should be 'openness' (the sixth principle), meaning that data handling practices ought to be transparent. The seventh principle of 'individual participation' should empower the data subject and give her

---

[69] See *Scope of the Guidelines* at <http://www.oecd.org/internet/ieconomy/oecdguidelinesontheprotectionofprivacyandtransborderflowsofpersonaldata.htm> for further insight. Since subject consent is needed only where appropriate, US regulation complies with the Guidelines despite its 'opt-out' approach, which I shall explain later.

the chance to access, confirm and/or request a modification of her stored personal data. The final principle – 'accountability' – requires those who handle data to be responsible for complying with the listed principles.[70]

3.1 US

It has been suggested that the OECD principles themselves relied, in fact, on the US Fair Information Practice Principles, published in 1973 by the US Department of Health, Education and Welfare.[71] Based on these principles, from 1970 on, the US Congress has passed a number of statutes protecting privacy in many sectors of the information economy.

The US legislation includes numerous specific laws, each focusing on a different aspect of social life, such as family, employment, health care and so on.[72] Not every piece of legislation was actually intended to protect privacy; some laws were conceived, for example, to facilitate government collection of data or law enforcement.[73] A number of federal statutes on privacy protection have been enacted following specific – often shocking – events, with the result that the approach is sectorial.[74] As well as these federal laws, states have also passed statutes protecting privacy in many contexts. Nevertheless, none of them has ever enacted a general law to protect all aspects of privacy, especially in the private sector.[75] The above-mentioned sectorial approach has sometimes been

---

[70]   Solove and Rotenberg (n 4) 713–714.

[71]   See Daniel J Solove, 'Privacy Self-Management and the Consent Dilemma' [2013] Harvard Law Review 1880, 1882. For a history of these principles, see Robert Gellman, 'Fair Information Practices: A Basic History – V. 2.17', 22 December 2016 <http://bobgellman.com/rg-docs/rg-FIPshistory.pdf> accessed 25 February 2017.

[72]   For a complete list of the statutes related to privacy see Solove and Schwartz, *Information Privacy Law* (n 15) 37ff or Solove and Rotenberg (n 4) 23–24.

[73]   See, for example, the USA-PATRIOT (Uniting and Strengthening America by Providing Appropriate Tools Required to Intercept and Obstruct Terrorism) Act of 2001, signed on October 26, to deter and punish terrorist acts in the United States and around the world, to enhance law enforcement investigative tools, and for other purposes – Pub. Law No. 107-56, 11 Stat. 271, briefly described below in this section.

[74]   Soma and Rynerson (n 15) 48. See also Jeff Sovern, 'Opting In, Opting Out, or No Options At All: The Fight for Control of Personal Information' [1999] Washington Law Review 1033, 1042: 'Laws regulating personal information … are a patchwork of *ad hoc* responses to outrage over past invasions of privacy rather than a coherent set of rules based on fundamental principles and policies.'

[75]   Solove and Schwartz, *Privacy, Information and Technology* (n 15) 38.

criticized, especially, but not exclusively, by scholars living in legal
systems where the approach to the protection of privacy is more
comprehensive.[76] The result of this pattern of law is that, in most
day-to-day situations, unlike in Canada or the EU, no protection of
privacy applies, other than privacy torts or contractual agreements.[77]

The most complete and wide-ranging of the US statutes on privacy is
the Privacy Act of 1974,[78] generally recognized to have been a response
to the 'Watergate scandal', which led to President Richard Nixon's
resignation. Although the Privacy Act is usually considered an omnibus
law for privacy protection in the public sector, it actually only applies to
certain agencies (federal, state or local government, or any other organization which has an information system containing personal information) and to certain uses of information. Congress intended this statute
to enable individuals to control and manage their personal information,
which was threatened by the government's increasing use of computers
and other information technologies. Through the Privacy Act, citizens
were provided with some rights regarding their personal information
stored in government record systems – i.e. the right to see one's records,
and to modify them when inaccurate.[79] Information can only be kept
when relevant and necessary to accomplish the purposes of the governmental agency that collected it; if an individual asks for an explanation
about the use of her information, this must be provided. These provisions
clearly accomplished some of the objectives of the OECD Guidelines.
Should a plaintiff attempt to claim a Privacy Act violation, she must
prove that the information disclosed was a 'record'. In this case, a record

---

[76]   See, for example, Sovern (n 74) 1042. Another scholar claimed that '[t]his
piece-meal approach to personal data protection makes it impossible for an
individual to know her privacy rights' and therefore suggested the adoption of a
more comprehensive approach for the private sector; see Joshua D Blackman,
'Proposal for Federal Legislation Protecting Informational Privacy Across the
Private Sector' [1993] Santa Clara Computer & High Tech Law Journal 431, 456.
For his proposal, based on the draft of what later became European Directive
95/46/EC; see in particular 465ff.

[77]   Note that not all privacy torts are recognized in every state. See Soma and
Rynerson (n 15) 48.

[78]   An Act to amend Title 5, United States Code, by adding a Section 552a,
to safeguard individual privacy from the misuse of Federal records, to provide
that individuals be granted access to records concerning them which are
maintained by Federal agencies, to establish a Privacy Protection Study Commission, and for other purposes – U.S.C. § 552a – Pub. Law No. 93-579, 88 Stat.
1896 – December 31, 1974.

[79]   Solove and Schwartz, *Privacy, Information, and Technology* (n 15) 304.

is understood as information about an individual maintained by an agency, i.e. information about her education, financial transactions, medical history, or criminal or employment history and which contains her name, or an identifying number, symbol or other particular, such as a finger or voice print or a photograph.[80]

Other statutes were introduced before and after the Privacy Act, such as the Freedom of Information Act (FOIA).[81] The FOIA itself is actually a substantial exception to the applicability of the Privacy Act, even though it pre-dates it. The FOIA permits public access to government records and gives everybody the right to inspect and copy records maintained by any federal agency: if the FOIA requires the release of records, the Privacy Act does not apply.[82] The FOIA itself contains some exemptions, two of which are 'privacy related'. The first exempts from disclosure 'personnel and medical files and similar files the disclosure of which would constitute a clearly unwarranted invasion of personal privacy'; the second exempts from disclosure 'records or information compiled for law enforcement purposes, but only to the extent that the production of such law enforcement records or information ... could reasonably be expected to constitute an unwarranted invasion of personal privacy'.[83] Given this combination of exemptions, and, in particular, in light of the interaction between the Privacy Act and the FOIA, a FOIA exemption on privacy would mean that the Privacy Act required the government to refrain from disclosing certain records.[84]

Prior to the enactment of the Privacy Act, another influential Act had been passed: the Fair Credit Reporting Act of 1970, which legislated on the use and disclosure of citizens' personal information handled by credit

---

[80] See § 552a(a)(4) for the definition. Moreover, such information needs to be contained in a 'system of records', i.e. 'a group of any records under the control of any agency from which information is retrieved using the name of the individual or by some identifying number, symbol, or other identifying particular assigned to the individual' (§ 552a(a)(5)(5)).

[81] An Act to amend section 3 of the Administrative Procedure Act, chapter 324, of the Act of June 11, 1946 (60 Stat. 238), to clarify and protect the right of the public to information, and for other purposes – Pub. Law No. 89-554, 80 Stat. 383 – July 4, 1966 – 5 U.S.C. § 552.

[82] See § 552a(k)(1).

[83] See § 552(b)(6) and § 552(b)(7)(C). For details, see Solove and Schwartz, *Privacy, Information, and Technology* (n 15) 249ff.

[84] Solove and Schwartz, *Privacy, Information, and Technology* (n 15) 322. For an analysis of the exemption cited, and further bibliographical references, see Anthony T Kronman, 'The Privacy Exemption to the Freedom of Information Act' [1980] Journal of Legal Studies 731.

reporting agencies.[85] As credit purchases became more and more common, the credit reporting agencies became significant economic actors.
The Fair Credit Reporting Act was an answer to credit agencies' failure
to respond to consumer complaints. In particular, the purpose of the Act
was to 'ensure that consumer reporting agencies exercise their grave
responsibilities with fairness, impartiality, and a respect for the consumer's right to privacy'.[86] Numerous measures were introduced with the
statute, mainly designed to limit the information that credit agencies
could provide in their credit reports. Moreover, an investigative consumer
report could now only be produced when the consumer had been given
clear, precise evidence that such a report was legitimate.[87]

In 1978 Congress adopted another Act concerning financial information: the Right to Financial Privacy Act,[88] probably enacted in
response to the *United States v. Miller* case,[89] in which the Supreme
Court held that a bank customer had no reasonable expectation of privacy
in transaction records held by her bank. In the Court's view, the bank had
control of that personal information and was entitled to handle and hold
it due to the existence of a federal statute that compelled retention. The
Right to Financial Privacy Act introduced the requirement of a subpoena
or a search warrant for law enforcement if government officials wanted to
obtain an individual's financial records. It also required a notice to the
individual before the disclosure of any information so that the individual
could challenge its release. This protection covers only individuals or
small partnerships.[90]

---

[85] An Act to amend the Federal Deposit Insurance Act, to require insured
banks to maintain certain records, to require that certain transactions in United
States currency be reported to the Department of the Treasury, and for other
purposes – Pub. Law No. 91-508, 84 Stat. 1114 – October 26, 1970 – 15 U.S.C.
§§ 1681 et seq. The Act was an amendment to title VI of the Consumer Credit
Protection Act, Pub. Law No. 90-321, 82 Stat. 146 – June 29, 1968. The Act was
passed together with the Bank Secrecy Act of 1970 (Pub. Law No. 91-508, 84
Stat. 1114 – 12 U.S.C., 15 U.S.C., 18 U.S.C. and 31 U.S.C.). See Soma and
Rynerson (n 15) 76ff for the two Acts.

[86] See § 602(a)(4) [15 U.S.C. § 1681].

[87] On this Act see Solove and Schwartz, *Privacy, Information, and Technology* (n 15) 361ff; Solove and Rotenberg (n 4) 519ff.

[88] Pub Law 95-630, 92 Stat. 3697 – November 10, 1978 – 12 U.S.C.
§§ 3401–3422.

[89] 425 U.S. 435 (1976). See Soma and Rynerson (n 15) 71.

[90] See Soma and Rynerson (n 15) 89ff.

Two years later, in 1980, the Privacy Protection Act was passed.[91] The Act imposes restrictions on the search and seizure of product materials that were reasonably made as a form of public communication; it therefore covers First Amendment matters. It also obliges officials to acquire a subpoena to obtain such information in order to enforce the law.

In the 1980s Congress passed a number of new Acts intended to combat data misuse through new technologies and communications, including the Cable Communications Policy Act of 1984,[92] on privacy protection for records held by cable companies, and the Computer Matching and Privacy Protection Act of 1988,[93] which regulates the use of computer files during government agency investigations. Many other Acts were enacted in the following decades, covering a variety of areas, such as unsolicited phone calls by telemarketers,[94] unsolicited e-mails,[95] and the protection of drivers' information[96] and of children's online privacy.[97]

---

[91] Pub. Law No. 96-440, 94 Stat. 1879, 42 U.S.C. §§ 2000aaff.

[92] An Act to amend the Communications Act of 1934 to provide a national policy regarding cable television Pub. Law No. 98-549, 98 Stat. 2780 – October 31, 1984.

[93] The Act amended the Privacy Act of 1974; see 5 U.S.C. §552a – Pub. Law No. 100-503, 102 Stat. 2507 – June 16, 1989. The Act was a response to government matching its employee records with records of individuals enjoying federal benefits in an attempt to catch people engaged in fraud, see Priscilla M Regan, *Legislating Privacy* (University of North Carolina Press 1995) 95ff.

[94] Telephone Consumer Protection Act of 1991, to amend the Communications Act of 1934 to prohibit certain practices involving the use of telephone devices. Pub. Law No. 120-243 – 47 U.S.C. § 227.

[95] CAN-SPAM Act of 2003 to regulate interstate commerce by imposing limitations and penalties on the transmission of unsolicited commercial electronic mail via the Internet – Pub. Law No. 108, 187-117 Stat. 2699 – 15 U.S.C. §§ 7701ff – December 16, 2003.

[96] Driver's Privacy Protection Act of 1994, to amend title 18, United States Code, to protect the personal privacy and safety of licensed drivers, taking into account the legitimate needs of government and business – Pub. Law No. 103-322, 18 U.S.C. §§ 2721–2725 – October 26, 1993. The Act prevents states from disclosing or selling personal information recorded in their motor vehicle records.

[97] Children's Online Privacy Protection Act of 1998 – Pub. Law No. 105-277, 112, Stat. 2581-72815 – U.S.C. §§ 6501–6506, October 21, 1998. The Act restricts the possible uses of information gathered from children under the age of 13 by Internet websites.

Of particular relevance to us now is the Electronic Communications
Privacy Act of 1986, which updated federal electronic surveillance in
order to keep up with new technologies.[98] The Act broadened the existing
protection for communications to include all forms of electronic transmission. It has three parts: the Wiretap Act, the Stored Communications
Act and the Pen Register Act.[99] The Electronic Communications Act
classifies communications into three types: wire, oral and electronic
communication, defining 'electronic communication' as 'any transfer of
signs, signals, writing, images, sounds, data or intelligence of any nature
transmitted in whole or in part by a wire, radio, electromagnetic,
photoelectronic or photooptical system that affects interstate or foreign
commerce, but does not include (A) any wire or oral communication
…'.[100] Electronic communications are, therefore, all communications
other than wire or oral communications – e-mails, for instance.[101] The
Stored Communications Act protects communications in storage, the
Wiretap Act those in transmission.

In the Internet environment, electronic service providers store information on communications and subscribers. The Stored Communications
Act forbids service providers from disclosing the contents of stored
communications. There are a number of exceptions, including disclosure
to law enforcement agencies under certain circumstances and with
specific guarantees.[102] Section 2703(c) – focusing on access to and
disclosure of subscribers' records – provides that a governmental entity
may require a provider to disclose records, or other information pertaining to a subscriber, or a customer, only when the entity:

> (a) obtains a warrant issued using the procedures described in the Federal
> Rules of Criminal Procedure (or, in the case of a State court, issued using
> State warrant procedures) by a court of competent jurisdiction; (B) obtains a

---

[98]   An Act to amend title 18, United States Code, with respect to the
interception of certain communications, other forms of surveillance, and for other
purposes – 18 U.S.C. § 2510-22 – Pub. Law No. 99-508, 100 Stat. 1848 –
October 21, 1986.
[99]   The Wiretap Act is codified in Title I of the Electronic Communications
Privacy Act, 18 U.S.C. §§2510–2522 and governs the interception of communications. The Stored Communications Act can be found in 18 U.S.C. §§ 2701–
2711. The Pen Register Act is at 18 U.S.C. §§ 3121–3127 and concerns pen
registers and trap and trace devices, as well as more modern analogous devices.
[100]   18 U.S.C. § 2510(12).
[101]   Solove and Rotenberg (n 4) 330; Solove and Schwartz, *Privacy, Information, and Technology* (n 15) 142.
[102]   18 U.S.C. § 2702(b).

court order for such disclosure under subsection (d) of this section; (C) has the consent of the subscriber or customer to such disclosure; ... (E) seeks information under paragraph (2).

Paragraph (2) establishes that the providers shall disclose the following data to the entity: name, address, local and long distance telephone connection records, or records of session times and durations, length of service and types of service utilized, telephone or instrument number or other subscriber number or identity, including any temporarily assigned network address. It is worth underlining that the government body receiving records or information under this subsection is not required to provide notice to a subscriber or customer.

The US courts have dealt with cases concerning government agency requests for the disclosure of ISP records. In the *United States v. Hambrick* case,[103] the Federal Court applied the 'reasonable expectation of privacy test' on providers' records and concluded that there was no reasonable expectation of privacy. In the Court's view, a person cannot have a legitimate expectation of privacy in information she has given voluntarily to other parties.[104] When a subscriber has revealed her information to an ISP, she cannot then claim to have a Fourth Amend ment privacy interest in that information.[105] The same approach was applied in another case, related to IP addresses[106] and URLs.[107] Since e-mail and Internet users rely on third-party equipment to communicate online, they

> have no expectation of privacy in the to/from addresses of their messages or the IP addresses of the websites they visit because they should know that this information is provided to and used by Internet service providers for the specific purpose of directing the routing of information [... It is] voluntarily turned over in order to direct the third party's servers.[108]

---

[103] 55 F. Supp. 2d 504 (1999). The text of the statute was different at that time, but for the purposes of this brief account of the case this is not relevant.

[104] This is the so-called 'third party doctrine' developed by the Supreme Court in the case *Smith v. Maryland*, 442 U.S. 735 (1979), 742ff.

[105] See *United States v. Kennedy*, 81 F. Supp. 2d 1103 (D. Kan. 2000), 1110.

[106] See the definition provided in Chapter 1.

[107] URL is an abbreviation for 'Uniform Resource Locator' or 'Universal Resource Locator'. It is the address system used on the Internet, for example, to specify the location of documents on the World Wide Web. See Entry: *URL* in John Daintith and Edmund Wright (eds), *A Dictionary of Computing* (Oxford University Press 2008).

[108] *United States v. Forrester*, 512 F. 3d 500 (9th Cir. 2008), 510.

The Court also reasoned that this kind of address only reveals unprotected addressing information, and none of the contents of the communication. The Court also compared e-mail to physical mail: the outside part of a physical mail is not covered by Fourth Amendment protection since what is on the envelope is considered visible and therefore voluntarily transmitted to third parties. The 'visible' part of e-mails, such as to/from addresses, should therefore be considered to have the same status.[109] In this decision, however, the Court also observed that applying the same analysis to URLs might be more problematic, because '[a] URL, unlike an IP address, identifies the particular document within a website that a person views and thus reveals much more information about the person's Internet activity',[110] in other words it could also reveal the specific article that a person had read on the website.

At the beginning of this century, new statutes were introduced, including the very controversial USA PATRIOT Act.[111] Enacted in the immediate aftermath of the 9/11 terrorist attacks, the PATRIOT Act contains some provisions that affect individual privacy. Intended to strengthen anti-terrorist measures, the Act makes provision for a network of electronic crimes task forces, thereby requiring information sharing among federal agencies. Furthermore, it mandates a new information system that allows the State Department access to some of the FBI's criminal files. It also includes a provision that permits government investigators to search educational records without a court order.[112] The Act has been harshly criticized for the high levels of intrusion into people's lives and privacy that it permits; its relevance to the purposes for which it was enacted has also been widely questioned.[113]

---

[109] Ibid. See Solove and Schwartz, *Privacy, Information, and Technology* (n 15) 184–185.

[110] *United States v. Forrester* (n 108) 510 fn 6.

[111] USA-PATRIOT (n 73). The USA-PATRIOT was not the only Act enacted as a response to 9/11. See, for instance, the Aviation and Transportation Security Act (Pub. Law No. 107-71, 115 Stat. 597; of November 19, 2001).

[112] See Soma and Rynerson (n 15) 141–143 and 101ff.

[113] See, for instance, Jennifer C Evans, 'Hijacking Civil Liberties: The USA PATRIOT Act of 2001' [2002] 33 Loyola University Chicago Law Journal 933; Susan N Herman, 'The USA PATRIOT Act and the Submajoritarian Fourth Amendment' [2006] Harvard Civil Rights-Civil Liberties Law Review 67.

In 2015 the PATRIOT Act was amended by the USA FREEDOM Act[114] in order to limit National Security Agency surveillance of American citizens, in the light of Edward Snowden's disclosures on the Agency's espionage activities. The Act was considered a victory by civil rights and privacy advocates[115] although some criticisms remain.[116]

That same year the US Congress passed the Cybersecurity Information Sharing Act (CISA).[117] Subject to certain requirements, the Act allows the sharing of Internet traffic information between technology companies and the government, with the aim of preventing cybersecurity threats. Numerous privacy advocates and associations have warned that this Act exceeds the bounds of cybersecurity.[118] Information can be shared 'notwithstanding any other provision of law', meaning that the Act takes

---

[114] Uniting and Strengthening America by Fulfilling Rights and Ensuring Effective Discipline Over Monitoring Act, 129 Stat. 268 Pub. Law No. 114-23 – June 2, 2015.

[115] Cindy Cohn and Rainey Reitman, 'USA Freedom Act Passes: What We Celebrate, What We Mourn, and Where We Go From Here', *eff.org* (2 June 2015) <www.cff.org/deeplinks/2015/05/usa-freedom-act-passes-what-we-celebrate-what-we-mourn-and-where-we-go-here> accessed 25 February 2017.

[116] Jon Queally, '"Fake" Reform: Little to Celebrate as USA Freedom Act Passes House', *commondreams.org* (14 May 2015) <www.commondreams.org/news/2015/05/14/fake-reform-little-celebrate-usa-freedom-act-passes-house> accessed 25 February 2017; Erin Kelly, 'Senate approves USA Freedom Act', *usatoday.com* (2 June 2015) <www.usatoday.com/story/news/politics/2015/06/02/patriot-act-usa-freedom-act-senate-vote/28345747/> accessed 25 February 2017.

[117] An Act to improve cybersecurity in the United States through enhanced sharing of information about cybersecurity threats, and for other purposes, Pub. Law No. 114-113 of December 18, 2015. The Act had been preceded in 2011 by another Bill with a similar name: Cyber Intelligence Sharing and Protection Act (CISPA) A Bill to provide for the sharing of certain cyber threat intelligence and cyber threat information between the intelligence community and cyber-security entities, and for other purposes, 112th Congress, 2d Session, H.R. 3523, May 7, 2012.

[118] See the open letter signed by a number of academics and non-profit associations: <https://d1ovv0c9tw0h0c.cloudfront.net/files/2015/03/CISA-2015-Sign-On-Letter.pdf > accessed 25 February 2017; see also Lee Tien, 'Senate Intelligence Committee Advances Terrible Surveillance Bill in Secret Session', *eff.org* (19 March 2015) <www.eff.org/deeplinks/2015/03/senate-intelligence-committee-advances-terrible-cybersecurity-bill-surveillance> accessed 25 February 2017 [barred texts in original].

precedence over other privacy laws, including the Electronic Communications Privacy Act and the Privacy Act.[119] Moreover, the information gathered can be shared with the intelligence agencies and the National Security Agency, which, as Snowden's revelations have shown, is not only a clear deterioration of privacy protection, but also has more worrying undertones.

At the time of writing, a number of Bills are still pending. While some of them could enhance privacy and personal data protection, some other would put these rights under threat. Among the latter ones there is the Law Enforcement Access to Data Stored Abroad (LEADS) Act.[120] The LEADS Act Bill was introduced at the beginning of 2015 and was intended to facilitate the gathering of electronic information stored by 'US persons' in other countries. The process would involve the issuance of a court warrant to an ISP; the latter, however, could try to have the warrant modified, if compliance would place it in violation of the law of the country where the data is actually stored.[121] If passed, the Act will modify the Electronic Communications Privacy Act with the aim of regulating the new digital world, cloud computing included.[122]

Along with these 'privacy-threatening' Bills, another, with a different aim, is pending in Congress. In 2012 President Obama set out a proposal for a 'Consumer Privacy Bill of Rights' to protect user privacy in the digital age.[123] The Bill was welcomed as a step towards better, more

---

[119]   Andy Greenberg, 'CISA Security Bill: An F For Security But An A+ For Spying', *wired.com* (20 March 2015) <www.wired.com/2015/03/cisa-security-bill-gets-f-security-spying/> accessed 25 February 2017.

[120]   A Bill to amend title 18, United States Code, to safeguard data stored abroad from improper government access, and for other purposes, S. 512, 114th Congress.

[121]   Daniel J Solove, 'Surveillance Law in Dire Need of Reform: The Promise of the LEADS Act' (17 March 2015) *linkedin.com* <www.linkedin.com/pulse/surveillance-law-dire-need-reform-promise-leads-act-daniel-solove> accessed 25 February 2017. The Bill draws on the *Microsoft v. US* (*In the Matter of a Warrant to Search a Certain E-Mail Account Controlled and Maintained by Microsoft Corporation*) case before the District Court of the Southern District of New York.

[122]   Solove, 'Surveillance Law' (n 121); Kurt Wimmer, 'Updating the Electronic Communications Privacy Act: An Essential Legislative Goal for Media Companies and the Public They Serve', mediainstitute.org (March 2015) <www.mediainstitute.org/PDFs/Policy%20Views%206%20LEADS%2031815.pdf> accessed 25 February 2017.

[123]   White House Report, 'Consumer Data Privacy in a Networked World: A Framework for Protecting Privacy and Promoting Innovation in the Global

comprehensive privacy protection although it has been criticized.[124] Under Sections 101–107 the Bill lists certain principles, such as individual control; transparency; respect for context; security; access and accuracy; focused collection; and accountability. These principles clearly track the Fair Information Practice Principles and the OECD Guidelines but are supposed to be applied only with regard to the 'privacy risk' the data poses. 'Privacy risk' is understood as either emotional, physical or financial harm to an individual. Unfortunately, the Bill does not consider that a consumer might want to limit the diffusion of her information regardless of the existence of such harms. Moreover, many businesses are not subject to the application of the Bill as broad exceptions have been included.[125] An 'opt-in' approach is only adopted for certain cases, namely when the information is collected 'out-of-context'.[126] While leaving room for improvement, the Bill is a clear attempt to increase protection of consumers' informational privacy.

Another aspect of the US legislation for privacy is of interest: the so-called 'privacy torts', mentioned earlier. The category of privacy torts can be traced back to a seminal 1960 article by William Prosser, in which the author analysed more than 300 privacy cases which had been settled since Warren and Brandeis' publication. Prosser classified the cases under four different categories of torts, which were later introduced in the *Restatement of Torts*. He maintained that the extreme confusion regarding privacy and its protection was due to a failure to distinguish between these categories.[127] The four torts are collectively known as 'invasion of privacy' and include: intrusion upon seclusion, public disclosure of private facts, false light and appropriation.[128] According to the *Restatement (Second) of Torts*, the four torts can now be described as follows:

1.   *Public disclosure of private facts*: the act of giving publicity to facts or acts regarding a person, which are embarrassing and which were otherwise not as widely known. This tort can be broken down into four elements: dissemination of true information (1), offensive to a

---

Digital Economy' [2013] Journal of Privacy and Confidentiality 95 <http://repository.cmu.edu/jpc/vol4/iss2/5/> accessed 25 February 2017.

[124]   Center for Democracy & Technology, 'Analysis of the Consumer Privacy Bill of Rights Act' (2 March 2015) <https://cdt.org/insight/analysis-of-the-consumer-privacy-bill-of-rights-act/> accessed 25 February 2017.

[125]   Ibid 3–4.

[126]   Section 103(a)(1).

[127]   Prosser (n 18) 407.

[128]   Ibid 389ff.

reasonable person (2), not of public concern (3) and so intimate that it is contrary to the public's sense of decency (4).[129]

2.   *Intrusion upon seclusion*: is the only one of the four privacy torts that does not require publicity. It is the gathering of information from someone's private space that provokes an invasion of that person's private affairs or solitude. The wrongdoing occurs at the time of the intrusion, not at the moment of the possible publication of the gathered personal information. The intrusion does not need to be physical, and may also be visual or audio.[130]

3.   *False light*: this figure of tort is close to defamation and concerns individuals who are shown in a 'false light' in the public eye, for example through the publication of misrepresentative facts, which are normally highly offensive. According to the *Restatement (Second) of Torts*, the offensiveness of false light has to be evaluated from a reasonable point of view and the offender had to have undertaken publication with knowledge or with reckless disregard.[131]

4.   *Appropriation*: intended to prevent unjust enrichment deriving from the theft of a person's name or likeness.[132]

Privacy is also protected by other torts. 'Breach of confidentiality' provides a remedy when a professional discloses a patient's or client's confidential information. 'Defamation' consists of the tort of libel and slander, for which a person is liable if they make false statements about another and harm their reputation. The tort of 'infliction of emotional distress' offers a remedy when a person 'by extreme and outrageous conduct intentionally or recklessly causes severe emotional distress to another'.[133]

---

[129]   The American Law Institute, *Restatement (Second) of Torts*, 1977, § 652D – 'Publicity Given to Private Life'. Soma and Rynerson (n 15) 38ff. This privacy tort is the one in clearest conflict with the freedom of speech and press protected by the First Amendment. See Prosser (n 18) 392–398.

[130]   *Restatement (Second) of Torts*, § 652B – 'Intrusion upon Seclusion'. See Soma and Rynerson (n 15) 41ff. See Prosser (n 18) 389–392.

[131]   *Restatement (Second) of Torts*, § 652E – 'Publicity Placing Persons in a False Light'. See Soma and Rynerson (n 15) 35ff. See also Prosser (n 18) 398–401.

[132]   *Restatement (Second) of Torts*, § 652C – 'Appropriation of Name or Likeness'. Soma and Rynerson (n 15) 32ff. See Prosser (n 18) 401–407 and for a more comprehensive explanation ibid 408.

[133]   *Restatement (Second) of Torts*, § 46. Due to the requirement for 'extreme and outrageous conduct', the actual application of this tort is limited; See Solove

The sectorial, fragmented, incoherent American privacy regulation has resulted in legislation that protects some data 'while allowing virtually identical records to remain unregulated', considered by some to be a reflection of the overall American approach to law and public policy.[134] It has been argued that an omnibus privacy regulation would be unlikely to succeed in the US due to 'American demands of detailed regulatory instruments'.[135] Moreover, as we have seen, many Acts were enacted in the aftermath of scandals or crimes, with the result that the legal innovation concentrates more on specific sectors than on the overall picture.[136]

The developments traced in this chapter are intended to illustrate the fact that despite Warren and Brandeis' seminal article on the invasion of privacy by private entities (such as newspapers, and the paparazzi), privacy regulation in the US has since acquired a different flavour; nowadays, the protection of privacy is very often conceived as protection from governmental intrusion into one's private life.[137] Nor does the US approach allow a coherent, comprehensive protection of privacy. All in all, US privacy regulation appears rooted in an attitude very unlike that of either the Italian or the Canadian systems, as I shall now illustrate.

---

and Schwartz, *Privacy, Information, and Technology* (n 15) 31. Solove proposed a different and expanded classification of privacy torts in order to obtain a framework better tailored to the new technological landscape. The author proposed a taxonomy of four groups of harmful activities: (1) information collection, (2) information processing, (3) information dissemination, and (4) invasion, each of which encompasses many different harmful situations. See Daniel J Solove, 'A Taxonomy of Privacy' [2006] University of Pennsylvania Law Review 477, 488ff.

[134] Robert Gellman, 'A Better Way to Approach Privacy Policy in the United States: Establish a Non-Regulatory Privacy Protection Board' [2003] Hastings Law Journal 1183, 1216. The author compares video rental, which is protected by the Video Privacy Protection Act, with other rentals – such as book rental – which are not covered by law.

[135] Ibid 1207.

[136] Robert Gellman, 'Fragmented, Incomplete, and Discontinuous: The Failure of Federal Privacy Regulatory Proposal and Institutions' [1993] Software Law Journal 199, 236.

[137] Authors explain this peculiarity in different ways. See, for example, Westin's hypothesis, Westin (n 15) 330, that this approach was a sort of reaction to the 'over-surveyed' European society, from which a [large?] segment of North American society was escaping/originated. For an explanation of this attitude and for a comparison with the European approach, see the seminal article by James Q Whitman, 'The Two Western Cultures of Privacy: Dignity versus Liberty' [2004] Yale Law Journal 1153.

3.2 Italy

As we have seen, the right to privacy in Italy emerged quite late in comparison with the US, and particularly so far as the judicial acknowledgement of a right to privacy is concerned: statutes protecting privacy and personal data were first enacted in Italy in 1996, after the US had passed similar privacy legislation.

As previously mentioned, at least until the enactment of the first regulation on privacy in 1996, when called upon to decide in cases related to privacy, the Italian Supreme Court relied on the Constitution and/or other existing provisions that covered and protected such a right, although not always directly. Certain provisions of Legge 633/1941, on *diritto d'autore*, for example, were referred to: arts. 93, 96 and 97 concern the secrecy of correspondence and rights related to portrayals. In addition, art. 10 of the Italian Civil Code protects use of a person's image. These provisions were already in force at the time of the decisions – in, for example, the *Caruso* and the *Petacci* cases, which ignored the existence of a right to privacy.

In 1950 Italy signed the European Convention for the Protection of Human Rights and Fundamental Freedoms, art. 8 of which proclaims the 'Right to respect for private and family life'. This international Charter has been added to the Universal Declaration of Human Rights; Italy is bound by both institutions.[138]

Furthermore, since the enactment of the Criminal Code in 1930, people's rights to privacy within the home have been protected by criminal provisions.[139] In particular, art. 615*bis* was introduced in 1974 to protect people's private lives from illicit interference. The provision, which has rarely been applied,[140] punishes with imprisonment both anyone who makes videos or recordings of people's private life taking place in private residences, and anyone who reveals or publishes news or images thus obtained, via any public medium.

---

[138] As time went on, more laws, such as those concerning workers' privacy (regulated by Legge 20.5.1970, no. 300), were introduced/passed. This statute is called *Statuto dei lavoratori*, meaning 'Charter of workers' rights'. According to Rodotà (n 11) 205, this is the first real acknowledgement of the right to privacy in the Italian system. For an account of the sources of law that protected privacy to a certain extent in the 1970s, see Stefano Rodotà, *Elaboratori elettronici e controllo sociale* (Il Mulino 1973) 56ff.

[139] Arts. 614 and 615 of the Italian Criminal Code – *Codice Penale* – which is the main source of criminal provisions in Italy. It was enacted by R.D. 19.10.1930, n. 1398.

[140] Pardolesi (n 65) 17, fn 33.

Excepting the above provisions, the first legislation for the protection of physical, as well as informational, privacy was introduced as late as 1996, prompted partly by a European Directive. At the time of the enactment of Directive 95/46/EC, many European countries had already adopted national legislation on privacy.[141] By 1981 Italy and Greece were the only European states that had not yet implemented any form of privacy regulation.[142] And still, despite many attempts to adopt such regulation, during the 1980s no Bill in the Italian Parliament ever got beyond the draft stage.[143]

Directive 95/46/EC was heavily influenced by both the OECD Guidelines and the activities of the Council of Europe.[144] The latter had, indeed, already adopted two resolutions: the first in 1973, concerning private databases, and the second, in 1974, concerning public databases. These resolutions were incorporated into the Strasbourg Convention no. 108 of 1981, for the Protection of Individuals with regard to Automatic Processing of Personal Data.[145] In drawing up a comprehensive regulation for privacy, the Council considered the need to protect not only electronically processed data, but also data stored in analogue archives.[146] On 24 October 1995 the European Community adopted Directive 95/46/EC, which dealt with the protection of individuals with regard to the

---

[141] For an overview of the Directive, see David I Bainbridge and Nick Platten, *EC Data Protection Directive* (Butterworths 1996).

[142] Vittorio Frosini, 'La protezione della riservatezza nella società informatica' [1981] Informatica e Diritto 5. The first law was enacted in two German *Länder* in 1970. Pardolesi (n 65) 32.

[143] For details, see Pardolesi (n 65) 40–41; Niger (n 55) 109–110; Buttarelli (n 12) 110–121.

[144] See Pardolesi (n 65) 33.

[145] The Convention, signed on 28 January 1981 by the Member States of the Council of Europe, is available at: <http://conventions.coe.int/Treaty/en/Treaties/html/108.htm> accessed 25 February 2017. In Italy the Convention was ratified by Legge 21.2.1989, n. 98. For the history of the documents and agreements which led to the Convention, as well as for an account of the contents and of the consequences of the Convention, see Buttarelli (n 12) 3–71. In 2001 an 'Additional Protocol to the Convention for the Protection of Individuals with regard to Automatic Processing of Personal Data regarding supervisory authorities and transborder data flows' was added to the Convention: <http://conventions.coe.int/Treaty/en/Treaties/Html/181.htm> accessed 25 February 2017. The Council of Europe has been working to update the Convention; see Graham Greenleaf, '"Modernising" Data Protection Convention 108: A Safe Basis for a Global Privacy Treaty?' [2013] Computer Law & Security Review 430.

[146] Pardolesi (n 65) 34. See recital no. 27, Directive 95/46/EC.

processing and free movement of personal data. The Directive stated that 'in order to remove the obstacles to flows of personal data, the level of protection of the rights and freedoms of individuals with regard to the processing of such data must be equivalent in all Member States'.[147] This homogenization was vital for the internal market, since it obviated the need for barriers to the free movement of data within the Community.[148] The Directive's goal of protecting fundamental rights and freedoms was key, especially with regard to the right to privacy, as recognized by both the general principle of Community law and art. 8 of the European Convention for the Protection of Human Rights and Fundamental Freedoms.[149] This protection was to be granted to 'all processing of personal data by any person whose activities [were] governed by Community law, excluding private use of personal data'.[150]

The year after the enactment of the Directive, Italy adopted Legge 31.12.1996, no. 675,[151] finally introducing privacy regulation into the Italian system. Although this statute is not a formal implementation of Directive 95/46, it broadly integrates the European legislation into its text.[152] Italian regulation differed from the European Directive in some

---

[147] Recital no. 8, Directive 95/46/EC.

[148] See recital no. 9, Directive 95/46/EC.

[149] See recital no. 10, Directive 95/46/EC. Although the European Constitution project has never been enacted, it is relevant to cite its art. I-51: 'Protection of personal data. 1. Everyone has the right to the protection of personal data concerning him or her. 2. European laws or framework laws shall lay down the rules relating to the protection of individuals with regard to the processing of personal data by Union institutions, bodies, offices and agencies, and by the Member States when carrying out activities which fall within the scope of Union law, and the rules relating to the free movement of such data. Compliance with these rules shall be subject to the control of independent authorities.' For a more in-depth analysis of the fundamental right to data protection, see Gloria González Fuster, *The Emergence of Personal Data Protection as a Fundamental Right of the EU* (Springer 2014).

[150] See recital no. 12, Directive 95/46/EC.

[151] I will only refer to some principles of this law since it was repealed by decreto legislativo 30.6.2003, no. 196. For a thorough analysis of Legge 675/96 and for further bibliographical references, see Buttarelli (n 12); Ettore Giannantonio, Mario Giuseppe Losano and Vincenzo Zeno Zencovich (eds), *La tutela dei dati personali. Commentario alla L. 675/1996* (2nd edn, Cedam 1999); Roberto Pardolesi (ed), *Diritto alla riservatezza e circolazione dei dati personali* (Giuffrè 2003).

[152] Giorgio Resta, 'Il diritto alla protezione dei dati personali' in Francesco Cardarelli, Salvatore Sica and Vincenzo Zeno-Zencovich (eds), *Il codice dei dati personali: temi e problemi* (Giuffrè 2004) 11.

areas, two of which are worth highlighting: first, Legge 675/96 also protected the dignity of the natural person; second, it gave the protection of personal identity and that of privacy equal consideration.[153]

The statute was modified several times and finally repealed in 2003,[154] with the introduction of the 'Codice in materia di protezione dei dati personali',[155] usually called *Codice Privacy*. The Italian Privacy Code does not differ greatly from the previously existing Legge 675/96, which was applicable to both automatic and manual processing.[156] Article 1, co. 2, letter b) of Legge 675/96 defines 'data processing' (*trattamento*) as every operation or set of operations, done with or without the use of electronic or other automated means. This relates to the collection, recording, organization, storage, elaboration, modification, selection, drawing, comparison, use, interconnection, blocking, diffusion, erasure or destruction of data.[157] The same article also supplied the interpreters with the definition of 'personal data', understood as any information relating to a natural or legal person, body or association, identified or identifiable, even indirectly, by reference to any other information, including an identification number.[158]

Article 1, co. 1, of Legge 675/96 prescribes that the processing of personal data has to respect the rights and fundamental freedoms, as well as the dignity of persons, with particular reference to the right to privacy and to personal identity. This text eventually confirmed the existence of the right to personal identity, which had previously only been considered as a creation of case law. This provision highlights an increasing awareness that identity can be harmed not only by misrepresentation in the mass media, but also when information regarding a person is handled without transparency or without the necessary warranties. In the digital

---

[153]   Rodotà, 'Persona, riservatezza, identità' (n 59) 583–584.

[154]   Legge 675/96 had been modified by decreto legislativo 9.5.1997, no. 123; 28.7.1997, no. 255; 8.5.1998, no. 135; 13.5.1998, no. 171; 6.11.1998, no. 389; 26.2.1999, no. 51; 11.5.1999, no. 135; 30.7.1999, n. 281; 30.7.1999, no. 282; 28.12.2001, no. 467.

[155]   Literally: 'Code on personal data protection matters'.

[156]   For an explanation see Andrea Giannaccari, 'L'ambito di applicazione della legge, l'importazione e l'esportazione dei dati personali' in Pardolesi (n 151) 141, 142ff. See also, Paolo Cerina, 'Art. 2. Ambito di applicazione' in Giannantonio, Losano and Zeno Zencovich (n 151) 21ff.

[157]   The definition implements verbatim art. 2, letter b) of Directive 95/46.

[158]   See art. 2, letter a) of Directive 95/46. For an explanation of the different kinds of data processing, see Luigi Lambo, 'La disciplina sul trattamento dei dati personali: profili esegetici e comparatistici delle definizioni' in Pardolesi (n 151) 59, 74ff.

environment the ease with which fragmented data can be processed greatly increases the possibility that a person may be partially, or prejudicially, represented; thus becoming no more than the sum of her electronic information.[159]

Specific provisions were introduced for certain categories of data, the most important being 'sensitive data'. The European legislators believed this data deserved a specific category because its possession could open the door to discrimination; it was therefore decided that the written consent of the data subject was a prerequisite for the processing of sensitive data, and the prior authorization of the Privacy Authority was also required.[160] According to art. 22, sensitive data is data which reveals racial or ethnic origin; religious, philosophical or other kind of beliefs; political opinions; or political affiliation, union membership, or data which could reveal facts about someone's health or sexual habits. This definition of 'sensitive data' introduces two extremely important aspects of Italian privacy regulation: first, the consent of the data subject; second, the Privacy Authority. Both elements will be analysed in more depth later in this chapter.

In 1997 Europe enacted another Directive concerning 'the processing of personal data and the protection of privacy in the telecommunications sector' (97/66/EC). The Directive was implemented in Italy through decreto legislativo 13.5.1998, no. 171, which modified Legge 675/96, with reference to journalism and personal data.[161] Article 1 of the Directive explains that the Directive was enacted to reconcile Member States' provisions for personal data protection in the telecommunications sector: the Directive is intended to complement Directive 95/46. Directive 97/66 refers to telecommunications services as services 'whose provision consists wholly or partly in the transmission and routing of signals on telecommunications networks, with the exception of radio- and television broadcasting'. Natural and legal persons received the protection of this Directive as 'subscribers' or 'users' of telecommunication services.[162]

---

[159]   See Giorgio Resta, 'Identità personale e identità digitale' [2007] Dir. informazione e informatica 522. An individual's identity might be protected through the cancellation, modification or blocking of processing. Nor is identity ever static. See Rodotà, 'Persona, riservatezza, identità' (n 59) 605–607.

[160]   See art. 8 of Directive 95/46/EC.

[161]   Salvatore Sica, 'Sicurezza e riservatezza nelle telecomunicazioni: il d.lgs. n. 171/98 nel "sistema" della protezione dei dati personali' [1998] Dir. informazione e informatica 776. See art 12, decreto legislativo 171/98.

[162]   A user is different from a subscriber since the former does not buy a subscription, see Paolo Pallaro, 'La privacy nel settore delle telecomunicazioni:

The regulation introduced with decreto legislativo 171/98 focused on the 'dynamic phase', meaning the circulation of data through a network or a telecommunication service. However, when data was stored in a database or was subject to processing, Legge 675/96 applied. Particular provisions were contemplated for data related to traffic calls: this data was supposed to be cancelled or anonymized at the end of the call, unless needed for invoicing. However, even in the latter case, data had to be erased after the period necessary for the resolving of any complaints regarding invoices or payments.[163]

Both the above Directives were repealed and substituted by Directive 2002/58/EC. This important Directive, enacted on 12 July 2002, concerns 'personal data processing and the protection of privacy in the electronic communications sector' (commonly known as 'Directive on privacy and electronic communications').[164] To implement this Directive, Italy also repealed Legge 675/96 and created an organic body of laws: the previously mentioned *Codice in materia di protezione dei dati personali*, enacted by decreto legislativo 30.6.2003, no. 196.[165] This Code, which – finally – also formally implements Directive 95/46, represents an attempt to create a single, comprehensive regulation on the matter of privacy. Article 1, using the same wording as art. 8 of the European Convention on Human Rights, proclaims that 'everyone has a right to the protection of personal data concerning him or her'. Like Legge 675/96, the Code accepts that personal data processing is carried out in fulfilment of

---

la direttiva comunitaria n. 97/66' [1998] Rivista diritto europeo 541, 545. See the same work for a brief comment on the entire Directive.

[163] See arts. 4ff, decreto legislativo 171/98.

[164] Directive 2002/58/EC of the European Parliament and of the Council of 12 July 2002 concerning the processing of personal data and the protection of privacy in the electronic communications sector (Directive on privacy and electronic communications) [2002] OJ L 201/37. Although it is not of great importance and therefore will not be summarized here, it is worth mentioning another piece of legislation, namely Regulation (EC) no. 45/2001 of the European Parliament and of the Council of 18 December 2000 on the protection of individuals with regard to the processing of personal data by the Community institutions and bodies and on the free movement of such data [2001] OJ L 8/1. This Regulation introduced the European Data Protection Supervisor.

[165] For a detailed analysis of this legislation and for further bibliographical references, see Cardarelli, Sica and Zeno-Zencovich (n 152); Juri Monducci and Giovanni Sartor (eds), *Il codice in materia di protezione dei dati personali* (Cedam 2004); Cesare Massimo Bianca and Francesco Donato Busnelli (eds), *La protezione dei dati personali: commentario al d.lgs. 30 giugno 2003, n. 196 (Codice della privacy)* (Cedam 2007).

fundamental rights and freedoms, and in respect of the subject's dignity, with particular reference to *privacy, personal identity, and the right to personal data protection.*[166] In specifying these terms, the legislator finally explicitly acknowledges the existence of the aforesaid rights,[167] in contrast with the text of Legge 675/96, which made no reference at all to a right to personal data protection. This sentence, although it might appear to be purely rhetorical, has actually been interpreted as introducing a quasi-constitutional protection to informational privacy, and is key to the interpretation of the entire *Codice.*[168]

This *Codice* is applicable to every person processing personal data within Italian territory.[169] The choice of the words 'each person' was intended to make the law applicable to both the private and the public sector; however, some provisions apply only to one or the other of them.[170] The expression 'each person' reflects a global approach to the protection of personal data; this approach, however, is undermined by many exceptions.[171]

The Code is divided into three parts. The first contains general duties and rights, with reference to both the private and public sectors. The second looks at specific areas where data is processed: by the police, by insurance companies or by banks, in the health sector, in journalism and so on. The third part provides for administrative and jurisdictional

---

[166]   See art. 2, decreto legislativo 196/03.

[167]   According to Sergio Niger, 'Il diritto alla protezione dei dati personali' in Monducci and Sartor (eds) (n 165) 7, the right to data protection differs from the traditional rights of personality: it seems to concern something external to the person, while other rights to personality directly concern the actual person. For a more in-depth analysis, see the works on the rights of personality cited above (n 59) and Resta, 'Il diritto alla protezione dei dati personali' (n 152) 23ff. The right to personal data protection has now been accepted as a fundamental right and freedom, according to Stefano Rodotà, 'Tra diritti fondamentali ed elasticità della normativa: il nuovo codice sulla privacy' [2004] Europa e Dir. Privato 1, 3.

[168]   See Resta, 'Il diritto alla protezione dei dati personali' (n 152) 14, and spec. 41–42. This right has also been considered a precondition for the full enjoyment of the other fundamental rights, see Rodotà, 'Tra diritti fondamentali' (n 167) 4; see also Id, 'Diritto, scienza, tecnologia: modelli e scelte di regolamentazione' [2004] Riv. critica dir. privato 368.

[169]   Art. 5, decreto legislative 196/03.

[170]   Arts. 18–22 apply only to public entities; arts. 23–27 apply to private entities and public companies.

[171]   Apart from specific exemptions related, for instance, to journalism (art. 25) or to scientific research (art. 12, letter d)), art. 4 provides for a special regime for processing with a public scope, such as that undertaken by the criminal records office (*Casellario giudiziale*). See Giannaccari (n 156) 165.

protection; it establishes the penalties applicable for violating the Code, and regulates the Privacy Authority bureau.

Article 4 gives a long list of definitions, which had also been included in Legge 675/96. With regard to 'processing', letter a) of art. 1 considers many different activities, which form four distinct stages:[172]

1.   the preliminary phase of data collection and registration;
2.   use, including organization, examination,[173] elaboration, modification, selection, extraction, comparison and interconnection of data;
3.   circulation, including communication and diffusion, of data;
4.   the last phase, which includes data conservation, blocking, erasure and destruction.

Article 4 also introduces a fundamental definition of 'personal data', which differs only slightly from the one included in Legge 675/96. In fact, the current definition comprises all information concerning a natural person, identified or identifiable, even indirectly, through reference made to any other information, including a personal identification number. Originally the definition also comprised 'legal persons' as data subjects; currently, due to a specific amendment, legal persons are no longer covered by the *Codice Privacy*.[174]

Article 4 also provides a definition of 'sensitive data', using the same formulation as in previous legislation. The definition of 'identifying data' is also covered, given as any data which allows the direct identification of a data subject.[175] Data can be considered 'anonymous' if it is impossible to associate it with an identified or identifiable subject, from the moment of its generation to after its processing.[176]

---

[172]   See the following classification proposed by Pascuzzi and Giovanella (n 57) 55.

[173]   This kind of action was not considered in Legge 675/96, see Niger, 'Il diritto alla protezione dei dati personali' (n 167) 13.

[174]   The current wording of art. 4, letter b), decreto legislativo 196/03 is the result of the amendments introduced by art. 40, co. 2, letter a), decreto legge 6.12.2011, no. 201, of which the consolidated version is Legge 22.12.2011, no. 214.

[175]   See art. 4, letters d) and c), decreto legislativo 196/03, respectively.

[176]   See art. 4, letter n), decreto legislativo 196/03. A recommendation of the European Council stated that data cannot be considered identifiable when identification requires an unreasonable amount of time and manpower, see Council Recommendation (EC) R97/5, 13 February 1997, on the protection of medical data. With reference to the issue of anonymity in Italian law, see

Data subject rights are essentially the same as those already recognized by Legge 675/96. Article 7, decreto legislativo 196/03 recognizes the data subject's right to know the origin, processing scope and methods of the data, and the identifying data of those responsible for the processing. The data subject also has the right to access her data and to obtain the modification and update of incomplete or obsolete information; and the right to have the data cancelled when it is no longer required for its original aim. Finally, the individual has the right to completely oppose any data processing.

Article 11 describes the way in which data has to be handled. It has to be processed lawfully and with fairness; it needs to be collected and registered for specific, explicit and legitimate aims and used in other processing operations only if compatible with those aims; data has to be correct and, when necessary, updated. The data also needs to be pertinent and complete, and must not exceed the scope for which it was collected or processed. Finally, data has to be stored in such a manner that allows the identification of the data subject for a period of time no longer than needed for the scope for which it was collected or processed. In addition, co. 2 of the same article introduces an important provision, which has proven to be very protective of privacy in the case studies illustrated in this book. According to this provision, data processed without complying with the discipline on personal data protection cannot be used for any other purpose, even if that purpose is itself legitimate.

The *Codice Privacy* also substituted decreto legislativo 171/98, which had implemented Directive 97/66;[177] the corresponding provisions can now be found in arts. 121–132. Article 133 confers a particular task on the *Garante* (Privacy Authority): the *Garante* shall encourage ISPs to draw up and adopt deontological codes for personal data processing. These codes should consider specific criteria through which the adequacy and uniformity of users' knowledge and awareness in electronic communications can be ensured. Providers and web managers should supply these codes and information directly on their websites in such a way that they can easily be accessed. These codes are intended to favour transparency and fairness towards users, in line with art. 11 of the Code.

When storing user data, providers are subject to the regulations applicable to every private individual, since the providers' collection of

---

Giusella Finocchiaro, 'Anonymity and the Law in Italy' in Ian Kerr, Carole Lucock and Valerie Steeves (eds), *Lessons from the Identity Trail: Anonymity, Privacy and Identity in a Networked Society* (OUP 2009) 523.

[177] See arts. 121–132, *Codice Privacy*.

data can be considered a 'database', as defined by letter p) of art. 4.[178] Providers shall cancel or anonymize telephonic traffic data when it is not necessary for the transmission of electronic communications. Article 123 states that providers can keep this data for up to six months, for invoicing or payment reasons.

Article 132 looks at data storage for aims other than those considered in art. 123; it has been subject to countless amendments.[179] Since the enactment of the *Codice Privacy*, Europe has introduced new, anti-terrorism, provisions on data retention: specifically Directive 2006/24/EU, the so-called 'Data retention Directive',[180] which was implemented in Italy through decreto legislativo 30.5.2008, no. 109. Following this implementation, art. 123 adds that providers shall store telephonic data for 24 months from the date the call occurred, to facilitate the investigation and repression of crimes. Digital telecommunications data, on the other hand, is to be kept for 12 months from the date the communication occurred.[181]

The 'Data retention Directive' has been criticized for intruding excessively into consumers' privacy, posing unnecessary burdens on ISPs, and undermining the entire structure of European privacy protection.[182] After

---

[178]   Letter p), art. 4 defines 'database' as any organized group of personal data, divided into one or more units, situated in one or more sites. See Silvia Gorini and Sergio Niger, 'Privacy e comunicazioni elettroniche' in Monducci and Sartor (n 165) 387.

[179]   For example, art. 123 was modified by decreto legge 24.12.2003, no. 354, the consolidated version of which is Legge 26.2.2004, no. 45; by decreto legge 27.7.2005, no. 144 (consolidated version Legge 31.7.2005, no. 155 (introducing laws to contrast international terrorism)); by Legge 18.3.2008, no. 48, which ratifies and executes the European Convention on Cybercrime, signed in Budapest in 2001; by decreto legislativo 30.5.2008, no. 109, which implements European Directive 2006/24. For a brief account of the modifications introduced, see Antonio Tolone, 'La disciplina degli obblighi di conservazione dei dati telematici da parte dei providers' [2008] Riv. informazione e informatica 856.

[180]   Directive 2006/24/EC of the European Parliament and of the Council of 15 March 2006 on the retention of data generated or processed in connection with the provision of publicly available electronic communications services or of public communications networks and amending Directive 2002/58/EC [2006] L 105/54.

[181]   See art. 132, co. 1 and 1*bis*, decreto legislativo 196/03.

[182]   Lilian Mitrou, 'Communications Data Retention: A Pandora's Box for Rights and Liberties?' in Alessandro Acquisti, Stefanos Gritzalis, Costos Lambrinoudakis and Sabrina di Vimercati (eds), *Digital Privacy: Theory, Technologies, and Practices* (Auerbach Publications 2008) 409; Lukas Feiler, 'The Legality of the Data Retention Directive in Light of the Fundamental Rights to

a number of national courts had declared the Directive invalid,[183] the European Court of Justice reached the same conclusion in the spring of 2014,[184] largely due to the disproportionate effects of the Directive on the fundamental rights concerned, primarily arts. 7 and 8 of the Charter.[185]

In 2009 Europe enacted another Directive that affects personal data protection law. Directive 2009/136/EC amended Directive 2002/58 and introduced an important change related to the so-called 'security breach

---

Privacy and Data Protection' [2010] European Journal of Law and Technology <http://ejlt.org//article/view/29/75> accessed 25 February 2017; Stephen McGarvey, 'The 2006 EC Data Retention Directive: A Systematic Failure' [2011] Hibernian Law Journal 119. See also the Article 29 Working Party, 'Opinion 3/2006 on the Directive 2006/24/EC' (25 March 2006) <http://ec.europa.eu/justice/policies/privacy/docs/wpdocs/2006/wp119_en.pdf> accessed 25 February 2017; and the Joint letter of 22 June 2010 to Cecilia Malmström, European Commissioner for Home Affairs, Viviane Reding, European Commission Vice-President with responsibility for Justice, Fundamental Rights and Citizenship and Neelie Kroes, European Commission Vice-President with responsibility for the Digital Agenda, signed by more than 100 privacy and technologies experts, associations and the like <www.vorratsdatenspeicherung.de/images/DRletter_Malmstroem.pdf> accessed 25 February 2017. For a different vision, see Francesca Bignami, 'Privacy and Law Enforcement in the European Union: The Data Retention Directive' [2007] Chicago Journal of International Law 233.

[183] See the cases of Romania: Romanian Constitutional Court Decision no. 1258 of 8 October 2009, Official Gazette no. 798 of 23 November 2009; and of Germany: Bundesverfassungsgericht, 2 March 2010, 1 BvR 256/08. See Eleni Kosta, 'The Way to Luxemburg: National Court Decisions on the Compatibility of the Data Retention Directive with the Rights to Privacy and Data Protection' [2013] SCRIPTed 339 <http://script-ed.org/wp-content/uploads/2013/10/kosta.pdf> accessed 25 February 2017.

[184] Joint cases C-293/12 and C-594/12 *Digital Rights Ireland Ltd v Minister for Communications, Marine and Natural Resources, Minister for Justice, Equality and Law Reform, The Commissioner of the Garda Síochána, Ireland and the Attorney General,* and *Kärntner Landesregierung, Michael Seitlinger, Christof Tschohl and Others* [2014] ECLI:EU:C:2014:238. Among numerous comments, see Simone Scagliarini, 'La Corte di Giustizia bilancia diritto alla vita privata e lotta alla criminalità: alcuni pro e alcuni contra' [2014] Dir. Info e info 873; Marie-Pierre Granger and Kristina Irion, 'The Court of Justice and the Data Retention Directive in Digital Rights Ireland: Telling Off the EU Legislator and Teaching a Lesson in Privacy and Data Protection' [2014] European Law Review 835; Alessandro Spina, 'Risk Regulation of Big Data: Has the Time Arrived for a Paradigm Shift in EU Data Protection Law?' [2014] European Journal of Risk Regulation 248.

[185] See especially para 69 of ECJ, C-293/12.

notification'; amendments also included specific provisions for 'cookies'.[186] Italy implemented this Directive in 2012, with two decrees, namely decreto legislativo 28.5.2012, nos. 69 and 70; security breach notification obligations are described in the new provision of art. 32*bis* of the Privacy Code. The main question that the Directive and its implementation address is how to deal with 'the storing of information, or the gaining of access to information already stored, in the terminal equipment of a subscriber or user' (art. 3, para 5, Directive 2009/136). The Directive requires that this information, mainly cookies, only be processed with users' consent. The Italian transposition explicitly requires *preliminary* consent (art. 123, *Codice Privacy*). This approach should strengthen the position of users vis-à-vis the online management of their information.[187]

As we have seen, the Italian framework for data protection is based on an all-encompassing regulation, applicable to all sectors of public and private life. This *Code* includes special provisions for particular kinds of data, rules for the intervention of the Privacy Authority in the public debate on data protection, particular forms of processing managed by the Authority, and many other provisions that show a specific dedication to personal data protection.

A further important aspect of privacy protection in Italy is its protection under tort law. According to art. 15 of the Privacy Code, whoever causes damage to someone as a consequence of the processing of her personal data must compensate the victim pursuant to art. 2050 of the Civil Code.[188] Article 2050 introduces a particular case of extra-contractual liability which contains a reverse onus clause, i.e. the wrongdoer has to demonstrate she could not have avoided the damage, thus making it easier for the victim to obtain compensation for the damage suffered. This explicit provision puts the subject who suffered 'privacy-related' damage in a better position than any other subject

---

[186] Article 29 Working Party, 'Opinion 04/2012 on Cookie Consent Exemption' (7 June 2012) <http://ec.europa.eu/justice/data-protection/article-29/documentation/opinion-recommendation/files/2012/wp194_en.pdf> accessed 25 February 2017; Article 29 Working Party, 'Working Document 02/2013 providing guidance on obtaining consent for cookies' (2 October 2013) <http://ec.europa.eu/justice/data-protection/article-29/documentation/opinion-recommendation/files/2013/wp208_en.pdf> accessed 25 February 2017.

[187] 'Individuazione delle modalità semplificate per l'informativa e l'acquisizione del consenso per l'uso dei cookie – 8 maggio 2014', Italian Privacy Authority (G.U. n. 126, 3 June 2014).

[188] For an explanation, see Cesare Massimo Bianca, *Diritto Civile. Vol. V – La responsabilità* (Giuffrè 2012) 707ff.

suffering harm for other violations of personal rights. Article 11 also provides that victims are entitled to non-pecuniary damages if data has been processed illicitly (i.e. contrary to art. 11). This provision further strengthens the situation of potential victims. Under the current interpretation, privacy in any event enjoys non-pecuniary damages compensation as a constitutionally protected right; nevertheless, an explicit provision obviously smoothes the path to such an interpretation.

In 2015 Italy adopted a 'Declaration for Internet Rights'.[189] The draft declaration, written by experts and scholars, was also discussed with citizens. The declaration is intended to sensitize Italy, and other countries, to the importance of the Internet as a space for fundamental rights. Article 5 declares that '[e]veryone has the right to the protection of the data that concern them in order to ensure respect for their dignity, identity and privacy'. Articles 9 to 11 respectively address the 'right to one's identity', the 'protection of anonymity' and the 'right to be forgotten'. The declaration represents a further step towards ensuring the protection of privacy and personal data, and of citizens' rights more generally in the online world.

As previously mentioned, most Italian legislation on privacy has been prompted by EU interventions. With the adoption of the Treaty of Lisbon,[190] Europe has increased its authority to intervene in the field of privacy and data protection. While previously such regulations centred around the concepts of competition and the internal market, art. 16 of the Treaty on European Union currently states that '[e]veryone has the right to the protection of personal data concerning them'. This provision sanctions the distinction between privacy and protection of personal data and the emancipation of the latter from the former.[191] Article 16 also provides that the Parliament and the Council shall lay down rules on the processing of personal data.[192]

---

189   The English version is available at <www.camera.it/application/ xmanager/projects/leg17/commissione_internet/testo_definitivo_inglese.pdf> accessed 25 February 2017.

190   Amending the Treaty on European Union and the Treaty establishing the European Community, signed in Lisbon, 13 December 2007, OJ C 306, 17.12.2007, pp. 1–271.

191   Paul De Hert, 'The Right to Protection of Personal Data. Incapable of Autonomous Standing in the Basic EU Constituting Documents?' [2015] Utrecht Journal of International and European Law 1, 2.

192   See Bernardo Cortese, 'La protezione dei dati di carattere personale nel diritto dell'Unione Europea dopo il Trattato di Lisbona' [2013] Diritto dell'Unione Europea 313.

The entire structure of the EU privacy regulatory framework will change in the next few years, with the entry into force of a new Regulation. In January 2012 the European Commission published a 'Proposal for a Regulation of the European Parliament and of the Council on the protection of individuals with regard to the processing of personal data and on the free movement of such data', commonly known as the 'General Data Protection Regulation'.[193] After a few years of discussion, the Regulation was finally adopted in April 2016.[194]

The text includes some significant innovations, of which the most important is actually the decision to intervene on privacy through a Regulation instead of adopting a Directive: a first for the EU. EU Directives, of course, need to be implemented by each Member State, through internal legislation, whereas EU Regulations are directly applicable – verbatim and uniformly – in each Member State, as an automatic consequence of their adoption at the European level. The Regulation repeals Directive 95/46 and amends Directive 2002/58 and will enter into force on 25 May 2018. A Directive on the processing of personal data for criminal aims was adopted at the same time as the Regulation;[195] Member States must transpose it into their national systems by 8 May 2018.

The European Regulation contains some of the existing provisions and also introduces a number of new ones. The Regulation introduces new

---

[193]   The proposal (COM(2012) 11 final) is available at: <http://ec.europa.eu/justice/data-protection/document/review2012/com_2012_11_en.pdf> accessed 25 February 2017. For a preliminary comment on the main changes that the Regulation should introduce, see Paul De Hert and Vasilis Papakonstantinou, 'The Proposed Data Protection Regulation Replacing Directive 95/46/EC: A Sound System for the Protection of Individuals' [2012] Computer law & Security Review 130; Luiz Costa and Yves Poullet, 'Privacy and the Regulation of 2012' [2012] Computer Law & Security Review 254.

[194]   Regulation (EU) 2016/679 of the European Parliament and of the Council of 27 April 2016 on the protection of natural persons with regard to the processing of personal data and on the free movement of such data, and repealing Directive 95/46/EC (General Data Protection Regulation) [2016] L 119/1.

[195]   Directive (EU) 2016/680 of the European Parliament and of the Council of 27 April 2016 on the protection of natural persons with regard to the processing of personal data by competent authorities for the purposes of the prevention, investigation, detection or prosecution of criminal offences or the execution of criminal penalties, and on the free movement of such data, and repealing Council Framework Decision 2008/977/JHA [2016] L 119/89.

definitions of the data that nowadays needs strong protection, such as 'biometric data', 'data concerning health' and 'genetic data'.[196]

'Data protection officers' are another novelty: they will liaise with national privacy authorities and serve as contact points for data subjects; their main role will be to monitor the implementation of the Regulation inside the institution for which they work. All public authorities or bodies will have to employ a data protection officer, as will any enterprise whose core activity is either data processing that requires the regular and systematic monitoring of data subjects on a large scale or that involves large-scale processing of special categories of data.[197]

In addition, when the processing operations present specific risks to the rights and freedoms of the subjects to whom the data refers – for example in relation to the purposes for which the data is collected – each institution shall adopt a 'data protection impact assessment', i.e. 'an assessment of the impact of the envisaged processing operations on the protection of personal data'.[198]

The Regulation also introduces two important concepts, developed over recent years, namely 'privacy by design' and 'privacy by default'. The controller shall implement technical and organizational measures and procedures in order to ensure that the processing meets the requirements of the Regulation and thus guarantees the protection of personal data (privacy by design). In addition, the controller shall implement mechanisms to ensure that, for each specific purpose, only the necessary personal data is processed by default and that this data is not collected or kept beyond the minimum period necessary (privacy by default).

Another meaningful change is the acknowledgement of the 'right to be forgotten', sometimes also referred to as the 'right to oblivion'.[199] This right, which has been subject to much scholarly attention in recent years,[200] gained huge popularity after the so-called 'Google Spain' case, in which the Court of Justice stated that search engine operators must

---

[196] Art. 4, Reg. 2016/679.

[197] Arts. 37ff., Reg. 2016/679.

[198] Art. 35, Reg. 2016/679. On this issue see David Wright and Paul De Hert (eds), *Privacy Impact Assessment* (Springer 2012).

[199] Art. 17 introduces the 'right to erasure'.

[200] Among the most recent contributions see Steven C Bennett, 'The "Right to Be Forgotten": Reconciling EU and US Perspectives' [2012] Berkeley Journal of International Law 161; Dominic McGoldrick, 'Developments in the Right to be Forgotten' [2013] Human Rights Law Review 761; Alessandro Mantelero, 'The EU Proposal for a General Data Protection Regulation and the Roots of the "Right To Be Forgotten"' [2013] Computer Law & Security Review 229.

consider individuals' requests to remove links resulting from a search on their name, when these links connect to pages containing data that are inaccurate, i.e. 'inadequate, irrelevant or excessive in relation to the purposes of the processing, that they are not kept up to date, or that they are kept for longer than is necessary unless they are required to be kept for historical, statistical or scientific purposes'.[201] The Regulation considers the right to be forgotten as the right to obtain from the controller the erasure of personal data without undue delay. This right concerns data that is no longer necessary for the purposes for which it was collected; data for which the subject withdraws her consent, or for which the consented storage period has expired; or data whose processing does not comply with the Regulation for any other reason. In the event that the controller has made the data public, it shall take all reasonable measures to inform third parties that the data subject asked to have it erased. The controller shall expeditiously carry out the erasure, unless there are specific grounds for not doing so, for example the exercise of freedom of expression. In some other cases, instead of erasing the data, the controller can restrict its processing.[202]

Although the Regulation does not directly affect the cases analysed here, it sheds light on the European conception of the right to privacy and to personal data protection, and will allow us a better understanding of the solutions adopted by the Court of Justice of the EU and their influence on the Italian system analysed in the next chapter.

---

[201] C-131/12 *Google Spain SL, Google Inc. v. Agencia Española de Protección de Datos (AEPD), Mario Costeja González* [2014] ECLI:EU:C:2014:317, paras 92–94. The decision provoked an outcry, particularly with reference to the limitation on the freedom of expression; see, for example: Alessandro Mantelero, 'Il futuro regolamento EU sui dati personali e la valenza "politica" del caso Google: ricordare e dimenticare nella digital economy' [2014] Dir. Inf. e Informatica 681; Stefan Kulk and Frederik Zuiderveen Borgesius, 'Google Spain v. González: Did the Court Forget About Freedom of Expression?' [2014] European Journal of Risk Regulation 389; Hielke Hijmans, 'Right to Have Links Removed: Evidence of Effective Data Protection' [2014] Maastricht Journal of European and Comparative Law 555; Giovanni Sartor, 'The Right to Be Forgotten: Balancing Interests in the Flux of Time' [2015] International Journal of Law and Information Technology 72.

[202] Art. 17. See Giovanni Sartor, 'The Right to Be Forgotten in the Draft Data Protection Regulation' [2015] International Data Privacy Law 64.

3.3 Canada

The outline of the Canadian framework for personal data protection arising from the Charter of Rights and Freedoms (discussed in Section 2) has been supplemented by two important pieces of legislation. The first – the Privacy Act – enacted in 1985,[203] applies only to public entities; the second, which was adopted in 2001 and entered into force in 2004, the Personal Information Protection and Electronic Documents Act (PIPEDA),[204] regulates privacy and data protection in the private sector. PIPEDA changed the existing regulative landscape significantly. The Act itself – as the first ever to regulate the collection, use and disclosure of personal information in the private sector – was completely novel.[205] Previously, regulation of personal information in the private sector had been patchy and referred only to some sectors of the economy.[206]

Like both the US Privacy Act and the European legislation, PIPEDA is based on the OECD Guidelines,[207] while also explicitly incorporating the principles contained in the Canadian Standards Association's *Model Code for the Protection of Personal Information* of 1996.[208]

---

[203]   R.S.C. 1985, c. H-6. For a history of the enactment of the Canadian Privacy Act, see David H Flaherty, 'Reflection on Reform of Federal Privacy Act', Publications of the Office of the Privacy Commissioner of Canada, 2008, 6ff <www.priv.gc.ca/media/2044/pa_ref_df_e.pdf> accessed 25 February 2017. For a chronological list of Canadian federal legislation on privacy see David H Flaherty, *Protecting Privacy in Surveillance Societies* (North Carolina University Press 1992) 244.

[204]   S.C. 2000, c. 5. From 1 January 2004 the Act is applicable to all commercial activities in each province that has not passed 'substantially similar' legislation. For a history of the adoption of PIPEDA, see Perrin and others (n 54) 1ff.

[205]   See especially Part 1; Parts 2–5 are then aimed at 'moving federal legislation out of the "age of paper"', see Perrin and others (n 54) 125ff and Colin HH McNairn, *A Guide to the Personal Information Protection and Electronic Documents Act* (5th edn, LexisNexis 2010) 93ff for a comment.

[206]   McIsaac, Shields and Klein (n 6) 1-51.

[207]   Perrin and others (n 54) 22; William A Charnetski, Patrick Flaherty and Jeremy Robinson, *The Personal Information Protection and Electronic Documents Act. A Comprehensive Guide* (Canada Law Book 2001) 9.

[208]   CAN/CSA-Q830-96; see Schedule 1 of PIPEDA. For an overview of the principles: McIsaac, Shields and Klein (n 6) 4-31ff; Charnetski, Flaherty and Robinson (n 207) 38ff; for an explanation on how and why the CSA's principles were used as a base for PIPEDA and the strengths and weaknesses of this approach, see also Perrin and others (n 54) 3ff.

The first part of PIPEDA, entitled 'Protection of personal information in the private sector', was a response to both the fears and worries linked to digital technologies[209] and, very probably, to the European Privacy Directive 95/46. The Directive, and the laws consequently enacted by the Member States, restricted the transmission of personal information to foreign jurisdictions that lack privacy safeguards. In this regard, Canada's approach differs from that of the US, which, as previously seen, does not contemplate comprehensive private sector privacy legislation.[210]

After the amendments introduced in 2015, PIPEDA's current definition of 'personal information' is: 'information about an identifiable individual'.[211] The concept of 'identifiability' is key: when specific data, or a compilation of data, is attributable to a specific person, then it can constitute personal information. At the same time, data which could potentially identify a person, such as a first name, does not constitute personal information if, in the circumstances of the case, the organization does not hold any other information on the same person.[212] The Federal Court has adopted the following definition: '[i]nformation will be about an identifiable individual where there is a serious possibility that an individual could be identified through the use of that information, alone or in combination with other available information'.[213]

PIPEDA does not distinguish between sensitive and other kinds of data. The rationale behind this choice is that it is difficult to state a priori what information may be sensitive since there is no generally accepted view of what constitutes sensitive data.[214] Here we find a clear difference between the otherwise close legislation of Canada and Europe-Italy.

PIPEDA applies to all organizations and covers all the personal information that the organization collects, uses or discloses in its commercial activities. It also applies to the information, related to an organization's employees, that the organization collects, uses or discloses in connection with any federal work, undertaking or business. It is not

---

[209] Section 3, PIPEDA.

[210] See McIsaac, Shields and Klein (n 6) 4-4; Power (n 36) 61. The mechanism by which the EU regulated the transfer of European citizens' data to third countries will be briefly explained in Chapter 5, Section 2.

[211] Section 2, PIPEDA.

[212] This is the interpretation of the Office of the Privacy Commissioner, 'Your Privacy Responsibilities – A Guide for Businesses and Organizations' (2000) 2 <http://publications.gc.ca/collections/Collection/IP34-7-2000E.pdf> accessed 25 February 2017.

[213] *Gordon v. Canada*, 2008 FC 258, para 34.

[214] Perrin and others (n 54) 23.

applicable to any federal governmental institution to which the Privacy Act applies; nor to individuals that collect, use or disclose personal information only and solely for personal or domestic purposes; nor to organizations which collect, use or disclose this personal data for journalistic, artistic or literary purposes and not for any other purposes.[215]

The 2015 Digital Privacy Act included the definition of 'business contact information',[216] which is exempted from the application of PIPEDA and is intended as 'any information that is used for the purpose of communicating or facilitating communication with an individual in relation to their employment, business or profession such as the individual's name, position name or title, work address, work telephone number, work fax number or work electronic address'.[217]

One of the most important and perhaps most controversial principles of PIPEDA is 'consent', about which I shall later write, comparing the Italian and US experiences. Parallel to data subject consent is the requirement of 'appropriate purposes'. According to Section 5(3), '[a]n organization may collect, use or disclose personal information only for purposes that a reasonable person would consider are appropriate in the circumstances'. This means that a data subject's consent itself is not sufficient to lawfully collect her personal data. The 2015 amendments also intervened on the issue of 'consent', as I shall later illustrate.

PIPEDA empowers the Privacy Commissioner – already responsible for the enforcement of the federal Privacy Act – to receive complaints, conduct investigations and issue reports on her findings;[218] the Privacy Act can be considered the first effective Canadian regulation for privacy.

Prior to the decree of PIPEDA, privacy protection in Canada relied on multiple sources. In 1977 the Canadian Human Rights Act was enacted.[219] Its Section 2(b) stated that 'the privacy of individuals and their right of access to records containing personal information concerning them by any purpose including the purpose of ensuring accuracy and completeness should be protected to the greatest extent consistent with the public interest'. In 1983 this provision was repealed and not

---

[215] Sections 4(1) and 4(2) PIPEDA.
[216] Digital Privacy Act, S.C. 2015, c. 32, An Act to amend the Personal Information Protection and Electronic Documents Act and to make a consequential amendment to another Act.
[217] Section 4.01, PIPEDA.
[218] Sections 11–12 and 18–19, PIPEDA. See infra, section 5 for further details.
[219] S.C. 1976–77, c. 33. An earlier Act had been passed in 1974, the so-called Privacy Act, concerning wiretapping.

substituted; the matter has since been regulated by the Privacy Act. The Act concerns both the collection and use of personal information by federal government departments and agencies, and individuals' right of access to their data. The Privacy Act also introduced the figure of the Privacy Commissioner.

In addition, the Privacy Act introduced a parliamentary standing committee for the first time in order to establish a direct relationship between data protectors and the legislative body.[220]

This Act applies to government institutions, i.e. to all government departments, bodies and offices. The Privacy Act differs from the more recent PIPEDA not only in the range of its application, but also in the very definition of 'personal information'. While PIPEDA provides a loose definition,[221] the Privacy Act specifically details what should and should not be considered as personal data. Section 3 of the Privacy Act states that '*"personal information"* means information about an identifiable individual that is recorded in any form', including, but not limited to, information relating to the race, national or ethnic origin, colour, religion, age or marital status of the individual; information on the education or the medical, criminal or employment history of the individual; information relating to financial transactions in which the individual has been involved; identifying numbers, symbols or other particulars assigned to the individual; the individual's address, fingerprints or blood type; the individual's personal opinions or views; the individual's name where it appears with other personal information relating to the individual, or where the disclosure of the name itself would reveal information about the individual.[222] Clearly, much of this data would be classified as 'sensitive' in the European legislation.

The enactment of the PIPEDA decree has led to government departments and agencies now being subject to a lower standard in their management of personal data than they were prior to its enactment. Considering this negative effect of PIPEDA and given that the Privacy

---

[220] Flaherty, *Protecting Privacy* (n 203) 246.

[221] Possible amendments proposed in Bill S-4 (see below) also include a modification of the definition of 'personal information'.

[222] These are only some examples; many other cases, with some explicit exceptions, are listed. See Section 3 of the Privacy Act. For a comparison between the definition provided by PIPEDA and the one provided by the Privacy Act, see McNairn (n 205) 30ff.

Act is more than 30 years old, scholars have claimed that the latter should be reformed.[223]

As well as the federal Privacy Act, the provinces and territories of Canada – with the exception of New Brunswick – enacted regulations for access to information and privacy.[224] In the private sector, however, at the time of PIPEDA's decree, only Québec had already (in 1994) passed its own legislation.[225] After the introduction of PIPEDA, other Canadian states passed specific laws. In 2004 British Columbia and Alberta promulgated their statutes.[226] In the same year Ontario approved an Act to regulate personal information in the health sector.[227] In 2008 New-foundland and Labrador passed legislation, as did New Brunswick in 2009.[228]

---

[223] Flaherty, 'Reflection on Reform' (n 203) 12ff. The author also includes some previous efforts at reform (see spec. 9ff).

[224] See Freedom of Information and Protection of Privacy Act, R.S.B.C. 1996, c. 165 (B.C.); Freedom of Information and Protection of Privacy Act, S.A. 1994, c. F-18.5 (Alberta); Freedom of Information and Protection of Privacy Act, S.S. 1990–91, c. F-22.01 (Sask.); Local Authority Freedom of Information and Protection of Privacy Act, S.M. 1997 c. 50 (Man.); Freedom of Information and Protection of Privacy Act, R.S.O. 1990, F.31, c. M. 56 (ON); Municipal Freedom of Information and Protection of Privacy Act, R.S.O. 1990, c. M. 56 (ON); An Act respecting Access to documents held by public bodies and the Protection of Personal Information, R.S.Q., c. A-2.1 (Qc); Freedom of Information and Protection of Privacy Act, S.N.S. 1993, c. 5 (N.S.); Access to Information and Protection of Privacy Act, S.N.L. 2002, c. A-1.1; Access to Information and Protection of Privacy Act, S.Y.T. 1995, c. 1 (Yukon); Access to Information and Protection of Privacy Act, S.N.W.T. 1994, c. 20 (N.W.T.). See Power (n 36) 7–11; McIsaac, Shields and Klein (n 6) 3-34.1ff.

[225] Act respecting the protection of personal information in the private sector, R.S.Q., c. P-39.1. Québec had also included a constitutional protection for privacy: Section 5 of the Québec Charter of Human Rights and Freedoms states that '[e]very person has a right to respect for his private life', see R.S.Q., c. C-12, Section 5. Furthermore, the Civil Code of Québec, as amended in 1987, recognizes a right to privacy in its art. 3, and provides in its Chapter III norms for the 'Respect of Reputation and Privacy' (S.Q., 1991, c. 64, arts. 35–41).

[226] British Columbia Personal Information Protection Act, S.B.C. 2003, c. 63 and Alberta Personal Information Protection Act, S.A. 2003, c. P-6.5. Both these Acts and the Québec one have a wider range than the federal Act: see McIsaac, Shields and Klein (n 6) 4-56ff, also with regard to problems concerning the relation between the provincial and federal Personal Information Acts.

[227] Personal Health Information Protection Act, 2004, S.O. 2004, c. 3, Schedule A [PHIPA].

[228] Respectively: Personal Health Information Act, SNL 2008, c P-7.01; Personal Health Information Privacy and Access Act, SNB 2009, c P-7.05.

PIPEDA allows any state law 'substantially similar' to PIPEDA itself to be applicable instead of the federal Act. As all of the above regulations are considered 'substantially similar' to PIPEDA, in these provinces the collection, use and disclosure of personal information is governed by provincial law. However, in the event that a law for any specific sector has not been decreed, PIPEDA applies. The same system works for laws relating solely to employers' privacy. When personal information goes outside the province, federal legislation applies. Unfortunately, in certain cases it is not clear whether PIPEDA, or the provincial regulation, or both, are applicable.[229]

In 2010 the Canadian Parliament passed an 'anti-spam law', a part of which came into force in 2014, the remainder in 2015.[230] The law relates to a number of different issues concerning electronic messages and computer programs, including e-address harvesting; misleading online representations in the promotion of products or services; installation of computer programs without the computer owner's consent; and collection of personal information via access to a computer in violation of federal law.

Some other Bills, based on specific requests, have been introduced in the last few years and will encroach on PIPEDA.[231] The Bills are, in fact, a response to Section 29 of PIPEDA: this section requires the Canadian Parliament to review Part 1 – which deals with data protection – of the Act, every five years. One of these Bills, the Digital Privacy Act, which

---

[229] McIsaac, Shields and Klein (n 6) 4-55–56.

[230] An Act to promote the efficiency and adaptability of the Canadian economy by regulating certain activities that discourage reliance on electronic means of carrying out commercial activities, and to amend the Canadian Radio-television and Telecommunications Commission Act, the Competition Act, the Personal Information Protection and Electronic Documents Act and the Telecommunications Act (S.C. 2010, c. 23).

[231] Office of the Privacy Commissioner of Canada, 'The Case For Reforming The Personal Information Protection and Electronic Documents Act (May 2013) <www.priv.gc.ca/en/privacy-topics/privacy-laws-in-canada/the-personal-information-protection-and-electronic-documents-act-pipeda/pipeda_r/pipeda_r_201305/> accessed 25 February 2017. Bill C-29, An Act to amend the Personal Information Protection and Electronic Documents Act (Safeguarding Canadians' Personal Information Act), 40th Parliament, 3rd Session, May 25, 2010; Bill C-12 (identical to Bill C-29), An Act to amend the Personal Information Protection and Electronic Documents Act, 40th Parliament, 1st Session, September 29, 2011; Bill C-475, An Act to amend the Personal Information Protection and Electronic Documents Act (order-making power), 41st Parliament, 2nd Session, October 16, 2013. Defeated January 29, 2014.

became law in 2015, has considerably modified PIPEDA. As already mentioned, this Act amended the PIPEDA definition of 'personal information'. It also affected the issue of subject consent, upgrading the requirements needed to obtain consent, and added exemptions where data can be used without the data subject's consent. The Digital Privacy Act also introduced a security breach notification regime, similar to the Italian. This includes offences of failing to comply with obligations related to data security breaches.

Many other modifications relate to the issue of consent and to the exceptions under which consent is not needed.[232]

2015 also saw the passing of the 'Anti-Terrorism Act'.[233] In response to the attack on the Parliament of Ottawa in October 2014, the main scope of the Act is to allow the disclosure of citizens' information in order to prevent terrorism and to strengthen national security. Although the Act does not specifically amend any of the privacy Acts, it has nevertheless been criticized for undermining privacy protection.[234] Indeed, the Act was immediately constitutionally challenged by civil liberties associations, which considered it too broad and excessively intrusive.[235]

---

[232]   See below next section. For a short account and some criticism, see Office of the Privacy Commissioner of Canada, 'Bill S-4, An Act to amend the Personal Information Protection and Electronic Documents Act and to make a consequential amendment to another Act. Submission to the Senate Standing Committee on Transport and Communications' (4 June 2014) <www.priv.gc.ca/en/opc-actions-and-decisions/advice-to-parliament/2015/parl_sub_150212/> accessed 25 February 2017; Dara Lithwick, 'Bill S-4: An Act to amend the Personal Information Protection and Electronic Documents Act and to make a consequential amendment to another Act, Legislative Summary, Library of the Parliament', Publication n. 41-2-S-4E (11 June 2014) <www.parl.gc.ca/Content/LOP/LegislativeSummaries/41/2/s4-e.pdf> accessed 25 February 2017.

[233]   S.C. 2015, c. 20, An Act to enact the Security of Canada Information Sharing Act and the Secure Air Travel Act, to amend the Criminal Code, the Canadian Security Intelligence Service Act and the Immigration and Refugee Protection Act and to make related and consequential amendments to other Acts.

[234]   Michael Geist, 'Privacy Under Attack in Anti-Terror Bill', *The Toronto Star* (24 March 2015) <www.thestar.com/business/2015/03/13/privacy-under-attack-in-anti-terror-bill-geist.htm> accessed 25 February 2017.

[235]   Dan Taekama, 'Journalist group and civil liberties association start constitutional challenge to anti-terrorism Bill C-51', *The Toronto Star* (21 July 2015) <www.thestar.com/news/gta/2015/07/21/journalist-group-and-civil-liberties-association-start-constitutional-challenge-to-anti-terrorism-bill-c-51.html> accessed 25 February 2017.

Parallel to the provisions described above, privacy is also protected by some tort law provisions. However, unlike in the US, these tort statutes have only been introduced at a provincial level, and only by some provinces, under the name of 'tort of invasion of privacy'. They all contain similar prescriptions: when a person, wilfully and without a claim of right, violates the privacy of another. In determining whether the act of one person violates the privacy of another, courts shall consider the nature, incidence and occasion of the act. Importance is also given to the kind of relationship existing between the parties.[236] In the remaining provinces there is no privacy tort. The courts have never recognized common law privacy torts, with a few exceptions, such as a 2012 decision by the Court of Appeal for Ontario,[237] when the Court explicitly recognized a 'right of action for intrusion upon seclusion'. The Court recognized that such a right would be appropriate to the court's role in developing 'common law in a manner consistent with the changing needs of society'.[238] The phrasing 'Intrusion upon seclusion' clearly recalls the US tort with the same name; the Court, indeed, frequently referred to the work of William Prosser.[239] In 2016, again referring to Prosser's classification, the Ontario Superior Court of Justice introduced the tort of 'public disclosure of private facts'.[240]

---

[236] British Columbia (R.S.B.C. 1996, c. 373); Manitoba (R.S.M. 1987, c. P125); Newfoundland and Labrador (S.N. 1981, c.6) and Saskatchewan (R.S.S 1978, c. P-24). All these Acts are called 'Privacy Acts'. Wilfulness is not required in the tort figure of Manitoba. The Québec Civil Code includes provisions that also cover privacy as a delict. Sec McIsaac, Shields and Klein (n 6) 2-58-51ff; Power (n 36) 193ff; McNairn and Scott (n 10) 41ff. In favour of an introduction of a common law tort of invasion of privacy, see Craig (n 10); David A Cornfield, 'The Right to Privacy in Canada' [1967] Toronto Faculty of Law Review 103; Alex Cameron and Mimi Palmer, 'Invasion of Privacy as a Common Law Tort in Canada' [2009] Canadian Privacy Law Review 105. See as early as 1976 Peter Burns, 'The Law and Privacy: The Canadian Experience' [1976] Revue du Barreau Canadien/Canadian Bar Review 1, spec. 12–28.

[237] *Jones v. Tsige*, 2012 ONCA 32, reversing *Jones v. Tsige*, 2011 ONCA 1475. For previous Ontario cases where a common law right of privacy emerged, see Craig (n 10) 367–369.

[238] *Jones v. Tsige*, 2012 (n 237) para 65.

[239] Ibid, passim, spec. paras 16–22.

[240] *Doe 464533 v. ND*, 2016 ONSC 541.

Other torts have been applied to protect privacy: breach of confidence, defamation, breach of copyright and nuisance, among others.[241] Nonetheless, these torts cannot cover all aspects of privacy, particularly those related to information.[242]

The above outline of the Canadian framework for privacy and personal data protection clearly demonstrates its greater proximity to the Italian than to the American framework. This similarity between the Canadian and Italian approaches also extends to the manner in which two critical but crucial issues – the subject's consent and the data protection authorities – which are discussed in the following sections.

4. A CONTROVERSIAL ISSUE: SUBJECT'S CONSENT

The data subject's consent is a very critical issue in any regulation for privacy and personal data. As previously mentioned, consent is one of the cornerstones of all Italian and Canadian legislation. In contrast, US regulation does not normally rely on the subject's permission, apart from in some specific cases.[243]

In systems such as the Canadian or Italian, consent represents a way for an individual to exercise her right to personal identity. Indeed, consent is the only tool with which the data subject can control her data flows. Whenever a person denies her consent, she is deciding to keep her information secret. On the other hand, whenever a person gives her consent, she is deciding to move from a secret identity to a 'controlled' identity.[244]

---

[241]   *Jones v. Tsige*, 2012 (n 237) para 15. See, again, Burns (n 236) spec. 12–28.

[242]   For a detailed examination of the existing torts and their role in defending privacy, see Craig (n 10) 381ff.

[243]   Consider, for instance, the Videotape Privacy Protection Act of 1988 (Pub. Law No. 100–618), § 2710(b)(2): 'A video tape service provider may disclose personally identifiable information concerning any consumer … to any person with the *informed, written consent* (including through an electronic means using the Internet) of the consumer' (emphasis added).

[244]   See Antonio Fici and Enza Pellecchia, 'Il consenso al trattamento' in Pardolesi, *Diritto alla riservatezza* (n 151) 499. Consent is the most complete expression of the right to control the movement of one's own personal data out of one's privacy sphere; see Giovanni Comandè, 'Artt. 11 e 12 (Consenso – Casi di esclusione del consenso)' in Giannantonio, Losano and Zeno Zencovich (n 151) 133; Buttarelli (n 12) 489ff.

Despite its centrality in protecting privacy, the requirement for subject consent has been criticized for frequently being overlooked in practice.[245] This is especially true in the online environment, where simple 'ticks' or 'clicks' habitually substitute oral and even written consent, often as 'default settings'.[246]

Many studies highlight the psychological-cognitive limits of consent, even when it is informed.[247] As is well known, the documents detailing the reasons and methods of data processing are usually so long and complicated that the data subjects concerned very rarely read them, particularly given the previously mentioned cognitive limits.

The OECD Guidelines included the 'use limitation principle', according to which 'personal data should not be disclosed, made available or otherwise used for purposes other than those specified in accordance with [purpose specification principle] except: a) *with the consent of the data subject*; or b) by the authority of law'.[248] The countries that implemented

---

[245] For issues relating to consent in Italian legislation, see Salvatore Patti, 'Il consenso dell'interessato al trattamento dei dati personali' [1999] Riv. dir. Civile, part II 455; Niger (n 55) 150ff. The actual efficacy of the consent expressed by the data subject was questioned as early as 1973 by Rodotà, *Elaboratori elettronici* (n 138) 45ff, who talks of 'the myth of consent'. For a critical approach to the centrality of consent in PIPEDA, see Lisa M Austin, 'Is Consent the Foundation of Fair Information Practices? Canada's Experience under Pipeda' [2006] University of Toronto Law Journal 181. For a thoroughly researched account of consent in the European legislation, see Eleni Kosta, *Consent in European Data Protection Law* (Brill Publishing 2013).

[246] Recital no. 17 of EU Directive 2002/58, states '... Consent may be given by any appropriate method enabling a freely given specific and informed indication of the user's wishes, *including by ticking a box* when visiting an Internet website' (emphasis added). The Working Party emphasized that this way of collecting personal data does not comply with the requirements of Directive 95/46, see Article 29 Working Party, 'Opinion 15/2011 on the Definition of Consent', WP 187 (12 July 2011) *passim* <http://ec.europa.eu/justice/policies/privacy/docs/wpdocs/2011/wp187_en.pdf> accessed 25 February 2017.

[247] See the works cited by Solove, 'Privacy Self-Management' (n 71) 1883ff, where the author explains the cognitive problems of consent. See also Alessandro Acquisti and Jens Grossklags, 'Privacy Attitudes and Privacy Behavior. Losses, Gains, and Hyperbolic Discounting' in L Jean Camp and Stephen Lewis (eds), *The Economics of Information Security* (Springer 2004) 165; Alessandro Acquisti, 'Privacy in Electronic Commerce and the Economics of Immediate Gratification' in *Proceedings of the 5th ACM conference on Electronic commerce* (ACM 2004) 21.

[248] Emphasis added.

these principles in their legislation approached the issue of consent in different ways.

Directive 95/46 provides its own definition of consent in art. 2(h): 'any freely given specific and informed indication of his wishes by which the data subject signifies his agreement to personal data relating to him being processed'.[249] Article 7 of the same Directive affirms that Member States shall ensure that data are processed only with the *unambiguous* consent of the data subject.[250]

The text of the 1995 Directive neither explicitly requires an 'opt-in' system nor excludes an 'opt-out'. Nonetheless, the requirement that the data subject give her consent seems to imply that simple inaction does not constitute consent.[251]

Ten years after the enactment of the Directive, the Article 29 Working Party indicated four criteria for legally valid consent:

1. Consent must be a clear and unambiguous indication of wishes.
2. Consent must be given freely.
3. Consent must be specific.
4. Consent must be informed.[252]

With the exception of sensitive data, it should be highlighted that under no circumstances is there either a total absence of protection or an absolute impossibility to process information. This means that no data is characterized by absolute publicity, since even the processing of data already in the public domain can be legitimately opposed by its data subject.[253]

As a result of the EU approach, Italian regulation on privacy and data protection has always taken the issue of consent very seriously. Article 11 of Legge 675/96 provided that the processing of personal data by private people or public entities was allowed only with the expressed consent of the data subject. The subject could consent to the entire processing or to

---

[249] For a detailed analysis of how 'consent' was drafted in the European legislation, see Kosta (n 245) 85ff.

[250] Directive 95/46/EC, art. 7(a); emphasis added.

[251] Christopher Kuner, *European Data Protection Law. Corporate Compliance and Regulation* (OUP 2007) 69.

[252] Article 29 Working Party, 'Working document on a common interpretation of Article 26(1) of Directive 95/46/EC of 24 October 1995' (25 November 2005) 10–12 <http://ec.europa.eu/justice/policies/privacy/docs/wpdocs/2005/wp114_en.pdf> accessed 25 February 2017.

[253] Rodotà, 'Persona, riservatezza, identità' (n 59) 591–592.

one or more parts of it. Furthermore, consent was valid only when given freely, in a written, specific form, and only if certain information, described in art. 10, had previously been given to the subject. Article 12 then listed the specific and exclusive cases in which consent was not needed.

The current *Codice Privacy* contains the same structure. Article 13 prescribes the content of the information that must precede the data subject's consent: it needs to cover the scope and methods of the data processing; the compulsory or optional nature of data conferring; the consequences of an eventual refusal to confer; the subject or category of subjects to whom the data can be communicated, and the range of diffusion of the same; and the identification information of the people handling the data. The information sheet must also list the subject's rights provided by art. 7, linked to the possibility of data access, modification, rectification, updating, cancellation and so on.

As in Legge 675/96, consent needs to be expressed, freely given, and documented; it can cover all, or part of, the processing. When consent refers to sensitive data it must be given in written form (art. 23).[254]

Directive 95/46 and the subsequent Italian implementation allow for a number of exceptions that accept the processing of personal data without the subject's consent. Article 24 of the Privacy Code considers consent unnecessary – for instance – in the event that data is needed to comply with an obligation according to national or European law; processing is necessary to execute contractual obligations; data comes from public registers, lists or acts that can be easily accessed by anyone; or it is needed to protect the life of a third person. Furthermore, Part II of the Code, which relates to specific sectors, also lists some particular exceptions in certain sectors, such as the judicial, or law and order. In some cases, consent is needed only if and when data is communicated to a third person: this is the case for data processed within an association or other non-profit entity on behalf of that body's members.

Article 25 further specifies that the communication and the diffusion of data is forbidden when the subject has asked for the deletion of the data; when the time for which the data was collected has expired; and when

---

[254] See, also, art. 26 for the warranties adopted for the protection of sensitive data. Although the request for specific written consent also existed in Legge 675/96, it was included in art. 22 on sensitive data. Some authors have claimed that the part played by consent in the processing of personal data has changed as it is now only necessary when dealing with sensitive data. See Maria Antonia Garzia, 'Art. 24. Casi nei quali può essere effettuato il trattamento senza consenso' in Bianca and Busnelli (eds) (n 165) 559–560.

communication or diffusion would be made for purposes different from those for which data was collected.

No exceptions other than those provided by the law can be applied.

The above concerns only what might be termed 'normal' data. As already mentioned, sensitive data receives different treatment, since it can only be processed with the prior authorization of the Privacy Authority and the explicit written consent of the data subject.

While explicit consent is currently needed only for sensitive data, the General Data Protection Regulation requires that consent always be 'explicit'. In the Explanatory memorandum for the Regulation proposal, the European Commission clarified that 'in the definition of consent, the criterion "explicit" is added to avoid confusing parallelism with "un-ambiguous" consent and in order to have one single and consistent definition of consent, ensuring the awareness of the data subject that, and to what, he or she gives consent'.[255]

Finally, it is important to note that art. 8 of the EU Charter of Fundamental Rights also recognizes that consent is paramount, when stating that personal data can be processed 'on the basis of the consent of the person concerned or some other legitimate basis laid down by law'.

The General Data Protection Regulation not only confirms the approach of the pre-existing legislation, but also strengthens the protection of privacy since it introduces new, specific requirements.[256] For instance, a completely new provision regulates children's consent in relation to information society services.[257]

The Canadian legislative approach is quite similar to the Italian one. As a general principle, PIPEDA requires the knowledge and consent of the person concerned for the collection, use or disclosure of her personal data, except where inappropriate. 'Informed consent' means that the organization must make a reasonable effort to ensure that the person is advised of the purposes for which her data is used. The purposes must be formulated in a manner that the person can reasonably understand.[258]

---

[255]   Explanatory Memorandum of the Proposal for a General Data Protection Regulation, Section 3.4.1: <www.europarl.europa.eu/RegData/docs_autres_institutions/commission_europeenne/com/2012/0011/COM_COM(2012)0011_EN.pdf> accessed 25 February 2017.

[256]   Art. 7, Reg. 2016/679.

[257]   Art. 8, Reg. 2016/679.

[258]   PIPEDA, Schedule 1 – 'Principles Set Out in the National Standard of Canada Entitled *Model Code for the Protection of Personal Information*, CAN/CSA-Q830-96' – 4.3 Principle 3 Consent. For an overview of the requirement for consent in provincial legislations, see Power (n 36) 71–74.

Consent may be given in many different ways and may be withdrawn at any time.[259] Nevertheless, in some circumstances, PIPEDA considers consent to be to some extent 'presumed' and provides some exceptions for the collection, use and disclosure without either the data subject's knowledge or her consent. For instance, data can be collected when it is clearly in the interest of the individual to do so and the latter's consent could not be obtained in a timely way; when it is reasonable to expect that the individual's consent would compromise the availability or the accuracy of the information, and the collection is reasonable for purposes related to a breach of law; when the information is publicly available; and when the information is used only for journalistic, artistic or literary purposes.[260] Collected data can, in some instances, be used at a later date without consent. For instance, this is possible when data is needed in a situation in which the life, health or security of an individual is threatened,[261] very much as under Italian law. PIPEDA also lists some cases in which disclosure is possible without either the knowledge or the consent of the subject. These cases usually involve government requests, law enforcement and court orders.[262] Specifically, Section 7(3)(c) permits the disclosure of personal information in response to 'a subpoena or warrant issued or an order made by a court, person or body with jurisdiction to compel the production of information, or to comply with rules of court relating to the production of records'. This provision has proved to be particularly significant in the judicial cases analysed in this book.

Following the 2015 amendments, PIPEDA currently requires consent to be 'valid'. The Act itself specifies that consent is valid 'if it is reasonable to expect that the individual understands the nature, purpose and consequences of the collection, use or disclosure of personal information to which they are consenting'.[263] This amendment asks organizations to make a greater effort to clarify the purposes for and the ways in which data are collected; it is intended to ensure that individuals are not misleadingly forced to give personal data.[264] The Canadian

---

[259] Perrin and others (n 54) 22ff.
[260] Section 7(1) PIPEDA.
[261] Section 7(2) PIPEDA.
[262] Section 7(3) PIPEDA. The Act also includes cases in which data can be used and disclosed without consent, provided that the subject has knowledge of the processing. See Section 7(4) and Section 7(5). See Power (n 36) 74–76, for the exceptions to consent in provincial privacy regulations.
[263] Section 6(1) PIPEDA.
[264] Lithwick (n 232) 4.

Privacy Commissioner's Office considers that this measure will make consent more meaningful, especially for young people living in the digital world.[265] The Digital Privacy Act has added other exceptions to the requirement of consent.[266]

The Privacy Act of 1983 also contains specific provisions about data subject consent. Under Section 7 of the Act, personal information possessed by a government institution can be used without the individual's consent for the purpose for which the information was collected, or for a use consistent with that purpose. Section 8 lists the cases in which disclosure is possible without the consent of the individual. These cases are, again, mainly linked to government requests, compliance with law, court orders and legal enforcement.

The 2010 Canadian anti-spam law includes particular provisions for consent: it creates an 'opt-in' regime applicable to a large variety of electronic messages, including instant messages and messages for commercial purposes. The Act also prescribes that the express consent of an individual must be obtained before a computer program can be installed on that person's computer, mainly in order to combat spyware. This Act is obviously intended to increase the ability of the subject to manage her data effectively, especially online. It remains to be seen how this regulation will actually modify the existing scenario. Nonetheless, it clearly represents another attempt to improve the protection of personal data.

It is worth noting the Privacy Commissioner's observation that the fact that a collection of personal data is 'reasonable' does not in itself obviate the need for consent.[267]

The American approach to consent is much less clear than the Canadian and Italian frameworks; it is also rather flimsy. As already mentioned, consent plays a marginal role in the American context: personal data is usually collected, used and disclosed without the subject's consent; the latter normally only has the choice of 'opting out'. This means, for example, that whenever a consumer buys a product, her data is automatically processed by the sales company. The default rule allows the data holder to keep the data, with broad discretion in handling

---

[265] See Office of the Privacy Commissioner of Canada (n 232).
[266] Section 7(1)(b.1), (b.2); Section 7(2)(b.1), (b.2), (c.1); Section (3)(c.1), (c.2), (d.1), (d.2), (d.3), (d.4), (e.1), (e.2), (h.1), (h.2).
[267] McIsaac, Shields and Klein (n 6) 4-51.

it. If the consumer wants to halt this processing of her data, she has to opt out, which few people actually do.[268]

Some parts of the US regulation request information notice to individuals, with a system termed 'notice and choice': these entities provide the individual with information and give them 'a choice to *opt out* of *some* of the forms of data collection and use described in the notices'.[269] An example of legislation that allows users to opt out is the Gramm-Leach-Bliley Act,[270] which requires financial institutions to provide customers with information concerning the disclosure of personal data to third parties and allows them to opt out of data sharing with third parties.

In accordance with the FOIA, disclosure of an individual's information to any person or to another agency is subject to the individual's own consent. However, there are exceptions – related, for example, to law enforcement or to the sharing of information among federal agencies, – when that information is to be used in civil or criminal law enforcement. Among these exceptions is that of 'routine use': whenever disclosure is compatible with the purposes for which the first agency initially collected the record, the information can be disclosed to another federal agency without the consent of the person to whom the information is related.[271] The same approach is taken within the Privacy Act. The Act itself, in its Section 3(b), requires the prior consent of the data subject but, at the same time, again provides the 'routine use' exception, which greatly undermines the very idea of consent.

Overall, provisions asking for consent prior to data collection, like those in the Videotape Privacy Protection Act of 1988,[272] are rare.

State laws also sometimes require prior consent.[273] However, these same laws often provide quite large exceptions to consent, similarly to

---

[268] Soma and Rynerson (n 15) 180; Solove, 'Privacy Self-Management' (n 71) 1884.

[269] Solove, 'Privacy Self-Management' (n 71) 1183–1884 (emphasis added).

[270] Pub. Law No. 106-102, 113 Stat. 1338, codified in the U.S.C. See, in particular, 15 U.S.C. § 6802(a)–(b). For an analysis of the default rules introduced by this Act, see Edward J Janger and Paul M Schwartz, 'The Gramm-Leach-Bliley Act, Information Privacy, and the Limits of Default Rules' [2002] Minnesota Law Review 1219, 1230.

[271] See 5 U.S. Code § 552a(b)(3). Conditions of disclosure are listed in § 552a(b)(1)–(12), and in § 552a(k) and 552a(j).

[272] See, for instance, the Video Privacy Protection Act of 1988, Pub. Law No. 100-618, 18 U.S.C. §§ 2710–2711.

[273] As an example see the Vermont opt-in approach, in Department of Banking, Insurance, Securities & Health Care Administration Banking Division,

the federal Acts. In other words, US laws usually allow personal data processing, unless a particular law specifically prohibits the activity[274] or users opt out – when this is possible.

Research has shown that so much time and money has to be spent understanding how to opt out that consumers do not bother to do so. Many people find it difficult – or impossible – to understand the information given to them. Moreover, opting-out systems seem to generate higher transaction costs than do opting-in systems. Businesses may, of course, have a vested interest in not lowering opt-out transaction costs. Opting in thus appears preferable since it makes it more likely that consumers choose according to their preferences.[275] Other studies suggest the opposite. Some scholars have claimed that an opt-in system would be more costly than an opt-out one since the former would restrict the free flow of information that is vital for current economic activity. Companies would have to obtain consumers' consent, contacting them individually to ask if they want to 'opt in'. This extra step would render an opt-in system much more expensive than an opt-out one, which assumes the permission of consumers who do not explicitly object.[276]

Although the positive and negative sides of both opt-in and opt-out have frequently been pointed out, in fact the two systems probably do not actually differ greatly. This is especially true online, where consent is simply de facto neglected.[277] It is, however, true that the Canadian and European-Italian approaches tend towards higher protection of personal data and privacy, trying to give subjects the tools with which to manage their own information through consent. In contrast, in the US the

---

Regulation B-2001-01 – 'Privacy of Consumer Financial and Health Information Regulation'.

[274]   Paul M Schwartz, 'The EU–US Privacy Collision: A Turn to Institutions and Procedures' [2013] Harvard Law Review 1966, 1976. This is what the author calls 'regulatory parsimony'.

[275]   Sovern (n 74) 1081ff.

[276]   See Michael E Staten and Fred H Cate, 'The Impact of Opt-in Privacy Rules on Retail Credit Markets: A Case Study of MBNA' [2003] Duke Law Journal 745, 765–766. On some issues of opt-in, see Nicklas Lundblad and Betsy Masiello, 'Opt-in Dystopias' [2010] SCRIPTed 155, spec. 162ff <https://script-ed. org/wp-content/uploads/2016/07/7-1-Lundblad.pdf> accessed 25 February 2017.

[277]   See Solove, 'Privacy Self-Management' (n 71) spec. 1897, who finds that in the online environment there are no differences between the two approaches. See Article 29 Working Party, 'The Future of Privacy' (1 December 2009) 8 and 17   <http://ec.europa.eu/justice/policies/privacy/docs/wpdocs/2009/wp168_en. pdf> accessed 25 February 2017, which states that confusion between opt-in and opt-out should be avoided.

majority of cases are governed by an opt-out scheme and data processing does not require the prior consent of the subject.

5. DATA PROTECTION AUTHORITIES AND THEIR ROLE

The last aspect of the current privacy situation in the three countries that we will consider is their data protection authorities or comparable entities. An understanding of the functions and roles of these institutions – different in the three countries – gives us greater insight into the countries' underlying conceptions of privacy and data protection.

Once again, as I shall now illustrate, Canada and Italy followed one path, and the US another.

The European Directive of 1995 required Member States to set up a national Supervisory Authority and each Member State now has at least one Supervisory Authority. However, the structures of these authorities vary quite considerably.[278] Some people see this requirement for a public body as typical of the EU's approach since the Union usually prefers that such roles be fulfilled by public authorities.[279]

The Italian *Garante per la tutela delle persone e di altri soggetti rispetto al trattamento dei dati personali*, whose title was later modified to *Garante per la protezione dei dati personali* (usually known as the *Garante della privacy*), was introduced with Legge 675/96.[280]

The Authority's powers and regulations have remained the same under the Privacy Code, art. 153 of which states that the Authority operates autonomously, with judicial independence and the right to make its own evaluations. The *Garante* is a four-member collective body, elected by the two branches of the Parliament. Its members are chosen on the basis of their expertise in the fields of law or informatics, and in the hope that they can be trusted to safeguard independence; they choose one of their fellows as president.

---

[278] See Art. 28, Directive 95/46/EC. Germany is an exception since it has a Federal Data Protection Commissioner (Bundesbeauftragte für den Datenschutz und die Informationsfreiheit), and each *Land* has its own Authority. On the organization of national Privacy Authorities, see Kuner (n 251) 14–15.

[279] Peter Hustinx, 'The Role of Data Protection Authorities' in Serge Gutwirth, Yves Poullet, Paul de Hert, Cécile de Terwangne and Sjaak Nouwt (eds), *Reinventing Data Protection?* (Springer 2009) 131, 133.

[280] For an overview, see Roberto D'Orazio, 'Art. 30. Istituzione del Garante' in Giannantonio, Losano and Zeno Zencovich (n 151) 397.

To ensure the independence of the board, the members of the Authority are appointed for seven years, and can serve only one term, during which they are not allowed to hold elective office.

Article 154 describes the Authority's tasks, which can be divided into four main categories: control, jurisdiction, advice and information.[281] Control involves monitoring the processing of personal data and ensuring that such processing is in compliance with privacy regulations and the other formalities required by the Privacy Code. The Authority keeps a general register of the processing of data, based on the notifications it receives. This register is intended to allow everyone to know what data is collected and which database it is being stored in, thus increasing the transparency of data processing and storage.

The *Garante*'s jurisdictional tasks include receiving notices and complaints from individuals and associations and, when necessary, applying appropriate measures. Although it cannot apply sanctions, the *Garante* can inhibit illicit behaviour and it has the power to decide cases related to privacy or data protection: art. 145 allows data subjects to enforce their rights listed under art. 7 by filing a claim before either the judicial authorities or the *Garante della privacy*.[282]

This jurisdictional power clearly complements the control function: the Authority begins the process of controlling an entity's compliance with the Privacy Code in its data processing after receiving notification from a private person. Subsequent to this process, the *Garante* can adopt any suitable measures,[283] among which the prohibition or blocking – either partial or total – of processing.

The *Garante* can also participate in existing lawsuits involving issues of privacy and data protection; this capacity has proved to be very important in some cases, including the lawsuits analysed in this book.

In its advisory role, the Authority can suggest the adoption of new regulations to protect privacy and data protection to Parliament and government. Moreover, the government has to consult the Authority when planning norms or acts which could affect personal data protection,[284] thus enabling the *Garante* to evaluate any possible conflict of the

---

[281] I borrow this classification from Giulia Pasetti, 'Il garante per la protezione dei dati personali' in Monducci and Sartor (n 165) 513.

[282] Massimiliano Granieri, 'Il sistema della tutela diritti nella legge 675/1996' in Pardolesi (ed) (n 151) 437; Buttarelli (n 12) 463ff.

[283] See Granieri (n 282) and Beatrice Cunegatti, 'Tutela amministrativa e giurisdizionale' in Monducci and Sartor (eds) (n 165) 487ff.

[284] Art. 154, co. 4 Privacy Code.

would-be norms with principles preserving privacy before the new legislation is passed.

The *Garante* is also required to take steps to increase citizens' awareness of privacy regulation, with a particular duty to encourage the adoption of deontological codes, whose accordance with the law the Authority must ensure.[285] In addition, the *Garante* formulates guidelines which help institutions, such as schools, associations, enterprises etc., to deal with personal data in a manner consistent with the law.

The General Data Protection Regulation confirms the need to have at least one Privacy Authority in each Member State. In comparison with the text of Directive 95/46, the Regulation introduces more precise requirements for data processing and provides for more specific powers for the Authority.[286] It remains to be seen how deep the changes to each national Privacy Authority will be.

The EU, in addition to the national authorities, has also set up two other entities: the European Data Protection Supervisor (EDPS) and the 'Article 29 Working Party'. The EDPS – prescribed by the Treaty of Amsterdam[287] and introduced by Regulation 45/2001[288] – is responsible for the monitoring of the personal data processing carried out by EU institutions and bodies. It can issue opinions on specific subjects related to data protection, thereby influencing European-level policy making,[289] and also intervene before the European Court of Justice in cases involving data protection.[290]

The Article 29 Working Party, introduced by art. 29 of the General Directive of 1995, is an independent advisory board made up of representatives from the Member State Authorities. Its main role is to examine questions related to how the Directive of 1995 may best be implemented at the national level, in as uniform a manner as possible. The Working Party advises the Commission on proposed amendments to the Directive and on additional measures to safeguard the rights covered by that same Directive. The Working Party is also tasked with informing the Commission of possible divergences between the laws of Member

---

[285] See Annex 1 to the Privacy Code, which contains the journalists' deontological code.

[286] Arts. 51ff, Reg. 2016/679.

[287] See art. 16, Consolidated Version of the Treaty Establishing the European Community.

[288] Reg. (EC) No 45/2001 (n 164).

[289] Kuner (n 251) 8.

[290] See art. 47(1)(i), Reg. 45/2001.

States which might undermine the equivalence of personal data protection in the European Union area. It can also make recommendations, on its own initiative, on matters relating to the protection of personal data. Like the national authorities, the Article 29 Working Party is required to produce an annual report on the current level of protection afforded to natural persons with regard to the processing of personal data, both within and outside the Community; the report is transmitted to the Commission, the Parliament and the Council.[291]

Although the 1995 Directive states that the Working Party has an 'advisory status',[292] its declarations can have an important impact on the application of European and national law on personal data protection.[293]

The General Data Protection Regulation provides for some significant changes in this sector: art. 68 establishes a new 'European Data Protection Board' to replace the Article 29 Working Party. It will be composed of the heads of the Supervisory Authority of each Member State and of the EDPS. The tasks of the new Board are very similar to those of the current Working Party, with some additions, to deal with the new issues introduced by the Regulation.[294]

The introduction of national and European authorities by European law is linked to the EU's Charter of Fundamental Rights. In fact, section 3 of art. 8 states that compliance with the rules contained in the first two sections related to personal data 'shall be subject to control by an independent authority'.

The European approach is, once again, similar to the Canadian approach, although the latter is in many ways weaker.

The Privacy Act of 1983 introduced the Canadian Privacy Commissioner, whose functions and range of action increased with the introduction of PIPEDA. The Commissioner is appointed by the Governor in Council, after consultation with the leaders of the recognized parties in both the Senate and the House of Commons; the appointment must then be approved by the two chambers.[295]

The Federal Commissioner has the power to make recommendations on the collection and use of personal information and to give an opinion on the correctness of decisions denying access to personal information; it

---

[291] See art. 30, Directive 95/46/EC.
[292] Art. 29(1), Directive 95/46/EC.
[293] Kuner (n 251) 10.
[294] Arts. 68ff., Reg. 2016/679.
[295] Section 53(1), Privacy Act.

does not have the power to make binding orders, which power resides solely in the Federal Court.[296]

The Commissioner has investigative powers, listed under Sections 31–35 of the Privacy Act, and can 'summon and enforce the appearance of persons before' its office and 'compel them to give oral or written evidence on oath and to produce such documents and things as the Commissioner deems requisite to the full investigation and consideration of the complaint'. It also has some complementary powers, such as to 'examine or obtain copies of or extracts from books or other records … containing any matter relevant to the investigation'. In some specific cases and under some circumstances, the Commissioner can apply for a review before the Federal Court in the event that its recommendations have not been respected.[297]

PIPEDA also grants the Privacy Commissioner auditing powers, entitling it to audit the management of an organization if there are grounds to believe that that organization is acting in contravention of the Act.[298]

In addition, PIPEDA has given the Commissioner an educational role (unlike under the Privacy Act): it is required to develop programmes and disseminate information to enhance public understanding of PIPEDA; to carry out, and publish, research on matters related to the protection of personal information; and to encourage organizations to adopt appropriate practices.[299] It can also carry out studies of specific sectors. This power, which already existed under the Privacy Act, has been used to investigate issues such as AIDS and genetic testing. The educational branch of the Office also provides guidelines to illustrate how businesses can comply with PIPEDA and encourages the adoption of codes of practice.[300]

The Federal Privacy Commissioner is not alone in carrying out its duties: a number of other offices and agencies also oversee the application of privacy laws, provide legal advice or, more generally, perform

---

[296] McIsaac, Shields and Klein (n 6) 3-26. See Sections 41ff, Privacy Act.

[297] These powers, however, have not often been used; the Commissioner relies instead on mediation and conciliation. See Colin J Bennett, 'The Privacy Commissioner of Canada: Multiple Roles, Diverse Expectations and Structural Dilemmas' [2003] Canadian Public Administration 218, 226. It should be noted that this article refers to the history of the Privacy Commissioner before PIPEDA came into force.

[298] Section 18, PIPEDA.

[299] Section 24, PIPEDA.

[300] Bennett, 'The Privacy Commissioner of Canada' (n 297) 229.

policy functions.[301] In addition, each province and territory – regardless of whether or not it has adopted its own state legislation – has a commissioner or an ombudsman responsible for monitoring privacy legislation. All privacy commissioners have a primary duty to receive and investigate complaints although their decisions do not all have the same binding force.[302]

PIPEDA also provides that, if appropriate or if requested by an interested person, the Federal Commissioner may consult with other entities that have similar powers and duties under provincial legislation.[303] This helps to ensure a more consistent application of the Act.

The Commissioners are also authorized to comment on Bills pending and on other regulation initiatives, with the aim of shaping laws to make them more 'privacy-compliant'. This mechanism, however, has been criticized by the Privacy Commissioners for not enabling them to intervene seriously and expeditiously in the process.[304] Finally, although no less importantly, some of the national Commissioners also have order-making powers.[305]

Each state government has, in addition to the Privacy Commissioner, an internal unit devoted to privacy policy responsibility.[306]

As mentioned, the Canadian Privacy Commissioner regulation has some weaknesses. First, it is not responsible for the personal information processing carried out by all organizations within Canada.[307] Furthermore, as previously seen, the powers of the Canadian Commissioner are different under the Privacy Act and under PIPEDA. The Commissioner itself has highlighted its limited power, mainly regarding its lack of 'order-making powers'. It proposed, in the event of a reform of the Privacy Act, that more powers, of mediation and conciliation for example, should be attributed to its office.[308] Scholars consider the order-making power 'powerful and influential' and argue that the Commissioner should also have 'a statutory mandate to educate and inform

---

[301]　Ibid 225.

[302]　Robin M Bayley and Colin J Bennett, 'Privacy Impact Assessments in Canada' in Wright and De Hert (eds) (n 198) 161, 163.

[303]　Section 23, PIPEDA.

[304]　Reported by Bayley and Bennett (n 302) 163.

[305]　Power (n 36) 155.

[306]　Bayley and Bennett (n 302) 163.

[307]　Bennett, 'The Privacy Commissioner of Canada' (n 297) 223.

[308]　Office of the Privacy Commissioner of Canada, 'Governmental Accountability for Personal Information. Reforming the Privacy Act' (June 2006) part III <www.priv.gc.ca/en/privacy-topics/privacy-laws-in-canada/the-privacy-act/pa_r/pa_reform_060605> accessed 25 February 2017.

Canadians about their privacy rights'. Additionally, order-making powers would strengthen the jurisprudence of privacy.[309] On the other hand, limited powers do not influence governmental decisions and might put 'the fundamental informational privacy rights of all Canadians profoundly at risk'.[310] It has also been suggested that the advisory functions of the Commissioner should become compulsory and binding.[311]

These being the concerns of prominent scholars regarding the Canadian Privacy Commissioner, it is no surprise that some of them have also expressed serious concerns about the US, where there is no formal privacy commission.

The 'Federal Privacy Board' was one of the fundamental novelties introduced by the Privacy Act of 1974. Following strong opposition, the Board was replaced by a committee, the Privacy Protection Study Commission.[312] This very Commission then concluded that the implementation of a Privacy Board was necessary; it recommended the creation of an ombudsman, to monitor the application of privacy laws and eventual privacy abuses,[313] to issue binding interpretations of the Privacy Act and to advise lawmakers on the privacy implications of proposed regulations.[314]

During the 1970s four study groups were created to understand the needs and problems related to privacy protection in the US. Three of these stressed the importance of establishing a federal entity that could supervise privacy issues.[315] In one case, the committee considered that society in the US was not mature enough to accept the creation of an ombudsman protecting privacy and personal data processing.[316]

---

[309] Citation from Flaherty, 'Reflection on Reform' (n 203) 26. The author claims that the success of some provincial commissioners lies in their order-making powers.

[310] Office of the Privacy Commissioner of Canada (n 308), part III.

[311] Flaherty, 'Reflection on Reform' (n 203) 27.

[312] For the process that led to the creation of a commission instead of a board, see Gellman, 'Fragmented, Incomplete, and Discontinuous' (n 136) 203–206; Flaherty, *Protecting Privacy* (n 203) 309–314.

[313] Marc Rotenberg, 'In Support of a Data Protection Board in the United States' [1991] Government Information Quarterly 79, 86.

[314] Privacy Protection Study Commission, Personal Privacy in an Information Society, 1977 <www.ncjrs.gov/pdffiles1/Digitization/49602NCJRS.pdf> accessed 25 February 2017.

[315] Gellman, 'Fragmented, Incomplete, and Discontinuous' (n 136) 208.

[316] Ibid 211, citing the U.S. Department of Health, Education & Welfare, Secretary's Advisory Committee on Automated Personal Data Systems,

Many years later, there are still frequent pleas from scholars for the introduction of an authority to oversee privacy protection. There have been many attempts to establish a Privacy Board.[317] In the 1990s it was asserted that a data protection board was 'the missing piece in the privacy protection framework of the United States' and would be a 'modest first step' towards shedding some light on privacy in the US; its task would also be to propose possible solutions.[318] Scholars have also suggested appropriate functions for any future privacy protection board.[319]

Other agencies and bureaus have been involved to a greater or lesser extent in privacy protection, but none of them has really fulfilled the functions of a board or of an authority.[320] For instance, the Fair Credit Reporting Act provided that the Federal Trade Commission (FTC) oversee the administration of certain practices but this does not seem to have covered the entire range of privacy issues.[321] Moreover, since the main role of the FTC is not to protect privacy, but rather to facilitate commerce, the entire model should be rearranged, in order to obtain better privacy protection.[322]

Currently, a number of different entities are tasked with safeguarding citizens' privacy but none of them is as powerful as the institutions of Italy and Canada, nor are they invested with the same authority as are these bodies.[323] In 1975 the Defense Privacy Board was created, as

---

'Records, Computers, and The Rights of Citizens' (1973) <www.justice.gov/opcl/docs/rec-com-rights.pdf> accessed 25 February 2017.

[317]   Gellman, 'A Better Way to Approach Privacy Policy' (n 134) 1192–1196. The author also proposed a possible model for a privacy agency (see esp. 1220ff). See also Gellman, 'Fragmented, Incomplete, and Discontinuous' (n 136) 207–208.

[318]   Rotenberg (n 313) 86 and 89.

[319]   Ibid 88.

[320]   Ibid 87; William S Challis and Ann Cavoukian, 'The Case For a U.S. Privacy Commissioner: A Canadian Commissioner's Perspective' [2000] John Marshall Journal of Computer & Information Law 1, 8.

[321]   Federal Trade Commission Act, 15 U.S.C. § 45(a). See Challis and Cavoukian (n 320) 24.

[322]   Challis and Cavoukian (n 320) 24; with emphasis on privacy in the workplace, see Jack Karns, 'Protecting Individual Online Privacy Rights: Making the Case for a Separately Dedicated, Independent Regulatory Agency' [2000] John Marshall Journal of Computer & Information Law 93, 95.

[323]   In addition to the institutions mentioned here, the following federal agencies also have privacy policy responsibilities: the Office of Management and Budget (OMB) in the Executive Office of the President; the National Telecommunications and Information Administration at the Department of Commerce; and the Bureau of International Communications and Information Policy

provided for by the Privacy Act of 1974. The Board's main role was to implement the Privacy Act. The Board still exists, now called the 'Defense Privacy and Civil Liberties Division' of the Department of Defense. In 1996 the Department of Health and Human Services established a Privacy Advocate and the Internal Revenue Service also established a Privacy Advocate as early as 1993.[324] Two other noteworthy bodies are the 'Division of Privacy and Identity Protection' of the FTC and the 'Privacy and Civil Liberties Oversight Board' (PCLOB).

The former is the most recent Division of the FTC – the Consumer Protection Bureau.[325] This Division, created in 2006, deals with consumer privacy and data security matters through enforcement, rule making and policy development. It monitors issues of consumer privacy, identity theft, information security and credit reporting, educates citizens and businesses about these issues, and develops policies in these areas. The Division is in charge of enforcing certain Acts, such as the Fair Credit Reporting Act and the Children's Online Privacy Protection Act.[326]

The Division's limited influence is demonstrated by the fact that it is not mentioned in any of the decisions analysed in this study. This could, of course, be due to the fact that the Division is a new institution and therefore has not yet had time to contribute to the issue when the cases discussed in this book were decided. Perhaps the Division's recent creation is not as significant as the fact that it is just a division of another institution. Canada and Italy, which have created bodies dedicated to privacy regulation, seem to accord more importance to both the issue in general and, consequently, to the role of the Privacy Authority.

The same argument also applies to the PCLOB, an independent agency within the executive branch, established by the Implementing Recommendations of the 9/11 Commission Act of 2007,[327] amending the

---

at the Department of State. See Gellman, 'Fragmented, Incomplete, and Discontinuous' (n 136) 220. According to Flaherty, *Protecting Privacy* (n 203) 316, the OMB was 'the closest approximation to a data protection agency' although it did not actually use its powers.

[324] Gellman, 'A Better Way to Approach Privacy Policy' (n 134) 1188.

[325] Colin J Bennett, *Regulating Privacy. Data Protection and Public Policy in Europe and the United States* (Cornell University Press 1992) 170ff, explains why the US did not create an institutional mechanism solely responsible for privacy. It seems that this decision followed discussions involving a wide range of different authorities.

[326] See <www.ftc.gov/about-ftc/bureaus-offices/bureau-consumer-protection/our-divisions/division-privacy-and-identity> accessed 25 February 2017.

[327] Implementing Recommendations of the 9/11 Commission Act, Pub. Law No. 110-53, August 3, 2007, Sections 801ff. The final report of the National

Intelligence Reform and Terrorism Prevention Act of 2004.[328] The Board was originally created by Section 1061 of the Terrorism Prevention Act; this version did not require bipartisan representation, and the Board had no subpoena powers to obtain any documents it might need. Furthermore, because the Board operated within the Executive Office of the President, it was considered by some to be a mere appendage of the President.[329] For these reasons, bipartisan Bills, such as the Implementing Recommendations of the 9/11 Commission Act of 2007, were introduced to modify the Board's structure and functioning: it is currently made up of five members, who are appointed by the President and confirmed by the Senate; only the Chairman serves in a full-time position. No more than three members can be chosen from the same political party. The members are appointed according to their expertise and knowledge of privacy and civil liberties. Unfortunately, the Board did not function effectively until 2013 due to budget constraints and disagreements about the nominees.[330]

The Board's mission is to review proposed regulations, laws and policies, and to check whether privacy and civil liberties are being appropriately considered in the development and implementation of such legal tools. The Board is also tasked with ensuring that the government's counter-terrorism activities do not trespass excessively on citizens' privacy and civil liberties.[331]

Commission on Terrorist Attacks Upon the United States (9/11 Commission), released on 22 July 2004, recommended the creation of 'a board within the executive branch to oversee adherence to the guidelines we recommend and the commitment the government makes to defend our civil liberties'. See U.S. National Commission on Terrorist Attacks Upon the United States, 'The 9/11 Commission Report' (2004), 395 <http://govinfo.library.unt.edu/911/report/911Report.pdf> accessed 25 February 2017.

[328]   Pub. Law No. 108-458; 118 Stat. 3688, December 17, 2004, Section 1061.

[329]   Fred H Cate, 'Security, Privacy, and the Role of Law' [2009] IEEE Security and Privacy 60, 61. For a more detailed explanation, see Garrett Hatch, 'Privacy and Civil Liberties Oversight Board: New Independent Agency Status' (27 August 2012) CRS Reports for Congress, 1–3 <www.fas.org/sgp/crs/misc/RL34385.pdf> accessed 25 February 2017.

[330]   Hatch (n 329) 5–12; Rachel Weiner, 'Never heard of the Privacy and Civil Liberties Oversight Board? You Should', *Washingtonpost.com* (10 June 2013) <www.washingtonpost.com/blogs/the-fix/wp/2013/06/10/never-heard-of-the-privacy-and-civil-liberties-oversight-board-you-should/> accessed 25 February 2017.

[331]   Intelligence Reform and Terrorism Prevention Act of 2004, Section 1061(c). See also <www.pclob.gov/about-us.html> accessed 25 February 2017.

Although the creation of the Division of Privacy and Identity Protection and the PCLOB has undoubtedly improved privacy protection, it should be noted that neither entity is similar to the privacy authorities of Italy and Canada. While both the US institutions have certain powers which resemble those of the Italian and Canadian authorities, such as their educational role and their power to supervise regulation, neither has judicial power. That the US, Canada and Italy have failed to adopt similar privacy authorities may be due to the fact that the OECD Guidelines contain no such requirement. Another possible explanation might be corporate lobbying;[332] as is well known, the business community has an ever-growing interest in the unrestricted handling of citizens' data. At the same time, interest groups for the protection of privacy have played only a marginal role.[333]

The importance of privacy boards has been stressed by the most prominent scholars in the field of privacy and data protection:[334] 'it is not enough simply to pass a data protection law in order to control surveillance; it is essential that an agency charged with implementation is duty bound to make the law work in practice. A statute by itself is an insufficient countervailing force to the ideological and political pressures for efficiency and monitoring of the population that are at work in Western society'.[335]

---

[332] Gellman, 'Fragmented, Incomplete, and Discontinuous' (n 136) 237; Andrew Charlesworth, 'Clash of the Data Titans? US and EU Data Privacy Regulation' [2000] European Public Law 253, 255.

[333] Bennett, *Regulating Privacy* (n 325) 205–206.

[334] Flaherty, *Protecting Privacy* (n 203) 381ff; Colin J Bennett and Charles D Raab, *The Governance of Privacy* (MIT Press 2006) 133ff.

[335] Flaherty, *Protecting Privacy* (n 203) 381.

4. Copyright vs. data protection: case studies

1. A BRIEF HISTORY OF COPYRIGHT ENFORCEMENT AGAINST FILE-SHARING

The cases cited below represent just one of the measures adopted by the copyright industry to enforce their rights against illegal file-sharing. The reasons behind the strategy of targeting users are mainly linked to the technological development of file-sharing, which, in turn, is linked to copyright enforcement strategies. This section summarizes the development of copyright enforcement in the online environment. A first important remark to be made is that the US Supreme Court and other lower courts have given interpretations that have influenced the development of file-sharing technologies, in the sense that the latter have evolved to be as 'enforcement-proof' as possible.[1]

Historically, the first cases were initiated by the Recording Industry Association of America (RIAA), which represents the interests of both the US recording industry and other music copyright holders.[2] As soon as MP3 technology hit the market, the RIAA understood that the free downloading of MP3 files could threaten its affiliates' business and, consequently, *its* business too. MP3 technology allows the compression

---

[1] Tim Wu, 'When Code Isn't Law' [2003] Virginia Law Review 679, 726ff; Niva Elkin-Koren, 'Making Technology Visible: Liability of Internet Service Providers for Peer-to-peer Traffic' [2005] New York University Journal of Legislation and Public Policy 15, 19ff; Monica Horten, *The Copyright Enforcement Enigma. Internet Politics and the 'Telecom Package'* (Palgrave 2012) 28ff.
[2] Robert P Merges, Peter S Menell and Mark A Lemley, *Intellectual Property in the New Technological Age* (5th edn, Aspen 2010) 682, holds that the RIAA represents more than 500 companies related to the creation, manufacturing, and distribution of sound recordings.

of files, resulting in much smaller files than previous data formats.[3] This, in turn, allows files to circulate on the Internet with greater ease and speed.

The RIAA's first move was an attempt to stop the production and sale of MP3 players.[4] However, the 'Diamond Rio' case was decided in favour of the company which produced the players, largely because the Court applied the reasoning of the Supreme Court majority in *Sony Betamax*, analogizing the 'time-shifting' of the Betamax to the 'space-shifting' of the MP3 player.[5]

The RIAA then took on the websites facilitating the exchange of MP3 files. A 1999 case involved 'MP3board.com', a search engine that trawled the Internet for MP3 files and provided links to them. The key issue was whether or not hypertext linking created by automated processes was a copyright infringement, irrespective of the copyright status of the material to which the link was provided. After years of litigation, the parties eventually settled the dispute and MP3board.com dropped its MP3 search engine.[6]

In 2000 another web portal created a successful service that enabled subscribers to organize a virtual online music locker, through which they could access, from any computer connected to the Internet, music files copied and stored on MP3.com's servers. The system was again based on the concept of 'space-shifting'.[7] The RIAA claimed that the initial copying of CDs onto the service's server, as well as the distribution of

---

[3]   MP3 – full name MPEG audio level 3 – is 'a way of encoding digital audio data into a compressed data format that is approximately one twelfth the size of the original without perceptible loss of quality'. Entry: *MP3* in Simon MH Collin, *Dictionary of Computing* (Peter Collin Publishing 2004).

[4]   *RIAA v. Diamond Multimedia System, Inc.*, 29 F. Supp. 2d 624 (C.D. Cal. 1998) and *RIAA v. Diamond Multimedia System, Inc.*, 180 F.3d 1072 (9th Cir. 1999). For a comment: Ted J Barthel, 'RIAA v. Diamond Multimedia System, Inc.: The Sale of the Rio Player Forces the Music Industry to Dance to a New Beat' [1999] DePaul-LCA Journal of Art & Entertainment Law 279; Elizabeth R Gosse, 'Recording Industry Association of America v. Diamond Multimedia System, Inc.: The RIAA Could Not Stop the Rio-MP3 Files and the Audio Home Recording Act' [1999] University of San Francisco Law Review 575.

[5]   *RIAA v. Diamond Multimedia System, Inc.*, 180 F.3d 1072, 1079. Later on the two parties reached a settlement; see Gosse (n 4) 597. The decision also examined the possible applicability to the Diamond Rio of the Audio Home Recording Act (17 U.S.C.S. §§ 1001ff) (AHRA). See *RIAA v. Diamond Multimedia System, Inc.* (n 5) 1075–1078.

[6]   *Arista Records, Inc., et al. v. MP3Board, Inc.*, 2002 U.S. Dist. LEXIS 16165.

[7]   Merges, Menell and Lemley (n 2) 683.

the files, constituted copyright infringement. The trial court rejected the fair use defence of MP3.com,[8] which later settled the case.[9]

The RIAA then turned its sights on file-sharing systems. Napster was the first prominent example of the widespread diffusion of this architecture: a peer-to-peer (P2P) file-sharing network, in which users (mainly) illicitly exchanged copyrighted material in MP3 format. End users downloaded software from the Internet that enabled them to share hundreds of thousands of songs. In 2000, 18 recording companies sued Napster for contributory and vicarious copyright infringement.[10] Napster based its defences on fair use, substantial non-infringing uses (as in the 'Betamax case') and Digital Millennium Copyright Act (DMCA) safe harbours. Napster was not involved in the ripping of audio CDs on users' computers, nor did it store files on its system. However, the District Court found that, unlike in *Sony Betamax*, Napster facilitated the distribution of infringing MP3 files. In fact, Napster did not just manufacture and sell a product, it actually continuously controlled user access. Napster also encouraged and assisted users in the act of infringement: it facilitated the exchange of files stored on users' hard disks; it created a library on each user's computer; and it enabled both searches for MP3 files located in other users' computers and the direct transfer of MP3 files from peer to peer. Hence, the Court held that Napster could not enjoy the fair use harbour.[11] Since Napster was considered liable for vicarious infringement, the Court enjoined its activities.[12]

The Court of Appeals affirmed the District Court's decision[13] although it recognized that Napster also had some non-infringing uses, such as artists' distribution of their own music. The Court found that Napster was

---

[8]   See *UMG Recordings, Inc. v. MP3.com, Inc.*, 92 F. Supp. 2d 349 (S.D.N.Y. 2000).

[9]   Merges, Menell and Lemley (n 2); Michael Geist, *Internet Law in Canada* (Captus Press 2002) 521ff.

[10]   *A&M Records, Inc. v. Napster*, 114 F. Supp. 2d 896, 900 (N.D. Cal. 2000); see Russell P Beets, 'RIAA v. Napster: The Struggle to Protect Copyrights in the Internet Age' [2001] Georgia State University Law Review 507; Timothy J Ryan, 'Infringement.com: RIAA v. Napster and the War Against Online Music Piracy' [2002] Arizona Law Review 495. The case of Napster echoed around the world: Giovanni Pascuzzi, 'Opere musicali su Internet: il formato MP3' [2001] Foro it., part IV 101; Paolo Autieri, 'Il caso Napster alla luce del diritto comunitario' in Luigi Carlo Ubertazzi (ed), *TV, Internet e "new trends" di diritti d'autore e connessi* (Giuffrè 2003) 63.

[11]   *A&M Records, Inc. v. Napster 2000* (n 10) 913ff.

[12]   Ibid 927.

[13]   *A&M Record Inc. v. Napster, Inc.*, 239 F.3d 1004 (2001).

aware of user infringement, that it had the right and ability to control user activity, and that it encouraged and assisted them in their infringements. Users could only find and download music through the use of Napster's support services: this meant that Napster contributed to the infringement.[14] As far as vicarious liability was concerned, Napster only made a profit through its failure to stop users' infringing behaviour. The more users registered, the more music was available, and this in turn drew more users. This was particularly true for infringing material, by which users were most likely to be attracted: financial benefit for Napster was therefore directly linked to the infringement of copyright.[15] Vicarious liability requirements were thus met. Napster was later shut down, following an injunction granted to A&M Records.[16]

The music industry won this initial legal battle against P2P technologies but technology was fighting back hard and new networks soon appeared. Their decentralized architecture made it difficult to locate either the source of the infringing material or the infringers themselves. This created a loophole in the DMCA, since the 1998 Act had not been designed for application to such architectures.[17]

After the victory against Naspter, the recording industry sued other P2P software companies. The ensuing suit against Grokster became one of US copyright law's seminal cases, second perhaps only to *Sony Betamax.*[18]

---

[14] Ibid 1022, quoting *A&M Records, Inc. v. Napster 2000* (n 10) 919–920.

[15] *A&M Record Inc. v. Napster 2001* (n 13) 1023ff.

[16] *A&M Records, Inc. v. Napster, Inc.*, 2001 U.S. Dist. LEXIS 2186 (N.D. Cal., 2001). The suits against it eventually bankrupted Napster, which in 2008 was bought by a bigger company.

[17] Elkin-Koren (n 1) 17–18 and 34ff. Napster's initial successors were Aimster (see *In re Aimster Copyright Litigation*, 334 F.3d 643 (7th Cir. 2003), *cert. denied* 540 U.S. 1107 (2004)) and AudioGalaxy. These were supplanted by Morpheus and KaZaA, which were in turn overtaken by eDonkey and Bit Torrent. See John Borland, 'Peer to Peer: As the Revolution Recedes' *CNET News.com* (31 December 2001) <www.cnet.com/news/peer-to-peer-as-the-revolution-recedes/> accessed 3 March 2017; John Borland, 'P2P Users Traveling By eDonkey', *CNET News.com* (28 August 2005) <http://news.cnet.com/P2P-users-traveling-by-eDonkey/2100-1025_3-5843859.html> accessed 3 March 2017.

[18] *MGM Studios, Inc. v. Grokster, Ltd*, 259 F. Supp. 2d 1029 (C.D. Cal. 2003); *MGM Studios, Inc. v. Grokster, Ltd*, 380 F.3d 1154 (9th Cir. 2004); *MGM Studios, Inc. v. Grokster, Ltd*, 545 U.S. 913 (2005); see Dana R Levin, 'The Future of Copyright Infringement: Metro-Goldwyn-Mayer Studios, Inc. v. Grokster, Ltd.' [2006] St. John's Journal of Legal Comment 271. For an interesting parallel between Sony Betamax and Grokster, see Jessica Litman, 'The Story of

Grokster was a company that distributed software which enabled users to exchange digital media via a peer-to-peer network.[19] The software, downloadable free of charge, automatically connected users' computers to the network and made files available for transfer to other connected users. Grokster also provided ways for users to search the shared files.[20] Some organizations in the motion picture and music recording industries sued Grokster, contending that its conduct rendered it liable, based on contributory and vicarious liability. In order to demonstrate Grokster's liability, they had to prove users' direct infringement of copyright. Citing *Napster*, the District Court held that it was 'undisputed that at least some of the individuals who use[d] defendants' software [were] engaged in copyright infringement of plaintiffs' copyrighted works'.[21] The Court first analysed the alleged contributory infringement and its two structural factors, namely 'knowledge of' and 'material contribution to' the infringing conduct of another. Since Grokster marketed itself as 'the next Napster', it clearly knew that most of the individuals who downloaded its software used it to infringe copyright.[22] However, this knowledge was not sufficient for the Court to consider Grokster liable as *actual* knowledge of the infringement and a failure to act despite possession of this knowledge were required.[23] As far as 'material contribution in users' infringement' was concerned, the reasoning applied in *Napster* could not be applied to Grokster's conduct. In fact, unlike Napster, Grokster did not operate a centralized file-sharing network.[24] Grokster provided no facilities for direct infringement, nor was it in any way materially involved in infringement. Even if Grokster were to deactivate its computers, users would still be able to share files. Apart from some support services, Grokster did not substantially contribute to infringement.[25]

Sony v. Universal Studios: Mary Poppins Meets the Boston Strangler' in Jane Ginsburg and Rochelle Dreyfuss (eds), *Intellectual Property Stories* (Foundation Press 2006) 358, 387ff.

[19]   *MGM Studios, Inc. v. Grokster 2003* (n 18) 1032. Although there were a number of plaintiffs, I will refer only to MGM; the same will be done with the defendants, collectively referred to as Grokster.

[20]   Ibid 1032.

[21]   Ibid 1034 referring to *A&M Record Inc. v. Napster 2001* (n 13) 1013–1014.

[22]   *MGM Studios, Inc. v. Grokster 2003* (n 18) 1037–1038.

[23]   See *A&M Record Inc. v. Napster 2001* (n 13) 1021.

[24]   Initially, Grokster applied a centralized-type network, as can be seen in *MGM Studios, Inc. v. Grokster 2003* (n 18) 1032ff; see also *MGM Studios, Inc. v. Grokster 2004* (n 18) 1166.

[25]   *MGM Studios, Inc. v. Grokster 2003* (n 18) 1039–1043.

With regard to vicarious liability, two requirements must exist: a financial benefit and the right and ability to supervise the infringing conduct. Grokster clearly gained a financial benefit from the infringing conduct: despite the fact that the software was distributed for free, the company derived substantial revenues from advertising, just as Napster did.[26] However, in light of the fact that Grokster had no ability to control what users did and that the network was actually owned by another company,[27] the District Court found Grokster not liable.

MGM appealed to the same Ninth Circuit Court of Appeals that had, just a few years before, decided Napster's destiny. The judges observed that contributory infringement required knowledge as well as material contribution. Grokster had a decentralized structure and even when it stopped operating, users were still able to share files. To the Court this meant that the company had no knowledge of what users did.[28] As for material contribution, the Ninth Circuit found that Grokster was not contributing, since it did not provide either the site or the facilities for infringement, nor did the files reside on its computers. In addition, as the District Court found, even though Grokster claimed to be 'the next Napster',[29] its technology could be put to numerous other uses.[30]

The Court then evaluated the possibility of vicarious liability. In considering Grokster's power and ability to supervise, the Ninth Circuit found that the sort of monitoring and supervisory relationship usually present in vicarious liability cases was totally absent in this instance. In the judges' opinion, the relationship between Grokster and its users differed greatly from that between Napster and its users.[31] For these reasons, the Ninth Circuit affirmed the District Court's decision.

In the aftermath of these two decisions, major labels and other copyright holders started to realize that suing Internet Service Providers (ISPs) was no longer worthwhile. The design of decentralized P2P systems had created an alibi for the companies that produced the software since they no longer had an active role in the exchange of files. Copyright holders therefore launched a new wave of lawsuits, in which they sued end users for their infringing behaviours. These suits, which are the core of this book, are later analysed in detail.

---

26   Ibid 1043–1044.
27   Ibid 1045–1046.
28   Ibid 1161–1163.
29   Ibid 1036.
30   Ibid 1164.
31   Ibid 1164–1166.

Despite Grokster's success in the lower courts, MGM successfully challenged the Ninth Circuit Court's decision before the Supreme Court.[32] The Supreme Court was convinced that Grokster knew that its users employed its software primarily to download copyrighted files. It was proved that the company had learned about these infringements as it received users' e-mails pertaining to downloaded copyrighted files. The Court's opinion was that Grokster was more than simply a passive recipient of information. Not only did Grokster present itself as 'the new Napster', it also sent users a newsletter advertising its ability to provide copyrighted materials. The money gained by selling advertising space increased as the number of users increased. Although Grokster occasionally sent warning e-mails to its users about infringing content, it never blocked user access when content owners notified it of infringements.[33]

In the light of such widespread infringements, the Court felt that in this case imposing liability seemed mandatory[34] and it again considered the question of Grokster's possible liability – either contributory or vicarious. Delivering the opinion, Justice Souter held that 'inducing' or 'encouraging' direct infringement may constitute contributory infringement.[35] In particular, the act of advertising an infringing use, or of instructing others in how to engage in such a use, showed an affirmative intent that the product be used for that scope. This could make the distributor of a device liable for any infringement by third parties. Three of Grokster's actions in particular guided the Court: (1) the company tried to satisfy the market built and later abandoned by Napster; (2) the company did not make any attempt to develop filtering tools or to diminish infringing activities in anyway; and (3) Grokster made money by selling advertising space, whose value grew as the volume of use grew.[36] So, while the Supreme Court decided not to revisit the *Sony Betamax* doctrine formally, it did proceed to correct the misapplication of the Ninth Circuit

---

[32] There were two concurring opinions: one from Justice Ginsburg, joined by the Chief Justice and Justice Kennedy (*MGM Studios, Inc. v. Grokster* Supreme Court (n 18) 942ff) and one from Justice Breyer, joined by Justice Stevens and Justice O'Connor (ibid 949ff).

[33] *MGM Studios, Inc. v. Grokster* Supreme Court (n 18) 923–927.

[34] Ibid 929.

[35] Souter J referred to *Gershwin Publishing v. Columbia Artists Management*, cit., 1162.

[36] *MGM Studios, Inc. v. Grokster* Supreme Court (n 18) 935–941.

Court of Appeals.[37] Accordingly, the Supreme Court remanded the case for further proceedings consistent with its opinion, which held Grokster liable.

With this decision on their side, recording companies started a new wave of suits against software distributors, in which the former regained an increasing measure of success.[38] 'Third party injunctions' probably best represent this subsequent approach to online copyright infringement. In these controversies, copyright holders ask judges to order specific injunctions against intermediaries,[39] usually to block user access to websites that provide infringing download links, as, for example, in the case of the decision by the Court of Justice of the European Union (CJEU) involving the ISP 'UPC Telekabel'.[40] The CJEU interpreted art. 8(3) of Directive 2001/29, related to injunctions directed to an 'intermediary whose services are used to infringe a copyright or related right', holding that the types of injunction applicable under art. 8(3) of Directive 2001/29 are a matter of national law; although they must, nonetheless, observe the limits arising from the same Directive and from EU law more generally.[41] The fundamental rights at stake should be

---

[37]   Ibid 933–934.

[38]   Consider, for instance, the case of LimeWire: *Arista Records, LLC v. Lime Group, LLC*, 715 F. Supp. 2d 481 (2010). See also the cases of eDonkey – *Arista Records LLC v. MetaMachine, Inc.*, No. 06-cv-06991, 2006 U.S. Dist. Ct. Pleadings 6991 (S.D.N.Y. September 11, 2006). Parties settled and the website was later shut down: Caroline McCarthy, 'File-sharing site eDonkey kicks it', *CNET News.com* (13 September 2006) <www.cnet.com/news/file-sharing-site-edonkey-kicks-it/> accessed 3 March 2017.

[39]   Martin Husovec, 'Injunctions against Innocent Third Parties: The Case of Website Blocking' [2013] JIPITEC 116 <www.jipitec.eu/issues/jipitec-4-2-2013/3745/husovec.pdf> accessed 3 March 2017; Eleni Synodinou, 'Intermediaries' Liability for Online Copyright Infringement in the EU: Evolutions and Confusions' [2015] Computer Law & Security Review 57.

[40]   Case 314/12 *UPC Telekabel Wien GmbH v. Constantin Film Verleih GmbH, Wega Filmproduktionsgesellschaft mbH* [2014] ECLI:EU:C:2014:192; for a comment, see Giulia Dore, 'And They Lived Happily Ever After UPC Telekabel: A Copyright Fairy Tale or a Genuine Chance to Strike a Fair Balance for Fundamental Rights?' [2015] Queen Mary Journal of Intellectual Property 226.

[41]   The Court here refers to the *Scarlet* case: Case70/10 *Scarlet Extended SA v. SABAM* [2011] ECR I-11959; see below Section 5.3.

taken into particular consideration.[42] In the specific case, the Court considered copyright to collide with both the freedom to conduct a business and Internet users' right to freedom of information. These rights are protected, respectively, by art. 17(2), art. 16 and art. 11 of the Charter of Fundamental Rights.

The adoption of an injunction like the one in the main proceeding would clearly limit the ISP's freedom to conduct a business; however, given that in this particular case the ISP would still have some freedom to adopt measures best adapted to its business, the measure applied by the Austrian courts was not considered by the CJEU to be too strong. This measure also needed to be 'reasonable' so that the ISP would not have to make what the Court felt to be unsustainable sacrifices. It was also important that the ISP applied measures that respected users' fundamental right of freedom of information.

The Court also declared that intellectual property rights are not inviolable and do not need to be absolutely protected. However, the measure being adopted needs to be sufficiently effective; in other words, it needs to either prevent users from accessing copyrighted material without authorization, or at least make it very difficult for them to do so. The Court therefore considered the measure requested in the Austrian lawsuit to be compatible with EU law and with the requirement to strike a fair balance between the fundamental rights involved, and thus sanctioned the adoption of injunctions to stop copyright infringement, in so far as these injunctions are adopted in a balanced manner. National courts should bear the burden of evaluating the effectiveness and balance of the measure applied.

The controversies described above serve as examples of how far the legal battle to stop file-sharing is from conclusion.

The next sections will go into greater detail on some cases involving the copyright industries and final users, in which copyright enforcement collided with users' personal data protection.

---

[42]   The Court here refers to *Promusicae*: see Case C-275/06 *Productores de Música de España v. Telefónica de España SAU* [2008] ECR I-00271, on which see below Section 5.1.

2. US CASES

2.1 Digital Millennium Copyright Act Subpoenas

As already mentioned, one of the consequences of the decisions in *Grokster* was a shift in the copyright industry's strategy on copyright enforcement.

In the summer of 2003 the RIAA started to sue individuals that it had reason to believe had illicitly shared copyrighted files through P2P networks.[43]

To detect whether recordings owned by its affiliates were being shared illegally, the RIAA's investigators ran a program on their own computers, just as any other P2P user would do.[44] Then they searched for songs owned by their labels and collected the Internet Protocol (IP) addresses of the users who were offering these recordings. As explained in Chapter 1, the RIAA could not match IP addresses to 'real' identities without the intervention of ISPs. The Association used the subpoena power granted by the DMCA to force the ISPs to cooperate.[45]

The RIAA's strategy could not have been simpler: it filled out subpoena requests, which it then gave to federal clerks, thus obtaining personal information on the people it believed to be pirating and sharing copyrighted songs. Once in possession of these names and addresses, the RIAA could sue end users directly. The recording industry's favourite tool in seeking damages was the Digital Theft Deterrence and Copyright Damages Improvement Act of 1999, which allows copyright holders to sue infringers for damages ranging from $750 to $30,000.

Some ISPs complied with the requests of the RIAA, which subsequently sent letters to and filed lawsuits against hundreds of individuals.

---

[43] See Ray Backerman, 'How the RIAA Litigation Process Works' (recordingindustryvspeople.blogspot.it, 11 January 2008) <http://recordingindustryvs people.blogspot.it/2007/01/how-riaa-litigation-process-works.html> accessed 5 March 2017.

[44] Ray Backerman, 'Large Recording Companies v. the Defenseless – Some Common Sense Solutions to the Challenges of the RIAA Litigation' [2008] Judges' Journal 20, 20. Later on, the RIAA used another methodology: they put corrupted junk files with popular song titles into P2P networks (this technique is called 'spoofing' – see Entry: *IP spoofing* in Collin (n 3)); see Alice Kao, 'RIAA v. Verizon: Applying the Subpoena Provision of the DMCA' [2004] Berkeley Technology Law Journal 405, 425.

[45] Numerous cases deal with DMCA subpoenas. I shall here illustrate only some of them. These cases were chosen as being significant for this research. The same is true of the 'John Doe' actions illustrated below.

Verizon Online (Verizon) was the first ISP to refuse to comply with the RIAA's subpoena, choosing instead to fight back.

In July 2002 the RIAA served a subpoena on Verizon, seeking information to identify someone who seemed to be using P2P software for the illegal downloading of songs.[46] The subpoena included the user's IP address, to enable Verizon to locate the infringer's computer, as well as the time and date the songs had been downloaded. As requested by Section 512(h)(2)(c) of the DMCA, the RIAA presented a sworn declaration that the information was sought in good faith and that it would only be used to enforce the rights of its members.[47] The RIAA asked Verizon for immediate assistance to block the unauthorized activity of file-sharing, specifically asking that the ISP remove or disable access to the infringing sound files through it system.[48]

Verizon refused to comply with the RIAA's subpoena. In response, the RIAA filed a motion to compel production. Verizon opposed the motion interpreting Section 512(h) of the DMCA as applying only if the infringing material is stored on the service provider's system or network under Subsection 512(c).[49] Since Verizon was simply transmitting information from user to user, there was no material stored on its system and the subpoena could not be applied to its case.

Meanwhile the RIAA served a second subpoena on Verizon. The ISP again refused to comply, this time also raising constitutional issues.[50]

---

46   *In re Verizon Internet Services*, 240 F. Supp. 2d 24 (D.D.C. 2003). For a general overview of the case, consider: Kao (n 44); David Gorski, 'The Future of the Digital Millennium Copyright Act (DMCA) Subpoena Power on the Internet in Light of Verizon Cases' [2005] Review of Litigation 149; Trevor A Dutcher, 'A Discussion of the Mechanics of the DMCA Safe Harbor and Subpoena Power, as Applied in RIAA v. Verizon Internet Services' [2005] Santa Clara Computer & High Tech Law Journal 493; Katherine Raynolds, 'One Verizon, Two Verizon, Three Verizon, More? – A Comment: RIAA v. Verizon and How the DMCA Subpoena Power Became Powerless' [2005] 23 Cardozo Arts & Entertainment Law Journal 343.

47   *In re Verizon* (n 46) 28.

48   *RIAA v. Verizon Internet Services*, 351 F.3d 1229 (DC Cir. 2003), 1223.

49   17 U.S.C. § 512(c): Information residing on systems or networks at direction of users.

50   The same questions were also introduced by Verizon in appealing the District Court's orders, see below, in this same section, for explanation. For a discussion on the constitutional problem raised by § 512(h) of the DMCA, see Matthew Amedeo, 'Shifting the Burden: the Unconstitutionality of Section 512(h) of the Digital Millennium Copyright Act and its Impact on Internet Service Providers' [2003] CommLaw Conspectus 311, 317ff.

The trial-level decisions went against Verizon and the RIAA obtained rulings forcing the company to divulge user identities.[51] In the opinion of the District Court, Section 512(h) had to be applied to every kind of service provider.

However, the Court of Appeals reversed this decision.[52] The rulings turned on the nature of Verizon's services. According to the District Court's Judge Bates, '[t]he statutory text of the DMCA provides clear guidance for construing the subpoena authority of Subsection (h) to apply to all service providers under the Act'.[53] Under Section 512(k) the Act provides two definitions of 'service provider'. The definition in Subparagraph (A), as applied in Subsection (a), considers providers as entities 'offering the transmission, routing, or providing of connections for digital online communications, between or among points specified by a user, of material of the user's choosing, without modification to the content of the material as sent or received'. Whereas, as used in Section 512(k), other than in Subsection (a), the term 'service provider' is intended as a provider of online services or network access, or the operator of facilities therefor, and also includes any entity described in the previous paragraph.[54] Given these definitions, Judge Bates had no doubt that the subpoena power of Section (h) was applicable to all service providers and therefore also applicable to Verizon. Judge Bates held that the narrow definition of Section 512(k)(1)(A) was applicable only for Subsection (a). In all the other cases, such as Section (h), the applicable definition of 'service provider' was the one in Section 512(k)(1)(B), which also included the mere transmission of data, such as Verizon's.[55]

Verizon countered, sustaining that an essential condition for a valid subpoena under the DMCA is a notification to the ISP which complies with Subsection (c)(3)(A).[56] Verizon reasoned that, since Subsection (c) deals with 'Information Residing on Systems or Networks at Direction of Users', it could not be applied in this case, given that Verizon was simply providing Internet connectivity or acting as a passive conduit.[57] The District Court considered that Verizon's interpretation failed to address a

---

[51] See *In re Verizon* (n 46) and *In re Verizon Internet Services*, 257 F. Supp. 2d 244 (D.D.C. 2003) (*In re Verizon 2*).

[52] *RIAA v. Verizon* (n 48) 1239.

[53] *In re Verizon* (n 46) 30.

[54] 17 U.S.C. § 512(k)(1)(B).

[55] *In re Verizon* (n 46) 32.

[56] 17 U.S.C. § 512(h)(2)(A).

[57] *In re Verizon* (n 46) 32.

number of contexts for which the subpoena had actually been conceived.[58] Safe harbours represent a compromise between ISPs and the copyright industry in order for the latter to obtain assistance from the former in identifying infringers.[59] Hence, Judge Bates reasoned that if the DMCA subpoena were not applicable to mere conduit providers, these would receive liability protection without a corresponding obligation to assist copyright owners in the enforcement of their rights. Judge Bates' conclusion, based on the history, text and structure of the DMCA, was to grant the RIAA's motion and order Verizon to comply with it.[60]

Although the Court did not consider them, Verizon also identified the grounds for possible constitutional challenges to the subpoena power introduced by the DMCA, a matter further developed in the subsequent lawsuit. Verizon claimed that Section 512(h) violates Article III of the Constitution, since it authorizes federal courts to issue a binding process even when there is no pending case or controversy.[61] Article III of the US Constitution refers to the judicial branch and provides that the 'federal judicial power' is divided between the Supreme Court and other inferior courts. Section 2 of the article indicates the appropriate subject matter for the federal courts, speaking of 'cases' and 'controversies'. This affirmative grant of power has been read as also encompassing a negative limitation: judicial power cannot extend to anything but a case or controversy.[62] The Supreme Court interprets these words as requiring that litigation is presented to federal courts in an adversarial form and within a context capable of judicial resolution:[63] the matter has to be concrete and not merely hypothetical.[64] Verizon's opinion was that this necessary context was lacking.

In Judge Bates' view, the clerk's issuance of a Section 512(h) subpoena did not involve the exercise of either judicial or investigatory power. The

---

[58]   Ibid 34.

[59]   Analysing the DMCA § 152's legislative development, some scholars underlined the lobbying activity of both ISPs and copyright holders such as the RIAA: Cassandra Imfeld and Victoria Smith Ekstrand, 'The Music Industry and the Legislative Development of the Digital Millennium Copyright Act's Online Service Provider Provision' [2005] Communication Law & Policy 291.

[60]   *In re Verizon* (n 46) 38–44, *passim*.

[61]   *In re Verizon 2* (n 51) 247. In Verizon's view, § 512(h) also violates the First Amendment right of Internet users, see below in this section.

[62]   Kathleen M Sullivan and Gerald Gunther, *First Amendment Law* (3rd edn, Foundation Press 2007) 31.

[63]   *Flast v. Cohen*, 392 U.S. 83, 97 (1968); see also Laurence H Tribe, *American Constitutional Law* (Foundation Press 1978) 67ff.

[64]   Sullivan and Gunther (n 62) 31.

fact that when a proposed subpoena is in proper form and has the listed requirements the clerk must expeditiously issue and sign the subpoena would imply that the clerk only executes a *ministerial duty*, which is an operation which leaves no room for discretion. As a consequence, there seems to be no threat to the judicial power.[65]

Verizon had also introduced another constitutional challenge to the DMCA, claiming that the use of the DMCA subpoena would infringe users' First Amendment rights. The Court dealt quickly with this issue and stated clearly that the First Amendment does not protect copyright infringement. The Court acknowledged that while the Supreme Court states that the First Amendment protects anonymity, and that lower courts consider online expression to be covered by the same Amendment, in this case user anonymity did not need protection.[66] In Judge Bates' opinion, Verizon's customers should have little expectation of either privacy or anonymity when infringing copyright. Someone who has 'opened her computer to the world' by using peer-to-peer technologies cannot then claim privacy expectation.[67]

For all the reported reasons, the District Court denied the motion to quash and the request for a stay presented by Verizon.

Verizon appealed both the District Court's orders, based on the same three reasons, namely: the inapplicability of Section 512(h) to an ISP acting merely as a conduit; the unconstitutionality of a Section 512(h) subpoena under Article III of the Constitution; and the violation of users' First Amendment rights.[68] However, the Court of Appeal did not touch upon the First Amendment issue and granted the appeal on the basis of the other argumentations.

Starting their reasoning with an analysis of DMCA safe harbours, the Justices underlined the fact that the notice and take-down provision was significantly absent from Section 512(a), which only concerns providers transmitting, routing or providing connections. In order to obtain a subpoena, a claimant must submit 'a copy of a notification described in

---

[65] *In re Verizon 2* (n 51) 249–252, *passim*.

[66] *In re Verizon* (n 46) 42–44, *passim*. As Sonia K Katyal, 'Privacy v. Piracy' [2004] Yale Journal of Law & Technology 222, 324 acknowledges 'the court mistakenly presumed that the individual in question – indeed, every individual potentially subject to a DMCA notice – was already guilty of infringement, and thus was not entitled to any First Amendment protections'.

[67] *In re Verizon 2* (n 51) 267. A similar argument had already been made in *Katz v. United States*, 389 U.S. 347 (1967), 351.

[68] *RIAA v. Verizon* (n 48) 1231.

Subsection (c)(3)(A)'.[69] The subpoena required by the RIAA could not meet this condition since Verizon was not storing the infringing material, which, consequently, could not be removed; nor could Verizon disable the access to the same material.[70]

The RIAA pointed out that under Section 512(c)(3)(A) a notification is effective if it 'includes substantially' the required information. Since Verizon was able to identify the infringer with the information given by the RIAA, the notice proved sufficient. However, the Senate and House Reports read the term 'substantially' to apply to cases in which there are technical or spelling errors.[71] It was clear that the notification made by the RIAA was more than just formally wrong: the Court could not identify any infringing material at all. It therefore held that since a notification under Section 512(c)(3)(A) was needed and since such a notification could not be made for an ISP like Verizon, the subpoena could not be issued in the case.[72]

Considering the history of the DMCA, both the District Court and the Court of Appeal admitted that, while enacting the Act, Congress had not considered P2P networks, since they appeared only later.[73] Both courts recognized that it is the unique power of Congress to change copyright law.[74] However, in facing the tricky formulation of Section 512 and its applicability to mere transmission providers, the two Courts reached two different outcomes. The District Court thought that the subpoena was applicable since otherwise the statute could not address many of the cases for which the entire DMCA had been conceived. The Court of Appeal adopted the opposite interpretation and quashed the subpoena.[75]

---

[69]   17 U.S.C. § 512(h)(2)(A).

[70]   *RIAA v. Verizon* (n 48) 1234. The infringing material is stored on users' computers, which the ISP obviously cannot reach. The RIAA argued that instead of removing the material or disabling access, Verizon could simply have terminated a user's Internet account. Verizon argued – and the Court of Appeal agreed – that disabling an individual's access to infringing material is different from disabling access to the Internet.

[71]   Senate Rep. No. 105-190, at 47 (1998); House Rep. No. 105-551 pt. II, at 56 (1998). But for a different interpretation see *ALS Scan, Inc. v. RemarQ Cmtys, Inc.*, 239 F.3d 619, 625 (4th Cir. 2001).

[72]   *RIAA v. Verizon* (n 48) 1236.

[73]   *In re Verizon* (n 46) 38, citing Brief of *Amicus Curiae* Alliance for Public Technology, et al., at 6; see also *RIAA v. Verizon* (n 48) 1238.

[74]   See *In re Verizon* (n 46) 38; *RIAA v. Verizon* (n 48) 1238.

[75]   *RIAA v. Verizon* (n 48) 1238. Followed recently by *In Re Subpoena Issued To Birch Communications, Inc*, 2015 U.S. Dist. LEXIS 58485 (2015).

On 24 May 2004 the RIAA filed a Petition for a Writ of Certiorari with the Supreme Court, which was denied.[76]

Following the *Verizon* cases, other ISPs refused to comply with DMCA subpoenas served by the RIAA. At least two other cases were decided on the basis of *Verizon*: one with Charter Communications, one of the biggest cable operators in the US;[77] the other with the University of North Carolina.[78]

As in the *Verizon* cases, the RIAA obtained a subpoena from the clerk of the District Court of the Easter District of Missouri in order to acquire information on hundreds of Charter's subscribers. After many attempts to quash the subpoena, Charter finally succeeded before the Court of Appeals for the Eighth Circuit.[79] The appeal was built on the same assumptions as Verizon had made: Section 512(h) was applicable only to ISPs engaged in storing material and not to Charter, which was merely engaged in transmitting; a subpoena must be supported by a case or controversy, but there was no case or controversy pending when the subpoena was issued; and Section 512(h) violated the First Amendment right of Internet users. In addition, Charter argued that the application of Section 512(h) could violate subscribers' privacy, as regulated in the Communication Act of 1934.[80] The majority of the Court of Appeal simply retraced the reasoning of the appellate decision taken in *Verizon* and concluded by agreeing with it; this meant that the Court of Appeal did not address the constitutional arguments presented by the ISP.[81]

However, in this case there was a quite extensive dissenting opinion, delivered by Justice Murphy, who harshly criticized the interpretation adopted by the Court on the grounds that it blocked copyright holders

---

[76]   *Recording Ind. Assoc. v. Verizon Internet Servs.*, 543 U.S. 924 (2004).

[77]   *In re Charter Communications, Inc., Subpoena Enforcement Matter*, 393 F.3d 771, 773 (8th Cir., 2005). For an overview, see Mikel R Boeve, 'Will Internet Service Providers Be Forced to Turn In Their Copyright Infringing Customers? The Power of the Digital Millennium Copyright Act's Subpoena Provision After In Re Charter Communication' [2006] Hamline Law Review 177.

[78]   *In re Subpoena to University of North Carolina at Chapel Hill*, 367 F. Supp. 2d 945 (M.D.N.C., 2005). See also *Interscope Records v. Does 1–7*, 494 F. Supp. 2d 388 (E.D. Va. 2007).

[79]   *In re Charter* (n 77) 774–775.

[80]   An Act to provide for the regulation of interstate and foreign communication by wire or radio, and for other purposes, Pub. Law No. 73-416, 48 Stat. 1064 [47 U.S.C. § 551(c)(1)].

[81]   Nevertheless, the Court wrote that Section 512(h) '*may* unconstitutionally invade the power of the judiciary'. *In re Charter* (n 77) 777–778 (italics in original).

from obtaining the necessary protection against infringement. In her view, legal action against end users was the only possible practical method for protecting copyright holders' interests. She underlined that, contrary to what was sustained in *Verizon*, P2P file-sharing programs were already being developed when Congress passed the DMCA. Justice Murphy held that since there is no express reference to one or more kinds of service provider in Section 512(h), the provision can be applied to all types of ISP. If Congress had intended to restrict the application of Section 512(h) to some types of ISP only, it would have clearly stated as much.[82]

It is interesting to note that Justice Murphy also addressed Charter's arguments on user privacy listed above and the Communication Act. She considered that the DMCA states that the ISP must immediately disclose the information required by the subpoena, 'notwithstanding any other provision of law'.[83] In her interpretation, this means that the subpoena is intended to 'supersede ... other statutes that might interfere with or hinder the attainment of [its] objective'.[84] This would mean that ISPs can comply with the subpoena even though this appears to collide with the Communication Act and user privacy.

The RIAA also failed to obtain a subpoena in *In re University N.C.* In the matter, users allegedly downloading copyrighted songs were connecting to the Internet through the University of North Carolina at Chapel Hill or through North Carolina State University. The universities were acting as ISPs, more precisely as 'merely transmitting' ISPs. The RIAA obtained a subpoena directed to the universities, which at first appeared to be willing to comply, and notified the users about the subpoena. Two of the users filed a motion to intervene, as John and Jane Doe, and another to quash the subpoena. Both the defendants used statutory and constitutional arguments in their attempt to quash the subpoena,[85] including the argument employed by Verizon that since an ISP only transmitting information cannot be subject to a notification like the one in Section 512(c)(3), and given that the DMCA requires this notification for the issue of a subpoena, Section 512(h) could not be applied in their cases. The RIAA stuck to its usual arguments and asked the judges to look

---

    82   *In re Charter* (n 77) 778–780.
    83   17 U.S.C. § 512(h)(5).
    84   Judge Murphy cited *Campbell v. Minneapolis Pub. Hous. Auth. ex rel City of Minneapolis*, 168 F.3d 1069, 1075 (8th Cir. 1999), see *In re Charter* (n 77) 785.
    85   *In re University N.C.* (n 78) 946.

beyond the words of the Act and to embrace the congressional intent, which was to curtail Internet violations.[86]

The District Court's decision was based on *Verizon* and *In re Charter*. Applying Section 512(h) to mere transmission ISPs – such as universities – would require the court to craft rules and to exceed the purposes of Congress.[87]

As for the possibility that the subpoena was a violation of judicial power, the Court maintained that since Section 512(h) is ambiguous, clerks would need to interpret it and this would result in their function being more-than-ministerial.[88] Following this reasoning, the Court ordered both subpoenas to be quashed.[89]

2.2 'John Doe' Proceedings

In the first of the *Verizon* decisions, the ISP maintained that even though the DMCA subpoena was not applicable in its own case, copyright holders could still make use of 'John Doe' actions. Verizon thought that such actions would better protect user rights and that service providers would have an opportunity to try to quash the subpoena. Judge Bates explained that such an action would have required a great deal of effort and expense for the copyright holders, and would have been slower than the Section 512(h) subpoena, which was easier and less costly. The judge also considered the DMCA subpoena to better protect users, given the requirements that had to be fulfilled by the copyright holder prior to successfully obtaining an injunction.[90]

---

[86]   Ibid 952.

[87]   Ibid 954–955.

[88]   Ibid 955.

[89]   The decisions of *RIAA v. Verizon* (n 48), *In re Charter* (n 77) and *In re University N.C.* (n 78) have been widely criticized. See, for example, Zach Chaffee-McClure, 'Train in Vain: The Clash Between the RIAA and the Eighth Circuit over Whether the DMCA Subpoena Provision Applies to Peer-to-Peer Networks, and the Need to Steer the DMCA Back on Track with Congressional Intent' [2005] Washburn Law Journal 175, 189; Raynolds (n 46) 376; Boeve (n 77) 137ff; Dutcher (n 46) 502ff, spec. 514, where the author argues that the approach taken by these courts violated 'equal protection' since users of a § 512(a) ISP would be treated differently from users of § 512(b)–(d) ISPs.

[90]   *In re Verizon* (n 46) 39–41, *passim*. In the case *In re Charter* (n 77) the Court suggested that 'organizations such as the RIAA [could] also employ alternative avenues to seek this information, such as "John Doe" lawsuits', see *In re Charter* (n 77) 775. See also Michael Froomkin, 'Anonymity and the Law in the United States' in Ian Kerr, Carole Lucock and Valerie Steeves (eds), *Lessons*

As a consequence of the less than satisfactory results in the *Verizon* cases, given the authority and influence of the US Court of Appeals for the District of Columbia Circuit, and in a situation where *certiorari* to the Supreme Court was denied, the RIAA changed strategy and turned to a 'John Doe' proceeding.

The Motion Pictures Association of America (MPAA) also started 'John Doe' actions. Countless lawsuits have arisen from this procedure; only some of them will be explained here, with the aim of investigating whether the copyright holders' new tool led to different outcomes, and if it did, what those outcomes were.

In 2008 Arista Records and many other recording companies sued some John Does.[91] The plaintiffs alleged that the defendants had used a P2P program to download and distribute the former's copyrighted works to the public, without authorization. As usual, Arista could discover the IP addresses of the users, but not their names. The IP addresses were supplied by the California State University of Fresno, which acted as the ISP. In deciding the motion, Judge Austin acknowledged that the US courts did not have a unique vision on the feasibility of discovery in these processes, citing as many decisions in favour of disclosure as against it.[92] Judge Austin mainly considered the five following indicators:

1. the allegations of copyright infringement in the complaint;
2. the possibility that the ISP could destroy or delete information that might identify the Does identified in the complaint;
3. the fact that the discovery request was narrowly tailored;
4. that the request would substantially contribute to moving the case forward; and
5. that defendants would not be identifiable without this information.

Judge Austin decided that disclosure could be granted, including names, current and permanent addresses, telephone numbers and e-mail addresses, for each defendant as identified by the IP numbers listed in the complaint. Nevertheless, Judge Austin, in order to protect the Does' privacy and First Amendment rights, ordered that the University should

---

from the Identity Trail: Anonymity, Privacy and Identity in a Networked Society (OUP 2009) 441, spec. 453. Katyal (n 66) 286 saw the shift towards 'John Doe' processes as a positive impact of the *Verizon* cases.

[91]   *Arista Records, LLC v. Does 1–12*, 2008 U.S. Dist. LEXIS 82548.

[92]   Ibid 3–4.

make reasonable efforts to inform its subscribers about the subpoena, giving them an opportunity to bring a motion to quash it.[93]

That same year, the same companies sued other John Does, subscribers at State University of New York at Albany.[94] In July 2008 the District Court granted Arista permission to seek discovery from the University, which notified each Doe of their intention to disclose the requested information. Four defendants responded in order to quash the subpoena, raising a number of defences, one of which related to the infringement of the First Amendment. The Court, like others before it, claimed that even though under the First Amendment users have a right to anonymity on the Internet, this is a very limited right since P2P is not a real way of expressing oneself.[95] Users' privacy rights were also qualified as very limited: the Court considered that 'a defendant's First Amendment *privacy interests are exceedingly small* where the "speech" is the alleged infringement of copyrights'.[96] Following these arguments, the Court recognized that it should '*balance* the tension between this minimally protected constitutional right and a copyright owner's right to disclosure of the identity of a possible trespasser of its intellectual property interest'.[97] To carry out this balancing act, the Court relied on a five-factors test already adopted by other courts in previous cases:

1. whether plaintiffs have made a concrete showing of a *prima facie* claim of actionable harm;
2. the specificity of the discovery request;
3. the absence of alternative means to obtain the subpoenaed information;

---

[93] Ibid 5–6.

[94] *Arista Records, LLC v. Does 1–16*, 2009 U.S. Dist. LEXIS 12159.

[95] Citing the Supreme Court case *Reno v. ACLU*, 521 U.S. 844 (1997) at 870. On the issue of whether First Amendment protection should be given to speeches other than political ones, see Victoria Smith Ekstrand, 'Unmasking Jane and John Doe: Online Anonymity and the First Amendment' [2003] Communication Law & Policy 405, 413 fn 40; see *Sony Music Entertainment, Inc. v. Does 1–40*, 326 F. Supp. 2d 556 (S.D.N.Y. 2004) 564. Joshua Dickman, 'Anonymity and the Demands of Civil Procedure in Music Downloading Lawsuits' [2008] Tulane Law Review 1049, 1066 argues that when a user downloads and makes available to others music she likes, she is unquestionably exercising her free speech right coming directly from the First Amendment.

[96] *Arista Records, LLC v. Does 1–16* (n 94) 12, citing *Arista Records LLC v. John Does 1–19*, 551 F. Supp. 2d 1 (2008), 8 (emphasis added).

[97] *Arista Records, LLC v. Does 1–16* (n 94) 12 (emphasis added).

4.   a central need to obtain the subpoenaed information to advance the claim;

5.   the party's expectation of privacy.[98]

Referring also to the *Napster* and *Grokster* cases, the Court considered that file-sharing was undoubtedly a copyright-infringing activity. The plaintiffs' request for discovery was considered reasonable and specific; moreover, they had demonstrated that they had no alternative way of obtaining user identities. This information was also considered central and critical for the plaintiffs to obtain the enforcement of their rights. The first four factors thus clearly weighed in favour of the copyright holders. Users' expectation of privacy was the only factor left. The Court considered that the Does had a minimal expectation of privacy, given the way in which P2P networks work. Hence, the plaintiffs' need for disclosure outweighed the Does' First Amendment rights. The Does could not claim any expectation of privacy.[99] As a result, the Court granted the copyright holders' request.

In the same decision, the Court argued that even if the information had been illegally obtained, this would not have constituted an obstacle to its admissibility in a civil trial.[100] This last statement is particularly interesting in light of what the Italian courts have decided. As mentioned in Chapter 3, art. 11 of the Italian Privacy Code states that information obtained in violation of the Code itself cannot be used. This provision proved important for the Italian cases here analysed.

This decision by the District Court was based on a test that had already been applied by other judges in similar controversies. The test seems to have originated in a case involving Sony Music Entertainment, in which a number of Does tried to quash a subpoena.[101] In deciding the case, Justice Chin considered two questions related to the First Amendment. The first question was whether someone who downloads or distributes music without permission is engaging in speech. In the case of an affirmative answer, the second question asked is whether or not the First Amendment protects that person's identity from disclosure. The District Court, relying on other courts' earlier decisions, elaborated upon the 'balancing test' reproduced above to decide whether a subpoena seeking disclosure of user identities was to be quashed or not.[102] On the question

---

98   See *Sony Music Entm't Inc. v. Does 1–40* (n 95) 565–567.

99   *Arista Records, LLC v. Does 1–16* (n 94) 16–25.

100   Ibid 26.

101   *Sony Music Entm't Inc. v. Does 1–40* (n 95).

102   Ibid 565.

of the defendants' expectation of privacy, Justice Chin referred to the *Verizon* case and held that people using file-sharing programs should not expect to have privacy. Furthermore, the judge also considered the terms of service in the contract between the ISP and the users. In the specific case, the terms stated that the transmission or distribution of material in violation of any law or regulation, including copyrighted works without proper authorization, was prohibited. The same terms further stated that the ISP had the right to disclose any information necessary to satisfy any law, regulation or other governmental request. This clearly weighed against users' expectation of privacy. As a result, the Court decided that the plaintiffs' right to pursue copyright infringement claims outweighed the defendants' right of privacy and anonymity.[103]

The ruling of the case involving Sony was applied in many subsequent cases. The test applied in *Sony* is just one of many applied by US courts in lawsuits aiming at unmasking Does.[104] Most cases pertain to defamation versus free speech, rather than copyright versus privacy. Nonetheless, courts sometimes apply the tests interchangeably. Justice Chin's decision is still applied in current cases involving copyright against John and Jane Does, and decided by different courts throughout the US.[105] In many cases, courts considered users' right to privacy to be very weak, or non-existent, because a third party, namely the ISP, already owned the data requested by the plaintiff.[106]

As we have seen, the RIAA has tried to punish illegal P2P networks and users in a number of different ways. Since 2007 it has sent hundreds

---

[103]   Ibid 567.

[104]   Nathaniel Gleicher, 'John Doe Subpoenas: Toward A Consistent Legal Standard' [2008] 118 Yale Law Journal 320; Matthew Mazzotta, 'Balancing Act: Finding Consensus on Standards for Unmasking Anonymous Internet Speakers' [2010] Boston College Law Review 833, especially 839ff.

[105]   See as examples: *Achte/Neunte v. Does 1–4.577*, 736 F. Supp. 2d 212 (2010); *West Coast Productions, Inc. v. John Does 1–5829*, 275 F.R.D. 9 (2011); *Voltage Pictures, Llc, v. Does 1–22*, 2013 U.S. Dist. LEXIS 111138 (2013); *Patrick Collins, Inc. v. John Does 1–11, 13–18, and 20–23*, 2013 U.S. Dist. LEXIS 13414 (2013); *Good Man Productions, Inc. v. John Doe*, 2014 U.S. Dist. LEXIS 172175 (2014); *Malibu Media, Llc. v. John Doe*, 2015 U.S. Dist. LEXIS 94054 (2015); *Rotten Records, Inc, v. John Doe*, 2015 U.S. Dist. LEXIS 73024 (2015). See also *Well Go Usa, Inc. v. Unknown Participants In Filesharing*, 2012 U.S. Dist. LEXIS 137272 (2012); *Signature Management Team, Llc, v. Automattic, Inc.*, 941 F. Supp. 2d 1145 (2013), applying the test crafted in *Sony* to a motion to quash a DMCA subpoena.

[106]   See, for instance, *Alibu Media, LLC v. John Does # 1–30*, 2012 U.S. Dist. LEXIS 175919 (2012), 10–11.

of 'pre-litigation' letters to various universities, with the request to forward them to their students. These letters did not identify the infringers; they just contained their IP addresses. With the threat of a future suit, they offered a settlement of about $3,000, as long as the student paid within 20 days of receiving the letter.[107] If the student did not respond to the letter, the RIAA started the 'John Doe' phase described above. Once the RIAA got users' names and addresses, it stopped pursuing the John Doe lawsuits and either sent letters to users offering a settlement, or started suing the identified defendants. When a defendant defaulted, plaintiffs usually obtained a default judgment,[108] in which each song was valued at roughly 1,000 times the amount for which the defendant could have purchased it.[109] Several claims were filed but it seems that only two eventually went to trial.[110]

Other cases have been resolved with the courts granting the requested order but applying specific measures to preserve user privacy and anonymity. The Federal District Court of the Eastern District of New York, for instance, approved a subpoena but required that the Does' information be sealed and sent directly to the Court,[111] and the United States District Court for the Northern District of Illinois Eastern Division

---

[107]   EFF, 'RIAA v. The People: Four Years Later' (*eff.org*, 2007) <http://w2.eff.org/IP/P2P/riaa_at_four.pdf> accessed 5 March 2017, 8–9. This campaign was for some time supported through a website (www.p2plawsuits.com – not accessible anymore) where individuals receiving pre-litigation letters could simply settle their cases with a credit card payment.

[108]   Default judgments may exist in different situations. In this case, the defendant never appears or answers the plaintiff's complaint, see Jake H Friedenthal, Mary K Kane and Arthur R Miller, *Civil Procedure* (4th edn, Thomson West 2005) 480ff; see also Entry: *Default-judgment* in Henry C Black, *Black's Law Dictionary* (5th edn, West Publishing 1979) 376, according to which '[u]nder Rules of Civil Procedure, when a party against whom a judgment for affirmative relief is sought has failed to plead (*i.e.* answer) or otherwise defend, he is in default and a judgment by default may be entered by the clerk or the court'.

[109]   For a criticism of the award of these damages see J Cam Barker, 'Grossly Excessive Penalties in the Battle Against Illegal File-Sharing: The Troubling Effects of Aggregating Minimum Statutory Damages for Copyright Infringement' [2004] 83 Texas Law Review 525.

[110]   *Virgin Records Am., Inc. v. Thomas*, 2007 U.S. Dist. LEXIS 79585 (D. Minn. 2007), then renamed *Capitol Records Inc. v. Thomas*, 579 F. Supp. 2d 1210 (2008) and *Sony BMG Music Entm't v. Tenenbaum*, 672 F. Supp. 2d 217 (D. Mass. 2009).

[111]   *In re: BitTorrent Adult Film Copyright Infringement Cases*, 296 F.R.D. 80 (2012), 93.

allowed the Does to proceed anonymously to preserve their identities.[112] Another possibility was to allow defendants to proceed under pseudonyms.[113] Only some courts adopted these precautions; others, even when a request was made, refused to adopt any of these measures.[114]

3. CANADIAN CASES

3.1 *BMG v. Does* before the Federal Court

Soon after the first US cases against final users, Canadian copyright holders started their own war against file-sharing on Canadian soil.

In February 2004 BMG Canada, together with other companies holding copyright in sound recordings, filed a claim against 'John Doe, Jane Doe and All Those Persons Who Are Infringing the Plaintiffs' Copyright in Sound Recordings'. The plaintiffs were the largest record companies in Canada and are hereinafter collectively called CRIA, the acronym of the umbrella group 'Canadian Recording Industry Association', which represented them in the pleadings.[115] CRIA's suit was a sort of copycat version of the RIAA's: CRIA was the RIAA arm in Canada, and the suits had the same goals.[116]

The respondents were five ISPs: Shaw Communication Inc., Rogers Cable Communication Inc., Bell Sympatico, Telus Inc. and Vidéotron Ltée. CRIA's first move was to issue a statement of claim against 29 Does, identified by their IP addresses, and to move for discovery from the ISPs involved in order to ascertain the users' real identities.

CRIA actually started directly with what was, for the RIAA, a second step since, as previously explained, Canadian law does not provide an

---

[112] *Sunlust Pictures, LLC v. Does 1–75*, 2012 WL 3717768 (N.D. Ill. Aug. 27, 2012), 6.

[113] *TCYK, LLC v. Doe*, 2013 U.S. Dist. LEXIS 95817 (2013), 14.

[114] *Liberty Media Holdings, LLC v. Swarm Sharing Hash File*, 821 F. Supp. 2d 444, 453 (D. Mass. 2011); *West Coast Productions* (n 105).

[115] The Canadian Recording Industry Association is a non-profit organization, founded in the 1960s, to represent the interest of Canadian companies that create, manufacture and market sound recordings. The association also enforces the rights of its members. Starting from 2011, the CRIA changed its name to 'Music Canada'; see <https://musiccanada.com/tag/cria/> accessed 5 March 2017.

[116] Jane Bailey, 'The Substance of Procedure: Non-Party Disclosure in the Canadian and U.S. Online Music Sharing Litigation' [2006] Alberta Law Review 615, 625.

instrument equivalent to the DMCA subpoena. Therefore, the plaintiffs relied on Rules 233 and 238 of the Federal Court Rules and on so-called 'Norwich orders' to compel the providers to disclose individuals' information.

CRIA's notice of motion stated that an investigation had revealed that file-sharers had infringed the plaintiffs' copyright. CRIA had relied heavily on MediaSentry, a company which located and identified IP addresses engaged in file-sharing activities, using software that distributed bogus or inoperative files over the Internet which users, imagining them to be music files, would download,[117] thereby signalling their infringing conduct.

As in the RIAA cases, these people were only identifiable through their pseudonyms or IP addresses. CRIA claimed that without disclosure of the users' identities, its members could not enforce their rights. Therefore it asked to obtain users' data, including home, mailing and business addresses; telephone numbers; facsimile numbers; and e-mail addresses.[118]

Four of the five ISPs opposed the motion; only Vidéotron agreed to comply. The ISPs' defences were based on different arguments, however it is interesting to note that all four of the opponent responses included some privacy claims, such as:

● revealing subscribers' information could make ISPs liable under the Personal Information Protection and Electronic Documents Act (PIPEDA), especially in case of incorrect information;[119]
● customers had an expectation that their data would remain confidential;[120]

---

[117]   See *Shaw's Written representations*, at 14 <www.cippic.ca/documents/file-sharing-lawsuits/FurtherWrittenSubmissionsShaw.pdf> accessed 5 March 2017. The documents of the trial are available on the website of the Canadian Internet Policy and Public Interest Clinic – CIPPIC – which intervened in the process as a public interest group (<www.cippic.ca> accessed 5 March 2017), see CRIA's request order for ISPs available at <www.cippic.ca/documents/file-sharing-lawsuits/Schedule-A–Order.pdf> accessed 5 March 2017.

[118]   Paras 1(a)–(b) of the order in the controversy between BMG and Does (*BMG Canada Inc. v. John Doe* [2004] 3 F.C.R. 241) <www.cippic.ca/sites/default/files/file-sharing-lawsuits/Schedule-A–Order.pdf> accessed 5 March 2017.

[119]   *Shaw's Written representations* (n 117) 17.

[120]   Ibid.

- there is no provision in PIPEDA for making such an order on an *ex parte* basis vis-à-vis the person whose personal information is sought;[121]
- any potential order for the disclosure of personal information would need to comply with PIPEDA principles, which – inter alia – require that only reasonably necessary personal information be disclosed;[122]
- the disclosure should be limited to name and last known address, since asking for business addresses, telephone numbers, facsimile numbers, and e-mail addresses would be 'overbroad, excessive and should not be required'.[123]

The Canadian Internet Policy and Public Interest Clinic (CIPPIC) intervened with a memorandum of argument, which began by clearly stating that the 'case involve[d] the *balancing* of privacy rights of individuals against the need for disclosure by plaintiffs wishing to pursue civil actions' and that a high threshold test would be appropriate, given that fundamental privacy values were at stake.[124] Quoting Supreme Court judgments, CIPPIC pointed out that in modern societies, people know that in some situations they can reasonably expect that their data will not be divulged and will be protected.[125] This important conception was at the core of PIPEDA and of other provincial laws; CIPPIC also recalled the Supreme Court interpretation of Sections 7 and 8 of the Charter of Rights and Freedoms.

CIPPIC also touched upon the issue of online anonymity: if the court ordered the disclosure of a user's information, any subsequent action commenced by CRIA could make public other information regarding that same user, who would have believed her online behaviour to be covered by anonymity. In some cases, this could create significant embarrassment and even an irreparable harm to the user, with a corresponding chilling

---

[121] Ibid.

[122] See *Rogers' written representations*, 19 <www.cippic.ca/documents/file-sharing-lawsuits/Rogers_Written_Reps_Mar12.pdf> accessed 5 March 2017; *Bell's written representations*, 2–3 <www.cippic.ca/documents/file-sharing-lawsuits/Bell_Written_Submissions.pdf> accessed 5 March 2017.

[123] See *Rogers' written representations* (n 122).

[124] *CIPPIC's memorandum of argument* is available at <www.cippic.ca/documents/file-sharing-lawsuits/Memorandum_final_12pt.pdf> accessed 5 March 2017 (emphasis added).

[125] See *R. v. Dyment* [1988] 2 S.C.R. 417, para 33.

effect on free speech and online activity.[126] Reporting an important
decision by the Ontario Superior Court, CIPPIC stressed that, as far as
anonymity is concerned,

> [i]mplicit in the passage of information through the Internet by utilization of
> an alias or pseudonym is the mutual understanding that, to some degree, the
> identity of the source will be concealed. ... [S]ome degree of privacy or
> confidentiality with respect to the identity of the Internet protocol address of
> the originator of a message has significant safety value and is in keeping with
> what should be perceived as being good public policy.[127]

CIPPIC acknowledged that privacy online cannot be absolute, but at the
same time plaintiffs should not be allowed to uncover the identity of
users based on mere allegations. Setting low threshold tests would permit
plaintiffs to engage in 'fishing expeditions' and abuse the judicial
process. Moreover, the fact that the order would be invasive, and without
previous notice to the defendants[128] would irremediably remove users'
anonymity and breach PIPEDA principles.

Like CIPPIC, Electronic Frontier Canada (EFC)[129] asked for and
obtained the chance to intervene and serve a written memorandum. EFC
addressed the question of the correct test to be applied in deciding on the
disclosure and held that the judicial exercise of discretion should involve
the *balancing of competing public interests* against the disclosure. In
particular, according to EFC, evidence should be excluded when 'its
prejudicial effect outweighs its probative value'.[130]

As sustained by CIPPIC and by some of the respondent ISPs, EFC
stated that the Does had an expectation of privacy about their information. Given the possible unreliability of the data that might be
disclosed, the prejudice to the defendant would outweigh the probative
value of obtaining the information. EFC argued that CRIA had an
obligation to ensure that users' privacy rights were not needlessly

---

126   *CIPPIC's memorandum* (n 124) 5–7.
127   *Irwin Toy Ltd. v. Doe* [2000] O.T.C. 561, paras 10–11.
128   Except for those already noticed by their ISP, such as Roger's users.
129   EFC 'was founded to ensure that the principles embodied in the Canadian
Charter of Rights and Freedoms remain protected as new computing, communications, and information technologies are introduced into Canadian society', see
<www.efc.ca> accessed 5 March 2017. *EFC's memorandum of argument*,
4–5 <www.cippic.ca/documents/file-sharing-lawsuits/document-archives.html>
accessed 5 March 2017.
130   *EFC's memorandum* (n 129) 7, citing the House of Lords case *British
Steel v. Granada Television* [1981] 1 All ER 417.

violated and to prove that the information sought was relevant to the claim of copyright infringement.[131]

As can be clearly seen, all the defendants, and the interveners, stressed the importance of user privacy. Moreover, the opponent parties all proposed the application of a balancing test. Even though the proposed tests differed, they all included a step-by-step analysis designed to weigh user privacy against other values.

With reference to the issue of user privacy, CRIA stated that in the particular case there was no expectation of privacy and that the disclosure of the information sought would not breach PIPEDA given that the Act explicitly authorizes disclosure of personal information in cases provided under Section 7(3)(c). Further, the plaintiffs held that subscribers had consented to the disclosure of their information when they agreed to the terms of service with their ISP. CRIA argued that ISPs were the only practical source of information available and that, notwithstanding the different opinion of the ISPs, the data maintained by the providers would be reliable.[132]

With regard to showing a *prima facie* case, CRIA asserted that evidence showed that individuals had copied sound recordings, over which CRIA had exclusive rights, to publicly shared computer directories, thus making recordings available for copy, transmission and distribution to potentially millions of other file-sharers.[133]

The recording industry then acknowledged that in deciding whether to grant the order, the Court should have taken into account the *public interest both in favour of and against disclosure*.[134] CRIA asserted that on the one hand, the disclosure was the only way to sue the infringers and, on the other, there was nothing that could weigh against CRIA's opportunity to sue.

As for privacy issues, the CRIA held that the case was just 'a matter of private law'. Hence, even if common law should be interpreted in light of the Charter's principles in private law matters, this does not mean that the analysis usually applied in cases regarding governmental actions should be imported into private litigation.[135] More precisely, art. 8 of the Charter

---

[131]   *EFC's memorandum* (n 129) 8–10.

[132]   *CRIA's written representations* at 5–6 <www.cippic.ca/documents/file-sharing-lawsuits/Plaintiffs_Submissions_March_12.pdf> accessed 5 March 2017.

[133]   Ibid 7.

[134]   Ibid 10.

[135]   Citing *Hill v. Church of Scientology of Toronto* [1995] 2 S.C.R. 1130 and *R. v. Fegan* [1993] O.J. No. 733.

238 *Copyright and information privacy*

did not apply, as it only protects citizens against invasion of the state when there is a reasonable expectation of privacy.[136]

With regard to PIPEDA, CRIA recalled Section 4.3 of Schedule 1 related to 'consent', which states that sometimes the knowledge and consent of the individual to whom the information is related might be inappropriate. Indeed, as explained earlier in this book, Section 7(3)(c) provides an important exception to subjects' consent: an organization may disclose personal information without the individual's knowledge or consent when it is 'required to comply with a subpoena or warrant issued or an order made by a court, person or body with jurisdiction to compel the production of information, or to comply with rules of court relating to the production of records'. The plaintiffs held that this section was applicable to their case, given that the precise aim of CRIA's motion was to obtain an order for the production of information from the respondents.[137]

CRIA also referred to the contractual relationship between users and providers and its terms of agreement. CRIA submitted that these terms notified subscribers that their information could be disclosed if they engaged in prohibited activities, including the dissemination of material that violates copyright and the use of file-sharing systems. Apparently, all the necessary consents had been obtained from the subscribers; hence, the disclosure requested by CRIA could be ordered without problems. Given Section 7(3)(c) and given the acceptance of the terms of use, the plaintiffs argued that the Does could not have any reasonable expectation of anonymity, especially in light of such an evident *prima facie* case of copyright infringement. User privacy could not outweigh an ISP's duty to disclose the information requested.[138]

CRIA held that when a user copies files into a shared directory on her computer, connects to the Internet and runs the application, she actually makes those files available to be copied, transmitted and distributed.[139] CRIA contended that the Does had violated Sections 18 and 27 of the Copyright Act related to the right to reproduction and distribution of the plaintiffs.[140] CRIA also explicitly addressed the issue of the applicability of the exemption provided by Section 80 of the Copyright Act, regarding, as already illustrated, copies for private use. Citing a decision of the

---

[136] Referring to *R. v. Plant* [1993] 3 S.C.R. 281, paras 23–24.
[137] *CRIA's written representations* (n 132) 15.
[138] Ibid 17–19.
[139] CRIA clearly referred to the right to 'make available', using the words of WIPO Treaties.
[140] *CRIA's written representations* (n 132) 26–27.

Copyright Board, CRIA illustrated that exemption under Section 80 'expressly excludes ... distributing, communicating to the public by telecommunication ... the copy made. ... distributing this same copy to friends online is prohibited.'[141] The inclusion of the recording files in a shared directory would be an act of distribution and the consequent transmission of copies online would represent a communication to the public. This would have excluded the applicability of Section 80, which does not apply if the copying is done for 'the purpose of either distributing ... or communicating to the public by telecommunication'.[142] To support its view, CRIA cited the well-known *Tariff 22* decision by the Copyright Board, which considered the making available of a work as the authorization of the communication of a work.[143] CRIA then cited the seminal decision *CCH*, where, as seen, it was specified that 'authorization' has to be interpreted as 'give approval to, sanction, permit, favour, encourage'.[144]

In March 2004 Justice Von Finckenstein delivered his decision. The judge asked himself three initial questions:

1. What legal test should th[e] Court apply?
2. Have the plaintiffs met the test?
3. If an order is issued, what should the scope and terms of such an order be?[145]

The Court referred first of all to the cases *Norwich* and *Glaxo Wellcome*.[146] In both these cases non-parties were requested to produce documents which already existed as a result of their normal functions. The records sought were therefore easily available and their production was questioned under principles other than their actual existence. Both

---

[141] Copyright Board of Canada, *Private Copying 2003–2004*, 12 December 2003 <www.cb-cda.gc.ca/decisions/2003/20031212-c-b.pdf> accessed 5 March 2017, 20.

[142] Remember on this point CIPPIC argued that users did not distribute 'on purpose', since the file-sharing program allows transmission to other users, even without the knowledge of the computer owner; see above.

[143] Copyright Board of Canada, *Public Performance of Musical Works 1996, 1997, 1998 – Tariff 22*, October 1999 <www.cb-cda.gc.ca/decisions/1999/19991027-m-b.pdf> accessed 5 March 2017, 26.

[144] *CCH Canadian Ltd. v. Law Society of Upper Canada* [2004] S.C.R. 339, 361.

[145] *BMG* Federal Court (n 118) para 8.

[146] *Norwich Pharmacal Co. v. Commissioners of Customs and Exercise* [1974] A.C. 133 (HL); *Glaxo Wellcome PLC v. Minister of National Revenue* [1998] 4 F.C. 439. See Chapter 2, Section 6.

cases listed the criteria that courts should consider in deciding whether disclosure should be ordered or not.

Since the *Glaxo Wellcome* decision, the doctrine of equitable discovery has been firmly established in the Canadian system.[147] The increased applicability of this doctrine may also be linked to the increase in the number of lawsuits such as *BMG*, in which the defendants' names are known only by third parties. The *BMG* case was paradigmatic in this sense: it began as a 'John Doe' case, but was solved by applying the *Norwich* standard.[148] Indeed, *Norwich* and *Glaxo Wellcome* established that when applicants seek pre-action discovery to ascertain the identity of defendants, they can do so by means of an equitable bill of discovery, whereas, as Von Finckenstein J explained, when an action has been commenced, even if it is against a 'Doe' defendant, the plaintiff has to rely on Rules 233 and 238.

Despite their similarities, *BMG* and *Glaxo Wellcome* present one marked difference: while the latter deals with confidentiality (as did *Norwich*), the former deals with Does' privacy. Before *BMG* a defendant could not advance privacy rights as a defence, since the request did not concern her personal realm, but that of someone else. *BMG* is further peculiar since it was the first example of the application of a *Norwich* order after the PIPEDA implementation.[149]

Based on *Norwich* and *Glaxo Wellcome*, Von Finckenstein J listed the following five criteria, which in his opinion should also have been applied to motions promoted under Rule 238:

   (a) the applicant must establish a prima facie case against the unknown alleged wrongdoer;

   (b) the person from whom discovery is sought must be in some way involved in the matter under dispute, he must be more than an innocent bystander;

   (c) the person from whom discovery is sought must be the only practical source of information available to the applicants;

   (d) the person from whom discovery is sought must be reasonably compensated for his expenses arising out of compliance with the discovery order, in addition to his legal costs;

---

[147] For other cases applying the same principle, see Kevin LaRoche and Guy J Pratte, 'The Norwich Pharmacal Principle and Its Utility in Intellectual Property Litigation' [2001] 18 Canadian Intellectual Property Review 117, 127ff.

[148] This led one author to express concern that the *Norwich* standard would be the only standard applied in all the pre-action discoveries: Melody Yiu, 'A New Prescription for Disclosure: Reformulating the Rule for the Norwich Order' [2007] University of Toronto Faculty Law Review 41, 43–44.

[149] Ibid 63.

(e) the public interest in favour of disclosure must outweigh the legitimate privacy concerns.[150]

In the case of Rule 233, the Court determined that the rule itself was not broad enough to cover the requests of the plaintiffs. This rule applies to the production of existing documents, while the Court considered that in the particular case ISPs would have to specifically generate the documents, which were not already in existence.[151]

With regard to the criterion under letter (a), the Court could not find evidence of connection between the pseudonyms and the IP addresses. The plaintiffs did not explain, or give proof of, how the nicknames were linked to the IP addresses identified by MediaSentry. The Court therefore considered it would be irresponsible to order the disclosure of users' data without this evidence and without being able to ascertain its reliability.[152] Second, the Court maintained that the plaintiffs had not showed evidence of infringement of copyright. Referring to a specific decision of the Copyright Board, also cited by CRIA,[153] Von Finckenstein J concluded that downloading a song for personal use did not amount to infringement in the light of Section 80(1) of the Copyright Act. The judge considered that when Does put personal copies into their shared directories they do not *authorize* infringement.[154]

Citing *CCH*, the judge claimed that he could not see any 'difference between placing a photocopy machine in a room full of copyrighted material and a computer user that places a personal copy on a shared directory linked to a P2P service'.[155] For an act to constitute 'distribution' there should be a positive act, such as sending the copies or advertising their availability; in fact, the 'right to make available' was not part of Canadian copyright law, given that Canada implemented the World Intellectual Property Organization (WIPO) Treaties only in 2012. Finally, the plaintiffs had not demonstrated that users had in fact directly infringed copyright, and direct infringement is the precondition for a secondary infringement to occur.[156]

As for criterion (b), there was no doubt that ISPs were involved with the alleged infringer, given that the former provided the latter's access to

---

[150] *BMG* Federal Court (n 118) paras 13–14.
[151] Ibid para 15.
[152] Ibid para 20.
[153] *Private Copying 2003–2004* (n 141) 20.
[154] *BMG* Federal Court (n 118) paras 21–25.
[155] Ibid para 27.
[156] Ibid paras 26–29.

the Internet.[157] Criterion (d) provides that the person from whom the discovery is sought shall be compensated for the expenses borne due to compliance with the discovery order, as well as legal costs. From the ISPs' affidavits, the Court drew some conclusions. First of all, the kind of information sought by the plaintiffs was not normally kept by the ISPs. Furthermore, the older the information is, the more difficult to collect and unreliable it is. Given that some time had passed, linking some IP addresses to account holders might be impossible. Moreover, even if ISPs could find out the name of the account holder, they would never find the actual computer user, especially when the account holder was an institution. Quite apart from these problems, the process would be costly for the ISPs and they would need to be reimbursed for all the expenses.[158]

Von Finckenstein J then addressed the issue of the public interest arguments for and against the disclosure of the data. Taking user privacy into account, the judge stated that '[i]t is unquestionable but that the protection of privacy is of utmost importance to Canadian society'.[159] He then cited the words of Justice Lamer in *R. v. Dyment*: '[g]rounded in man's physical and moral autonomy, privacy is essential for the well-being of the individual. For this reason alone, it is worthy of constitutional protection, but it also has profound significance for the public order'.[160]

Concerning PIPEDA, the judge considered that even though, in enacting the said Act, Parliament had agreed on the need to protect privacy, this did not mean that privacy could be used to protect a person from the application of liability. In particular, PIPEDA does not restrict the ability of a court to order production of documents related to the identity of the same person, as the exemption provided by Section 7(3)(c) demonstrates. Therefore, both PIPEDA and the *Norwich/Glaxo Wellcome* test would have permitted the disclosure of the requested data. Indeed, previous cases demonstrated that privacy had never outweighed the interest in obtaining disclosure.[161]

---

157   Ibid para 30. Regarding letter (c) the Court did not make any determination.
158   Ibid paras 32–35.
159   Ibid para 36.
160   *R. v. Dyment* (n 125) para 28.
161   The Court cited *Irwin Toy Ltd. v. Doe* (n 127); *Loblaw Companies Ltd. v. Aliant Telecom, Inc.* [2003] N.B.R. (2d) (Supp.) No. 32; *Ontario First Nations Limited Partnership v. John Doe* (June 3, 2002) (Ont. S.C.J.); *Canadian Blood Services/Société Canadienne du Sang v. John Doe* (June 17, 2002) (Ont. S.C.J.);

The Court wanted to ensure the reliability of the information to be disclosed. As the evidence had been gathered some months before the motion was filed, the information might be difficult to obtain and be of limited reliability.[162] Since these problems could lead to the identification of the wrong people, the Court stated that 'the privacy concerns outweigh the public interest concerns in favour of disclosure'.[163]

Justice Von Finckenstein then analysed the second question, i.e. whether the plaintiffs had met the test. Following the premises, the judge concluded that the test had not been met. The plaintiffs had neither demonstrated a *prima facie* case, nor had they proved that ISPs were the only practical source of information, nor had they established that the public interest case for disclosure was greater than the privacy concerns.[164]

In its conclusion, the Court considered what measures would have had to have been adopted had the disclosure been granted. In order to protect the Does' privacy, their names would have been disclosed only to substitute 'John and Jane Doe': users' pseudonyms would have been used for the main part of the trial and their real names and addresses would have been inserted in an annex, subject to confidentiality.[165]

As a result, the judge denied the motion.

3.2 *BMG v. Does* before the Federal Court of Appeal

CRIA soon appealed Justice Von Finckenstein's decision.[166] The appellant held that the federal judge had mistakenly interpreted Section 80(1) of the Copyright Act. According to CRIA, the Does had copied the recordings in their shared directories with the aim of distributing and communicating the songs and not for their own private use. Such behaviour constituted an infringement of authorization rights under Sections 18(1) and 27(1) of the Copyright Act. Hence, the judge should have recognized the existence of a *prima facie* or bona fide standard. In

---

Wa'el Chehab v. John Doe (October 3, 2003) (Ont. S.C.J.); *Kibale v. Canada* [1991] F.C.J. No. 634 (QL) (FC).

[162] See *Shaw's Written representations* (n 117); *Telus's written representations*, 4–7 <www.cippic.ca/documents/file-sharing-lawsuits/Written_Representations.pdf> accessed 5 March 2017.

[163] *BMG Federal Court* (n 118) paras 36–42.

[164] Ibid para 43.

[165] Ibid paras 44–46.

[166] *CRIA's notice of appeal* <www.cippic.ca/documents/file-sharing-lawsuits/criaappealnotice.pdf> accessed 5 March 2017.

CRIA's view, Von Finckenstein J had erred in holding that the plaintiffs did not demonstrate the link between users' pseudonyms and the IP addresses and that ISPs were not the only practical source of the information sought. He had further erred in saying that it was common ground that subscribers had an expectation that their identity would be kept private and confidential and that the data were not reliable due to their obsolescence. Finally, the judge erred in holding that Rule 233 presupposes the existence of the requested documents, since computer data were already available on the computer systems of the ISPs.[167]

In May 2005 the Federal Court of Appeal delivered its decision, which went in the same direction as Justice Von Finckenstein's as regards the evidence, but was not completely in accordance with his view as regards Section 80.

Addressing the issue of the applicability of Rule 233, Sexton JA agreed with Von Finckenstein J in saying that the information sought did not currently exist and that it needed to be produced. Therefore, the mentioned Rule could not be applied. The Court wrote that the crucial evidence submitted by CRIA was inaccurate and could point towards the wrong people, creating the risk of invading the privacy of innocent account holders, who might be named as defendants. Justice Sexton stated that the appeal should have been dismissed for this reason alone.[168]

In contrast, in spite of the ISPs' arguments, Sexton J considered Rule 238 applicable in the case. Rule 238(2) provides that notice of the motion must be served 'on the other parties'. Since the other parties were not known (the Does), the ISPs argued that the service was not possible and therefore Rule 238 could not provide a procedure to discover the infringers' identities. However, Rule 238(1) provides that '[a] party to an action may bring a motion for leave to examine for discovery any person not a party to the action ... who might have information on an issue in the action'. As argued by the plaintiffs, the main issue on the motion was the identity of the alleged infringers and in the Court of Appeal's reasoning this was an issue in the action, and Rule 238 was broad enough to cover this case. Even though Justice Sexton admitted that examinations for discovery of third parties should not become common, he stated that orders under Rule 238 would be necessary when a plaintiff was frustrated

---

167   Ibid 6–8.
168   *BMG Canada Inc. v. John Doe* [2005] F.C.J. No. 858, paras 17–21.

in enforcing her rights because she was unaware of the identity of the alleged wrongdoers.[169]

Turning to the applicability of a bill of discovery, the Court cited *Glaxo Wellcome* again. Justice Sexton agreed with the Trial Division in holding that the criteria used for granting a bill of discovery should also have been applied under Rule 238, given that the same issue was at stake in both procedures.[170] However, while Justice Von Finckenstein had said that the plaintiff should provide evidence of a *prima facie* case, the appellate Court stated that the proper test was whether the applicant had a bona fide claim against the proposed defendant. Referring once again to *Glaxo Wellcome*,[171] Justice Sexton recognized that it was impossible for the plaintiffs to prove a *prima facie* case, given that they did not even know the identity of the alleged infringers, let alone their behaviour. For these reasons, the Court of Appeal suggested that the proper standard required a bona fide claim. As for the other criteria relating to the equitable bill of discovery, the appellate Court agreed with Justice Von Finckenstein.[172]

With reference to the delicate question of user privacy, Sexton JA opened the decision stating that the 'case illustrate[d] the tension existing between the privacy rights of those who use the Internet and those whose rights may be infringed or abused by anonymous Internet users'.[173] Sexton JA's reasoning with regard to privacy is interesting. He acknowledged that current unwarranted intrusions put individuals at great personal risk and subjected their views and beliefs to indefensible scrutiny[174] and agreed with the lower court in saying that in order for the disclosure to have been permitted, public interest would have had to outweigh legitimate privacy concerns. Under PIPEDA, ISPs are not entitled to voluntarily disclose their customers' personal information. Nevertheless, as we have seen, they can be compelled to reveal this

---

[169]   The Court of Appeal recalled the Ontarian decision (*Irwin Toy Ltd. v. Doe* (n 127)) applying the Ontario Rules of Civil Procedure, R.R.O. 1990 – *Production From Non-Parties With Leave – Order for Inspection – 30.10; Discovery of Non-Parties With Leave – General – 31.10.* A similar case was decided by the New Brunswick Court of Queen's Bench: *Loblaw Companies Ltd. v. Aliant Telecom Inc.* (n 161). See New Brunswick Rules of Court, N.B. Reg. 82-73 – *32.12 Discovery before Commencement of Proceeding.* See *BMG* Appeal (n 168) paras 23–27.

[170]   See *Glaxo Wellcome PLC* (n 146), para 20.

[171]   Ibid para 44.

[172]   *BMG* Appeal (n 168) paras 28–35, *passim*.

[173]   Ibid para 1.

[174]   Ibid para 4.

information pursuant to a court order. Moreover, when an organization receives a request for the release of personal information, it 'shall retain the information for as long as is necessary to allow the individual to exhaust any recourse' under the Act.[175] In order to protect people's privacy, PIPEDA provides that the disclosure of personal information handled by organizations is only legitimate in certain circumstances. The Court of Appeal held that even though modern technology has had great benefits for society, this should not mean that technology is allowed to 'obliterate those personal *property* rights which society ha[s] deemed important':[176] although privacy concerns had to be considered, they had to surrender to public concerns related to the infringement of intellectual property rights, where this *'infringement threatens to erode those rights'*. Therefore, if plaintiffs showed that they had a bona fide claim that unknown individuals infringed their copyrights, they had a *right* to obtain the identity of those persons in order to start a lawsuit. Nevertheless, this disclosure has to be made with caution to be sure that the alleged infringers' *privacy rights are invaded as minimally as possible.*[177]

Going back to the actual case, the Court considered the question of the lengthy delay between the request for the identities made by CRIA and the recording industry's collection of the information. The possible inaccuracy of the information, linked to the dynamicity of IP addresses, could have led to the infringement of the privacy rights of innocent persons, who could then have been sued by CRIA without justification. Furthermore, as CIPPIC had pointed out, Justice Sexton stressed that plaintiffs had to be careful not to extract defendants' private information unrelated to the infringement of copyright. This information could indeed be highly confidential and intrusion upon it could result in a breach of PIPEDA by the ISPs, with liability consequences. Finally, the Court held that if the disclosure were granted, specific direction would have to be given as to the type of information disclosed and the manner in which this information could be used.[178]

---

[175] PIPEDA – *Retention of information* – 8(8). After 2012 amendments, Section 41.26(1)(b) of the Copyright Act also prescribes that whoever receives a notice of claimed infringement (under the so-called 'notice & notice' system) shall retain any records that would allow the identity of the person to whom the electronic location belongs to be determined.

[176] *BMG* Appeal (n 168) para 41 (emphasis added).

[177] Ibid (emphasis added).

[178] E.g. users could be identified only through their initials; see ibid paras 35–45.

Lastly, in making its decision, the Court of Appeal turned to the question of copyright infringement. According to Justice Sexton, the lower Court had not correctly applied Subsection 80(1) of the Copyright Act. Indeed, the Trial Division judge relied upon *CCH* but he did not consider that copying the songs into a shared directory could constitute authorization because it invited and permitted other users to access and copy them. The Trial Division had stated that 'distribution' meant a 'positive act' by the owner of the shared folder but Sexton JA did not share this interpretation. Moreover, while Von Finckenstein J had stated that there could not be a secondary infringement – because users were not aware of the copying carried out by someone else – the appellate Court had a different opinion: indirect infringement could also exist when the user 'should have known' that there was infringement. Overall, Justice Sexton concluded by saying that Von Finckenstein J's findings were made too early in the case.[179]

The Court dismissed the appeal without prejudice to the plaintiffs' right to make a new application for disclosure of user identities, taking into account the Court's reasons.[180]

3.3 Following Cases

BMG is the most important case that the Canadian courts have faced to date in the matter of 'copyright vs. privacy'. The case remains a milestone, given the very low number of decisions delivered on this subject, as this short section demonstrates.

At the end of August 2011 the Federal Court released its decision on *Voltage Pictures LLC v. Jane Doe and John Doe.*[181] Voltage Pictures is a production company, which owns the copyright in the film *The Hurt Locker*. Exactly as had been done in the US, and as CRIA had done for music, Voltage Pictures traced the IP numbers of users allegedly downloading the movie. Again, as in the BMG cases, the plaintiff was not able to obtain user names without the help of the ISPs. Therefore, the claimant asked for a written examination for discovery of the ISPs in order to obtain the names and addresses corresponding to their users' IP numbers.[182]

Insofar as can be gleaned from reading the decision, the Federal Court, relying on an affidavit, accepted the claim that the defendants had

---

[179]   Ibid paras 46–54.
[180]   Ibid para 55. Richard CJ and Noël JA agreed.
[181]   *Voltage Pictures LLC v. Jane Doe and John Doe*, 2011 FC 1024.
[182]   Ibid paras 2–6.

downloaded and distributed the movie through P2P networks.[183] The Court failed to follow the more stringent test applied by the Trial Division in *BMG*, applying instead the more lenient, bona fide claim test required by the Court of Appeal in *BMG*. Citing the latter decision, Shore J held that a bona fide claim was enough, as long as caution was exercised by the courts when ordering the disclosure of identities, in order to minimize the invasion of privacy.[184]

With regard to Rule 238 of the Federal Courts Rules, the Court found that the ISPs had relevant information for the claimant, given that without their help Voltage Pictures could not know the names and addresses of the defendants. Hence, the Court considered it would be unfair not to allow the plaintiff to obtain that information.[185] As a result of its reasoning, the Court granted the motion, giving the ISPs two weeks to provide the plaintiff with the information.

An important difference between the *Voltage Pictures* and *BMG* suits is that in the former no ISPs contested the motion requested by the claimant.[186] Furthermore, in *Voltage Pictures*, P2P users downloaded a movie and not a song: this distinction is very relevant, since the private copying exemption of Section 80(1) only applies to music.

In 2014 Voltage Pictures introduced another lawsuit against John and Jane Doe, seeking information on thousands of users from an ISP through a *Norwich* order.[187] Although there had been no contestation by the ISPs, CIPPIC was granted leave to intervene. Voltage alleged that it had met all the requirements set out by the Federal Court of Appeal in *BMG*. CIPPIC sustained that no information should be revealed, given the users' right to privacy, and in accordance with Sections 7 and 8 of the Charter of Rights and Freedoms.

The Federal Court asked itself two main questions. The first was whether the Court should grant the order ensuring Voltage the right to obtain the information. In the event that the order were granted, the second question concerned the measures that should be adopted in granting the order so as to protect user privacy. The Court noticed that there were 'important *competing policy considerations* as to whether the Norwich order should be granted' and that an order like the one requested by Voltage was 'a *discretionary* and extraordinary' one.[188]

---

183   Ibid para 7.
184   Ibid para 14 citing *BMG* Appeal (n 168) paras 41–42.
185   *Voltage Pictures* 2011 (n 181) paras 18–26.
186   Ibid para 29.
187   *Voltage Pictures LLC v. John Doe* [2015] 2 F.C.R. 540.
188   Ibid paras 33–35 (emphasis added).

The Court devoted part of its decision to the question of whether the plaintiff should show a *prima facie* or a bona fide case. Considering the BMG decisions as well as other cases, the Federal Court held that a bona fide case was sufficient; a *prima facie* standard would have been a high threshold to reach, and the Court was persuaded that Voltage was not going on a 'fishing expedition'. The judge considered that there should be no differences between the cases in which privacy is involved and the cases in which other rights are involved: as Voltage had established a bona fide claim, the Court considered that the plaintiff's rights enforcement outweighed Internet users' privacy.[189]

To better assess its decision, the Court referred to some US cases on the same subject. The Canadian Court acknowledged that US judges normally consider the identification of alleged infringers in these cases to be meritorious. Nonetheless, there have been cases in which courts weighed against plaintiffs' requests. These cases were usually characterized by a high grade of unfairness on the part of the plaintiffs, who were making 'troll' requests to obtain user identities, with the sole aim of reaching quick and easy settlement. This strategy has been labelled a 'business model' by the courts.[190]

From the US cases, the Canadian Federal Court inferred that other aspects should be evaluated in addition to the test applied in *BMG*. This would help to reach a correct balance between the privacy right of potentially innocent users and the right of the plaintiffs to enforce their copyright. Nonetheless, in the specific case, the Court was persuaded that Voltage had demonstrated a serious intention to engage in litigation; the plaintiff also gave sufficient evidence of infringement and of a link between IP addresses and infringing activities. The Court consequently granted the order. However, three different measures to protect user privacy were adopted: first, a 'Case Management Judge' would be appointed to monitor the conduct of Voltage; second, the letter to be sent

---

[189]   Ibid paras 45–57.
[190]   Ibid paras 101–105. This is particularly true when dealing with the copyright enforcement of pornographic movies, where fear of embarrassment and high levels of shame lead users to settle cases very quickly (so-called 'copyright trolls', see the empirical study by Matthew Sag, 'Copyright Trolling, An Empirical Study' [2015] 100 Iowa Law Review 1105). Consider, for instance, the decision in *Ingenuity 13 LLC v. John Doe*, 2013 WL 1898633 (CD Cal, 2013).

to the users would be reviewed by the Court to ensure the appropriateness of the language; and third, the information would be limited to name and address.[191]

4. ITALIAN CASES

4.1 The *Peppermint* Case: Decisions in Favour of Disclosure

The Italian fundamental case on copyright enforcement against file-sharing is known as the *Peppermint* case. Peppermint is a German recording company, which holds the copyright on the music of many different artists. In autumn 2006 a law firm based in northern Italy started sending thousands of letters on behalf of Peppermint to Internet users accused of illegal file-sharing.[192] The letters claimed that, thanks to the collaboration of another company called Logistep, Peppermint was aware that the recipient of the letter had made available on her computer, and exchanged through a P2P system, sound recordings on which Peppermint held copyrights. Logistep was a Swiss company that used a modified version of file-sharing software in order to register IP addresses, pseudonyms and other user data. The letter, which said that the ISP had supplied users' data in response to an order from the Tribunal of Rome,[193] contained a sort of settlement agreement: if the user immediately deleted all the files and paid a sum in partial compensation for the damages, Peppermint would not sue the user or notify the public authority of her illegal behaviour, which was criminally punishable.[194]

---

[191] *Voltage Pictures* 2015 (n 187) paras 133–139.

[192] Examples of the letters sent can be found at <http://xp2p.altervista.org/?p=11> accessed 5 March 2017.

[193] Trib. Roma, ord., 18.8.2006 in Riv. dir. Ind., n. 4-5/2008, II, 328. For a criticism, see Marcello De Cata, 'Il caso "Peppermint". Ulteriori riflessioni anche alla luce del caso "Promusicae"' [2008] Riv. dir. Industriale 404, 411ff. See also Trib. Roma, ord., 19.8.2006, in Dir. Informatica, n. 4-5/2007, 815 and in Il civilista, n. 5/2008, 30. According to Guido Foglia, 'La privacy vale più del diritto d'autore: note in materia di filesharing e di sistemi peer-to-peer' [2007] Dir. industriale 598, this decision was further confirmed after Wind's appeal (Trib. Roma, ord., 22.9.2006), and the same conclusion was again reached in another lawsuit between the same parties (Trib. Roma, ord., 9.9.2007). Consider also the comparison made by the Italian case and the European ones by Marialuisa Gambini, *Dati personali e internet* (ESI 2008) 104ff.

[194] The point is questionable: in Italy most crimes can be prosecuted *ex officio* by the Prosecuting Attorney (*Pubblico Ministero*), without the need of any

As the letters said, they were sent on the basis of an order from the Tribunal of Rome. In June 2006 Peppermint had asked the Tribunal of Rome to order Wind Telecomunicazioni s.p.a., an ISP, to disclose the data associated to some of its users, who had allegedly infringed Peppermint's copyright. Peppermint explained that many songs in which it owned the copyright had been exchanged through a P2P network. The plaintiff also claimed that many of the IP addresses registered by Logistep belonged to Wind customers. As the RIAA and CRIA had done, Peppermint maintained that the IP addresses could only be linked to the customers' information by the ISP. For these reasons, the plaintiff asked the Tribunal to order Wind to disclose the data related to the alleged infringers. Peppermint made this request through a complaint under arts. 156 and 156*bis*, Legge 633/41, the Italian statute regulating copyright.

As previously explained, this article provides a remedy for a copyright holder, under specific requirements, to obtain a judicial order that requires the exhibition of, or asks for information needed by, the plaintiff. The article states that the plaintiff can obtain from the judge an order asking the counterparty to supply the elements for the identification of the subjects involved in the production or distribution of the products or services that constitute violation of copyright.

Courts have interpreted art. 156*bis* either as a 'precautionary measure' or as a sort of 'discovery tool'. The decision analysed here qualified it as a precautionary measure; therefore, Peppermint had to demonstrate the *fumus boni iuris* and the *periculum in mora*, as well as the instrumentality of the measure for a future lawsuit.

Peppermint claimed that the requested data needed to be disclosed without delay since ISPs only retained this information for six months.[195] Moreover, the longer the delay, the greater the damage to Peppermint would be. As for the instrumentality of the requested measure, Peppermint held that this request was needed in order to later sue Wind to obtain the exhibition of the alleged infringers' data.

Wind counterclaimed that the request was not admissible for many different reasons, one of which was that the plaintiff's action was not legitimate since Peppermint was not the actual holder of the economic rights on the allegedly uploaded songs. Wind also claimed that there was

---

notification by the victim. The crime punished by the former text of art. 171, co. 1 letter a-*bis*), Legge 633/41 is indeed prosecutable *ex officio*, meaning that Peppermint's promise not to notify the public authority of the illegal behaviour was ludicrous.

[195] This retention period was linked to the implementation of the Data Retention Directive 2006/24/EU, now repealed. See Chapter 3, Section 3.2.

no proof that the upload had been made by Wind users, and therefore Wind should not be the defendant. Finally, but importantly, Wind considered that Peppermint had collected user data in violation of privacy law.

Wind also held that it could not be considered an intermediary under art. 156, Legge 633/41 and, therefore, could not receive an order such as the one Peppermint had requested. In fact, art. 156 provides a remedy for cases in which a copyright holder fears the violation of her economic right or wants to prevent the perpetuation or repetition of an already existing violation. The copyright holder can prevent or stop the infringement by asking a judge either to stop the infringer or to stop the activity of an intermediary providing the services used as a means to the infringing activity. In its interpretation, Wind considered itself not to be an intermediary to which art. 156 could apply.

The defendant also claimed that only a criminal law judge, due to arts. 23 and 132 of the Privacy Code, could issue an order such as the one requested by Peppermint. Article 23 provides that the collection of data is only allowed with the subject's consent. In contrast, art. 132 at that time prescribed that intermediaries had to keep data related to telephone traffic for 30 months *for the scope of crime repression.*[196] Wind probably interpreted art. 132 as only being applicable within a criminal trial.

The judge notified the Privacy Authority of the existence of the lawsuit between Peppermint and Wind, as required by art. 152 of the Italian Privacy Code. Nonetheless, the Privacy Authority chose not to involve itself in the lawsuit.[197]

The Tribunal of Rome considered Peppermint's request to be admissible. As for instrumentality, the judge claimed that this was *in re ipsa*, given that the purpose of the subsequent lawsuit would be to obtain the users' data,[198] exactly as in the precautionary measures. As far as *fumus boni iuris* was concerned, the Tribunal held that Peppermint had proved to be the copyright holder of the allegedly illegally shared songs.[199] Furthermore, the judge was persuaded by the description of the way in which Peppermint had obtained user data. In the Tribunal's opinion, the way the data had been collected and processed by the company in charge

---

[196]   The current text of art. 132 requires shorter retention periods.

[197]   See Trib. Roma, ord., 18.8.2006 (n 193) paras 1–3.

[198]   This meant that, in the judge's view, the 'preliminary phase' and the subsequent lawsuit had the same aim.

[199]   The Tribunal based these argumentations on a report by someone who was probably a consultant for Peppermint. See Trib. Roma, ord., 18.8.2006 (n 193) para 5.

(i.e. Logistep), was *reliable, acceptable and also licit,* since a person using file-sharing software shows her acceptance of the fact that her IP address can be recognized by all other users of the same system. Moreover, the fact that it was well known that software like e-Mule or Gnutella was widely used for offering or obtaining songs was another element of proof of the facts alleged by Peppermint.[200] The Tribunal therefore held that it was beyond doubt that the users who had uploaded Peppermint's songs were Wind customers.

The Tribunal held that the requirement of *periculum in mora* was also to be considered *in re ipsa* for many reasons, all linked to the fact that P2P and the Internet are difficult to control. If Peppermint were unable to obtain alleged infringers' identities, users would be able to continue infringing copyright. The slower the intervention against the uploader, the higher the likelihood that other users would obtain the song, with a sort of multiplier effect.[201]

Then the judge turned to the question of whether a copyright holder could ask a third party to exhibit alleged infringers' data. The Tribunal made a comparison between the common *actio ad exhibendum* provided by art. 210 of the Italian Code of Civil Procedure[202] and the one provided by arts. 156 and 156*bis*, Legge 633/41. The former requires the person from whom the documents are requested to be one of the parties to the process. In contrast, the latter permits that a third party be requested to exhibit documents. Contrary to Wind's claim, in the Tribunal's opinion an ISP supplying access to the Internet is undoubtedly an intermediary as understood by art. 156 since its services allow the exchange of files through file-sharing systems. Article 156*bis*, then, permits the copyright holder to ask for the exhibition of 'documents, elements or information' held by the other party. Even though art. 156*bis* contains the expression 'counterparty', in the judge's view this term should be interpreted as 'the person holding the needed documents', which in this case was the ISP.[203]

---

[200] See ibid para 5.1.

[201] Ibid para 7.

[202] So-called *Codice di procedura civile* (c.p.c.), Regio Decreto 28.10.1940, no. 1443 and subsequent amendments.

[203] See Trib. Roma, ord., 18.8.2006 (n 193) paras 6–6.1. This provision creates problems of interpretation, probably due to the less than precise implementation in the Italian system of art. 8, Directive 2004/48. The European provision made reference to someone who effectively contributed to the infringement, and the provider, at least in this case, cannot be considered as such. See Carlo Blengino and Monica A Senor, 'Il caso "Peppermint": il prevedibile contrasto tra protezione del diritto d'autore e tutela della privacy nelle reti peer

With regard to privacy, the Tribunal considered art. 24, co. 1, letter (f) of the *Codice in materia di protezione dei dati personali*. This provision holds that personal information can be processed without the data subject's consent when it is necessary for the exercise or the defence of a right within a process and as long as it is not shared. In the Tribunal's interpretation, this was the case in Peppermint's request: in fact, the plaintiff had no other means of obtaining the users' real identities. However, art. 132, recalled by the defendant, was considered not pertinent to the lawsuit since it concerns the storage and not the handling of telephone traffic data.[204]

Following these argumentations, the Tribunal of Rome ordered Wind to give Peppermint the names, surnames, addresses, and places and dates of birth of the alleged infringers.

This decision was just one of those rendered by the Tribunal of Rome in the controversy initiated by Peppermint. At the end of 2006 the Tribunal adopted a decision dismissing the requests for user data.[205] Peppermint appealed and the appeal was decided by another section of the same Tribunal in February 2007.[206]

According to the interpretation given by this section of the Tribunal, art. 156*bis* obliges the counterparty, whether directly or indirectly involved in the illicit conduct, to exhibit data and information related to further subjects involved in the same illicit conduct. This interpretation leads to the conclusion that only those who are somehow, even indirectly, responsible for the violation of intellectual property rights can be subject to the order pursuant to art. 156*bis*. Such an interpretation would also be

---

to-peer' [2007] Dir. inf. e informatica 835, 838–839. Other scholars maintain that art. 156*bis* should be read as referring only to the parties to the lawsuit concerning the enforcement of copyright: Guido Scorza, 'Il conflitto tra copyright e privacy nelle reti Peer to Peer: il caso Peppermint – Profili di diritto interno' [2007] Dir. Internet 465, 467. However, such an interpretation would consider art. 156*bis* as a 'copy' of art. 210 cpc: De Cata (n 193) 414ff.

[204]   Trib. Roma, ord., 18.8.2006 (n 193) para 6.2.

[205]   In Italy not all judicial decisions are published. Therefore, there is no trace of the order of November 2006 but according to the text of the decision Trib. Roma, ord., 9.2.2007, the contested order was taken on 28–29.11.2006 by the Tribunal of Rome. See Trib. Roma, ord., 9.2.2007, in *Resp. civ. e prev.*, n. 7-8/2007, 1699. The decision does not mention the name of the defendants, which was Telecom Italia SpA; see Eugenio Prosperetti, 'The Peppermint "Jam": Peer-to-peer goes to Court in Italy' [2007] Entertainment Law Review 280, 282. For another decision ordering data disclosure, see Trib. Roma, 26.4.2007, in Riv. dir. ind., n. 4-5/2008, II, 328.

[206]   Trib. Roma, ord., 9.2.2007 (n 205).

in line with the exceptionality of this provision, which remains an invasive tool.[207]

This decision interpreted art. 156*bis* in the light of art. 8 of the 'Enforcement Directive': Under letters (a), (b) and (c) of art. 8 it should be possible to obtain information and data not only from the author of the violation, but also from someone who '(a) was found in possession of the infringing goods on a commercial scale; (b) was found to be using the infringing services on a commercial scale; (c) was found to be providing on a commercial scale services used in infringing activities'.[208] Therefore, art. 156*bis*'s term *controparte* should refer to persons other than the direct infringer and to whom no violation can be attributed. It follows from these considerations that art. 156*bis* provides intellectual property rights holders with a special tool with which to discover who is violating their rights, and what the actual extent of the illicit conduct is. In the Tribunal's opinion, no other interpretation was possible. If the term *controparte* referred only to the alleged infringer, then the provision itself would be useless since it would only duplicate that which is already introduced by art. 210 Code of Civil Procedure.

The Tribunal then considered the issue of privacy and, in particular, the objection made by the defendant that art. 156*bis* would collide with art. 24 of the *Codice Privacy*. The Tribunal considered that art. 156*bis* could not be in conflict with privacy legislation, given that European Directive 2004/48/EC, which is subsequent to the Italian Privacy Code, gives prevalence to the application of privacy legislation. Therefore, in the Tribunal's opinion, art. 24 is in harmony with the European legislation and, in fact, already balances information privacy protection and the need of copyright holders for justice.

Article 24 of the Italian Constitution, which provides that everyone can take judicial action to protect her own rights, would strengthen the interpretation explained above. In the Tribunal opinion, this constitutional provision concurs in supporting the conclusion that privacy can be subordinated to a person's need for judicial protection of her rights. Article 156*bis* requires that a number of key factors be assessed by the judges before they order the disclosure of any data: tribunals should order disclosure only when the case really needs to override privacy.

The Tribunal also considered an ISP's duty to collaborate in the enforcement of intellectual property rights, which is central to Directive

---

[207] See Trib. Roma, ord., 9.2.2007 (n 205).

[208] Letter (d) of art. 8 states that the same order can be made towards people mentioned by the subject indicated under letters (a), (b) and (c).

2000/31/EC and its implementation by decreto legislativo no. 70/03. In fact, as happens for the US DMCA, the ISP exemption from liability introduced by Directive 2000/31 was counterbalanced by their duty of collaboration in the battle for intellectual property rights enforcement. This duty is embedded within the structure of the Directive and is indeed fundamental since without the collaboration of the ISPs it might not be possible to discover who the infringers are.

Following this reasoning, the Tribunal granted the order to disclose. However, it did not specifically state which data should be disclosed, ordering only the disclosure of suitable information, thus in some ways worsening the situation for users.

4.2 The *Peppermint* Case: Decisions Against Disclosure

In the wake of the lawsuits that ruled in favour of user data disclosure, and because of the letters sent to users by the law firm representing the recording company, the *Peppermint* case drew the attention of scholars, users and consumer associations.

In a subsequent decision by the Tribunal of Rome in July 2007,[209] the plaintiffs were Peppermint and Techlands Sp. z o.o., a videogame company. The lawsuit was once again based on art. *156bis*, Legge 633/41. In their claim, the two companies stressed that art. 24 of the *Codice in materia di protezione dei dati personali* did not constitute an obstacle to the disclosure of data since this data was needed for the judicial protection of intellectual property rights, even though this was a civil and not a criminal trial. In its counterclaim, Wind recalled art. 132 of the Privacy Code and held that the communication of personal data could be ordered only within a limited period, in connection with specific crimes listed by law,[210] and when requested by the Public Prosecutor. Furthermore, art. 132 had to be considered exceptional and therefore could not be interpreted extensively for application to similar cases.[211] Wind reiterated its interpretation of arts. 156 and 156*bis* as excluding

---

[209]   See Trib. Roma, ord., 16.7.2007 in Dir. informatica, n. 4-5/2007, 828. See also Trib. Roma, ord., 14.7.2007 in Riv. dir. ind., n. 4-5/2008, II, 330.

[210]   Crimes are those listed in art. 407, co. 2, letter (a), of the Italian Criminal Procedure Code, D.P.R. 22.9.1988 n. 447.

[211]   The Italian Civil Code opens with some preliminary provisions, which are usually applied to all branches of the law. In particular, art. 14 provides a rule for interpretation of 'exceptions to law': they cannot be applied beyond the cases and the time for which they were introduced.

ISPs from the list of subjects towards whom courts could order disclosure. The defendant also added that art. 123 of the Privacy Code prescribed that ISPs had to delete or at least anonymize the kind of data requested by plaintiffs.[212] This meant that it was legally and technically impossible to disclose the requested data.

Wind also claimed that the collected IP addresses could not be used since they had been acquired in violation of privacy law, as art. 11 of the Privacy Code states. When this data was being acquired, users should have been informed of the collection of their information. If this had happened, users, after having been informed, could have consented to the data's processing. The exemption provided by art. 24 of the *Codice dei dati personali* mentioned by Peppermint refers only to the judicial phase and not to any previous stage, such as when Logistep collected the users' data.

Unlike in the previous cases, this time the Privacy Authority voluntarily stepped into the lawsuit and offered its remarks on the privacy issues. The Authority held that the processing of personal data related to electronic services in the 'information society' was restricted to criminal judgments. In particular, it should be limited to criminal investigations made by public authorities in charge of national security and defence. In the opinion of the Privacy Authority (*Garante*) a different interpretation would lead to a violation of the fundamental rights of privacy and secrecy of communications, protected by the Italian Constitution as well as by European law and by the European Convention on Human Rights. In the Privacy Authority's view, the compression of these fundamental rights is possible *only* when required for the safeguarding of superior principles protected by criminal law. The requests of Peppermint and Techlands should have been rejected since they were related to matters of lesser importance than the secrecy of communications.

The Authority argued that Directive 2002/58/EC has been imposed on Member States to enhance the privacy of electronic communications. At the same time, the Directive prohibits the storage of traffic data (including IP addresses and users' personal data) with the exception of data retained for the aim of preventing and prosecuting crimes. However, this exception does not cover civil offences.

Directive 2004/48 on the enforcement of intellectual property rights carries a provision imposing the disclosure of information on the origin and distribution of goods and services prejudicial to the rights of persons who are not the author of the violation. At the same time, as mentioned,

---

[212] The text of art. 123 is now different.

the Directive reserves the limitations inserted in the privacy regulations. The Authority held that this construction of the Directive meant that the European legislator considered privacy to prevail over intellectual property enforcement. Decreto legislativo no. 196/03, implementing Directive 2002/58/EC, introduced the same limitation as did the latter. The only exception to the conservation of personal data and electronic communications traffic data was the one mentioned by Wind, namely the repression of some specific crimes.[213]

The Authority additionally held that the collection and processing of user data carried out by the plaintiffs was illicit because it violated the Privacy Code: Logistep's monitoring activity should have been previously authorized by the Privacy Authority, as well as by the data subjects themselves, as required respectively by arts. 37 and 13 of the same Code. The lack of authorization meant that the collecting was illicit and that the data could not therefore be used for any other processing, as prescribed again by the Code (art. 11).[214]

Lastly, the Privacy Authority explained that arts. 156 and 156*bis* of Legge 633/41 had to be interpreted in the light of the Constitution and, in particular, in the light of arts. 2 and 15 regarding privacy and secrecy of communications. These fundamental rights can only be limited when in conflict with collective values embodied in criminal laws and criminal sanctions: private interests cannot limit them.

The decision of the Tribunal, which was heavily influenced by the intervention of the Privacy Authority, ruled against the disclosure of user data.

The Tribunal considered that arts. 156 and 156*bis* can be applied neither to information related to electronic communications nor to the traffic data produced. Indeed, the Italian and European laws on the secrecy and privacy of communications between private persons prohibit the processing and diffusion of these data. The only exception to such bans concerns the protection of values considered more important than intellectual property, such as in the case of criminal laws protecting collective interests. This means that the use of electronic communications data to enforce 'private' rights is not allowed. More precisely, according to the interpretation of the Tribunal of Rome, art. 24 of the *Codice Privacy* does also allow the use of personal data without the data subject's consent for the enforcement of private rights but only when the

---

[213] This had also been confirmed by the Italian Constitutional Court in the sentence n. 372/2006, see below.

[214] See next section for a fuller explanation.

plaintiff already holds the information and, above all, when the information has been lawfully collected. In the case before the court, the plaintiffs had instead asked to obtain users' personal data in a phase *preceding* the trial, therefore art. 24 could not constitute the basis upon which the plaintiffs could obtain the disclosure of the information. Furthermore, as illustrated by the Authority in its intervention, Logistep's collection of user data was illicit due to the lack of authorization by either the Authority or the data subjects. For both these reasons, art. 24 did not justify the disclosure of data. The illicit collection of the information meant that it could not be used for any other purpose, as prescribed by art. 11 of the Privacy Code.

The Tribunal added that a fundamental reason to reject the plaintiffs' request was the limit imposed by the secrecy of communication between people, a value protected directly by arts. 2 and 15 of the Constitution. The right to secrecy could only be overridden by other interests with the same or higher constitutional importance and, in all cases, adopting a balanced and comparative approach.

Although Directive 2004/48/EC introduced a number of measures to improve the enforcement of intellectual property rights, the same Directive expressly yields to the protection of privacy. It would be in contrast with the Enforcement Directive to allow the disclosure of data under art. 156*bis*.

At the same time, Directive 2002/58/EC expressly prohibits the conservation of electronic communications traffic data, except under some specific circumstances provided by its art. 15. The Italian Constitutional Court intervened on exactly this point, with decision n. 372/06 pertaining to art. 132 of the *Codice Privacy*. The constitutional judges clarified that the conservation of data for a longer period than the one required by art. 132 of the *Codice Privacy* was legitimate given that it was needed in order to balance privacy and collective interests. In fact, the fundamental right to privacy can vary according to the actual need against which it must be weighed, provided that the latter is recognized by the Constitution. The comparative weight given to the protection of privacy also depends on the gravity of the possible crimes in question. However, this evaluation is in the hands of the legislator.[215]

---

[215] Corte Cost., 14.11.2006, n. 372 (especially paras 5ff) in Dir. Informatica, n. 1/2007, 133.

Following the reasoning above, the Tribunal of Rome rejected the claim of Peppermint and Techlands.[216]

Some months later the Tribunal of Rome delivered another decision in a case again started by Peppermint and Techland.[217] This time, the two companies sued another provider, Tiscali s.p.a., which responded with a number of counterclaims, including one concerning users' privacy. The Privacy Authority intervened in the trial, as did Codacons and Adiconsum, the most important Italian consumer rights associations. The three entities asked for the request to be rejected since it violated consumer privacy. Adiconsum also requested that the judge ask for a Constitutional Court judgment on the constitutionality of art. 156*bis*, Legge 633/41. In the opinion of Adiconsum, art. 156*bis* contravened art. 15 of the Constitution on the freedom and secrecy of correspondence and communications. The association also wanted the judge to ask for a preliminary ruling by the CJEU on the existence of a duty for Member States to grant the disclosure of personal data in a civil proceeding on copyright infringement.

In its decision the Tribunal considered that the claimants' claim should be interpreted as a discovery request. This meant that, through the application of art. 156*bis*, the claimant could obtain evidence for a subsequent trial but not an injunction. This provision was based on two rationales: on the one hand, the need to compensate for the information asymmetry in the intellectual property enforcement process; on the other, the need to increase the effectiveness of protection against counterfeiting.

The interpretation of art. 156*bis* as a discovery tool affected the overall interpretation of the necessary requirements for the granting of the order requested by the plaintiffs. For example, the Tribunal held that the instrumentality of the request had to be considered with regard to a possible trial in which the evidence found through the discovery could be used. Previous decisions had, in contrast, evaluated the instrumentality of the request with regard to a possible subsequent case against the provider, in which instance it would have been considered to be an extension of the precautionary measure phase. Considering art. 156*bis* to be a discovery tool made it unnecessary to consider the existence of a *periculum in mora*; rather, it was important to consider the possibility that the evidence would disappear while the parties were waiting for the lawsuit to

---

[216] The plaintiffs' requests were also rejected by Trib. Roma, ord., 22.11.2007, in Foro it. 2008, 4, I, 1329.

[217] Trib. Roma, ord., 17.3.2008 in *Giur. it.*, n. 7/2008, 1738.

commence. In the judge's view, the way file-sharing works would make the identification of individual consumers more and more difficult as time passed.

As for the conflict between information privacy and copyright enforcement, the Tribunal of Rome noted that there had been a decision by the CJEU in the *Promusicae* case.[218] The Tribunal acknowledged that, as I shall illustrate in the following pages, the decision of the CJEU had given the national judge the burden of balancing the conflicting interests. The judge therefore considered the following Italian norms:

- art. 4 of the Privacy Code, giving the definition of 'data processing';
- art. 24, letter (f) of the same Code, which allows the processing of data without the data subject's consent to enforce a right before a judge;
- art. 123 of the Code, which prohibits the storage of traffic data;
- art. 132, which provides for a duty to store traffic data for 24 months for the investigation and repression of crimes; and for a further 24 months for the same reasons for certain crimes.

Analysing these norms, the Tribunal concluded that art. 132 of the *Codice Privacy* was a special provision, as compared to that contained in art. 24, letter (f). In particular, the fact that the Italian legislator considered the possibility of a longer period of storage *only* for crime prosecution led to the conclusion that exceptions to a data subject's consent could *only* be applied in those cases.

The Italian legislator had chosen to limit the protection of personal data in criminal cases only. This choice was compatible with the interpretation given by the CJEU in the *Promusicae* decision, in which the Court said that there was no duty for the Member States to impose the disclosure of information in civil proceedings. Hence, in the Tribunal's opinion, the legislator had already decided how to balance the two rights. Both are fundamental rights: the enforcement of intellectual property shall prevail over privacy only when there are public interests that are protected by the existence of criminal rules and penalties; when the only violated interest is the copyright holder's, however, personal data protection must prevail.

As required by the *Promusicae* decision, national judges must interpret the national law in compliance with Community law, these fundamental

---

[218] See below, Section 5.1 for details on this case.

rights, and the principle of proportionality. The Italian judge must therefore acknowledge the choice made by the legislator not to protect copyright when to do so would entail a violation of privacy rights.

In the judge's view, the prevalence of privacy over enforcement measures for intellectual property did not mean that the copyright owners have no protection against file-sharing. The Tribunal suggested that P2P network managers or file-sharing software producers could be sued to stop the infringement of copyright.[219]

The judge finally concluded that granting the claimants' request would mean the disclosure of consumers' personal data without any consent, violating their right to privacy, and rejected the claim.

4.3 The *Peppermint* Case: The Key Role of the Privacy Authority

As can be seen above, the Privacy Authority had a fundamental role in the decision of the *Peppermint* case, acknowledged by the Tribunal in the case.

In addition to its intervention in the lawsuit, the Privacy Authority issued some decisions that help to shed light on the problematic situation arising from the enforcement of copyright against file-sharing.

In February 2008, for instance, following the *Peppermint* cases, the Privacy Authority delivered a decision on Logistep's data processing.[220] In order to decide whether or not this process had been licit, the Authority divided the company's activities into two different phases:

---

[219]   The judge cited the case of *Napster* as an example. This suggestion of the Tribunal was criticized for conflicting in some ways with the Italian regulation for ISP liability. See Andrea Sirotti Gaudenzi, 'Violazione della proprietà intellettuale: non è ammesso il provvedimento di discovery in caso di peer to peer' [2008] Giur. it. 1742, 1744.

[220]   Privacy Authority, 28.2.2008, Bulletin no. 91/February 2008 <www. garanteprivacy.it/garante/doc.jsp?ID=1495246> accessed 5 March 2017. In its decision, the Authority referred to the judgment of the European Court of Justice in the *Promusicae* case (see below Section 5.1). In the opinion of the Privacy Authority, the decision of the European Court had to be interpreted as an exclusion of the possibility to disclose the data requested by copyright holders in civil proceedings. As early as September 2007, the Authority had issued a deliberation relating to the conservation of electronic communications data. Probably due to the cases summarized here, the Privacy Authority wrote that providers are not allowed to provide/reveal data requested by other parties within a civil proceeding, see Privacy Authority, 19.9.2007, Bulletin no. 86/September 2007 para 5 <www.garanteprivacy.it/garante/doc.jsp?ID=1442463> accessed 5 March 2017.

(1) the collection and automated processing of a huge amount of personal data, obtained through the use of software called 'file sharing monitoring' (fsm); (2) the request made to the Italian judges, in a civil proceeding, to require that users' real identities be communicated by ISPs.

The Authority specified that the exchange of files on the Internet had to be considered as 'communication', since the notion states: '"communication" means any information exchanged or conveyed between a finite number of parties by means of a publicly available electronic communications service'.[221] The existence of a 'finite number of parties' distinguishes a private communication from a communication to the public. Even though a P2P system allows communication to a very high number of people, this does not mean that the number is indefinite or absolutely not determinable. The communication is, in fact, directed to determined subjects, who can be identified. Furthermore, a communication to the public requires simultaneity and uniqueness of transmission, neither of which applies to P2P systems.

The Privacy Authority considered Logistep's data collection to be illicit. Although the software did not carry out intrusive activities on users' computers, the Authority concluded that the company's processing did not respect the Privacy Code. In particular, the collection violated the principle of 'lawfulness' as it had been done without any legal grounds; the processing also violated the principle of 'purpose' since the systematic registration of data was made for purposes other than those of P2P networks. This was especially true for those subscribers who were not necessarily engaged in file-sharing. Lastly, the principle of proportionality, too, had been violated since secrecy of communication should only be limited when in conflict with a right of equal importance, and consequently not in a civil proceeding.

Logistep's processing was massive and widespread and lasted for a prolonged period. The company kept track of the operations of an indefinite number of single users with regard to specified copyrighted contents. The Authority considered the collection made by Logistep as contrary to art. 5, European Directive 2002/58, and art. 122, decreto legislativo no. 196/03.

The processing was also problematic in terms of transparency and fairness given that users had not been given any previous information on the collection or use of their data. As we have just seen, the Tribunal of

---

[221] See art. 2, letter (d), Directive 2002/58 and art. 4, letter (l) of the Italian Privacy Code.

Rome considered this data to be personal information related to identifiable users, therefore the collector should have informed users of this further processing. With regard to this point, the Authority cited an interesting document of the Article 29 Working Party; the document focuses on the conflict between data protection and the enforcement of intellectual property rights.[222] In this document, the group stated that no personal data can be collected unless the data subject has been rightly and previously informed of the possible methods of control and of the identity of the person processing the data. The user must receive this information before the collection starts and before giving her personal data through any download.

Following the reasoning summarized above, under arts. 143 and 154 of the Privacy Code, the Authority enjoined Peppermint, Techland and Logistep from any further use of user data. The Authority also ordered the three companies to erase the data by the end of March of the same year.

Before this decision was released, the Privacy Authority had issued another decision concerning the security of traffic data and its retention for crime repression. Among the various provisions included in their first decision, one is of particular relevance to our current analysis. The Authority held that since the aim of data retention was crime repression, the disclosure of the retained data ought to be limited: it expressly stated, moreover, that providers were not allowed to comply with requests made within *civil* or *administrative* lawsuits. Retained data could be disclosed only if requested by a justified judicial order, in relation to particular *crimes*, specified by the law.[223]

No subsequent cases applied art. 156*bis* for the enforcement of copyright against file-sharing: the Tribunal of Rome's – eventual – decisive rejection of the copyright holders' requests may well have deterred any new lawsuits.

---

[222]   Article 29 Working Party, 'Working document on data protection issues related to intellectual property rights' (18 January 2005) <http://ec.europa.eu/justice/data-protection/article-29/documentation/opinion-recommendation/files/2005/wp104_en.pdf> accessed 5 March 2017.

[223]   Privacy Authority, 17.1.2008 (spec. para 5) <www.garanteprivacy.it/web/guest/home/docweb/-/docweb-display/docweb/1482111> accessed 5 March 2017. See also the previously cited document by the Privacy Authority issued on 19.9.2007 (n 222).

5. EUROPEAN COURT OF JUSTICE CASES

5.1 The *Promusicae* Case

In June 2006 the Juzgado de lo Mercantil no. 5 of Madrid asked for a preliminary ruling by the CJEU under art. 234 of the Treaty Establishing the European Community (TEC).[224]

The lawsuit exactly mirrored the *Peppermint* cases.[225] In the Spanish case Productores de Música de España (Promusicae), a trade group representing the Spanish recording industry, sued Telefónica de España SAU, a national telephone operator and ISP, to obtain the data of alleged infringers. In the same situation as the Tribunal of Rome, not knowing how to balance user privacy and copyright enforcement, the Judgado de lo Mercantil asked the CJEU to intervene.[226]

As mentioned, the Spanish case was identical to Peppermint's: in November 2005, Promusicae had made an application to the Juzgado de lo Mercantil asking for an order to oblige Telefónica to disclose the identities and physical addresses of some of its customers, allegedly infringers of Promusicae's copyright. In December 2005 the Spanish judge ordered the preliminary measure requested by Promusicae. Telefónica appealed, claiming that under the Spanish Ley 34/2002[227] the communication of the information requested by Promusicae could only be authorized in a criminal investigation, for public security or national defence purposes. This implied that it could not be obtained in a civil procedure. Promusicae counterclaimed that art. 12 of Ley 34/2002 on the duty of retaining customer information should be interpreted in accordance with many different provisions of European Directives 2000/31, 2001/29 and 2004/48, as well as with art. 47 of the European Charter of Fundamental Rights, protecting the right to an effective remedy in law.[228]

---

[224] The current numbering of art. 234 TEC is 267 Treaty on the Functioning of the European Union (TFEU).

[225] Similar cases occurred in other EU Member States; for references, see Irini A Stamatoudi, 'Data Protection, Secrecy of Communications and Copyright: Conflicts and Convergences – The Example of Promusicae v. Telefonica' in Irina A Stamatoudi, *Copyright Enforcement and the Internet* (Kluwer 2010) 199, 223ff.

[226] *Productores de Música de España v. Telefónica* (n 42) paras 29ff.

[227] This refers to LSSI (*Ley 34/2002 de servicios de la sociedad de la información y de comercio electrónico*) of 11 July 2002, by which European Directive 2000/31/EC was implemented in Spain.

[228] Art. 47 of the Charter of Fundamental Rights of the EU's text is close to the mentioned art. 24 of the Italian Constitution.

The Juzgado could not move beyond this impasse and asked the CJEU whether European law, in particular Directives 2000/31, 2001/29 and 2004/48, also taking the Charter of Fundamental Rights into account, had to be interpreted as imposing upon the Member States the duty to implement an obligation to communicate personal data in the context of civil lawsuits.[229]

The first observation of the CJEU was that Community law has to ensure the effective protection of intellectual property, and that this is especially important in the information society. However, the Spanish Court was worried that the provision of art. 12 of Ley 34/2002 could undermine this protection. Ley 34/2002 is the implementation of Directive 2000/31 and its art. 12 sanctions the protection of privacy, as required by Directives 95/46 and 2002/58.[230]

The European judges clarified that the disclosure requested by Promusicae involved the making available of users' personal data. The information did indeed relate to identified or identifiable natural persons, as described by the definition of art. 2(a) of Directive 95/46.[231] The data stored by Telefónica was a processing of personal data as meant in art. 2 of Directive 2002/58, read together with art. 2(b) of Directive 95/46. The communication requested by Promusicae therefore fell within the scope of Directive 2002/58.

The Court explained that it remained to be ascertained whether Directive 2002/58 precluded Member States from implementing, in order to protect copyright, an obligation to communicate personal data in civil proceedings. If it did not, it ought to be considered whether this obligation followed from one of the other Directives mentioned by the Spanish judge (2000/31, 2001/29, 2004/48). If this was not the case either, the CJEU should consider whether Community law – including the European Charter of Fundamental Rights – would anyway require a different reading of the mentioned Directives.

The Court therefore started to analyse each of the three Directives. Directive 2002/58, art. 5(1) provides that Member States must ensure the confidentiality of electronic communications and related traffic data. The

---

[229] See *Productores de Música de España v. Telefónica* (n 42) para 34.

[230] Ibid paras 41–44.

[231] Article 2. Definitions: 'For the purposes of this Directive: (a) "personal data" shall mean any information relating to an identified or identifiable natural person ("data subject"); an identifiable person is one who can be identified, directly or indirectly, in particular by reference to an identification number or to one or more factors specific to his physical, physiological, mental, economic, cultural or social identity.'

storage of a user's personal data by any other person, unless explicitly consented to, is prohibited although the Directive does provide some exceptions. Article 6(1) of the Directive states that stored traffic information must be erased or at least anonymized when it is no longer needed for the purposes of the transmission of the communication: this provision concerns the processing of traffic data for the requirements of billing or marketing services, not the sharing of data with persons other than those acting for the providers. Article 15(1) of the same Directive provides that Member States can introduce measures to restrict the confidentiality of traffic data when this restriction constitutes a necessary, proportionate and appropriate measure to safeguard state security, defence or public security; or to prevent, investigate and prosecute criminal offences or the unauthorized use of electronic communications systems. But none of these exceptions, listed in art. 13(1) of Directive 95/46, seems to be linked to civil proceedings, such as the one between Promusicae and Telefónica.

However, art. 15(1) of Directive 2002/58 closes with an express reference to art. 13(1) of Directive 95/46, which, under letter (g), authorizes Member States to implement legislative measures restricting the obligation of confidentiality of personal data when this restriction is necessary for the protection of the rights and freedoms of others. According to the opinion of the CJEU, since art. 13 does not specify the rights and freedoms concerned, the provision has to be interpreted as not excluding the possibility of protection of the right to property or other situations where authors seek to obtain protection in civil proceedings. This means that Directive 2002/58 does not preclude the possibility for Member States to lay down an obligation to disclose personal data in civil lawsuits. At the same time, however, art. 15(1) does not *compel* Member States to lay down such an obligation in the situations listed by the article.[232]

Since Directive 2002/58 does not require Member States to implement such legislation, the CJEU started to analyse the three Directives mentioned by the Juzgado and noted that their purpose was to protect industrial property, including copyright. Nevertheless, all three Directives prescribe that such protection cannot affect the protection of personal data.[233]

---

[232] See *Productores de Música de España v. Telefónica* (n 42) paras 45–56.
[233] See art. 1(5)(b) of Directive 2000/31; art. 9 of Directive 2001/20; art. 8(3)(e) of Directive 2004/48.

Article 8(1) of Directive 2004/48 expressly requires Member States to ensure that, in the case of proceedings concerning an infringement of an intellectual property right and in response to a justified request of the claimant, the competent judge may order information to be provided on the origin and distribution networks of the goods or services that infringe the right. This provision, which has to be read along with paragraph 3(e) of the same article, does not, however, require Member States to lay down an obligation to communicate the data. Nor do arts. 15(2) and 18 of Directive 2002/31 or art. 8(1) and (2) of Directive 2001/29 require such an obligation.

The CJEU then turned to the question of fundamental rights. The Spanish Court referred to arts. 17 and 47 of the Charter. As already noted, the former concerns the protection of the right to property, including intellectual property. The latter provides for the right to an effective remedy. By referring to these articles, the Juzgado probably meant to clarify whether an interpretation of the EU Directive according to which Member States did not have an obligation to communicate personal information in civil proceedings would infringe the fundamental rights contemplated by arts. 17 and 47 of the Charter.

The CJEU held that the rights to both (intellectual) property and to effective judicial protection are general principles of Community law. However, another fundamental right was at stake in this particular case, namely the right to the protection of personal data and, hence, to a private life. Directive 2002/58 itself, in its recital no. 2, declares the respect for fundamental rights protected by the Charter, especially under arts. 7 and 8 on the respect for private life and the right to the protection of personal data.[234]

Following these considerations, the CJEU found itself in the difficult position of having to 'reconcile the requirements of the protection of different fundamental rights, namely the right to respect for private life on the one hand and the rights to protection of property and to an effective remedy on the other'.[235]

The CJEU identified two main mechanisms which would, it its opinion, allow the balancing of these different rights. The first was provided by both Directive 2002/58 and by the three Directives mentioned by the Juzgado. Directive 2002/58 provides rules that determine when and to what extent the processing of personal data is lawful and which safeguards are needed. Directives 2000/31, 2001/29 and 2004/48

---

[234] See *Productores de Música de España v. Telefónica* (n 42) paras 57–65.
[235] Ibid para 66.

introduce exceptions for the cases in which the measures adopted to protect intellectual property under their provisions can affect the protection of personal data. The second mechanism was to be found in the Member States' national provisions implementing the Directives and in their application by national authorities.

Indeed, as Directives have to be applied to a large number of different situations in many different countries, they necessarily contain general provisions and allow each Member State discretion in their transposition: when transposing European Directives Member States must ensure that they rely on an interpretation of the Directive that allows a fair balance between the different fundamental rights protected by Community law. Furthermore, when courts and authorities apply these rules, they must not only interpret their national law in a way consistent with the European Directives, but also rely on an interpretation of them which is consistent with these fundamental rights and with other general principles of Community law as well. Among these principles, the Court pointed out, is the principle of proportionality.[236]

In addition, the Court recalled that art. 15(1) of Directive 2002/58 requires that all the measures adopted be in compliance with art. 6(1) and (2) of the Treaty on European Union (TEU), which recognizes the rights, freedoms and principles set out by the Charter.[237]

In the light of all these considerations, the CJEU concluded that Community law does not require Member States to lay down an obligation to communicate personal data to ensure effective protection of copyright in the context of civil proceedings in situations such as the one in which the Spanish lawsuit originated. However, Community law requires that, in transposing European Directives, Member States rely on an interpretation of them that allows a fair balance between the fundamental rights protected by the European legal order. Finally, the Court warned authorities and courts of Member States that when implementing national laws transposing European Directives they should rely on an interpretation consistent with the Directives. At the same time, they should ensure that they do not rely on an interpretation which conflicts with the fundamental rights or principles of Community law, one of which is the principle of proportionality.

---

[236] Ibid paras 67–68.
[237] The current numbering of art. 6 TEU is still art. 6 TEU.

5.2 The *Bonnier* Audio Case

The *Promusicae* decision did not provide clear guidance and was not fully satisfactory; it was in fact followed by other requests for preliminary rulings on the same, or closely related, questions.[238]

In 2010 the High Court of Sweden (Högsta domstolen) asked for a reference for a preliminary ruling from the CJEU in a lawsuit between Bonnier Audio AB and other audio book publishers, and Perfect Communication Sweden AB, an ISP.[239] The plaintiffs had sued the ISP in order to obtain an injunction ordering the disclosure of data on some of their customers allegedly involved in illegal file-sharing of audio books. The interpretation of the CJEU was requested in relation to arts. 3–5 and 11 of Directive 2006/24/EC – 'Data Retention Directive' that will be declared invalid in 2014 – and art. 8 of Directive 2004/48/EC – the IPR Enforcement Directive.

As mentioned, art. 8, Directive 2004/48 provides a tool for copyright holders, in response to a justified and proportionate request, to obtain from a court an order of disclosure of information on the origin and distribution networks of the goods or services which infringe an intellectual property right. The information, which can be requested from any person, can include the identifying data of the infringers as well as that of the producers, distributors, suppliers and so on. This mechanism shall apply without prejudice to statutory provisions that govern the protection of confidentiality of information sources or the processing of personal data.

The CJEU considered the definition of 'personal data' under Directive 95/46 and the already-mentioned restrictions to its application provided by art. 13(1), especially those related to 'the protection of the data subject or of the rights and freedoms of others'. In addition, the Court considered the definitions of 'traffic data' and 'communication' provided by art. 2, Directive 2002/58, both of which were applicable to the case before the Court. Under art. 5(1) of the same Directive, Member States must ensure the confidentiality of communications and of traffic data.

---

[238] The CJEU applied the same reasoning (and the same wording) in the order with which it decided *Oberster Gerichtshof* (Case 557/07 *LSG-Gesellschaft zur Wahrnehmung von Leistungsschutzrechten GmbH v. Tele2 Telecommunication GmbH* [2009] I-01227). See Pierluigi Di Mico, 'Il rapporto tra diritto di autore e diritto alla riservatezza: recenti sviluppi nella giurisprudenza comunitaria' [2010] Il diritto di autore 1.

[239] Case 461/10 *Bonnier Audio AB v. Perfect Communication Sweden AB* [2013] ECLI:EU:C:2012:219.

These data must be erased or made anonymous when they are no longer needed for the purpose of the transmission of a communication, in compliance with art. 6 of Directive 2002/58. The same article allows the processing of users' data for billing and payment purposes, for the period during which the bill may be lawfully challenged and payment pursued. The same Directive, under art. 15, again provides the restrictions listed above, and already introduced by art. 13(1), Directive 95/46.

The Court then considered Directive 2006/24, which extended the application of art. 15(1) of Directive 2002/58 to any data not specifically affected by Directive 2006/24 itself. As we have seen, the Data Retention Directive was intended to harmonize Member States' provisions concerning the retention of certain users' data by providers of publicly available electronic communications services, or of public communications networks, in order to ensure that those data were available for the purpose of the investigation, detection and prosecution of serious crime. Article 4 of the Directive stated that Member States should 'adopt measures to ensure that data retained in accordance with this Directive are provided only to the competent national authorities in specific cases and in accordance with national law'. Each Member State could choose the procedures to be followed, as far as these procedures were in accordance with both the relevant provisions of EU law and the European Charter.

The data affected by Directive 2006/24 were listed in art. 5 and included, among others: data necessary to trace and identify the source of a communication, for example the names, addresses and IP addresses of the subscribers; data necessary to identify the destination of a communication; data necessary to identify the date, time and duration of a communication; and data necessary to identify the type of communication. The Directive did not allow the retention of the content of the communication.

Directive 2006/24 also amended Directive 2002/58 and, specifically, provided that the mentioned provisions contained in art. 15 were not applicable to the data to be retained under Directive 2006/24 itself.

The Court also analysed Swedish laws on copyright. The law implementing Directive 2004/48 provided as follows:

> If the applicant shows clear evidence that someone has committed an infringement ... the court may order one or more of the persons referred to in the second paragraph below, on penalty of a fine, to provide the applicant with information on the origin and distribution network of the goods or services affected by the infringement (order for disclosure of information). Such an order may be made at the request of an author or a successor in title of an author or a person who, on the basis of a licence, is entitled to exploit the work. It may be made only if the information can be regarded as

facilitating the investigation into an infringement concerning the goods or services. The obligation to disclose information applies to any person who: (1) has carried out or contributed to the infringement; (2) has, on a commercial scale, exploited the goods affected by the infringement; (3) has, on a commercial scale, exploited a service affected by the infringement; (4) has, on a commercial scale, provided an electronic communications service or another service used in the infringement, or (5) has been identified by a person referred to in points (2) to (4) as participating in the production or distribution of goods or the supply of services affected by the infringement.

Paragraph 53d of the same law also specifies that '[a]n order for disclosure of information may be made only *if the reasons for the measure outweigh the nuisance or other harm which the measure entails for the person affected by it or for some other conflicting interest'.*[240] The obligation to disclose information does not cover information that would reveal that a person had committed a criminal act.

As for privacy, the Swedish law transposing Directive 2002/58 provides that 'a person who, in connection with the provision of an electronic communications network or an electronic communications service, has acquired or been given access to, inter alia, data on subscriptions may not without authorisation disseminate or exploit the data which he has acquired or to which he has been given access'. At the time of the lawsuit, Directive 2006/24 had not yet been transposed, although the time limit prescribed had already expired.[241]

The plaintiffs claimed that their exclusive rights to the reproduction, publication and distribution of audiobooks had been infringed by means of an FTP ('file transfer protocol') server which allowed file-sharing. They applied to the Solna District Court to obtain an order for the disclosure of the name and address of the person using the IP address from which it appeared that the files were distributed. The service provider challenged the application arguing that it was contrary to Directive 2006/24. Nonetheless, the Court granted the application. The service provider appealed before the Stockholm Court of Appeal to obtain a dismissal of the order and requested a referral to the CJEU to obtain clarification on whether Directive 2006/24 precluded the disclosure to persons other than the authorities referred to in the Directive of information relating to a subscriber to whom an IP address had been allocated. The Court of Appeal held that no provision in Directive 2006/24 precluded the disclosure of subscribers' data and rejected the

---

[240] Emphasis added.
[241] For more details, see *Bonnier Audio AB v. Perfect Communication Sweden AB* (n 239) paras 1–23.

application for a referral to the CJEU. However, since the Swedish Court found that the applicant had not proved that there was an infringement, it reversed the order of the lower Court.

The publishers appealed to the Högsta domstolen. The Swedish highest Court considered that, despite the decision in *Promusicae*, there were still doubts as to whether EU law allows or precludes the application of the piece of Swedish copyright law illustrated above. Therefore the Court decided to ask for a preliminary ruling and posed two questions.[242]

The CJEU summarized the two questions posed by the Swedish Court as follows:

> the national court asks, in essence, whether Directive 2006/24 is to be interpreted as precluding the application of a national provision based on Article 8 of [Directive 2004/48] which, in order to identify a particular subscriber, permits an Internet service provider in civil proceedings to be ordered to give a copyright holder or its representative information on the subscriber to whom the Internet service provider provided an IP address which was allegedly used in the infringement, and whether the fact that the Member State concerned has not yet transposed Directive 2006/24, despite the period for doing so having expired, affects the answer to that question.

On the premise that the data at issue in the main proceedings had been retained in accordance with Swedish law and in compliance with art. 15(1), Directive 2002/58, the Court stressed how under Directive 2006/24 the data had to be retained for the purpose of investigation, detection and prosecution of serious crimes, as defined by the national law of each Member State. These data were to be provided only to the competent national authorities in specific cases and in accordance with the national law concerned. Directive 2006/24 only dealt with these specific data; its scope is provided by art. 11, which considered art. 15(1) of Directive 2002/58 not to be applicable to the same data.

On the other hand, art. 15(1) continued to be applicable to data retained for purposes different from those included in Directive 2006/24. Therefore, due to arts. 11 and 12 of Directive 2006/24, this Directive was a special set of rules, derogating art. 15(1) of Directive 2002/58. The Court then stated that the legislation applicable in the case at issue fell out of the scope of Directive 2006/24; therefore the fact that Sweden had not yet implemented it was not relevant.

The preliminary observation made by the CJEU was that the data sought by the applicants in the main proceeding had to be considered as personal data, and their communication was a 'processing of personal

---

[242] Ibid paras 25–35.

data', implying the applicability of Directive 2002/58. In addition, the disclosure of data was requested in a civil proceeding by a copyright holder, that is by a private person and not for the benefit of a competent national authority.

Swedish law includes a tool that could require the communication of personal information to private individuals in civil proceedings. To obtain such a result, copyright holders need to demonstrate: (1) clear evidence of infringement; (2) that the information facilitates the investigation into an infringement of copyright; and (3) that the reasons for granting the measure outweigh the harm to the person affected by it or to some other conflicting interest.

As we have seen, in *Promusicae* the Court held that art. 8(3) of Directive 2004/48, read in conjunction with art. 15(1) of Directive 2002/58, does not preclude Member States from imposing an obligation to disclose personal data within civil proceedings. At the same time, European law does not require Member States to lay down such an obligation. In *Promusicae* the CJEU also held that Member States should interpret national law in a manner consistent with EU law, and taking into account the general principles of EU law, including the principle of proportionality.

Given the peculiarities of the Swedish law, the CJEU considered that the legislation enabled the national court to weigh the conflicting interests involved based on the facts of each case, taking into account the principle of proportionality. This seemed to ensure a fair balance between the protection of copyright and the protection of users' personal data.

The conclusions of the Court were therefore that Directives 2002/58 and 2004/48 did not preclude national legislation such as that at issue in the main proceedings insofar as the legislation in question enables the national court to weigh the conflicting interests involved, on the basis of the facts of each case and taking due account of the principle of proportionality.[243]

Comparing this decision with the one in *Promusicae*, two important remarks can be made. First, the Court did not, in either decision, state clearly whether copyright or data protection should prevail. Second, in contrast to the *Promusicae* decision, the *Bonnier Audio* judgment at least gives courts a key to interpretation: to apply a 'case-by-case' analysis.

The application of the 'case-by-case' approach of course puts judges in the position of having to make a choice that is very likely to be

---

[243]   Ibid paras 36–62.

influenced by many different factors, including that which is defined in this book as the 'conception' of each of the conflicting rights.

5.3 Other European Cases Involving the Conflict Between Copyright and Privacy

The CJEU has been dealing with the problem of balancing rights in an increasing number of cases. This section briefly illustrates three of them, in which copyright and privacy collided once again, although in a manner unlike that in the cases described above.

In 2011 the CJEU decided a case between four Belgian companies representing the authors, composers and editors of musical works (hereinafter considered under the name of just one of them, SABAM: Société d'Auteurs Belge – Belgische Auteurs Maatschappij) and a Belgian access provider, Scarlet Extended SA.[244]

In 2004 SABAM discovered that some of Scarlet's users employed P2P networks to share SABAM's works illicitly. SABAM brought interlocutory proceedings against Scarlet before the President of the Brussels Tribunal de première instance, claiming that Scarlet, as an ISP, was in the best position to take measures to stop users' infringing activities. SABAM wanted Scarlet to block or in some way make it impossible for its customers to share files through P2P networks without the authorization of copyright holders. This request was made on the basis of the Belgian law transposing art. 8 of Directive 2001/29.

The President of the Tribunal, considering that copyright had been violated, appointed an expert to investigate whether the solutions proposed by SABAM were technically feasible; in particular, if it was possible to filter the unlawful content of file-sharing, or to monitor the use of P2P networks. The expert concluded that, despite some obstacles, the measures requested by SABAM could not be entirely ruled out. Accordingly, in 2007, the President of the Tribunal ordered Scarlet to make it impossible for its users to share SABAM's copyrighted works through P2P systems.

Scarlet appealed, stating that it was impossible to comply with the injunction; the system would not be effective and it would affect the network capacity. In addition, Scarlet claimed that such a measure would contravene art. 15 of Directive 2000/31 since it would impose a general obligation to monitor communications, requiring, as it did, the general surveillance of all communications made on its network. Scarlet added

---

[244] Case 70/10 *Scarlet Extended SA v. SABAM* [2011] ECR 000.

that this filtering system would breach EU laws on personal data protection and secrecy of communications because filtering would involve the processing of IP addresses, and these are personal data.

The Court of Appeal of Brussels decided to ask for a reference for a preliminary ruling to ascertain whether the measures imposed on Scarlet were in accordance with EU law or not. The Belgian Court asked whether Directives 2001/29 and 2004/48, in conjunction with Directives 95/46, 2000/31 and 2002/58, construed in particular in the light of arts. 8 and 10 of the European Convention on the Protection of Human Rights and Fundamental Freedoms, allowed a national court to order a provider to install a preventive measure for all its customers for an unlimited period, with the aim of filtering all electronic communications, especially those involving P2P software, in order to identify electronic files on which the applicant claimed to hold rights, and subsequently block these transfers. The Court also asked, in the event of an affirmative answer, whether national judges 'called upon to give a ruling on an application for an injunction against an intermediary whose services are used by a third party to infringe a copyright [should] apply the principle of proportionality when deciding on the effectiveness and dissuasive effect of the measure sought'. The injunction requested by SABAM would have concerned 'all electronic communications passing via its services, in particular those involving the use of peer-to-peer software' and would have applied 'indiscriminately to all [Scarlet's] customers; as a preventive measure; exclusively at [the provider's] expense; and for an unlimited period'.[245]

The CJEU considered art. 8 of Directive 2001/29, which, as already mentioned, allows holders of intellectual property rights to apply for an injunction against intermediaries, whose services are being used by a third party to infringe their rights, with the aim of preventing further infringement. The way these injunctions work is clearly a matter of national law, as long as they respect the limitations arising from EU Directives.

These rules must in particular respect art. 15 of Directive 2000/31, which prohibits the adoption of measures that require ISPs to monitor communications on their networks. In the words of the court, a system like the one requested by SABAM would require

> first, that the ISP identify, within all of the electronic communications of all its customers, the files relating to peer-to-peer traffic; secondly, that it identify, within that traffic, the files containing works in respect of which

---

245   Ibid paras 1–29.

holders of intellectual-property rights claim to hold rights; thirdly, that it determine which of those files are being shared unlawfully; and fourthly, that it block file sharing that it considers to be unlawful.

Such monitoring would require the active observation of the communication, and it would therefore be banned by art. 15(1).[246]

The Court considered whether such an injunction would nonetheless be consistent with EU law and analysed the necessary protection of fundamental rights. Even though these injunctions aim at protecting intellectual property, considered a fundamental right in art. 17(2) of the Charter, nothing in either the Charter itself, or in the CJEU's case law, suggests that intellectual property rights are inviolable and need to be absolutely protected. In this sense, the *Promusicae* decision must be read as requiring judges to balance intellectual property rights with the protection of other rights. Freedom to conduct a business can be considered one of these rights: a filtering system like the one requested by SABAM would place an excessive burden and excessive costs on the ISP. The Court therefore ruled that such a filtering system would not reflect the necessary fair balance between conflicting rights. The CJEU went further and stated that such a filtering system would also infringe ISPs' customers' fundamental right to protection of their personal data and freedom to communicate. Filtering would collect and identify users' IP addresses, which are '*personal data because they allow those users to be precisely identified*'.[247]

In addition, the injunction requested by SABAM might also undermine freedom of information because a filtering system would not distinguish between lawful and unlawful content. This is particularly true when exceptions to copyright need to be applied.

At least four different rights must therefore be taken into account when ordering a filtering system: on the one hand, intellectual property rights; on the other, the freedom to conduct a business, the right to protection of personal data, and the freedom of communications and information. All this considered, the CJEU held that EU law precludes an injunction such as the one requested by SABAM, which would require the ISP to adopt a filtering system.[248]

A very similar case to the one above was decided by the CJEU only some months later. The request for a preliminary ruling was again made by the Court of First Instance of Brussels in a lawsuit involving SABAM

---

[246] Ibid paras 30–50.
[247] Ibid para 51 (emphasis added).
[248] Ibid paras 52–54.

against Netlog, a company running a typical online social network platform.[249] SABAM claimed that Netlog offered users the possibility to make use of works on which SABAM held copyright, making these works available to the public through their profiles, so that other users could access them without SABAM's consent. Given that SABAM's requests were very similar to those it had already made in the case against Scarlet, the CJEU applied the same reasoning and decided that a filtering system such as the one requested by SABAM would not strike a fair balance among the rights considered and that EU law precluded the adoption of such a measure.

6. COMPARING APPROACHES: CRITICISMS AND COMMENTS

6.1 Comparing Approaches

The approaches taken by the US, Italian and Canadian systems to resolve the conflict between privacy and copyright are somewhat different; they can be broadly distinguished between those of the US and Canada, which adopt specific tests in order to understand whether users' privacy should prevail over copyright holders' rights, and Italy, which does not apply such a test, although, when interpreting art. 156*bis* as a precautionary measure, courts need to evaluate the *fumus boni iuris* and the *periculum in mora*.

The CJEU's reasoning does not fit easily into either of these categories, as the court's task is not actually to resolve the conflict, but rather to give guidance to the courts of the Member States on how to apply European laws. It is nonetheless intriguing to consider the steps followed by the CJEU in determining whether one particular right should prevail, and if so, which.

Another possible classification is related to the enforcement provision applied in the particular case. As we have seen, while Italy and the US have a specific tool for copyright protection, the Canadian system relies on the subpoena provision applicable in all civil proceedings.[250] This difference, however, is decreased by the fact that US copyright holders have been forced to employ the usual 'John Doe' tool, thus approximating more closely the Canadian position.

---

[249] Case 260/10 *SABAM v. Netlog NV* [2012] ECLI:EU:C:2012:85.
[250] US: 17 U.S.C. § 512(h), known as the DMCA subpoena. Italy: art. 156*bis*, Legge 633/41. Canada: Rules 233 and 238 of the Federal Court Rules.

It is clear that the decisions given vary not only between the three systems, but also within each system, due to differing interpretations of the rules relating to copyright and privacy and – more generally, and typically – to the interpretative role proper to judges. Despite these divergences, it is possible to outline a main line of decision for each of the three systems.

Prima facie, in the US, the majority of cases are resolved in favour of copyright. This is true regardless of whether the conflicting right taken into account is to anonymity, to privacy or to both. In Canada, although the sample is limited, it is clear that information privacy prevails over copyright. Finally, in Italy, most decisions have been in favour of privacy.

As we have seen, in the American system claimants have been forced to apply 'John Doe' processes to ask for users' identities. This approach has sometimes led to the application of a test that examines the following factors: (1) whether plaintiffs have made a concrete showing of a *prima facie* claim of actionable harm; (2) the specificity of the discovery request; (3) the absence of alternative means to obtain the subpoenaed information; (4) a central need to obtain the subpoenaed information to advance the claim; and (5) the party's expectation of privacy.[251]

Similarly, the Canadian approach has considered the following criteria:

(a) the applicant must establish a *prima facie* case against the unknown alleged wrongdoer;
(b) the person from whom discovery is sought must be in some way involved in the matter under dispute, he must be more than an innocent bystander;
(c) the person from whom discovery is sought must be the only practical source of information available to the applicants;
(d) the person from whom discovery is sought must be reasonably compensated for his expenses arising out of compliance with the discovery order in addition to his legal costs;
(e) the public interests in favour of disclosure must outweigh the legitimate privacy concerns.[252]

Finally, the Italian application of precautionary measures requires only two elements: *fumus boni iuris* and *periculum in mora*, meaning a summary finding that (1) the claim is founded and (2) there is a danger that the right may be impaired by the lapse of time.

---

[251] See *Sony Music Entm't Inc. v. Does 1–40* (n 95); *Arista Records, LLC v. Does 1–16* (n 94) 12. I am aware that not all the cases considered have applied this test; nevertheless, I find it useful to consider it for the purposes of this chapter.

[252] *BMG Canada Inc. v. John Doe* (n 118) paras 13–14.

Although the three approaches differ, they also have commonalities. First, even though none of the three provisions regarding disclosure of third-party documents or data mentions the need to consider third-party rights to privacy, judges have always taken this issue into account. This is probably linked to the fact that user privacy has always been used as a counterclaim by defendants.

The second point the systems' provisions have in common is that they all leave a lot of space for the judge's interpretation. This may be one explanation why privacy has been given so much weight in the balancing processes in all three jurisdictions. In the US test, for instance, 'expectation of privacy' is still a somewhat hazy concept. The same can be said about letter (e) of the Canadian test quoted above, which involves the public interest in the disclosure of data. The Italian approach may be the least discretional of the three as it does not include references to privacy or data protection. However, art. 156*bis*, co. 3, Legge 633/41 states that, in ordering the disclosure, judges shall consider the necessary measures to protect confidential information. The law does not define 'confidential information', which could, however, also include personal data held by ISPs. Indeed, in the cases described – at least in the Canadian and American contexts – the judges also considered the 'terms of services' between users and ISPs, and the confidentiality by which intermediaries were thereby bound.

The previous sections have demonstrated that a conflict between copyright and privacy – and anonymity – exists. The conflict is persistent, and absolutely challenging, regardless of the outcome of any one lawsuit.

Given that there are no clear legislative solutions, judges have to apply their own ideas, perceptions and conception of the institutions involved. Judges have to decide all cases brought to them by a party, even in the absence of any applicable norm. Nowadays, technology seems to run ever faster than law. This means that judges face (and will probably continue to face) situations in which they have to decide on the basis of laws that are obsolete and unhelpful, having been conceived for times now past. Under these circumstances, judges use their discretion more than in other contexts: the existence of room for manoeuvre and open clauses gives courts the space to adopt different decisions.[253]

The direction taken by each decision may therefore be influenced by a number of factors. The last chapter of this book is devoted to explaining

---

[253]   See Xavier Groussot, 'Rock the KaZaA: Another Clash of Fundamental Rights' [2008] Common Market Law Review 1745, 1761.

exactly how the conception of privacy and copyright in each system has affected court decisions in the weighing of these conflicting rights.

6.2 Criticisms and Comments

This last section illustrates some of the criticisms made by scholars of the cases and decisions described above. Indeed, all the tools applied are open to criticism.

First, the DMCA, which has been said to have a chilling effect on free speech because it destroys users' anonymity. The majority of the US decisions have been in favour of disclosure, stating, for example, that the subpoena should only apply to user identity and does not involve First Amendment issues, because it does not require disclosure of the underlying speech.[254] In the *Verizon* case, Judge Bates considered the DMCA requirements to be a sufficiently high burden to act as a warranty against the unfounded disclosure of users' identities.[255] The same judge also considered that copyright holders' interests easily outweighed users' anonymity rights, given that it is difficult to imagine that someone who essentially opens their computer to the world can reasonably expect privacy.[256]

Not all the courts have reasoned in this way. In *Capitol Records, Inc. v. Does 1–16* Judge Garcia underlined that the 'disclosure of subscriber log files may contain highly confidential and sensitive files, disclosure of which could well be violative of the subscribers' privacy rights'. The Court concluded that 'the harm related to disclosure of confidential information in a student or faculty member's Internet files [could] be equally harmful' as the damages suffered by the plaintiff.[257]

Authors have also pointed out that the ease with which someone can obtain a subpoena from a clerk could lead malicious people to use such a tool for nefarious purposes.[258] This has also raised the question of

---

[254] *In re Verizon 2* (n 51) 262.

[255] Ibid 263–264.

[256] Ibid 265–267.

[257] *Capitol Records, Inc. v. Does 1–16*, 2007 U.S. Dist. LEXIS 97930 (2007), 2–3.

[258] Jordana Boag, 'The Battle of Piracy versus Privacy: How the Recording Industry Association of America (RIAA) Is Using the Digital Millennium Copyright Act (DMCA) As Its Weapon Against Internet Users' Privacy Rights' [2004] California Western Law Review 241, 243. The same worry was underlined by Senator Brownback when discussing the Bill 'Consumers, Schools, and Libraries Digital Rights Management Act' in 2003, referring to the District

whether such conduct could constitute an illegal search and seizure under the Fourth Amendment.[259]

In the case of the RIAA, which relied on bots as a monitoring device, the identities of some people were wrongly uncovered. This means that innocent people have been, and can still be, exposed, with consequent loss of anonymity, in violation of First Amendment protection for anonymous online speech.[260]

The discovery tool applied in 'John Doe' trials does not differ greatly from the DMCA subpoena as regards privacy and anonymity issues. As we have seen, when Does tried to quash subpoenas on the basis of privacy concerns, courts sometimes shifted their attention to the relationship between the ISP and the user, considering the terms of services governing the contract between the two. This approach was taken, in particular, in *Sony Music Entertainment, Inc. v. Does 1–40*.[261] As we saw, the Court applied a five-step test and also considered the 'party's expectation of privacy'. In the judge's opinion, the defendants could only have a minimal expectation of privacy; the terms of service specifically stated that the transmission or distribution of material in violation of any law or regulation, including copyrighted works without proper authorization, was prohibited. The same terms further stated that the ISP had the right to disclose any information necessary to satisfy any law, regulation or other governmental request.[262] As a result of this analysis, the Court decided that the plaintiffs' right to pursue copyright infringement claims outweighed the defendants' right to anonymity.[263]

Even though anonymity and privacy partially overlap, especially in the US, anonymity has been taken into account much more often than privacy by courts deciding on user identity disclosure. In the early cases, the courts were not very worried about First Amendment issues and let

---

Court's decision in *Verizon*; see Congressional Record – Senate, September 16, 2003, S11571ff.

[259] Amedeo (n 50) 320–321.

[260] Ibid 321.

[261] *Sony Music Entm't Inc. v. Does 1–40* (n 95). Followed by *London-Sire Records, INC. et al. v. DOE 1 et al.*, 542 F. Supp. 2d 153, 158 (S.D.N.Y. 2009).

[262] The court also relied on *In re Verizon 2* (n 51) 260–261, 267–268. *Sony Music Entm't Inc. v. Does 1–40* (n 95) reasoning about privacy expectation was followed in *Doe I v. Individuals*, 561 F. Supp. 2d 249, 255 (D. Conn. 2008).

[263] *Sony Music Entm't Inc. v. Does 1–40* (n 95) 567.

plaintiffs proceed with little or no discussion.[264] Later they started showing greater sensitivity to speech and privacy issues, subsequently recognizing the need for balance. Courts defined the different standards or specific criteria that parties should meet when seeking to identify anonymous people.[265] These standards normally require that parties seeking the identities of anonymous speakers demonstrate:

(a) that they have made reasonable attempts to provide notice of the subpoena to the anonymous speakers,[266] typically an adequate notice and reasonable opportunity to respond;
(b) that there is some evidence on the merits of the claim; and
(c) that they have a real need for the identifying information.[267]

The second requirement has been understood in different ways: (a) as a demonstration that the claim was brought in good faith; (b) as a demonstration that the claim could withstand a motion to dismiss; (c) as a demonstration that the claim could withstand a motion for summary

---

[264] See, for example, *In re Subpoena Duces Tecum to America Online, Inc.*, 52 Va. Cir. 26 (Va. Cir. Ct. 2000). See also Lyrissa Barnett Lidsky, 'Silencing John Doe: Defamation & Discourse in Cyberspace' [2000] Duke Law Journal 855.

[265] Lyrissa Barnett Lidsky, 'Anonymity in Cyberspace: What Can We Learn from John Doe?' [2009] Boston College Law Review 1373, 1376. See also Mazzotta (n 104) 866ff, surveying 10 different unmasking standards; Smith Ekstrand (n 95) 417ff; Gleicher (n 104) 338ff; Clay Calvert and others, 'David Doe v. Goliath, Inc.: Judicial Ferment in 2009 for Business Plaintiffs Seeking the Identities of Anonymous Online Speakers' [2009] John Marshall Law Review 1, spec. 41ff, where the authors compare the tests used by different courts between 2008 and 2009; Jonathan D Jones, 'Cybersmears and John Doe: How Far Should First Amendment Protection of Anonymous Internet Speakers Extend?' [2009] First Amendment Law Review 421.

[266] When the subpoenaed party is an ISP, it often does not notify anonymous speakers about the subpoena; see Mazzotta (n 104) 843. When the identity of the defendant is unknown, this requirement cannot be applied too strictly. Courts have sometimes held that posting notice of the suit in the forum where Doe posted his allegedly defamatory statement was sufficient; see, for example, *Doe v. Cahill*, 884 A.2d 451, 461 (Del. Supr. 2005).

[267] Need-based inquiries have also been defined in different ways, investigating whether there were other means of obtaining information, or the scope of the identifying request, or whether the information sought was relevant or otherwise important for the lawsuit, and so on; see Mazzotta (n 104) 854.

judgment; and (d) as the demonstration of prima facie evidence for all elements of the claim.[268]

Some courts have considered an additional 'First Amendment balancing prong' to fully protect users' rights to (anonymous) free speech and some measure of privacy. The first court to apply this additional requirement was the Superior Court of New Jersey.[269] The Court stated that the application of a 'motion-to-dismiss standard in isolation fails to provide a basis for an analysis and balancing of Dendrite's request for disclosure in light of John Doe No. 3's competing right of anonymity in the exercise of his right of free speech'.[270]

In the cases analysed here, the courts have mainly rejected First Amendment claims, stating that copyright infringement does not amount to free speech.[271] Hence, the degree of anonymity protection is considered minimal when dealing with copyright infringement.[272] It has been argued that the contents and context of the speech should be considered before compelling the disclosure of the speaker's identity.[273] The context in which a violation occurs might be, indeed, often embarrassing or even a cause for harassment. As we have seen, many copyright infringement cases have arisen from the downloading of pornographic movies; some cases also concerned homosexual pornography, making it highly likely that the people involved would face social stigma.

The Canadian decisions also applied a specific test. With regard to *BMG*, the decisions given both by the Federal Court and the Federal

---

[268]   Mazzotta (n 104) 850–851; Barnett Lidsky, 'Anonymity in Cyberspace' (n 265) 1378, who asserts that (d) is the dominant standard.

[269]   *Dendrite International, Inc. v. Doe, no. 3*, 775 A.2d 756 (NJ Super. 2001); the standard applied in this case seems to be 'gaining ground as the dominant standard': Barnett Lidsky, 'Anonymity in Cyberspace' (n 265) 1378. See also Froomkin (n 90) 454.

[270]   *Dendrite International, Inc. v. Doe, no. 3* (n 269) 770. Other courts then applied different balancing benchmarks for the First Amendment, or no benchmark at all: see Mazzotta (n 104) 857ff.

[271]   *In re Verizon 2* (n 51) 260, quoting *Universal City Studios, Inc. v. Reimerdes*, 82 F. Supp. 2d 211, 220 (S.D.N.Y. 2000); *Harper & Row Publishers, Inc. v. Nation Enterprises*, 471 U.S. 539, 568 (1985); *Zacchini v. Scripps-Howard*, 433 U.S. 562, 574–78 (1977). '[T]he First Amendment is not a license to trammel on legally recognized rights in intellectual property', see *In re Capital Cities/ABC, Inc.*, 918 F.2d 140, 143 (11th Cir. 1990).

[272]   *In re Verizon 2* (n 51) 260.

[273]   Barnett Lidsky, 'Anonymity in Cyberspace' (n 265) 1380, spec. fn 40; Lyrissa Barnett Lidsky and Thomas F Cotter, 'Authorship, Ardencies, and Anonymous Speech' [2007] Notre Dame Law Review 1537, spec. 1601ff; Mazzotta (n 104) 864.

Court of Appeal left some questions unanswered.[274] Two main points, however, can be considered to be uncontested. First, ISP account holders have an expectation that their identities will be kept confidential. This statement is based on the terms of agreement between ISPs and users, as well as on Sections 3 and 5 of PIPEDA. Second, Section 7(3)(c) of PIPEDA was applicable in the case, which meant that ISPs could disclose users' personal information without consent pursuant to a court order.[275]

A question remains about whether courts should apply a 'bona fide claim' or a '*prima facie* claim'. The Federal Court of Appeal, in requiring a bona fide claim threshold, lowered the requirements to be met for the disclosure of information. The Court even stated that, once a plaintiff has shown a bona fide claim that somebody is infringing her copyright, she has a *right* to have the infringer's identity revealed. However, the Court immediately went on to state that 'caution must be exercised by the courts in ordering such disclosure, to make sure that privacy rights are invaded in the most minimal way'.[276] Nonetheless, the attitude here seems to be different from other cases, such as *Tariff 22*,[277] in which, delivering his dissenting opinion, Justice LeBel stressed that the privacy of individuals would be directly implicated if copyright owners could collect their data from ISPs. Hence, courts should be cautious in applying a test that could stimulate the monitoring of user data: they should also adopt an interpretation of PIPEDA that respects user privacy, and eschew an interpretation that encourages the monitoring of personal data.[278]

An important difference between the *BMG* decisions and the other Canadian ones is that the latter were adopted before the approval of PIPEDA. This difference is particularly relevant to considerations of the *Glaxo Wellcome* case, where the plaintiffs were seeking production of

---

[274]   For comments, see Bailey (n 116); Ian Kerr and Alex Cameron, 'Nymity, P2P & ISPs: Lessons from BMG Canada Inc. v. John Doe' in Katherine J Standburg and Daniela Stan Raicu (eds), *Privacy and Technologies of Identity: a Cross Disciplinary Conversation* (Springer 2006) 269; Margaret A Wilkinson, 'Battleground Between New and Old Orders: Control Conflicts Between Copyright and Personal Data Protection' in Ysolde Gendreau (ed), *An Emerging Intellectual Property Paradigm: Perspectives from Canada* (Edward Elgar Publishing 2008) 227.

[275]   *BMG* Federal Court (n 118) para 9.

[276]   *BMG* Appeal (n 168) para 42.

[277]   Wilkinson (n 274) 237.

[278]   *Society of Composers, Authors and Music Publishers of Canada (SOCAN) v. Canadian Association of Internet Providers* [2004] 2 S.C.R. 427, paras 153–155.

documents in the possession of a public institution. Public institutions are governed by access legislation, in particular by the Access to Information Act.[279] Furthermore, *Glaxo Wellcome* involved information held by a corporate person, while PIPEDA focuses only on individuals. For these reasons, it was argued that the reliance on *Glaxo Wellcome* by both courts was 'entirely misplaced':[280] the existence of PIPEDA at the time *BMG* was decided might or even should have rendered the older cases inapplicable to these later ones.[281]

Beyond these issues, it is important to stress that the Courts in *BMG* would have ordered the disclosure of the data had the plaintiffs met the evidentiary requirements, or even if the evidence were simply up to date. It should therefore not come as a surprise that the *Voltage* case was decided differently. However, it was suggested that cases like *BMG* should be resolved by looking at the Charter of Rights and Freedoms: although the Charter only applies to state activities, common law should not grow in conflict or even inconsistently, with the Charter itself.[282]

One author also suggested that a different result might have been reached if a criminal lawsuit had been started by CRIA. Criminal law is usually differently perceived from private law; in criminal proceedings, the public interest is normally more easily recognizable than in disputes between private parties (and the Charter applies).[283] Indeed, one of the issues in the *Promusicae* case was precisely the fact that the disclosure was requested within a civil rather than a criminal lawsuit.

Even though the problem of protecting anonymity has arisen within the Canadian system, no case appears to have properly considered this fuller account of privacy.[284] *BMG* can be seen as a first step towards a more thorough consideration of the issue of privacy, perhaps due to the participation of CIPPIC. The courts did, at least, give indications on the

---

[279]   Access to Information Act, R.S.C. 1985, c. A-1.

[280]   Wilkinson (n 274) 244.

[281]   Ibid 262.

[282]   See Amy Min Chee-Fong, 'Unmasking the John Does of Cyberspace: Surveillance by Private Copyright Owners' [2005] Canadian Journal of Law and Technology 169, 176, citing *Retail, Wholesale and Department Store Union, Local 580 v. Dolphin Delivery Ltd* [1986] 2 S.C.R. 573, paras 32ff. Nevertheless, the same decision clearly stated that the Charter does not apply to private litigation.

[283]   Wilkinson (n 274) 263–264.

[284]   Bailey (n 116) 638. But see Wilkinson (n 274) 234ff, who mentioned *Society of Composers, Authors and Music Publishers of Canada (SOCAN) v. Canadian Association of Internet Providers* (n 278) as a decision which raised privacy concerns.

need to minimize data disclosure; they also accepted that data should be protected through anonymization as such an approach was also expected by the public.[285]

All in all, the Canadian approach, even though it requires the lower, bona fide threshold of DMCA Section 512(h), seems to better protect privacy, due to the different structure of the test applied.[286] The Canadian approach under *BMG* appears to give more importance to privacy than to copyright. The requirement of current and complete evidence is undoubtedly a barrier to the disclosure of data; moreover, ISPs have demonstrated a reluctance to supply CRIA with information that could lead to a breach of the obligation deriving from PIPEDA with respect to their customers.[287] As we have seen, the subsequent *Voltage* case took a different position.

Some critics consider it wrong to apply privacy expectations to user names[288] but Canadian courts and administrative bodies have expressed the opinion that even general web-browsing habits can be considered personal.[289] In addition to the strictly indemnificatory data, two other categories of information have been identified. The first is related to the files on a user's computer that are accessible to others through the network; the second – closely linked to the first – refers to the files actually exchanged among users.[290] Users have an expectation that their data will be kept confidential; ISPs can be considered as the gatekeepers of users' personal information;[291] it would be no surprise if a user sued

---

[285]   *BMG* Federal Court (n 118) paras 44ff.

[286]   Bailey (n 116) 640.

[287]   See for example *Shaw's Written representations* (n 117) 17.

[288]   Thoughts and quotations from Yiu (n 148) 64.

[289]   See, for example, the dissenting opinion of LeBel J in a case before the Supreme Court, which stated that web surfing and downloading 'habits tend to reveal core biographical information about a person' (*Society of Composers, Authors and Music Publishers of Canada (SOCAN) v. Canadian Association of Internet Providers* (n 278) para 155). The Canadian federal Privacy Commissioner had the same opinion in a case where a broadcaster was accused of collecting personal data through a website, see PIPEDA Case Summary no. 2001-25 – *A broadcaster accused of collecting personal information via Web site* <www.priv.gc.ca/en/opc-actions-and-decisions/investigations/investigations-into-businesses/2001/pipeda-2001-025> accessed 5 March 2017.

[290]   Min Chee-Fong (n 282) 170–171.

[291]   Kerr and Cameron (n 274) 272.

her ISP for breach of fiduciary duties.[292] In fact, ISPs usually include one or more provisions regarding respect for user privacy in their contracts with clients. As already mentioned, confidentiality and privacy are not necessarily the same thing and their overlap may be confusing.[293] However, confidentiality can prove to be a (contractual) means through which to protect privacy.

It is worth noting that in 2009 the Canadian Radio and Telecommunications Commission (CRTC) imposed a different, higher standard of protection for the personal information collected by ISPs.[294] This change was intended to balance the right of Canadians to use the Internet for their own purposes with the interest of ISPs in managing the traffic generated in their networks; the policy document was adopted in response to concerns which emerged during a public consultation process.[295]

Furthermore, the Privacy Commissioner of Canada stated that a *subpoena duces tecum* – initially used by the RIAA in the US – would not be a sufficient basis, in and of itself, for the disclosure of personal information without the consent of the individual as a subpoena does not compel actual production.[296] This Privacy Commissioner has clearly stated, on more than one occasion, that IP addresses are indeed personal information.[297]

---

[292]   Ibid 273. For an interesting analysis of the relationship between ISPs and users, see Ian Kerr, 'The Legal Relationship Between Online Service Providers and Users' [2001] Canadian Business Law Journal 419.

[293]   Wilkinson (n 274) 253ff.

[294]   See Canadian Radio and Telecommunications Commission (CRTC), 'Review of the Internet Traffic Management Practices of Internet Service Providers', Telecom Public Notice 2008-19, October 21, 2009, para 102 <www.crtc.gc.ca/eng/archive/2009/2009-657.htm> accessed 5 March 2017.

[295]   Alex Cameron, 'CRTC Imposes Super-PIPEDA Privacy Protection for Personal Information Collected by ISPs' [2009] Internet and E-Commerce Law in Canada 94.

[296]   See PIPEDA Case Summary no. 2009/05 – *Husband's financial information disclosed to wife's lawyers by accounting firm improperly complying with Summons to Witness* <www.priv.gc.ca/en/opc-actions-and-decisions/investigations/investigations-into-businesses/2009/pipeda-2009-005/> accessed 5 March 2017.

[297]   PIPEDA Case Summary no. 25/2001 (n 289); no. 2005/315 – *Web-centred company's safeguards and handling of access request and privacy complaint questioned* <www.priv.gc.ca/en/opc-actions-and-decisions/investigations/investigations-into-businesses/2005/pipeda-2005-315/>; no. 2005/319 – *ISP's anti-spam measures questioned* <www.priv.gc.ca/en/opc-actions-and-decisions/investigations/investigations-into-businesses/2005/pipeda-2005-319/> all accessed 5 March 2017.

However, courts in Canada have not considered that privacy may be part of the Charter of Rights, while copyright is not. Such a consideration could help in balancing these two rights, which, in the end, means balancing copyright holders' and users' rights.[298]

The vast majority of scholarly comment on (and criticism of) the conflict between privacy and copyright in the Canadian context came in the wake of the *BMG* decisions. As we have seen, the *Voltage* and *BMG* decisions reached opposite conclusions. It is nonetheless interesting to notice that here too it was difficult for the Court to strike a correct balance between copyright and privacy. In the last case analysed, for instance, while the judge reached the conclusion that the enforcement of copyright had to prevail, he nevertheless introduced a number of measures to preserve user privacy, thus demonstrating that privacy is highly valued in the Canadian judicial context.

Further confirmation of this can be found in the fact that the American and Canadian courts approached the conflict between copyright and privacy with a very similar tool – a balancing test – but, although their tools entailed very similar requirements, the expectation of privacy was high in the *BMG* cases, but considered non-existent in most of the US cases.

I shall now turn to the Italian context, which, as we have seen, has been affected by the European decisions adopted by the CJEU. Although the tool applied differs greatly from the Canadian and American ones, it does not seem to be any more satisfactory.

The outcomes of the lawsuits have been criticized by scholars: the handling of the *Peppermint* case generated a fear that both privacy and freedom of speech could undergo a chilling effect.[299] This criticism has also been made of the American and the Canadian contexts: it seems that the fear is linked more to the question of the disclosure of user information than to the way in which the process of disclosure in general is managed.

---

[298] Gregory R Hagen and Nyall Engfield, 'Canadian Copyright Reform: P2P Sharing, Making Available and the Three-Step Test' [2006] University of Ottawa Law and Technology Journal 477 <www.uoltj.ca/articles/vol3.2/2006.3.2. uoltj.Hagen.477-516.pdf> 501. The same Authors, however, also express some doubts about the possibility of applying the Charter in the cases at issue.

[299] Roberto Caso, 'Il conflitto tra copyright e privacy nelle reti Peer to Peer: in margine al caso Peppermint – Profili di diritto comparato' [2007] Dir. Internet 471, 475.

In the *Peppermint* case, all Logistep's data processing contravened the Privacy Code. In particular, art. 122 of the Privacy Code prohibits the use of an electronic communication network to access information stored in a user's computer; the storage of such information and/or monitoring of user activities are also prohibited. In addition, if someone wants to monitor communication services for a reason not necessitated by the supplying of the service itself, this person shall notify such processing to the Privacy Authority (art. 37, co.1, letter (d), decreto legislativo no. 196/03). With these considerations in mind, scholars commenting on the Tribunal's decisions had already reached the conclusion of the Privacy Authority, later adopted by the Tribunal of Rome, which implied the prevalence of the protection of privacy over the enforcement of copyright.[300] As mentioned, the decisions of the Tribunal against disclosure seem to be a direct consequence of the intervention of the Privacy Authority in the lawsuit.[301]

In its initial decisions, the Tribunal did not consider some important issues that later became fundamental for resolving the conflict between the two rights. Neither the national nor the European system, in fact, allows the processing of data relating to electronic communication, or their acquisition, communication or use without the data subject's consent. In the Italian system this ban can be traced back to arts. 2 and 15 of the Constitution: the prohibition of processing should only be overridden by values or interests of higher importance, such as the common good.[302]

The decision adopted by the Tribunal of Rome on 19 August 2006 held that a person taking part in a file-sharing network implicitly accepts that other file-sharers know her IP number;[303] such an interpretation introduces an exception to the necessary consent of data subjects not contemplated by art. 24. The Privacy Authority has always asked for a strict interpretation of the aforesaid article, stating that such exceptions are to be considered narrow and cannot be extensively applied to other situations. The same decision also held that the processing of user data was legitimate since it was intended to enforce or defend a right before a

---

[300]   Ibid 476.
[301]   Blengino and Senor (n 203) 836; Scorza (n 203) 466; Foglia (n 193) 599.
[302]   Ibid 841.
[303]   Alessandro Mantelero, 'L'idea del peer to peer fra tutela della privacy ed enforcement dei diritti d'autore' [2008] Riv. trim. dir. e proc. civile 1481, 1488 fn 38, notes that file-sharing users do not communicate their IP and GUID codes expressively, rather, they are automatically detected by software such as Logistep's.

judicial authority under art. 24, letter (f). The decision of 16 July 2007, in contrast, considered this latter provision to be applicable only in cases in which the claimant already possesses the data and wants to use it to enforce her right, as long as this possession is legitimate.[304] In the *Peppermint* case, claimants did not have the data: they sued the provider to obtain it. The users' personal data was utilized in a phase *precedent* to the enforcement. A more coherent interpretation was given in the decision of 17 March 2008, where the Court considered art. 156*bis* to be a discovery tool which should not be used to identify the alleged infringer, but to detect the evidence needed in a subsequent lawsuit.[305] As mentioned, one of the questions was whether personal data should be disclosed within civil as well as criminal lawsuits. Some scholars maintained that disclosure would also be possible within a civil proceeding under the provision of art. 24 of the Constitution, concerning the right to be heard in court for the protection of one's rights.[306]

The final decision taken by the Tribunal of Rome, and the content of the Privacy Authority's judgment, are probably closely related to the fact that the violation of privacy occurred through an electronic communication network. Such networks obviously enable far greater intrusion upon people's lives than do analogue instruments.[307]

While the case of *Peppermint* was pending, the CJEU was called to rule on the *Promusicae* case. The intervention of the CJEU was seen as a chance to obtain clear definitions of personal data protection and copyright enforcement, and a resolution of the conflict between them. The constitutional importance of both rights, which are also included in the European Charter of Fundamental Rights, obviously increases the difficulty of finding a correct and solid resolution of the conflict. The delicate nature of the conflict requires particular caution in determining a 'one-size-fits-all' solution. Scholars have noted that it would be more appropriate to endeavour to find a concrete balance between the interests at play rather than a solution based on the nature of the protection (civil vs. criminal law) alone.[308] As the interests concerned are of constitutional

---

[304] Mantelero (n 303) 1489 is of the same opinion. For a criticism of this interpretation see instead Scorza (n 203) 469.

[305] Blengino and Senor (n 203) 844.

[306] Marialuisa Gambini, 'Diritto d'autore e tutela dei dati personali: una difficile convivenza in Rete' [2009] Giur. it. 509, 512–513.

[307] Roberto Caso, 'Il conflitto tra diritto d'autore e protezione dei dati personali: appunti dal fronte euro-italiano' [2008] Diritto dell'internet 470.

[308] Mantelero (n 303) 1495; Davide Sarti, 'Privacy e proprietà intellettuale: la Corte di giustizia in mezzo al guado' [2008] AIDA 435, 440–441. See also

relevance, they should enjoy equal levels of protection; it is therefore correct to apply a 'procedural balancing rule', involving the principle of proportionality, for example,[309] as the CJEU ruled.

The extent of the *Promusicae* decision has been interpreted in three different ways: some authors claimed that the decision was in favour of intellectual property enforcement;[310] some others considered the sentence to be a win for the protection of personal data;[311] however, the majority of scholars contended that the decision did not actually lean towards any solution, leaving the Member States to decide what to do and so increasing interpretative uncertainties and threatening harmonization.[312]

Stefano Rodotà, *Repertorio di fine secolo* (Laterza 1999) 221, according to whom the entire system of personal data protection should take a case-by-case approach because different contexts can give different meanings to the same data. Consider also Andrea Ottolia, 'Proprietà intellettuale e trattamento dei dati personali: riflessioni su privacy "per il sistema" e "nel sistema"' [2010] AIDA 319, 325.

[309]   Gino Scaccia, 'Il bilanciamento degli interessi come tecnica di controllo costituzionale' [1998] Giurisprudenza Costituzionale 3953, 203–205.

[310]   Mantelero (n 303) 1492ff; Di Mico (n 238) (referring to the copycat decision in the Austrian case).

[311]   Alfredo Trotta, 'Il traffico telefonico fra la tutela del diritto d'autore e quella della privacy' [2008] Dir. Industriale 76.

[312]   Sylvia Kierkegaard, 'ECJ Rules on ISP Disclosure of Subscribers' Personal Data in Civil Copyright Cases – Productores de Música de España (Promusicae) v Telefónica de España SAU (Case C-275/06)' [2008] Computer Law & Security Report 268, 273; Caso (n 307) 468–469; Fanny Coudert and Evi Werkers, 'In the Aftermath of the Promusicae Case: How to Strike the Balance?' [2008] International Journal of Law and Information Technology 50, 51; Kate Brimsted and Gavin Chesney, 'The ECJ's Judgement in Promusicae: The Unintended Consequences – Music to the Ears of Copyright Owners or a Privacy Headache for the Future? A Comment' [2008] Computer Law & Security Report 275, 277; Sarti (n 308) 438ff; Michal Koščík, 'Privacy Issues in Online Service Users' Details Disclosure in the Recent Case-Law. Analysis of Cases Youtube v. Viacom and Promusicae vs. Telefonica' [2009] Masaryk University Journal of Law & Technology 259, 264ff; Ottolia (n 308) 326–327; Giancarlo Frosio, 'Urban Guerrilla & Piracy Surveillance: Accidental Casualties in Fighting Piracy in P2P Networks in Europe' [2011] Rutgers University Computer & Technology Law Journal 1, 20; Lee A Bygrave, 'Data Protection vs. Copyright' in Dan JB Svantesson and Stanley Greenstein (eds), *Internationalisation of Law in the Digital Information Society: Nordic Yearbook of Law and Informatics 2010–2012* (Ex Tuto Publishing 2013) 55, 72; Luigi Carlo Ubertazzi, 'Proprietà intellettuale e privacy' [2014] AIDA 435, 446ff. Other scholars welcomed the decision more optimistically: 'I do not share [IP scholars' criticisms]. This judgment is unsurprising and makes perfect sense to me', see Groussot (n 253) 1758.

The decision of the CJEU, in its failure to specify which right should prevail, disappointed many scholars. Each Member State could still make its own judgement, thus (to some extent) undermining attempts to homogenize enforcement tools across Europe. Scholars have also suggested that the decision of the CJEU requires additional exceptions to be added to those existing in Directive 2002/58.[313]

The opinion of the Advocate General Kokott was probably more precise and concrete than the resolution reached in the judgment of the Court.[314] The Advocate General considered that Community law allows Member States to introduce a duty to disclose personal information in criminal matters. In civil proceedings Member States *may* provide for personal data to be communicated to state authorities, but are, nevertheless, not obliged to do so. AG Kokott wrote that the possibility to disclose personal data should be restricted to very serious copyright infringement: in cases where the infringer has a profit motive, or is seriously undermining copyright holders' profit capacity. In fact, in the opinion of the Advocate General, copyright protection is a public interest often defended by the EU. Therefore, given the importance of copyright, its protection can be considered fundamental, even when the interest to be protected is a private one. At the same time, however, file-sharing for private use, without profit, cannot be considered a real threat to copyright protection, even taking into account the controversial opinions on the effects of file-sharing on copyright profits.[315] In reaching this conclusion, the Advocate General considered a restrictive interpretation of art. 15, Directive 2002/58 and stated that the entire Directive should be considered as *lex specialis*, since it regulates the specific sector of personal data in electronic communications.[316]

The CJEU, however, did not apply the same reasoning. Its interpretation of art. 13 of Directive 95/46 seems to allow each Member State to include the protection of property rights in civil proceedings among the exceptions which permit the disclosure of personal data without the data subject's consent. The European judges thus lowered the protection of the personal information threshold since they did not stress the necessary

---

[313] Brimsted and Chesney (n 312) 277; Coudert and Werkers (n 312) 61; Chistopher Kuner, 'Data Protection and Rights Protection on the Internet: The Promusicae Judgment of the European Court of Justice' [2008] European Intellectual Property Review. 199, 202; Groussot (n 253) 1763ff.

[314] See Case 275/06 *Productores de Música de España v. Telefónica de España SAU* [2008] ECR I-00271, Opinion of AG Kokott.

[315] Ibid paras 105–106, 119–121.

[316] See ibid paras 85–89.

presence of a pressing social need for the application of such a measure.[317] As noted by the Advocate General, the question to be answered is 'when' a threat to intellectual property rights requires a necessary measure within a democratic society. It is at this point that the principle of proportionality recalled by the CJEU comes into play. The judge's role in any proceeding is thus fundamental.[318]

The decision reached by the CJEU in the *Bonnier Audio* case was perhaps more satisfactory. In fact, the Court clearly stated that the disclosure of personal data in civil proceedings is not contrary to European law as long as it is possible to decide on a case-by-case basis whether the disclosure should be granted or not. This is in line with the statement of Advocate General Jääskinen, who held that the right to privacy and intellectual property rights benefit from equal protection,[319] as both are fundamental rights.[320]

The Advocate held that for the disclosure of user data to be possible, EU law should first require that ISPs retain such data, and also record the purpose for, and period of retention of, such data. A disclosure from a database for purposes other than those for which the data was collected would be contrary to European law. Therefore, national legislation (in this case, Swedish) should already have provided for the exceptions and restrictions required to disclose user data. The retention and subsequent disclosure could not be carried out for purposes other than those provided by the law.[321]

As happened in *Promusicae*, in *Bonnier Audio* the Court did not strictly follow the Advocate General's opinion. Nonetheless, while the CJEU did not supply a predetermined resolution of the cases in which copyright and privacy collide, it did give Member States clearer guidance than in the previous case.

It is questionable whether the Court should explicitly state that privacy is more important than copyright, although some authors believe that this is the correct approach.[322] Many scholars have claimed that in order to solve the conflict between copyright and personal data the two rights

---

[317] Coudert and Werkers (n 312) 64.

[318] Ibid 65–71, *passim*.

[319] Case 461/10 *Bonnier Audio AB v. Perfect Communication Sweden AB* [2013] ECLI:EU:C:2012:219, Opinion of AG Jääskinen, para 62.

[320] Ibid para 3.

[321] Ibid paras 60–61.

[322] Zuzana Hecko, 'Data Retention by Internet Service Providers for IP rights protection: Bonnier Audio (C-461/10)' [2012] Journal of Intellectual Property Law & Practice 449, 452.

need to be in some way evaluated and scaled. It has, for example, been said that to reach a correct balance it is essential to understand the true nature and the public values of the conflicting rights.[323] If copyright were considered solely in economic terms, it would be easy to give prevalence to privacy.[324] However, it may not be so easy to make this distinction, although the plaintiffs in the cases analysed above undoubtedly only held economic copyrights.

The question of whether rights should be ranked is not the subject of this book although, as previously seen,[325] some scholars have considered the ranking of rights to be key to the solving of the thorny question of rights balancing.

---

[323] Bailey (n 116) 635.
[324] Blengino and Senor (n 203) 849–850.
[325] See Chapter 1.

5. Conclusions: conceptual balancing

1. FILE-SHARING AND THE CONCEPTION OF COPYRIGHT IN THE THREE SYSTEMS

This chapter is devoted to an analysis of what I call the 'conception' of the two conflicting rights. As previously stated, I consider the 'conception' of a right to be the expression of the general approach that a legal system has towards that right. Conception describes the approach of a legal system to a specific right as it emerges from the organic whole of laws and policies related to a specific institution. Conception expresses the epitome of a right while, at the same time, it constitutes a lens through which the interpreter can systematically read the norms concerning that right.

Since my claim is that the conception of copyright and information privacy has influenced the way in which judges have balanced the two rights when they conflict, I shall now explain these two conceptions.

In Chapters 2 and 3 I described copyright and information privacy regulation in the three countries. Starting with their history and constitutional dimensions, I went on to illustrate some of the most important aspects of these regulatory frameworks, paying special attention to the aspects that touched upon the conflict at stake.

Comparing the analyses conducted for each country, we see a form of duality emerging in the case of each of the two rights. With regard to copyright, the approaches adopted by the US and Italy appear stronger and more protective than that of Canada. In terms of information privacy, however, the US approach is the weakest, with Italy and Canada providing similar, more robust protection.

Copyright policy in each of the three legal systems has undoubtedly been influenced by a number of international Treaties. Whereas Canada was slow and, to some extent, reluctant to amend its regulation to comply with the Treaties and only revised its Copyright Act in 2012, after many failed attempts, the US and Europe – and consequently Italy – had already implemented international agreements at the beginning of the twenty-first century.

More generally, the attitude of Canada towards copyright is revealed as 'softer' than in the US and Europe/Italy. My analysis of the leading cases highlights that Canadian courts have interpreted copyright norms restrictively. In contrast, the US and Italy have shown a consistent interest in copyright: in both countries the legislation has been regularly updated. While the structure of both countries' copyright legislation has been maintained, many amendments have been introduced in an attempt to protect copyright from the increasingly widespread violations enabled by new technologies. The province of copyright has thus been enlarged and now comprises many works which were not contemplated when the original laws were enacted; moreover, copyright holders are now entitled to a greater number of different rights than previously.

Currently, the protection of original works of authorship is coherent and all-encompassing in all three countries. Music, in particular, enjoys comprehensive protection: musical works are protected from unwanted copying, public execution, communication and distribution. While the right to make available does not exist per se in the US system, it is nonetheless recognized as included in the right to distribute.[1]

Given the existence of many different rights in a single work, the copy of a musical work can potentially violate several aspects of copyright law. This may be the case, for instance, with file-sharing through P2P networks, an activity to which the three countries adopt different approaches. Both the US and Italy have modified their legislation to adapt it to this new phenomenon. In both systems, the unlawfulness of file-sharing is (relatively) clearly stated. A number of Bills have also been proposed to target copyright piracy specifically. Canada – in contrast – has not yet enacted any regulation to expressly punish file-sharing. Interestingly, although not surprisingly, the only judge to state (between the lines) that file-sharing of copyrighted songs should be considered legal is Canadian.[2] The modifications introduced by the Canadian Copyright Modernization Act may, however, soon change the landscape.

---

[1]   Michael Schlesinger, 'Legal Issues in Peer-to-peer File-sharing, Focusing on the Right to Make Available' in Alain Strowel (ed), *Peer-to-peer File-sharing and Secondary Liability in Copyright Law* (Edward Elgar Publishing 2009) 43, 47 and 64ff. See *Elektra v. Barker* – S.D.N.Y – 31.3.2008; *Motown Records Co. v. Theresa DePietro*, 2007; *Atlantic Recording v. Anderson*, S.D. Tex. 2008, but *contra* see *London-Sire Records v. Does*, D. Mass. 2008.

[2]   I am here referring to *BMG Canada Inc. v. John Doe* [2004] 3 F.C.R. 241, for an analysis of which see Chapter 4, Section 3.1.

Differences are also evident in the way copyright is limited to allow free use. The US famously relies on fair use, which, as a general clause, allows some uses to be considered non-infringing, although these uses are not explicitly listed in the law. Canadian fair dealing adopts an opposite approach and states precisely which uses are allowed and which are not. However, this precise wording has not prevented the Canadian Supreme Court from enlarging the scope of the exception.[3] Amendments introduced in 2012 followed this trend. The Italian exceptions and limitations differ from both of the above: not only are they worded precisely, they are also interpreted in a restrictive manner, as required by Italian rules on the interpretation of laws.

These different approaches have influenced file-sharing activities. Even though US fair use is an open clause, it has never exempted file-sharing, which is regarded as an infringing use. While both the US and Italy include a 'private use' exception, neither legal system includes file-sharing within this exception. A fair dealing clause of 'Reproduction for Private Purposes' now also exists in the Canadian regulation, where, in fact, Section 80(1) of the Copyright Act had already been considered to be exempt P2P from infringing uses.[4] Canada's framework differs in this respect from the other two, which are less permissive towards users' activities, or – the other side of the same coin – provide higher safeguards for copyright owners.

Divergences between the attitudes concerning copyright emerged clearly while studying enforcement tools too. Once more, Canada is the only country of the three that has not introduced an ad hoc tool to facilitate copyright enforceability.

This is perhaps the clearest indication of the difference between the Canadian approach and that of the other two countries. As mentioned, the Digital Millennium Copyright Act (DMCA) and EU 'IPR Enforcement Directive' result from implementation of the World Property Organization (WIPO) Treaties. However, while some years ago this difference might have been explained by Canada's delay in implementing the Treaties, this appears not to have been the only reason: Canada has now implemented the Treaties but has not yet introduced a special instrument to enforce copyright. This means that Canadian copyright holders who want to enforce their rights against file-sharers still have to rely on 'John Doe'

---

[3] See, in particular, the decision *CCH Canadian Ltd. v. Law Society of Upper Canada* [2004] S.C.R. 339.

[4] See again *BMG Canada Inc. v. John Doe* (n 2). Consider also CIPPIC's memorandum in the same lawsuit at 15 <www.cippic.ca/documents/file-sharing-lawsuits/Memorandum_final_12pt.pdf> accessed 10 March 2017.

procedures and on the Federal Rules of Civil Procedure applicable to any kind of lawsuit.

Even though the use of DMCA *subpoenas* did, in fact, prove fruitless and US copyright holders had to switch to John Doe procedures, the existence of a specific tool for the protection of copyright indicates the importance placed on this right. A similar argument can be made with regard to the Italian context, where the implementation of Directive 2004/48 introduced art. 156*bis*, Legge 633/41, a tool that some scholars and courts regarded as introducing 'discovery' into the Italian legal system.[5]

Finally, the liability of online intermediaries also demonstrates a different methodology, which, once again, points to the difference between Canada's position and that of the other two systems. The US introduced a specific liability regime in 1998 with the enactment of the DMCA; a similar approach was taken by the EU with Directive 2000/31. Canada, however, had no specific regulation for this thorny issue until 2012, although this gap had been partially filled by some Supreme Court decisions, particularly *CCH*.[6] The way provider liability for copyright infringement is framed is another indication of the overall approach of each country to copyright. While the US and Italy make it very difficult for providers to enjoy liability limitation, this is not the case in Canada.

The previous pages – and Chapter 2 – I hope, have provided a clear illustration of the conception of copyright in the US, Canada and Italy.

In general, the American regulatory framework for copyright is extremely protective, with numerous amendments intended to protect copyright from the possible threats arising out of technological developments. All legislation in recent decades has enlarged the province of copyright. Laws have been enacted to improve copyright enforceability, prolong it, and punish its violation with increasing penalties, including jail. The numerous Bills, proposed with great frequency, are another manifestation of the importance placed on copyright. The constitutional dimension of copyright is mirrored in the laws adopted by Congress. In other words, the US conception of copyright is that of an essential right that needs to be defended by a strong, coherent legal framework.

The Italian conception of copyright – as a right which needs to be properly safeguarded – is close to that of the US. As a consequence of

---

[5] *Peppermint* case, Trib. Rome, 17.3.2008, in Giur. It., n. 7/2008, 1738 on which see Chapter 4, Section 4. See also Luigi Carlo Ubertazzi, *Commentario breve alle leggi su proprietà intellettuale e concorrenza* (CEDAM 2016) 2074.

[6] *CCH* (n 3).

European interventions, Italy has amended Legge 633/41 very often. The law currently protects every aspect of a work of authorship for 70 years after the author's death and copyright violation can be punished with criminal sanctions. Although *diritto d'autore* is not explicitly mentioned in the Italian Constitution, it is considered to be a constitutional right, partly as a result of the introduction of, and in accordance with, art. 17 of the EU Charter of Fundamental Rights.

Canada has chosen to take a different stance. Before the enactment of the Copyright Modernization Act, Canadian copyright law differed profoundly from that of the US and Italy, and even now, after the implementation of the WIPO Treaties, Canada's legislation leaves more space for users' rights and is more protective of providers' functions than the other two; neither does it provide specific tools to enhance copyright enforceability. All in all, Canada allows a high degree of user freedom and while it does protect copyright owners, their rights are not very strongly defended. Indeed, Supreme Court case law to date demonstrates an intention not to let copyright expand beyond the necessary. The Canadian conception of copyright law is that of a right which undoubtedly has to be safeguarded, but does not have any particular characteristics that make it a priority.

The conceptions of copyright described above influenced judges' decisions in the cases analysed in Chapter 4, weighing either in favour, or against, copyright when courts were faced with the delicate task of balancing. The same can be said for the conception of information privacy, as illustrated in the next section.

2. THE CONCEPTION OF PRIVACY AND PERSONAL DATA PROTECTION IN THE THREE SYSTEMS

Before analysing the approaches to privacy, it is worth noting the importance of technology in the adoption of all legislation on data protection. In the 1970s developed countries began to consider the necessity of legislating on the new issue of computer technology. The core principles of data protection legislation were adopted by all legal systems, thanks to formal and informal relationships between countries and to a certain degree of supranational intervention.[7]

---

[7] Colin J Bennett, *Regulating Privacy. Data Protection and Public Policy in Europe and the United States* (Cornell University Press 1992) 118–123, mainly attributes the convergences in personal protection regulations to the threat from technology to society at that time.

None of the three Constitutions explicitly mentions privacy or information privacy as such. However, the Supreme Courts of the three countries have explicitly traced the right to both physical and informational privacy back to their Constitutions. This is really, however, as far as the similarities between them go.

I hope that Chapter 3 demonstrated satisfactorily that the US approach to privacy is very different from those of Italy and Canada. This difference may result from the fact that there are no international agreements designed to ensure greater homogeneity among the systems, unlike in the field of copyright where legislation has been converging, partly as a consequence of the implementation of international Treaties. At the international level, with regard to data protection, only non-binding guidelines exist, such as, for example, those of the Organisation for Economic Co-operation and Development, which are, in fact, no more than 'a fundamental statement of international consensus on communication policies'.[8] As a consequence, despite the fact that all three systems comply with these guidelines, their regulations can (and currently do) differ greatly.

US legislation for the protection of privacy is a patchwork of statutes: not only is regulation divided between state and federal rules, it also lacks uniformity and coherence. The enactment of specific statutes as a response to particular events has resulted in fragmented legislation that does not properly protect privacy – either informational or physical – in everyday life. US states can enhance their own laws, as can Canadian states. However, while in Canada state laws have to be 'substantially similar' to the Personal Information Protection and Electronic Documents Act (PIPEDA), in the US there is no similar benchmark.

The method followed by Canada and Italy clearly differs significantly from that of the US. Both the Canadian and the Italian approach include (at least) one important, all-encompassing statute, PIPEDA and the *Codice Privacy*, respectively; since 1985 Canada has also had a Privacy Act. Strict rules apply both to private and to public entities, and informed consent is the basis for processing personal data. Although the actual rationality and efficiency of consent can certainly be questioned, the existence of this principle indicates the centrality of the data subject and of her will.

Another key point that reveals the differences between the approaches is the existence of dedicated privacy authorities. Once more, the situations in Canada and Italy are similar. Both systems have a specific

---

[8] Quotation from Bennett, ibid 138.

Privacy Authority, which plays a particularly significant role in the protection of privacy. The importance of the authorities' roles is clearly demonstrated in the case studies analysed in this book. In the US, a body – the Division – to control the application of privacy regulation was only created in 2006 and is merely a division of another institution; Canada and Italy, however, seem to attach more importance to the role of the Privacy Authority, each having created a specific – largely independent – organ dedicated to privacy protection. This clearly indicates that both systems accord more importance to the right to privacy itself than does the US.

Another characteristic of privacy law in the US is that, very often, rights which would be considered autonomous in other countries are traced back to privacy.[9] In other words, the right to privacy is invoked in cases that would not be protected on the grounds of 'privacy' in other countries: the latter is closer to the 'right to self-determination' intro-duced by the German Bundesverfassungsgericht, and represents the right to 'construct one's own identity'.[10] In Canada and Italy privacy is considered to be a way to achieve self-determination, which – however – is a right in itself. The broad US interpretation of privacy at times strengthens, at times weakens, the concept and its protection. Privacy may be strengthened by the fact that it is often invoked and applied as a defence: the higher the number of a subject's interests that are protected, the more the core aspects of privacy – such as the right to be let alone – are respected. However, the right to privacy can also be weakened by this wide approach. It may become a sort of 'wild-card-right', used whenever a case has to be defended but no other right has been directly violated. In such a situation, privacy would be 'everywhere', and thus 'nowhere'.

The existence of the above divergences is confirmed by the EU's decisions on the adequacy of the American and Canadian data protection laws when it comes to 'transborder data flows'. European Directive 95/46 provides that personal data can be transferred to third countries only when they can grant an adequate level of protection for information

---

[9]   For instance, in the US privacy is frequently coupled with anonymity, as both are included under First Amendment protection. This is becoming more and more common in the Internet world, according to Daniel J Solove and Paul M Schwartz, *Information Privacy Law* (5th edn, Aspen Publishing 2015) 554.

[10]   Manuel José Cepeda Espinosa, 'Privacy' in Michel Rosenfeld and András Sajó (eds), *The Oxford Handbook of Comparative Constitutional Law* (OUP 2012) 966, 970.

privacy.[11] When Canada adopted PIPEDA, the European Commission issued a decision in which it stated that 'Canada is considered as providing an adequate level of protection for personal data transferred from the Community to recipients subject to the Personal Information Protection and Electronic Documents Act';[12] data can thus be transferred freely between Canada and the EU.

The European approach to the US was completely different: Directive 95/46 states that when a country does not provide an adequate level of protection 'the Commission shall enter into negotiations with a view to remedying the situation'.[13] As the EU considered the level of protection offered by the US to be inadequate, the EU Commission and the US Department of Commerce agreed on the well-known 'Safe Harbor Privacy Principles' framework.[14] Under this framework, US companies that wanted to process or store European citizens' personal data had to

---

[11] See Recitals nos. 56 and 57, as well as arts. 25 and 26 of Directive 95/46/EC of the European Parliament and of the Council of 24 October 1995 on the protection of individuals with regard to the processing of personal data and on the free movement of such data [1995] OJ L 281/31. This has led other countries to adopt new legislation. For an analysis of this 'emulation effect' see Steven Bellman, Eric J. Johnson, Stephen J. Kobrin and Gerald L. Lohse, 'International Differences in Information Privacy Concerns: A Global Survey of Consumers' [2004] The Information Society 313, 314; Bennet (n 7) 123–128.

[12] Art. 1, Commission Decision of 20 December 2001 pursuant to Directive 95/46/EC of the European Parliament and of the Council on the adequate protection of personal data provided by the Canadian Personal Information Protection and Electronic Documents Act [2002] OJ L 002/13.

[13] Art. 25, para 5, Directive 95/46/EC.

[14] 2000/520/EC: Commission Decision of 26 July 2000 pursuant to Directive 95/46/EC of the European Parliament and of the Council on the adequacy of the protection provided by the safe harbour privacy principles and related frequently asked questions issued by the US Department of Commerce [2000] OJ L 215/7. For a brief overview, see Sylvia Mercado Kierkegaard, 'Safe Harbor Agreement – Boon or Bane?' [2005] Shidler Journal of Law, Commerce, & Technology 10 <https://digital.law.washington.edu/dspace-law/bitstream/handle/1773.1/362/vol1_no3_art10.pdf?sequence=1> accessed 10 March 2017. It is also possible for US firms to implement 'Model Contract Clauses' or 'Corporate binding rules'. The latter are tools applied by corporate groups when transferring data from an EU Member State to a non-EU state within the same corporate group. The rules, which are a combination of technical measures, policies and internal training, must be approved by a Privacy Authority. Model contract clauses are sets of standard clauses that must be followed when transferring data out of, and into, the EU. The only applicable clauses are those issued by the Commission. For further details see <http://ec.europa.eu/justice/data-protection/international-transfers/index_en.htm> accessed 10 March 2017.

self-certify that they adhered to some basic principles, which were stated in the framework; adhesion to these principles meant that the company could handle personal data.

The framework was criticized for many years. Changes to US regulations after 9/11 and Snowden's revelations about US government surveillance of Internet users' personal data clearly demonstrated that the US system did not protect personal data adequately. In 2015 the Court of Justice of the European Union declared the Commission's Decision invalid.[15] As a consequence, the US and the EU had to negotiate a new agreement, adopted in 2016, and known as the 'Privacy Shield',[16] under which the US has a duty to ensure that American companies remain in compliance with the rules they commit to; non-compliance leads to sanctions and removal from the list of companies adhering to the Privacy Shield.

The US promised that the power of public authorities to access personal data for national security reasons would be subject to clear limitations. EU citizens will also have a redress mechanism and an opportunity to turn to a special Ombudsperson. Alternative Dispute Resolution systems will be introduced to allow citizens to obtain reparation. And lastly, the US and the EU agreed to a joint review mechanism on an annual basis.[17]

This brief explanation of how the EU Commission has dealt with transborder data flows should shed some light on the different conceptions of privacy in the three countries. In fact, although the right to privacy is in a sense a creature of the American system, Canada and Italy have been developing a more comprehensive, and therefore more protective, approach. The American conception of privacy is that of a right covered by the Constitution, but not deserving of all-encompassing laws to protect any of its facets. Personal data, in particular, is not safeguarded as it is in the Italian or Canadian systems. The latter countries present

---

[15] Case C-362/14 *Maximillian Schrems v. Data Protection Commissioner* [2015] ECLI:EU:C:2015:650.

[16] Martin A Weiss and Kristin Archick, 'U.S.-EU Data Privacy: From Safe Harbor to Privacy Shield', Congressional Research Service, 2016 <www.fas.org/sgp/crs/misc/R44257.pdf> accessed 10 March 2017.

[17] Within two months of its adoption, the agreement was challenged in the European Court of Justice: Cynthia O'Donoghue and Thomas C Evans, 'EU-US Privacy Shield challenged in the European Court of Justice', Technology Law Dispatch (5 December 2016) <www.technologylawdispatch.com/2016/12/privacy-data-protection/eu-us-privacy-shield-challenged-in-the-european-court-of-justice> accessed 10 March 2017.

more similar conceptions of privacy; both systems provide laws that cover every aspect of life, and these laws are supervised by an independent authority to which citizens can apply if they believe their rights to have been violated. Although the Canadian framework is divided between state and federal laws, PIPEDA's requirement for 'substantially similar' laws helps to ensure adequate levels of privacy protection throughout the country. The Italian regulatory framework, which mainly derives from European Directives, probably embodies the strongest of the three conceptions. Article 1 of the Privacy Code introduced the existence of a right to personal data protection, thus going further than the courts.

As an additional example, consider the idea of 'identifiability': while in Canada and the EU data that can potentially identify an individual is considered 'personal data' and protected as such, in the American system this data falls outside the scope of legislation. Canadian and Italian regulations only allow for the use of personal data on a legal basis and/or with the data subject's consent; the US system, however, allows the use of personal data unless it is harmful or is in some way restricted by law.[18]

The three conceptions of privacy can be labelled 'weak' – the US; 'strong' – Canada; and 'strong–very strong' – Italy. These attitudes to privacy laws have played a role in judges' decisions, as did the conception of copyright. I shall try to explain in the next (and final) section how judgments have been affected by these conceptions.

3. CONCLUSIONS: CONCEPTUAL BALANCING

Two prominent scholars maintain that 'EU law views privacy as a fundamental right, while the U.S. considers it one interest that is balanced against others'.[19] This statement is probably the best explanation we have of the outcome of the analysed lawsuits, at least of those that took place in the US and Italy. The present section will now try to demonstrate that the judges concerned decided the lawsuits by adhering to the conception of copyright and privacy of the country in which they were operating.

The solutions adopted by judges vary not only between the three systems, but also within each system. Such differences are the result of different interpretations of the rules relating to copyright and privacy;

---

[18] Paul M Schwartz and Daniel J Solove, 'Reconciling Personal Information in the United States and European Union' [2014] California Law Review 877, 880–881.

[19] Ibid 880.

these divergences are, indeed, the natural outcome of the interpretative role proper to a judge. Despite them, nevertheless, a main line of decision can be defined for each of the three systems.

In the US the majority of cases were resolved in favour of copyright, both in cases where the DMCA subpoena was applied, and those which followed the John Doe process. This is also true whether the opposing right taken into account is anonymity or privacy, or both. In Canada, although the sample is very small, information privacy undoubtedly prevailed over copyright, as it did in the Italian cases.

A very interesting similarity between the cases in all three systems is that even though none of the three provisions regarding disclosure of a third party's documents or data mentions the need to consider third-party rights to privacy, the judges always took this issue into consideration. While this may be a consequence of defendants' counterclaims, it may also be an indicator of the importance of users' rights to information privacy in the lawsuits analysed.

It is worth stressing that the provisions applied by judges in the three systems leave a lot of space for interpretation. For instance, in the US test, the concept of 'expectation of privacy' does not have well defined borders.[20] The same can be said about letter (e) of the Canadian test. How can a judge easily decide whether the disclosure of certain data is more important than privacy concerns? The Italian approach is probably the least discretional of the three since it includes no clear reference to the concept of 'privacy'.[21] Such spaces for interpretation are key to the idea of conceptual balancing, allowing judges to introduce some 'extra' factors, which would not be included if the law was worded narrowly, into the balancing mechanism.

The cases – and the conflict – analysed in this book are paradigmatic examples of the tensions created by digital technologies (or rather, by a specific use of those technologies) and of how legal systems react when facing technological evolution. Nowadays, technologies are advancing increasingly faster than the law. This means that judges are facing (and will continue to face) situations in which they have to decide on the basis

---

[20] This is also demonstrated by the attention that scholars have paid to this particular issue.

[21] Nonetheless, art. 156*bis*, co. 3, Legge 633/41 states that, in ordering the disclosure, the judge shall consider the measure necessary to protect confidential information. The expression 'confidential information' seems to me to refer more to questions of industrial secrets and business competition than to privacy and data protection, or to professional confidentiality (as in cases involving doctors or lawyers).

of obsolete norms, which cannot help them to find solutions because they were conceived for different times.[22] The existence of leeway and open clauses gives judges room to exercise their discretion.

The weight judges give to conflicting rights in the balancing process emerges from the text of the decisions adopted and can be inferred both from single words or sentences, and from the overall decision. In its decisions in the cases between the RIAA and Verizon[23] the United States District Court for the District of Columbia explicitly mentions policy issues. In the first judgment delivered by the Court, Judge Bates explains that the interpretation of the DMCA subpoena as proposed by Verizon would 'mak[e] little sense from a policy standpoint'.[24] What policy standpoint is the Court referring to? One which can be found throughout the entire decision: in enacting the DMCA subpoena, Congress – which is the only institution that has the power to regulate copyright[25] – wanted to create a tool to enforce copyright expeditiously, through increased prevention of copyright infringement online. Indeed, the *raison d'être* of the entire DMCA is to protect copyright holders from online piracy, as it is of the DMCA subpoena.

How should judges balance conflicting rights in such a situation? In this case, the Court stated that the balancing had already been done 'appropriately' by Congress.[26] Therefore, no further balancing was needed, and users' privacy and anonymity – or, indeed, freedom of speech – could not enter the balancing process at all.[27]

The second judgment in the case between the RIAA and Verizon includes an explicit balancing. In the words of the Court '[t]he recording industry has suffered substantial losses due to Internet piracy. Whatever marginal impact the DMCA subpoena authority may have on the

---

[22] 'The precedent will stand until and unless changes in law or technology make it obsolete. No greater certainty can reasonably be expected of law. Law must change as technology changes': Richard A Posner, *Reflections on Judging* (Harvard University Press 2013) 126.

[23] *In re Verizon Internet Services*, 240 F. Supp. 2d 24 (D.D.C. 2003).

[24] Ibid 30.

[25] Ibid 36–40.

[26] Ibid 37; also: *In re Verizon Internet Services*, 257 F. Supp. 2d 244 (D.D.C. 2003), 264.

[27] *In re Verizon* (n 23) 43. It was not in the courts' power to modify the balance reached by Congress in the DMCA: *In re Verizon Internet Services* (n 26) 274. The same argument is used to reach an opposite conclusion by the United States Court of Appeals for the District of Columbia Circuit in *RIAA v. Verizon Internet Services*, 351 F.3d 1229 (DC Cir. 2003), 1238.

expressive or anonymity rights of Internet users, then, is *vastly out-weighed* by the extent of copyright infringement over the Internet through peer-to-peer file sharing.'[28]

This statement explicitly clarifies that copyright is more important than users' anonymity, and that the latter is, in fact, greatly outweighed by the need to combat copyright infringement. Of course, anonymity related to file-sharing is weak and may not, in fact, deserve protection at all.[29] However, within the scope of this research Judge Bates' statement is enlightening: even free speech has to surrender to copyright enforcement.

In the case involving Charter Communications,[30] the provider argued that DMCA subpoenas would violate the Cable Communications Act.[31] Paragraph 551 of 47 U.S.C. protects subscribers' privacy and prohibits cable operators 'from disclosing personal information that could identify subscribers without obtaining their prior written or electronic consent, and operators are required to take actions to prevent unauthorized access to such information'.[32] A cable operator – in this case an Internet Service Provider – complying with a subpoena would violate the Communications Act. However, in the Court's opinion this interpretation was incorrect. The Congress had already considered subscribers' rights and copyright enforcement needs: the DMCA explicitly requires service providers to expeditiously disclose the information requested by the subpoena 'notwithstanding any other provision of law'.[33] This interpretation means that judges do not need to balance users' privacy with any colliding copyrights: the balancing has already been done by Congress. This reading of the norms would overcome the difficulties arising from the conflict on which the present book focuses; however, only the above judgment seems to refer to such an interpretation, while others approach the issue in a radically different manner.

The first decision by Judge Bates includes a useful comparison between the DMCA subpoena and the John Doe process. In fact, Verizon had suggested that as a DMCA subpoena was not applicable to access providers, copyright holders should consider bringing a John Doe action in the federal court. The Court recognized that in both cases user

---

[28] *In re Verizon Internet Services* (n 26) 265–266 (emphasis added).
[29] This is indeed the opinion of Judge Bates: *In re Verizon* (n 23) 42.
[30] *In re Charter Communications, Inc., Subpoena Enforcement Matter*, 393 F.3d 771 (8th Cir., 2005).
[31] Cable Communications Policy Act 1984, Pub. Law No. 98-549, 98 Stat. 2779, in particular: 47 U.S.C. § 551: 'Protection of subscriber privacy'.
[32] *In re Charter* (n 30) 784.
[33] DMCA § 512(h)(5). *In re Charter* (n 30) 784–785.

anonymity was at issue but it also claimed that the DMCA is more protective of users' rights than John Doe procedures, given that the requirements to obtain users' identities through a subpoena are more stringent than those needed to obtain them through a John Doe action.[34] The fact that in a DMCA subpoena the applicant must establish a *prima facie* case of copyright infringement would be – in the same judge's opinion – a sufficient safeguard for protecting free speech and, ultimately, individuals' identities.[35]

In addition, the Court considered the burden that copyright holders should bear to obtain users' identities through John Doe actions: the time and costs which copyright holders would incur would greatly undermine the effectiveness of the measures against copyright infringement.[36] However, as fully explained in Chapter 4, John Doe actions were actually used widely in order to obtain alleged infringers' information. Although the procedure is different from that of the DMCA subpoena, the substance of the decisions remains the same.

For instance, in *Sony Music Entertainment Inc. v. Does*,[37] the Terms of Service between provider and users were considered to indicate that users should have known that their information could be disclosed if laws or governmental entities, including – of course – judges so requested. A very similar reasoning had, in fact, been applied in one of the *Verizon* cases.[38]

Likewise, the arguments related to anonymity, free speech and P2P file-sharing were applied in the same way in DMCA subpoena cases and in John Doe actions. While file-sharing may, to some extent, be free speech entitled to First Amendment protection, such protection is very limited and would not be sufficient to outweigh copyright enforcement.[39] In addition, since file-sharing amounts to copyright infringement,[40] courts explicated that the First Amendment does not cover illegal activities.[41]

Expectation of privacy was one of the criteria upon which courts decided whether to allow users' information disclosure or not. Both

---

[34] *In re Verizon* (n 23) 40–41.

[35] *In re Verizon Internet Services* (n 26) 262–263.

[36] *In re Verizon* (n 23) 41.

[37] *Sony Music Entm't Inc. v. Does 1–40*, 326 F. Supp. 2d 556 (2004), 559.

[38] *In re Verizon Internet Services* (n 26) 267.

[39] *Sony Music Entm't Inc. v. Does 1–40*, 326 F. Supp. 2d 556 (2004), 564–565; *Arista Records, LLC v. Does 1–16*, 2009 U.S. Dist. LEXIS 12159, 10–11.

[40] Ibid 565.

[41] *In re Verizon* (n 23) 42; *Sony Music* (n 39) 562–563.

expectation of privacy and First Amendment protection were – in the judges' opinions – so small that they could only surrender to the plaintiff's right to use discovery to obtain users' identities.[42]

Going back to the *Verizon* cases, according to Judge Bates, users not only had little or no anonymity, they could not enjoy much expectation of privacy either. Here lies a great difference between the US approach and that of Italy or Canada: while the US considers expectation of privacy as the counter-value to copyright infringement, Canadian and Italian judges juxtapose copyright infringement to information privacy/data protection. Data protection/information privacy is infringed as soon as Internet Protocol (IP) numbers are collected, while (expectation of) privacy is not. Expectation of privacy was, in the judges' words, very low, since users should not expect to have privacy when carrying on an (allegedly) infringing activity.[43] However, information privacy linked to IP numbers (and other user information) is infringed at the moment in which this information is collected without respecting the law.

The differences of approach in the specific cases are just a reflection of the three countries' overall conceptions of privacy. In the US, where informational privacy does not enjoy all-encompassing protection, and instead expectation of privacy is the parameter to be considered, the mere collection of IP addresses is not seen as an invasion of privacy. IPs themselves do not fall into the category of 'personal data'. In sharp contrast, in both the Canadian and the European-Italian contexts, IP addresses have been explicitly qualified as personal data and their collection is therefore subject to legal procedures and requirements.[44] In addition, with regard to copyright, the illegal nature of file-sharing has never been doubted in the American decisions. Once again this decisive declaration of the illegality of file-sharing is born out of the strong conception of copyright described above.

In Canada and Italy, however, as we have seen, the illegality of file-sharing is at least questioned. Perhaps most strikingly, in the Canadian case *BMG v. Does*, Judge Von Finckenstein specified that 'downloading a song for personal use does not amount to infringement', as I have had cause to mention on a number of occasions.[45] One reason for

---

42   Consider, for instance, *Arista Records* (n 39) 21–22.
43   *In re Verizon Internet Services* (n 26) 267; *Sony Music* (n 39) 566–567; *Arista Records* (n 39) 10–11.
44   Consider the explanations found in Chapter 1 and references there cited, in particular Section 2 and references there cited.
45   *BMG Canada Inc. v. John Doe* [2004] 3 F.C.R. 241, para 25. Consider also paras 22–24.

this lack of clarity may well be the fact that at the time of the *BMG* case Canada had not yet implemented the WIPO Treaties and their 'right to make available'. However, it is also the result of a generally weak conception of copyright, which very often favours user rights over those of copyright holders. This weak conception is counterbalanced by a very strong approach to privacy, both physical and informational. As previously stated, in Canada IP addresses are considered as personal data. Judge Von Finckenstein recognized that IP addresses were valuable in the Internet environment and that their concealment should be seen as good policy.[46] While the Court clarified that privacy cannot be a shield behind which to carry out illegal activities, it also plainly stated that '[i]t is unquestionable but that the protection of privacy is of utmost importance to Canadian society'.[47] Courts are required by common law and by PIPEDA 'to balance privacy rights against the rights of other individuals and the public interest'.[48]

In the test applied by Judge Von Finckenstein, the public interest in favour of disclosure had to outweigh legitimate privacy concerns. The public interest in favour of disclosure would be the interest of copyright holders in obtaining users' identities in order to enforce the right alleged to have been infringed. In the Court's words, the plaintiff had not proved such a public interest. On the contrary, each respondent sustained that 'ISP account holders have an expectation that their identity will be kept private and confidential. This expectation of privacy is based on both the terms of their account agreements with the ISPs and sections 3 and 5 of the Personal Information Protection and Electronic Documents Act. (PIPEDA).'[49] The judge's concerns about the reliability of the data to be disclosed – due to the delay in the request for disclosure – led the Court to a decision in favour of users' privacy.

Although the Court did not grant the disclosure, it did prescribe what measures should be applied in case of disclosure in order for the invasion of privacy to be as limited as possible.[50]

The Court of Appeal also stressed the importance of privacy. Even though the appellate judges did not share Judge Von Finckenstein's view that file-sharing is not copyright infringement,[51] they considered user privacy to prevail. Adopting a test very similar to the one used by Judge

---

[46] Ibid para 37.
[47] Ibid paras 36, 39.
[48] Ibid paras 40.
[49] Ibid para 9.
[50] Ibid paras 44–46.
[51] Ibid paras 47–50.

Von Finckenstein, the Court of Appeal found that privacy outweighed the public interest in disclosing the information. The judges clarified that '[p]rivacy rights are significant and they must be protected'.[52] Such protection is achieved by means of PIPEDA, which provides procedures and exceptions for the collection and processing of personal data.[53]

Nonetheless, the Court pointed out that privacy should yield to public concerns about the protection of IPRs – copyright included – when infringement actually threatens to erode these rights. However, even in such cases, precautionary measures should be taken, both to ensure that privacy rights suffer the minimum invasion possible and to avoid the leakage of other, non-relevant, information.[54]

Again, privacy won over copyright in the Appellate Court.

Subsequent cases involving Voltage Pictures and the film *The Hurt Locker* had a different outcome, but nonetheless were very protective of privacy and personal data. In particular, the Federal Court, in acknowledging that the issues 'require[d] a delicate balancing of privacy rights versus the rights of copyright holders',[55] was concerned that information related to individuals not involved in file-sharing could be accidentally disclosed. The Court considered the plaintiff's copyright to be violated by file-sharing[56] but before ordering the disclosure, it made sure that specific procedures would be followed to 'ensure that privacy rights are invaded in the most minimal way possible'.[57]

The judgment is also interesting because the Court analyses the decisions made by US courts in similar cases. The Canadian judge recognized that only when information to be protected was linked to sensitive aspect of users' lives – i.e. the use of pornography – did US courts exercise particular care in allowing disclosure.[58] This finding further demonstrates that the US does not value personal information in the same way as Canada and Italy do. In the US, personal data only seems to gain meaning when it is linked to more sensitive information. In

---

[52]   *BMG Canada Inc. v. John Doe*, [2005] F.C.J. No. 858, para 38.

[53]   More in particular, S. 7(3) of PIPEDA listing the exceptions upon which disclosure of personal information can be made, even in the absence of a subject's consent.

[54]   *BMG Canada Inc. v. John Doe* (n 52) paras 41–41.

[55]   *Voltage Pictures LLC v. John Doe* [2015] 2 F.C.R. 540, para 1.

[56]   Ibid para 18.

[57]   Ibid paras 57–59; in particular, paras 137ff for the measures actually adopted.

[58]   Ibid paras 117ff.

contrast, Italy and Canada value personal data per se, with Italy giving sensitive data different, even more rigorous, protection.

The value placed on the protection of personal data in Italy also emerges from some of the judgments analysed in this book. While all the decisions considered file-sharing to be an illicit activity which violates plaintiff's copyright, only some of them qualified the collection of IP addresses as legal. One of the judgments seemed to take a sort of 'expectation of privacy' into consideration; the Tribunal stated that when someone uses a P2P technology, she shows a willingness to accept that her IP address could be known by any other user within the network.[59]

At the same time, the Court considered one of the exceptions to the need for a data subject's consent provided by the Privacy Code to be applicable to the case at stake.[60] The same reasoning was later applied in subsequent decisions,[61] such as the decision of the Tribunal of Rome of 9 February 2007, which granted the request of Peppermint in the appeal against a first instance decision of the same Tribunal.[62] The Tribunal of first instance had held privacy to prevail over copyright, taking into consideration the fact that the discovery tool introduced by EU Directive 2004/48 and used by Peppermint should be 'appl[ied] without prejudice to other statutory provisions which ... govern the protection of confidentiality of information sources or the processing of personal data'.[63] The appellate judge, however, construed art. 156*bis*, Legge 633/41 as allowing the disclosure of users' data on the basis of the above-mentioned exception to users' consent provided by the Privacy Code.

Key to these Italian decisions is the fact that they considered only the user's information (which would be disclosed) to be personal data, and not the IP addresses per se. On the contrary, since under European and Italian law IP addresses are personal data,[64] their collection is in itself illicit if the data subject has not previously given her consent. In addition, their collection should have been notified to the Privacy Authority.

---

[59] Trib. Roma, ord., 18.8.2006 in *Riv. dir. Ind.*, n. 4-5/2008, II, 328.
[60] Namely art. 24, co. 1, lett. f).
[61] For instance: Trib. Roma, ord., 9.2.2007, in Resp. civ. e prev., n. 7-8/2007, 1699.
[62] Trib. Roma, ord., 29.11.2006, as cited in Trib. Roma, ord., 9.2.2007.
[63] Art. 8, co. 3, Dir. 2004/48.
[64] See Chapter 1, Section 2.

The Privacy Authority, taking part in the lawsuit in order to safeguard information privacy, succeeded in balancing the conflicting rights.[65] It explicitly stated that privacy should only be superseded by rights with a higher degree of importance and that this was not the case for copyright. The Tribunal of Rome adopted the Privacy Authority's interpretation and – partly in light of the words of Directive 2004/48, quoted above[66] – clearly stated that copyright was not important enough to prevail over privacy. In reaching this outcome, the conclusions of Advocate General Kokott in the *Promusicae* case were also taken into consideration.[67]

In an earlier decision the same Tribunal had also applied what I call conceptual balancing.[68] Finding itself in an impasse generated by the application of art. 156*bis*, Legge 633/41, the Court took the entire system of Italian laws into account. Starting with the Constitution and the European regulatory framework for both of the conflicting rights, the judge sketched the conceptions of the conflicting rights and decided in favour of privacy. The text of the law was undoubtedly ambiguous and it is not surprising that different judges have interpreted the laws in conflicting ways. Confronted by uncertain laws governing the conflict between rights, judges can rely on conceptual balancing to understand the value that the entire legal system places upon a right and, following this evaluation, can decide that one of the two rights prevails.

A similar analysis was made in the last of the Italian controversies, delivered after the Court of Justice's decision in *Promusicae*. After acknowledging that a conflict existed between the interest of copyright holders and the need to protect users' data, the Court stated that the conflict had actually been solved by the Italian legislator. The fact that, in implementing the Directive, the Italian legislature did not introduce an explicit provision allowing the disclosure of personal information in civil procedures led the Tribunal of Rome to the conclusion that users' information could only be disclosed in criminal procedures. This decision was reached after having summarized the Italian legal system's overall conception of data protection and intellectual property rights.[69] Again,

---

[65]   Trib. Roma, ord., 22.11.2007, in *Foro it.* 2008, 4, I, 1329.

[66]   See Trib. Roma (n 65).

[67]   The *Promusicae* case was decided by the CJEU a few months after the Tribunal of Rome pronounced its judgment.

[68]   Trib. Roma, ord., 16.7.2007 in *Dir. informatica*, n. 4-5/2007, 828.

[69]   Italy's status as an EU Member State was also taken into consideration.

the concepts of the conflicting rights were the basis upon which the judge built her judgment.[70]

The texts of the judgments that I have analysed reveal the way in which judges balance rights. If we were to trace the balancing applied by the courts in these cases back to the categories illustrated in Chapter 1, the US and Canadian decisions might be included in the idea of 'definitional balancing'. The US and Canadian courts have, in fact, adopted a specific test, which has since been applied to many other cases. The Italian judgments, in contrast, seem to be closer to 'ad hoc balancing'.

In all three approaches, however, the concepts of privacy and copyright played a key role in helping judges to define which right should prevail. These decisions prove that when courts face difficulties in balancing rights, they rely (at least to a certain extent) on their legal system's overall policy approach to the rights in conflict.

The aim of this book is to shed some light on how judges balance conflicting rights. The idea of 'conceptual balancing' is not intended as an all-encompassing explanation of judges' reasoning, nor as a method that judges should feel obliged to apply. Nonetheless, judges, and lawyers in general, should be conscious that their interpretation and application of the law also reflects conceptions that, although not explicit or evident, shape the solutions adopted.

Conceptual balancing is, of course, only one of the concurring causes that lead judges to a given outcome. It represents only one of the many possible ways in which the 'act of' balancing carried out by judges can be described.

---

[70] A partially different opinion is hold by Marcello De Cata, 'Il caso "Peppermint". Ulteriori riflessioni anche alla luce del caso "Promusicae"' [2008] Rivista di diritto industriale 404, 443: he stressed the interesting point that the resolution of the conflict was arrived at by the Italian judges through the coordination of specific norms and not with reference to general principles. In the author's opinion this could mirror the conception of privacy, which is not yet seen as a fundamental right, but as a limit to other rights.

Bibliography

Abrams L.S. and McGuinnes K.P., *Canadian Civil Procedure Law* (2nd edn, Lexis Nexis 2010)

Abriani N., 'Le utilizzazioni libere nella società dell'informazione: considerazioni generali' [2002] AIDA 98

Abriani N., Cottino G. and Ricolfi M., *Diritto industriale in Trattato di diritto commerciale diretto da Cottino*, vol. 2 (Cedam 2001)

Acquisti A., 'Privacy in Electronic Commerce and the Economics of Immediate Gratification' in *Proceedings of the 5th ACM conference on Electronic commerce* (ACM 2004) 21

Acquisti A. and Grossklags J., 'Privacy Attitudes and Privacy Behavior. Losses, Gains, and Hyperbolic Discounting' in Camp L.J. and Lewis S. (eds), *The Economics of Information Security* (Springer 2004) 165

Aleinikoff T.A., 'Constitutional Law in the Age of Balancing' [1987] Yale Law Journal 943

Alexy R., *A Theory of Constitutional Rights* (Julian Rivers tr, OUP 2002)

Alexy R., 'Constitutional Rights, Balancing, and Rationality' [2003] Ratio Juris 131

Alexy R., 'On Balancing and Subsumption. A Structural Comparison' [2003] Ratio Juris 433

Alexy R., 'Balancing, Constitutional Review, and Representation' [2005] International Journal of Constitutional Law 572

Alexy R., 'The Construction of Constitutional Rights' [2010] Law & Ethics of Human Rights 21

Alvanini S., 'La responsabilità dei service provider' [2010] Dir. industriale 329

Alvanini S. and Cassinelli A., 'I (possibili) nuovi poteri di AGCom in material di diritto d'autore nel settore dei media' [2011] Dir. Industriale 543

Amedeo M., 'Shifting the Burden: the Unconstitutionality of Section 512(h) of the Digital Millennium Copyright Act and its Impact on Internet Service Providers' [2003] CommLaw Conspectus 311

Andrepont C., 'Digital Millennium Copyright Act: Copyright Protection for the Digital Age' [1999] DePaul-LCA Journal of Art & Entertainment Law 397

Angelopoulos C., 'Are Blocking Injunctions Against ISPs Allowed in Europe? Copyright Enforcement in the Post-Telekabel EU Legal Landscape' [2014] Journal of Intellectual Property Law & Practice 812

Article 29 Working Party, 'Working Document on Data Protection Issues Related to Intellectual Property Rights' (18 January 2005) <http://ec.europa.eu/justice/data-protection/article-29/documentation/opinion-recommendation/files/2005/wp104_en.pdf>

Article 29 Working Party, 'Working Document on a Common Interpretation of Article 26(1) of Directive 95/46/EC of 24 October 1995' (25 November 2005) 10-12 <http://ec.europa.eu/justice/policies/privacy/docs/wpdocs/2005/wp114_en.pdf>

Article 29 Working Party, 'Opinion 3/2006 on the Directive 2006/24/EC' (25 March 2006) <http://ec.europa.eu/justice/policies/privacy/docs/wpdocs/2006/wp119_en.pdf>

Article 29 Working Party, 'Opinion 15/2011 on the Definition of Consent', WP 187 (12 July 2011) <http://ec.europa.eu/justice/policies/privacy/docs/wpdocs/2011/wp187_en.pdf>

Article 29 Working Party, 'The Future of Privacy' (1 December 2009) 8 and 17 <http://ec.europa.eu/justice/policies/privacy/docs/wpdocs/2009/wp168_en.pdf>

Article 29 Working Party, 'Opinion 04/2012 on Cookie Consent Exemption' (7 June 2012) <http://ec.europa.eu/justice/data-protection/article-29/documentation/opinion-recommendation/files/2012/wp194_en.pdf>

Article 29 Working Party, 'Working Document 02/2013 providing guidance on obtaining consent for cookies' (2 October 2013) <http://ec.europa.eu/justice/data-protection/article-29/documentation/opinion-recommendation/files/2013/wp208_en.pdf>

Ashdown G.J., 'Legitimate Expectation of Privacy' [1981] Vanderbilt Law Review 1289

Atelli M., 'Riservatezza (diritto alla). III) Diritto Costituzionale', *Enciclopedia Giuridica Treccani*, vol. XXVII (1995)

Austin L.M., 'Is Consent the Foundation of Fair Information Practices? Canada's Experience under Pipeda' [2006] University of Toronto Law Journal 181

Australian Privacy Commissioner, *Information Privacy in Australia: A National Scheme for Fair Information Practices in the Private Sector*, August 1997 <http://austlii.edu.au/itlaw/national_scheme/national-PART.html>

Autieri P., 'Il caso Napster alla luce del diritto comunitario' in Ubertazzi L.C. (ed), *TV, Internet e 'new trends' di diritti d'autore e connessi* (Giuffrè 2003) 63

Autieri P., 'Diritti connessi al diritto d'autore' in Auteri P., Floridia G., Mangini V.M., Olivieri G., Ricolfi M., Romano R., and Spada P., *Diritto industriale. Proprietà intellettuale e concorrenza* (Giappichelli 2016) 675

Autieri P., 'Il contenuto del diritto d'autore' in Auteri P. P., Floridia G., Mangini V.M., Olivieri G., Ricolfi M., Romano R., and Spada P., *Diritto industriale. Proprietà intellettuale e concorrenza* (Giappichelli 2016) 623

Backerman R., 'How the RIAA Litigation Process Works' (recordingindustryvspeople.blogspot.it, 11 January 2008) <http://recordingindustry vspeople.blogspot.it/2007/01/how-riaa-litigation-process-works.html>

Backerman R., 'Large Recording Companies v. the Defenseless – Some Common Sense Solutions to the Challenges of the RIAA Litigation' [2008] Judges' Journal 20

Bailey J., 'The Substance of Procedure: Non-Party Disclosure in the Canadian and U.S. Online Music Sharing Litigation' [2006] Alberta Law Review 615

Bainbridge D.I. and Platten N., *EC Data Protection Directive* (Butterworths 1996)

Baistrocchi P., 'Liability of Intermediary Service Providers in the EU Directive on Electronic Commerce' [2002] Santa Clara Computer & High Technology Law Review 111

Ball H.G., *Law of Copyright and Literary Property* (Bender & Co. 1944)

Band J. and Schruers M., 'Safe Harbors Against The Liability Hurricane: The Communications Decency Act and The Digital Millennium Copyright Act' [2002] Cardozo Arts & Entertainment Law Journal 295

Barak A., 'Proportionality and Principled Balancing' [2010] Law & Ethics of Human Rights 1

Barak A., 'Proportionality (2)' in Rosenfeld M. and Sajó A (eds), *The Oxford Handbook of Comparative Constitutional Law* (OUP 2012) 738

Barak A., *Proportionality. Constitutional Rights and Their Limitations* (CUP 2012)

Barker J.C., 'Grossly Excessive Penalties in the Battle Against Illegal File-Sharing: The Troubling Effects of Aggregating Minimum Statutory Damages for Copyright Infringement' [2004] 83 Texas Law Review 525

Barnett Lidsky L., 'Silencing John Doe: Defamation & Discourse in Cyberspace' [2000] Duke Law Journal 855

Barnett Lidsky L., 'Anonymity in Cyberspace: What Can We Learn from John Doe?' [2009] Boston College Law Review 1373

Barnett Lidsky L. and Cotter T.F., 'Authorship, Ardencies, and Anonymous Speech' [2007] Notre Dame Law Review 1537

Barron J. and Dienes C.T., *Constitutional Law in a Nutshell* (4th edn, West Publishing 2005)

Barthel T.J., 'RIAA v. Diamond Multimedia System, Inc.: The Sale of the Rio Player Forces the Music Industry to Dance to a New Beat' [1999] DePaul-LCA Journal of Art & Entertainment Law 279

Basu D., 'Obtaining Disclosure from Non-parties' [2005] Journal of Personal Injury 198

Bayley R.M. and Bennett C.J., 'Privacy Impact Assessments in Canada' in Wright D. and De Hert P. (eds), *Privacy Impact Assessment* (Springer 2012) 161

Becker C., 'Criminal Enforcement of Intellectual Property Rights' [2003] Canadian Intellectual Property Review 183

Becker L.E. Jr, 'The Liability of Computer Bulletin Board Operators for Defamation Posted by Others' [1989] Connecticut Law Review 203

Beets R.P., 'RIAA v. Napster: The Struggle to Protect Copyrights in the Internet Age' [2001] Georgia State University Law Review 507

Bellman S., Johnson E.J., Kobrin S.J. and Lohse G.L., 'International Differences in Information Privacy Concerns: A Global Survey of Consumers' [2004] The Information Society 313

Benditt T.M., 'Law and the Balancing of Interests' [1975] Social Theory and Practice 321

Bennett C.J., *Regulating Privacy. Data Protection and Public Policy in Europe and the United States* (Cornell University Press 1992)

Bennett C.J., 'The Privacy Commissioner of Canada: Multiple Roles, Diverse Expectations and Structural Dilemmas' [2003] Canadian Public Administration 218

Bennett C.J., *The Privacy Advocates: Resisting the Spread of Surveillance* (MIT Press 2008)

Bennett C.J., 'The "Right to Be Forgotten": Reconciling EU and US Perspectives' [2012] Berkeley Journal of International Law 161

Bennett C.J. and Raab C.D., *The Governance of Privacy* (MIT Press 2006)

Benvenuto L., 'Il Sistema della discovery e del diritto di "informazione" nel codice della proprietà industriale' [2007] Rivista di Diritto Industriale II, 108

Bernal P., 'The EU, the US and Right to be Forgotten' in Gutwirth S., Leenes R. and de Hert P. (eds), *Reloading Data Protection. Multidisciplinary Insights and Contemporary Challenges* (Springer Verlag 2014) 61

Bernal Pulido C., 'The Rationality of Balancing' [2006] Archives for Philosophy of Law and Social Philosophy 195

Betti E., *Interpretazione della legge e degli atti giuridici* (Giuffrè 1949)

Bianca C.M., *Diritto Civile. Vol. V – La responsabilità* (Giuffrè 2012)

Bianca C.M. and Busnelli F.D. (eds), *La protezione dei dati personali: commentario al d.lgs. 30 giugno 2003, n. 196 (Codice della privacy)* (Cedam 2007)

Bignami F., 'Privacy and Law Enforcement in the European Union: The Data Retention Directive' [2007] Chicago Journal of International Law 233

Bin R., *Diritti e argomenti. Il bilanciamento degli interessi nella giurisprudenza costituzionali* (Giuffrè 1992)

Black H.C., *Black's Law Dictionary* (5th edn, West Publishing 1979)

Blackman J.D., 'Proposal for Federal Legislation Protecting Informational Privacy Across the Private Sector' [1993] Santa Clara Computer & High Tech Law Journal 431

Blengino C., 'La tutela penale del copyright digitale: un'onda confusa e asincrona' in Ardizzone A., Benussi L., Blengino C., Glorioso A., Ramello G.B., Ruffo G, and Travostino M., *Copyright digitale. L'impatto delle nuove tecnologie tra economia e diritto* (Giappichelli 2009) 69

Blengino C. and Senor M.A., 'Il caso "Peppermint": il prevedibile contrasto tra protezione del diritto d'autore e tutela della privacy nelle reti peer to-peer' [2007] Dir. inf. e informatica 835

Boag J., 'The Battle of Piracy versus Privacy: How the Recording Industry Association of America (RIAA) Is Using the Digital Millennium Copyright Act (DMCA) As Its Weapon Against Internet Users' Privacy Rights' [2004] California Western Law Review 241

Boeve M.R., 'Will Internet Service Providers Be Forced to Turn In Their Copyright Infringing Customers? The Power of the Digital Millennium Copyright Act's Subpoena Provision After In Re Charter Communication' [2006] Hamline Law Review 177

Bogen D.S., 'First Amendment Ancillary Doctrines' [1978] Maryland Law Review 679

Bolaños B., 'Balancing and Legal Decision Theory' in Sieckmann J-R. (ed), *Legal Reasoning: the Methods of Balancing* (Franz Steiner Verlag 2010) 63

Bomhoff J., 'Balancing, the Global and the Local: Judicial Balancing as a Problematic Topic in Comparative (Constitutional) Law' [2008] Hastings International & Comparative Law Review 555

Bomhoff J., 'Rights, Balancing & Proportionality' [2010] Law & Ethics of Human Rights 109

Bomhoff J., *Balancing Constitutional Rights. The Origin and Meaning of Postwar Legal Discourse* (CUP 2013)

Borland J., 'Peer to Peer: As the Revolution Recedes' *CNET News.com* (31 December 2001) <https://www.cnet.com/news/peer-to-peer-as-the-revolution-recedes/>

Borland J., 'P2P Users Traveling by eDonkey', *CNET News.com* (28 August 2005) <http://news.cnet.com/P2P-users-traveling-by-eDonkey/2100-1025_3-5843859.html>

Bridges A.P., 'Comment of the Right of Making Available Before the United State Copyright Office', Docket No. 2014-2 <www.copyright.gov/docs/making_available/comments/docket2014_2/Andrew_Bridges.pdf>

Brimsted K. and Chesney G., 'The ECJ's Judgement in Promusicae: The Unintended Consequences – Music to the Ears of Copyright Owners or a Privacy Headache for the Future? A Comment' [2008] Computer Law & Security Report 275

Brown B., 'Fortifying the Safe Harbors: Reevaluating the DMCA in a Web 2.0 World' [2008] Berkeley Technology Law Journal 437

Bugiolacchi L., 'La responsabilità dell'host provider alla luce del d.lgs. n. 70/2003: esegesi di una disciplina "dimezzata"' [2005] Resp. civ. prev. 188

Burns P., 'The Law and Privacy: The Canadian Experience' [1976] Revue du Barreau Canadien/Canadian Bar Review 1

Burri M., 'Permission to Link: Making Available via Hyperlinks in the European Union after Svensson' [2014] JIPITEC 245 <http://www.jipitec.eu/issues/jipitec-5-3-2014/4098>

Buttarelli G., *Banche dati e tutela della riservatezza. La privacy nella società dell'informazione* (Giuffrè 1997)

Bygrave L.A., 'International Agreements to Protect Personal Data' in Rule J.B. and Greenleaf G. (eds), *Global Privacy Protection: The First Generation* (Edward Elgar Publishing 2008) 15

Bygrave L.A., 'Privacy and Data Protection in an International Perspective' [2010] Scandinavian Studies in Law 165

Bygrave L.A., 'Data Protection vs. Copyright' in Svantesson D.J.B. and Greenstein S. (eds), Internationalisation of Law in the Digital Information Society: Nordic Yearbook of Law and Informatics 2010–2012 (Ex Tuto Publishing 2013) 55

Bygrave L.A., *Privacy and Data Protection in an International Perspective* (OUP 2014)

Calvert C., Gutierrez K., Kennedy K.D. and Murrhee K.C., 'David Doe v. Goliath, Inc.: Judicial Ferment in 2009 for Business Plaintiffs Seeking the Identities of Anonymous Online Speakers' [2009] John Marshall Law Review 1

Cameron A., 'CRTC Imposes Super-PIPEDA Privacy Protection for Personal Information Collected by ISPs' [2009] Internet and E-Commerce Law in Canada 94

Cameron A. and Palmer M., 'Invasion of Privacy as a Common Law Tort in Canada' [2009] Canadian Privacy Law Review 105

Cannon R., 'The Legislative History of Senator Exon's Communications Decency Act: Regulating Barbarians on the Information Superhighway' [1996] Federal Communications Law Journal 51

Caso R., 'Il conflitto tra copyright e privacy nelle reti Peer to Peer: in margine al caso Peppermint – Profili di diritto comparato' [2007] Dir. Internet 471

Caso R., 'Il conflitto tra diritto d'autore e protezione dei dati personali: appunti dal fronte euro-italiano [2008] Diritto dell'internet 470

Cassano G. and Cimino I.P., 'Il nuovo regime di responsabilità dei providers: verso la creazione di un novello "censore telematico"' [2004] I Contratti 88

Cate F.H., *Privacy in the Information Age* (Brookings Institution Press 1997)

Cate F.H., 'Security, Privacy, and the Role of Law' [2009] IEEE Security and Privacy 60

Center for Democracy & Technology, 'Analysis of the Consumer Privacy Bill of Rights Act' (2 March 2015) <https://cdt.org/insight/analysis-of-the-consumer-privacy-bill-of-rights-act/>

Cepeda Espinosa M.J., 'Privacy' in Rosenfeld M. and Sajó A. (eds), *The Oxford Handbook of Comparative Constitutional Law* (OUP 2012) 966

Cerina P., 'Art. 2. Ambito di applicazione' in Giannantonio E., Losano M.G. and Zeno Zencovich V. (eds), *La tutela dei dati personali. Commentario alla L. 675/1996* (2nd edn, Cedam 1999) 21

Chaffee-McClure Z., 'Train in Vain: The Clash Between the RIAA and the Eighth Circuit over Whether the DMCA Subpoena Provision Applies to Peer-to-Peer Networks, and the Need to Steer the DMCA Back on Track with Congressional Intent' [2005] Washburn Law Journal 175

Challis W.S. and Cavoukian A., 'The Case For a U.S. Privacy Commissioner: A Canadian Commissioner's Perspective' [2000] John Marshall Journal of Computer & Information Law 1

Charlesworth A., 'Clash of the Data Titans? US and EU Data Privacy Regulation' [2000] European Public Law 253

Charnetski W.A., Flaherty P. and Robinson J., *The Personal Information Protection and Electronic Documents Act. A Comprehensive Guide* (Canada Law Book 2001)

Choudhry S., 'So What Is the Real Legacy of Oakes? Two Decades of Proportionality Analysis under the Canadian Charter's Section 1' [2006] South Carolina Law Review 501

Cohn C. and Reitman R., 'USA Freedom Act Passes: What We Celebrate, What We Mourn, and Where We Go From Here', *eff.org* (2 June 2015) <www.eff.org/deeplinks/2015/05/usa-freedom-act-passes-what-we-celebrate-what-we-mourn-and-where-we-go-here>

Colangelo G., 'Comunicazioni elettroniche, contenuti digitali e diritto d'autore: commento al Regolamento AGCOM' [2011] Mercato concorrenza regole 576

Collin S.M.H., *Dictionary of Computing* (Peter Collin Publishing 2004)

Colucci A. and Fiore F., *La tutela penale nel diritto d'autore* (Giappichelli 1996)

Comandè G., 'Artt. 11 e 12 (Consenso – Casi di esclusione del consenso)' in Giannantonio E., Losano M.G. and Zeno Zencovich V. (eds), *La tutela dei dati personali. Commentario alla L. 675/1996* (2nd edn, Cedam 1999) 133

Committee on Judiciary, Subcommittee on Patents, Trademarks and Copyright, 86th Cong., 1st Sess., Copyright Law Revision, 'Study No. 3, The Meaning of "'Writings'" in the Copyright Clause of the Constitution', 1956 <http://www.copyright.gov/history/studies/study3. pdf> accessed on 15 February 2017

Comoglio L.P., 'Istruzione e discovery nei giudizi in materia di proprietà industriale' [2000] AIDA 270

Consolo C., *Spiegazioni di diritto processuale civile. Le tutele: di merito, sommarie ed esecutive* (Giappichelli 2010)

Copeland D., 'SOPA, PIPA Votes Indefinitely Delayed', *readwriteweb-.com* (20 January 2012) <http://readwrite.com/2012/01/19/sopa_pipa_votes_indefinitely_delayed/>

Cornfield D.A., 'The Right to Privacy in Canada' [1967] Toronto Faculty of Law Review 103

Cortese B., 'La protezione dei dati di carattere personale nel diritto dell'Unione Europea dopo il Trattato di Lisbona' [2013] Diritto dell'Unione Europea 313

Costa L. and Poullet Y., 'Privacy and the Regulation of 2012' [2012] Computer Law & Security Review 254

Coudert F. and Werkers E., 'In the Aftermath of the Promusicae Case: How to Strike the Balance?' [2008] International Journal of Law and Information Technology 50

Cox P., 'Evolution or Revolution? Norwich Pharmacal Orders over the Last 20 Years' [2004] Trademark World 40

Craig C.J., 'The Changing Face of Fair Dealing in Canadian Copyright Law: A Proposal for Legislative Reform' in Geist M. (ed), *In the Public Interest: The Future of Canadian Copyright Law* (Irwin Law 2005) 437

Craig J.D.R., 'Invasion of Privacy and Charter Values: The Common-Law Tort Awakens' [1997] McGill Law Journal 355

Cunegatti B., 'Tutela amministrativa e giurisdizionale' in Monducci J. and Sartor G. (eds), *Il codice in materia di protezione dei dati personali* (Cedam 2004) 487

D'Agostino G., 'Healing Fair Dealing? A Comparative Copyright Analysis of Canada's Fair Dealing to U.K. Fair Dealing and U.S. Fair Use' [2008] McGill Law Journal 309

D'Orazio R., 'Art. 30. Istituzione del Garante' in Giannantonio E., Losano M.G. and Zeno Zencovich V. (eds), *La tutela dei dati personali. Commentario alla L. 675/1996* (2nd edn, Cedam 1999) 396

Daintith J. and Wright E. (eds), *A Dictionary of Computing* (Oxford University Press 2008)

David R. and Brierley J.E.C., *Major Legal Systems in the World Today* (3rd edn, Stevens and Sons 1985)

De Beer J., 'Copyrights, Federalism, and the Constitutionality of Canada's Private Copying Levy' [2004] McGill Law Journal 735

De Beer J. and Burri M., 'Transatlantic Copyright Comparisons: Making Available via Hyperlinks in the European Union and Canada' [2014] EIPR 95

De Cata M., 'Il caso "Peppermint". Ulteriori riflessioni anche alla luce del caso "Promusicae"' [2008] Rivista di diritto industriale 404

De Cata M., *La responsabilità civile dell'Internet service provider* (Giuffrè 2010)

De Hert P., 'The Right to Protection of Personal Data. Incapable of Autonomous Standing in the Basic EU Constituting Documents?' [2015] Utrecht Journal of International and European Law 1

De Hert P. and Papakonstantinou V., 'The Proposed Data Protection Regulation Replacing Directive 95/46/EC: A Sound System for the Protection of Individuals' [2012] Computer Law & Security Review 130

Di Amato A., 'Musica on-line e tutela penale' [2007] Dir. Internet 329

Di Corinto A., 'Diritti d'autore, deciderà la Corte Costituzionale', *Repubblica.it* (20 October 2014) <www.repubblica.it/economia/affari-e-finanza/2014/10/20/news/diritti_dautore_decider_la_corte_costituzionale-98539164/>

Di Mico P., 'Il rapporto tra diritto di autore e diritto alla riservatezza: recenti sviluppi nella giurisprudenza comunitaria' [2010] Il diritto di autore 1

Dickman J., 'Anonymity and the Demands of Civil Procedure in Music Downloading Lawsuits' [2008] Tulane Law Review 1049

Djavaherian D.K., 'Reno v. ACLU' [1998] Berkeley Technology Law Journal 371

Donner I., 'The Copyright Clause of the U.S. Constitution: Why Did the Framers Include It With Unanimous Approval?' [1992] American Journal of Legal History 361

Dore G., 'And They Lived Happily Ever After UPC Telekabel: A Copyright Fairy Tale or a Genuine Chance to Strike a Fair Balance for

Fundamental Rights?' [2015] Queen Mary Journal of Intellectual Property 226

Drahos P., *A Philosophy of Intellectual Property* (ANU Press 1996)

Drassinower A., 'CCH Canadian Limited v. The Law Society of Upper Canada: A Primer' [2003] 28 Canadian Law Libraries 201

DuBose M.M., 'Criminal Enforcement of Intellectual Property Laws in the Twenty-First Century' [2006] Columbia Journal of Law & Arts 481

Dutcher T.A., 'A Discussion of the Mechanics of the DMCA Safe Harbor and Subpoena Power, as Applied in RIAA v. Verizon Internet Services' [2005] Santa Clara Computer & High Tech Law Journal 493

Dworkin R., *Taking Rights Seriously* (Duckworth 1977)

EFF, 'RIAA v. The People: Four Years Later' (*eff.org*, 2007) <http://w2.eff.org/IP/P2P/riaa_at_four.pdf>

Elkin-Koren N., 'Making Technology Visible: Liability of Internet Service Providers for Peer-to-peer Traffic' [2005] New York University Journal of Legislation and Public Policy 15

Elkin-Koren N., 'After Twenty Years: Revisiting Copyright Liability of Online Intermediaries' in Frankel S. and Gervais D.J. (eds), *The Evolution and Equilibrium of Copyright in the Digital Age* (CUP 2014) 29

Esmail P., 'CCH Canadian Ltd v. Law Society of Upper Canada: Case Comment on a Landmark Copyright Case' [2005] Appeal 13

Evans J.C., 'Hijacking Civil Liberties: The USA PATRIOT Act of 2001' [2002] 33 Loyola University Chicago Law Journal 933

Feiler L., 'The Legality of the Data Retention Directive in Light of the Fundamental Rights to Privacy and Data Protection' [2010] European Journal of Law and Technology <http://ejlt.org//article/view/29/75>

Fenning K., 'The Origin of the Patent and Copyright Clause of the Constitution' [1929] Georgetown Law Journal 109

Fici A. and Pellecchia E., 'Il consenso al trattamento' in Pardolesi R. (ed), *Diritto alla riservatezza e circolazione dei dati personali* (Giuffrè 2003) 499

Ficsor M., *The Law of Copyright and the Internet: the 1996 WIPO Treaties, Their Interpretation, and Implementation* (OUP 2002)

Finn R.L., Wright D. and Friedewald M., 'Seven Types of Privacy' in Gurthwirth S., Leenes R., de Hert P. and Poullet Y. (eds), *European Data Protection: Coming of Age* (Springer Verlag 2013)

Finocchiaro G., 'Anonymity and the Law in Italy' in Kerr I., Lucock C. and Steeves V. (eds), *Lessons from the Identity Trail: Anonymity, Privacy and Identity in a Networked Society* (OUP 2009) 523

Fisher W., 'Theories of Intellectual Property' in Munzer S.R. (ed), *New Essays in the Legal and Political Theory of Property* (CUP 2001) 168

Flaherty D.H., 'On the Utility of Constitutional Rights to Privacy and Data Protection' [1991] Case Western Reserve Law Review 831

Flaherty D.H., *Protecting Privacy in Surveillance Societies* (North Carolina University Press 1992)

Flaherty D.H., 'Reflection on Reform of Federal Privacy Act', Publications of the Office of the Privacy Commissioner of Canada, 2008, 6ff <www.priv.gc.ca/media/2044/pa_ref_df_e.pdf>

Flor R., *Tutela penale ed autotutela tecnologica dei diritti d'autore nell'epoca di Internet. Un'indagine comparata in prospettiva europea ed internazionale* (CEDAM 2010)

Focarelli C., *La privacy* (Il Mulino 2015)

Foglia G., 'La privacy vale più del diritto d'autore: note in materia di filesharing e di sistemi peer-to-peer' [2007] Dir. industriale 598

Franzoni M., 'La responsabilità del provider' [1997] AIDA 248

Freer R.D., *Civil Procedure* (Wolters Kluwer 2009)

Friedenthal J.H., Kane M.K. and Miller A.R., *Civil Procedure* (4th edn, Thomson West 2005)

Froomkin M., 'Anonymity and the Law in the United States' in Kerr I., Lucock C. and Steeves V. (eds), *Lessons from the Identity Trail: Anonymity, Privacy and Identity in a Networked Society* (OUP 2009) 441

Frosini V., 'La protezione della riservatezza nella società informatica' [1981] Informatica e Diritto 5

Frosio G., 'Urban Guerrilla & Piracy Surveillance: Accidental Casualties in Fighting Piracy in P2P Networks in Europe' [2011] Rutgers University Computer & Technology Law Journal 1

Gambini M., *Le responsabilità dell'Internet service provider* (ESI 2006)

Gambini M., 'Diritto d'autore e tutela dei dati personali: una difficile convivenza in Rete' [2009] Giur. it. 509

Gambini M., *Dati personali e internet* (ESI 2008)

Gambino A.M., 'Le utilizzazioni libere: cronaca, critica, parodia' [2002] AIDA 127

Gardini G., *Le regole dell'informazione. Principi giuridici, strumenti, casi* (Mondadori 2009)

Garzia M.A., 'Art. 24. Casi nei quali può essere effettuato il trattamento senza consenso' in Bianca C.M. and Busnelli F.D. (eds), *La protezione dei dati personali: commentario al d.lgs. 30 giugno 2003, n. 196 (Codice della privacy)* (Cedam 2007)

Gasser U. and Schulz W., 'Governance of Online Intermediaries: Observations from a Series of National Case Studies' (2015) The Berkman Center for Internet & Society Research Publication Series 15/5 https://papers.ssrn.com/sol3/papers.cfm?abstract_id=2566364

Geiger C., '"Constitutionalising" Intellectual Property Law? The Influence of Fundamental Rights on Intellectual Property in the European Union' [2006] International Review of Intellectual Property and Competition Law 371

Geiger C., 'Copyright's Fundamental Rights Dimension at EU Level' in Derclaye E. (ed), *Research Handbook on the Future of EU Copyright* (Edward Elgar Publishing 2009) 27

Geiger C., 'Intellectual Property Shall be Protected!? – Article 17 (2) of the Charter of Fundamental Rights of the European Union: a Mysterious Provision with an Unclear Scope' [2009] European Intellectual Property Review 113

Geiger C., 'The Anti-Counterfeiting Trade Agreement and Criminal Enforcement of Intellectual Property: What Consequences for the European Union?' in Rosen J. (ed), *IP Rights at the Crossroads of Trade* (Edward Elgar Publishing 2012) 167

Geiger C., Schönherr F., Stamatoudi I. and Torremans P., 'The Information Society Directive' in Stamatoudi I. and Torremans P. (eds), *EU Copyright Law* (Edward Elgar Publishing 2014) 395

Geist M., *Internet Law in Canada* (Captus Press 2002)

Geist M. (ed), *The Copyright Pentalogy: How the Supreme Court of Canada Shook the Foundations of Canadian Copyright Law* (University of Ottawa Press 2013)

Geist M., 'Privacy Under Attack in Anti-Terror Bill', *The Toronto Star* (24 March 2015) <www.thestar.com/business/2015/03/13/privacy-under-attack-in-anti-terror-bill-geist.htm>

Gellman R., 'Fragmented, Incomplete, and Discontinuous: The Failure of Federal Privacy Regulatory Proposal and Institutions' [1993] Software Law Journal 199

Gellman R., 'A Better Way to Approach Privacy Policy in the United States: Establish a Non-Regulatory Privacy Protection Board' [2003] Hastings Law Journal 1183

Gellman R., 'Fair Information Practices: A Basic History – V. 2.17', 22 December 2016 <http://bobgellman.com/rg-docs/rg-FIPshistory.pdf>

Gervais D.J., 'Transmissions of Music on the Internet: An Analysis of the Copyright Laws of Canada, France, Germany, Japan, the United Kingdom, and the United States' [2001] Vanderbilt Journal of Transnational Law 1363

Gervais D.J., 'Canadian Copyright Law Post-CCH' [2004] Intellectual Property Journal 131

Gervais D.J., 'A Uniquely Canadian Institution: the Copyright Board of Canada' in Gendreau Y. (ed), *An Emerging Intellectual Property Paradigm: Perspectives from Canada* (Edward Elgar Publishing 2008) 199

Gervais D.J., 'Criminal Enforcement in the US and Canada' in Geiger C. (ed), *Criminal Enforcement of Intellectual Property. A Handbook of Contemporary Research* (Edward Elgar Publishing 2012) 276

Gervais D.J., *The TRIPS Agreement. Drafting History and Analysis* (Sweet & Maxwell 2012)

Gervais D.J. (ed), *International Intellectual Property. A Handbook of Contemporary Research* (Edward Elgar Publishing 2015)

Ghidini G., *Profili evolutivi del diritto industriale* (Giuffrè 2015)

Giannaccari A., 'L'ambito di applicazione della legge, l'importazione e l'esportazione dei dati personali' in Pardolesi R. (ed), *Diritto alla riservatezza e circolazione dei dati personali* (Giuffrè 2003) 141

Giannantonio E., Losano M.G. and Zeno Zencovich V. (eds), *La tutela dei dati personali. Commentario alla L. 675/1996* (2nd edn, Cedam 1999)

Giovanella F., 'Effects of Culture on Judicial Decisions. Personal Data Protection vs. Copyright Enforcement' in Caso R. and Giovanella F. (eds), *Balancing Copyright Law in the Digital Age. Comparative Perspectives* (Springer Verlag 2015) 65

Giussani A., 'L'attuazione dell'accordo TRIPs e l'esibizione dei documenti' [2000] AIDA 256

Glatstein B.J., 'Tertiary Copyright Liability' [2004] University of Chicago Law Review 1605

Gleicher N., 'John Doe Subpoenas: Toward a Consistent Legal Standard' [2008] 118 Yale Law Journal 320

Glenn H.P., 'Comparative Legal Families and Comparative Legal Traditions' in Reimann M. and Zimmermann R. (eds), *The Oxford Handbook of Comparative Law* (OUP 2006) 422

Glenn H.P., *Legal Traditions of the World* (OUP 2014)

Goldstein P. and Hugenholtz P.B., *International Copyright. Principles, Law, and Practice* (OUP 2013)

González Fuster G., *The Emergence of Personal Data Protection as a Fundamental Right of the EU* (Springer 2014)

Gorini S. and Niger S., 'Privacy e comunicazioni elettroniche' in Monducci J. and Sartor G. (eds), *Il codice in materia di protezione dei dati personali* (Cedam 2004) 387

Gorski D., 'The Future of the Digital Millennium Copyright Act (DMCA) Subpoena Power on the Internet in Light of Verizon Cases' [2005] Review of Litigation 149

Gosse E.R., 'Recording Industry Association of America v. Diamond Multimedia System, Inc.: The RIAA Could Not Stop the Rio-MP3 Files and the Audio Home Recording Act' [1999] University of San Francisco Law Review 575

Granger M. and Irion K., 'The Court of Justice and the Data Retention Directive in Digital Rights Ireland: Telling Off the EU Legislator and Teaching a Lesson in Privacy and Data Protection [2014] European Law Review 835

Granieri M., 'Il sistema della tutela diritti nella legge 675/1996' in Pardolesi R. (ed), *Diritto alla riservatezza e circolazione dei dati personali* (Giuffrè 2003) 437

Greco P. and Vercellone P., *I diritti sulle opere dell'ingegno* (Utet 1974)

Greenberg A., 'CISA Security Bill: An F For Security But An A+ For Spying', *wired.com* (20 March 2015) <www.wired.com/2015/03/cisa-security-bill-gets-f-security-spying/>

Greenleaf G., 'APEC's Privacy Framework: A New Low Standard' [2005] Privacy Law and Policy Reporter 121

Greenleaf G., 'Five Years of the APEC Privacy Framework: Failure or Promise?' [2009] Computer Law & Security Report 28

Greenleaf G., '"Modernising" Data Protection Convention 108: A Safe Basis for a Global Privacy Treaty?' [2013] Computer Law & Security Review 430

Griffiths J., 'Criminal Liability for Intellectual Property Infringement in Europe – the Role of Fundamental Rights' in Christophe Geiger (ed), *Criminal Enforcement of Intellectual Property. A Handbook of Contemporary Research* (Edward Elgar Publishing 2012) 197

Griffiths J. and McDonagh L., 'Fundamental Rights and European Intellectual Property Law – The Case of Art 17(2) of the EU Charter' in Christophe Geiger (ed), *Constructing European Intellectual Property Achievements and New Perspectives* (Edward Elgar Publishing 2013) 80

Grimm D., 'Proportionality in Canadian and German Constitutional Jurisprudence' [2007] University of Toronto Law Journal 383

Grosso A., 'Legally Speaking: the Promise and Problems of the No Electronic Theft Act' [2000] Communications of the ACM 23

Groussot X., 'Rock the KaZaA: Another Clash of Fundamental Rights' [2008] Common Market Law Review 1745

Guastini R., 'Teoria e ideologia dell'interpretazione costituzionale' [2006] Giurisprudenza costituzionale 743

Guibourg R.A., 'On Alexy's Weighing Formula' in Jan-Reinard Sieckmann (ed), *Legal Reasoning: the Methods of Balancing* (Franz Steiner Verlag 2010) 145

Hagen G.R., '"Modernizing" ISP Copyright Liability' in Geist M. (ed), *From 'Radical Extremism' to 'Balanced Copyright'. Canadian Copyright and the Digital Agenda* (Irwin 2010) 361

Hagen G.R. and Engfield N., 'Canadian Copyright Reform: P2P Sharing, Making Available and the Three-Step Test' [2006] University of Ottawa

Law and Technology Journal 477 <www.uoltj.ca/articles/vol3.2/2006.3.2.uoltj.Hagen.477-516.pdf>

Hagen G.R., Hutchison C., Lametti D., Reynolds G., Scassa T. and Wilkinson M.A., *Canadian Intellectual Property Law. Cases and Materials* (Emond Publishing 2013)

Halpern S.E., 'New Protections for Internet Service Providers: An Analysis of "The Online Copyright Infringement Liability Limitation Act"' [1999] Seton Hall Legislative Journal 359

Halpern S.W., *Copyright Law. Protection of Original Expression* (2nd edn, Carolina Academic Press 2010)

Halpern S.W., Nard C.A. and Port K.L., *Fundamentals of United States Intellectual Property Law: Copyright, Patent, Trademark* (Wolters Kluwer Law 2012)

Hamilton S.N., 'Made in Canada: A Unique Approach to Internet Service Provider Liability and Copyright Infringement' in Geist M. (ed), *In The Public Interest: The Future of Canadian Copyright Law* (Irwin Law 2005) 285

Handa S., *Copyright Law in Canada* (Butterworths 2002)

Hatch G., 'Privacy and Civil Liberties Oversight Board: New Independent Agency Status' (27 August 2012) CRS Reports for Congress, 1–3 <www.fas.org/sgp/crs/misc/RL34385.pdf>

Hayes M.S., 'The Impact of Privacy on Intellectual Property in Canada' [2006] Intellectual Property Journal 67

Hayhurst W.L., 'The Canadian Supreme Court on Copyright: CCH Canadian Ltd. v Law Society of Upper Canada' [2004] Canadian Business Law Journal 134

Hecko Z., 'Data Retention by Internet Service Providers for IP Rights Protection: Bonnier Audio (C-461/10)' [2012] Journal of Intellectual Property Law & Practice 449

Helfer L.R., 'The New Innovation Frontier? Intellectual Property and the European Court of Human Rights' [2008] Harvard International Law Journal 1

Herman S.N., 'The USA PATRIOT Act and the Submajoritarian Fourth Amendment' [2006] Harvard Civil Rights-Civil Liberties Law Review 67

Hijmans H., 'Right to Have Links Removed: Evidence of Effective Data Protection' [2014] Maastricht Journal of European and Comparative Law 555

Hogg, P.W., *Constitutional Law of Canada* (Carswell 2010)

Holland A., Bavitz C., Hermes J., Sellars A., Budish R., Lambert M. and Decoster N., 'Online Intermediaries Case Studies Series: Intermediary Liability in the United States' (2015), The Global Network of Internet

& Society Research Centers <https://publixphere.net/i/noc/page/OI_Case_Study_Intermediary_Liability_in_the_United_States>

Hollander C., 'Norwich Pharmacal Takes Wings' [2009] Civil Justice Quarterly 458

Horten M., *The Copyright Enforcement Enigma. Internet Politics and the 'Telecom Package'* (Palgrave 2012)

Hughes J., 'The Philosophy of Intellectual Property' [1988] Georgetown Law Journal 287

Humphrey J.S., 'Recent Development: Debating the Proposed Peer-to-Peer Piracy Prevention Act: Should Copyright Owners be Permitted to Disrupt Illegal File Trading Over Peer-to-Peer Networks?' [2003] North Carolina Journal of Law & Technology 375

Husa J., 'The Future of Legal Families' [2016] Oxford Handbooks Online: Law 1, <www.oxfordhandbooks.com/view/10.1093/oxfordhb/9780199935352.001.0001/oxfordhb-9780199935352-e-26?print=pdf>

Husovec M., 'Injunctions against Innocent Third Parties: The Case of Website Blocking' [2013] JIPITEC 116 <www.jipitec.eu/issues/jipitec-4-2-2013/3745/husovec.pdf>

Hustinx P., 'The Role of Data Protection Authorities' in Serge Gutwirth S., Poullet Y., de Hert P., de Terwangne C. and Nouwt S. (eds), *Reinventing Data Protection?* (Springer 2009) 131

Imfeld C. and Smith Ekstrand V., 'The Music Industry and the Legislative Development of the Digital Millennium Copyright Act's Online Service Provider Provision' [2005] Communication Law & Policy 291

Jackson V.C., 'Constitutional Law in an Age of Proportionality' [2015] Yale Law Journal 3094

Janger E.J. and Schwartz P.M., 'The Gramm-Leach-Bliley Act, Information Privacy, and the Limits of Default Rules' [2002] Minnesota Law Review 1219

Jones J.D., 'Cybersmears and John Doe: How Far Should First Amendment Protection of Anonymous Internet Speakers Extend?' [2009] First Amendment Law Review 421

Joyce C. and Patterson L.R., 'Copyright in 1791: An Essay Concerning the Founders' View of the Copyright Power Granted to Congress in Article I, Section 8, Clause 8 of the US Constitution' [2003] Emory Law Journal 909

Judge E.F. and Gervais D.J., *Intellectual Property: The Law in Canada* (2nd edn, Carswell 2011)

Julià-Barceló R., 'On-line Intermediary Liability Issues: Comparing E.U. and U.S. Legal Frameworks' [2000] European Intellectual Property Review 105

Julià-Barceló R. and Koelman K.J., 'Intermediary Liability: Intermediary Liability in the E-Commerce Directive: So Far so Good, but It's not Enough' [2000] Computer Law & Security Review 231

Kao A., 'RIAA v. Verizon: Applying the Subpoena Provision of the DMCA' [2004] Berkeley Technology Law Journal 405

Karns J., 'Protecting Individual Online Privacy Rights: Making the Case for a Separately Dedicated, Independent Regulatory Agency' [2000] John Marshall Journal of Computer & Information Law 93

Katyal S.K., 'Privacy v. Piracy' [2004] Yale Journal of Law & Technology 222

Kelly E., 'Senate Approves USA Freedom Act', *usatoday.com* (2 June 2015) <www.usatoday.com/story/news/politics/2015/06/02/patriot-act-usa-freedom-act-senate-vote/28345747/>

Kerr I., 'The Legal Relationship Between Online Service Providers and Users' [2001] Canadian Business Law Journal 419

Kerr I. and Cameron A., 'Nymity, P2P & ISPs: Lessons from BMG Canada Inc. v. John Doe' in Standburg K.J. and Stan Raicu D. (eds), *Privacy and Technologies of Identity: a Cross Disciplinary Conversation* (Springer 2006) 269

Kierkegaard S., 'ECJ Rules on ISP Disclosure of Subscribers' Personal Data in Civil Copyright Cases – Productores de Música de España (Promusicae) v Telefónica de España SAU (Case C-275/06)' [2008] Computer Law & Security Report 268

Kokott J. and Sobotta C., 'The Distinction Between Privacy and Data Protection in the Jurisprudence of the CJEU and the ECtHR' [2013] International Data Privacy Law 222

Koščík M., 'Privacy Issues in Online Service Users' Details Disclosure in the Recent Case-Law. Analysis of Cases Youtube v. Viacom and Promusicae vs. Telefonica' [2009] Masaryk University Journal of Law & Technology 259

Kosta E., *Consent in European Data Protection Law* (Brill Publishing 2013)

Kosta E., 'The Way to Luxemburg: National Court Decisions on the Compatibility of the Data Retention Directive with the Rights to Privacy and Data Protection' [2013] SCRIPTed 339

Kronman A.T., 'The Privacy Exemption to the Freedom of Information Act' [1980] Journal of Legal Studies 731

Kuczerawy A., 'Intermediary Liability & Freedom of Expression: Recent Developments in the EU Notice & Action Initiative' [2015] Computer Law & Security Review 46

Kulk S. and Borgesius F.Z., 'Google Spain v. González: Did the Court Forget About Freedom of Expression?' [2014] European Journal of Risk Regulation 389

Kuner C., *European Data Protection Law. Corporate Compliance and Regulation* (OUP 2007)

Kuner C., 'Data Protection and Rights Protection on the Internet: The Promusicae Judgment of the European Court of Justice' [2008] European Intellectual Property Review 199

LaFrance M., *Copyright Law in a Nutshell* (1st edn, Thomson West 2008)

Lambo L., 'La disciplina sul trattamento dei dati personali: profili esegetici e comparatistici delle definizioni' in Pardolesi R. (ed), *Diritto alla riservatezza e circolazione dei dati personali* (Giuffrè 2003) 59

Landes W.A. and Posner R.A., *The Economic Structure of Intellectual Property Law* (Harvard University Press 2003)

Lane F.S., *American Privacy. The 400-Year History of Our Most Contested Right* (Beacon Press 2010)

LaRoche K. and Pratte G.J., 'The Norwich Pharmacal Principle and Its Utility in Intellectual Property Litigation' [2001] 18 Canadian Intellectual Property Review 117

Larson R.G. and Godfread P.A., 'Bringing John Doe to Court: Procedural Issues in Unmasking Anonymous Internet Defendants' [2009] William Mitchell Law Review 328

Lefranc D., 'Historical Perspective on Criminal Enforcement' in Christophe Geiger (ed), *Criminal Enforcement of Intellectual Property. A Handbook of Contemporary Research* (Edward Elgar Publishing 2012) 101

Leval P.N., 'Toward a Fair Use Standard' [1990] Harvard Law Review 1105

Levin D.R., 'The Future of Copyright Infringement: Metro-Goldwyn-Mayer Studios, Inc., v. Grokster, Ltd.' [2006] St. John's Journal of Legal Comment 271

Lewis E.P., 'Unmasking "Anon12345": Applying an Appropriate Standard When Private Citizens Seek the Identity of Anonymous Internet Defamation Defendants' [2009] University of Illinois Law Review 947

Libeu A., 'What Is a Reasonable Expectation of Privacy?' [1985] Western State University Law Review 849

Lithwick D., 'Bill S-4: An Act to amend the Personal Information Protection and Electronic Documents Act and to make a consequential amendment to another Act, Legislative Summary, Library of the Parliament', Publication n. 41-2-S-4E (11 June 2014) <www.parl.gc.ca/Content/LOP/LegislativeSummaries/41/2/s4-e.pdf>

Litman J., 'The Story of Sony v. Universal Studios: Mary Poppins Meets the Boston Strangler' in Ginsburg J. and Dreyfuss R. (eds), *Intellectual Property Stories* (Foundation Press 2006) 358

Liu J., 'Copyright Injunctions after eBay: An Empirical Study' [2012] Lewis & Clark Law Review 215

Lock T., 'Oops! We Did It Again – the CJEU's Opinion on EU Accession to the ECHR' (VerfBlog, 19 December 2014) <www.verfassungsblog.de/en/oops-das-gutachten-des-eugh-zum-emrk-beitritt-der-eu>

Loo A.W.S., *Peer-to-peer Computing: Building Supercomputers with Web Technologies* (Springer Verlag 2007)

Luizzi V., 'Balancing of Interests in Courts' [1980] Jurimetrics 373

Lundblad N. and Masiello B., 'Opt-in Dystopias' [2010] SCRIPTed 155 <https://script-ed.org/wp-content/uploads/2016/07/7-1-Lundblad.pdf>

Mandrioli C., *Corso di diritto processuale civile. Editio minor*, vol. III (9th edn, Giappichelli 2011) 240

Manta I.D., 'The Puzzle of Criminal Sanctions for Intellectual Property Infringement' [2011] Harvard Journal of Law & Technology 469

Mantelero A., 'L'idea del peer to peer fra tutela della privacy ed enforcement dei diritti d'autore'[2008] Riv. trim. dir. e proc. civile 1481

Mantelero A., 'The EU Proposal for a General Data Protection Regulation and the Roots of the "Right to Be Forgotten"' [2013] Computer law & Security Review 229

Mantelero A., 'Il futuro regolamento EU sui dati personali e la valenza "politica" del caso Google: ricordare e dimenticare nella digital economy' [2014] Dir. Inf. e Informatica 681

Marco Ricolfi and others, 'Osservazioni del Centro Nexa for Internet & Society sullo schema di regolamento di cui all'allegato A) alla delibera n. 452/13/CONS del 25 luglio 2013' (2013) <http://nexa.polito.it/nexacenterfiles/nexa_consultazione_agcom_452_13.pdf>

Margoni T., 'Eccezioni e limitazioni al diritto d'autore' [2011] Giurisprudenza Italiana 1959

Marshall D.S., 'First Impressions of a Troubling Case: Some Comments on CCH Canadian Limited v. The Law Society of Upper Canada' [2000] Canadian Law Libraries 19

Martin B. and Newhall J., 'Criminal Copyright Enforcement Against File Sharing Services' [2013] North Carolina Journal of Law & Technology 101

Martin R.M., 'Freezing the Net: Rejecting a One-Size-Fits-All Standard For Unmasking Anonymous Internet Speakers in Defamation Lawsuits' [2007] 75 University of Cincinnati Law Review 1217

Massey C.R., *American Constitutional Law: Powers and Liberties* (Aspen Publishing 2001)

Mastroianni R., *Diritto internazionale e diritto d'autore* (Giuffrè 1997)

Mastroianni R., 'Proprietà intellettuale e costituzioni europee' [2005] AIDA 11

Matthews D. and Žikovská P., 'The Rise and Fall of the Anti-Counterfeiting Trade Agreement (ACTA): Lessons for the European Union' [2013] IIC 626

Mazzotta M., 'Balancing Act: Finding Consensus on Standards for Unmasking Anonymous Internet Speakers' [2010] Boston College Law Review 833

McCarthy C., 'File-sharing Site eDonkey Kicks It', *CNET News.com* (13 September 2006) <https://www.cnet.com/news/file-sharing-site-edonkey-kicks-it/>

McCullagh D., '"Pirate Act" Raises Civil Rights Concerns' *CNETNews. com* (26 May 2004) <http://news.cnet.com/'Pirate-Act'-raises-civil-rights-concerns/2100-1027_3-5220480.html>

McFadden P.M., 'The Balancing Test' [1988] Boston College Law Review 585

McGarvey S., 'The 2006 EC Data Retention Directive: A Systematic Failure' [2011] Hibernian Law Journal 119

McGoldrick D., 'Developments in the Right to Be Forgotten' [2013] Human Rights Law Review 761

McIsaac B., Shields R. and Klein K., *The Law of Privacy in Canada* (Carswell 2011)

McKeown J.S., *Fox on Canadian Law of Copyright and Industrial Designs* (3rd edn, Carswell 2000)

McKeown J.S., *Canadian Intellectual Property Law and Strategy* (OUP 2010)

McNairn C.H.H., *A Guide to the Personal Information Protection and Electronic Documents Act* (5th edn, LexisNexis 2010)

McNairn C.H.H. and Scott A.K., *Privacy Law in Canada* (Butterworths 2001)

Mclody Yiu, 'A New Prescription for Disclosure: Reformulating the Rule for the Norwich Order' [2007] University of Toronto Faculty Law Review 41

Menell P.S., 'Intellectual Property: General Theories' in Boudewijn Bouckaert and Gerrit de Geest (eds), *Encyclopedia of Law & Economics*, vol 2 (Edward Elgar Publishing 2000) 129

Menell P.S., 'In Search of Copyright's Lost Ark: Interpreting the Right to Distribute in the Internet Age' [2011] Journal of Copyright Society USA 1

Mengoni L., *Ermeneutica e dogmatica giuridica* (Giuffrè 1996)

Mercado Kierkegaard S., 'Safe Harbor Agreement – Boon or Bane?' [2005] 1 Shidler Journal of Law, Commerce, & Technology 10

<https://digital.law.washington.edu/dspace-law/bitstream/handle/1773.
1/362/vol1_no3_art10.pdf?sequence=1>

Merges R.P. and Ginsburg J.G., *Foundations of Intellectual Property* (Foundation Press 2004)

Merges R.P., Menell P.S. and Lemley M.A., *Intellectual Property in the New Technological Age* (5th edn, Aspen 2010)

Min Chee-Fong A., 'Unmasking the John Does of Cyberspace: Surveillance by Private Copyright Owners' [2005] Canadian Journal of Law and Technology 169

Mitchell J., 'Wikipedia: So How Do You Like Censorship?' *readwrite web.com*, (19 January 2012) <http://readwrite.com/2012/01/19/wikipedia_so_how_do_you_like_censorship-2/>

Mitrou L., 'Communications Data Retention: A Pandora's Box for Rights and Liberties?' in Acquisti A., Gritzalis S., Lambrinoudakis C., and di Vimercati S. (eds), *Digital Privacy: Theory, Technologies, and Practices* (Auerbach Publications 2008) 409

Moiny J., 'Are Internet Protocol Addresses Personal Data? The Fight Against Online Copyright Infringement' [2011] Computer Law & Security Review 348

Möller K., 'Balancing and the Structure of Constitutional Rights' [2007] International Journal of Constitutional Law 453

Monaghan H.P., 'Overbreadth' [1981] Supreme Court Review 1

Monateri P.G. (ed), *Methods of Comparative Law* (Edward Elgar Publishing 2012)

Monducci J. and Sartor G. (eds), *Il codice in materia di protezione dei dati personali* (Cedam 2004)

Moore S., 'The Challenge of Internet Anonymity: Protecting John Doe on the Internet' [2009] John Marshall Journal Computer & Information Law 469

Morra M., *I reati in materia di diritto d'autore* (Giuffrè 2008)

Mota S.A., 'Neither Dead nor Forgotten: The Past, Present, and Future of the Communications Decency Act in Light of Reno v. ACLU' [1998] Computer Law Review & Technology Journal 1

Netanel N.W., 'Impose a Noncommercial Use Levy to Allow Free Peer-to-Peer File-sharing' [2003] Harvard Journal of Law & Technology 1

Niger S., 'Il diritto alla protezione dei dati personali' in Monducci J. and Sartor G. (eds), *Il codice in materia di protezione dei dati personali* (Cedam 2004) 7

Niger S., *Le nuove dimensioni della privacy: dal diritto alla riservatezza alla protezione dei dati personali* (Cedam 2006)

Nimmer D., 'Appreciating Legislative History: The Sweet and Sour Spots of the DMCA's Commentary' [2002] Cardozo Law Review 917

Nimmer D., *Copyright: Sacred Test, Technology, and the DMCA* (Kluwer Law International 2003)

Nimmer M.B., 'The Right to Speak from *Times* to *Time*: First Amendment Theory Applied to Libel and Misapplied to Privacy' [1968] California Law Review 935

Nissenbaum H., *Privacy in Context. Technology, Policy, and the Integrity of Social Life* (Stanford University Press 2010)

Nivarra L., 'L'enforcement dei diritti di proprietà intellettuale dopo la Direttiva 2004/48/CE' [2005] Rivista di Diritto Industriale I, 33

Noel W. and Davis L.B.Z., 'Some Constitutional Consideration in Canadian Copyright Law Revision' [1981] Canadian Patent Reporter 17

Note, 'The First Amendment Overbreadth Doctrine' [1970] Harvard Law Review 844

Note, 'Computer Bulletin Board Operator Liability for User Misuse' [1985] Fordham Law Review 439

Note, 'Computer Bulletin Boards and Defamation: Who Should Be Liable? Under What Standard?' [1987] Journal of Law and Technology 121

O'Donoghue C. and Evans T.C., 'EU-US Privacy Shield challenged in the European Court of Justice', Technology Law Dispatch (5 December 2016) <www.technologylawdispatch.com/2016/12/privacy-data-protection/eu-us-privacy-shield-challenged-in-the-european-court-of-justice>

O'Flynn T., 'File-sharing: An Holistic Approach to the Problem' [2006] Entertainment Law Review 218

O'Hare J. and Browne K., *Civil Litigation* (14th edn, Sweet & Maxwell 2009)

Odermatt J., 'A Giant Step Backwards? Opinion 2/13 on the EU's Accession to the European Convention on Human Rights', KU Leuven Working Paper No. 150 – February 2015 <https://ghum.kuleuven.be/ggs/wp150-odermatt.pdf>

Office of the Privacy Commissioner, 'Your Privacy Responsibilities – A Guide for Businesses and Organizations' (2000) <http://publications.gc.ca/collections/Collection/IP34-7-2000E.pdf>

Office of the Privacy Commissioner, 'Governmental Accountability for Personal Information. Reforming the Privacy Act' (June 2006) part III <www.priv.gc.ca/en/privacy-topics/privacy-laws-in-canada/the-privacy-act/pa_r/pa_reform_060605>

Office of the Privacy Commissioner, 'The Case For Reforming The Personal Information Protection and Electronic Documents Act (May

2013)	<www.priv.gc.ca/en/privacy-topics/privacy-laws-in-canada/the-personal-information-protection-and-electronic-documents-act-pipeda/pipeda_r/pipeda_r_201305/>

Office of the Privacy Commissioner, 'Bill S-4, An Act to amend the Personal Information Protection and Electronic Documents Act and to make a consequential amendment to another Act. Submission to the Senate Standing Committee on Transport and Communications' (4 June 2014) <www.priv.gc.ca/en/opc-actions-and-decisions/advice-to-parliament/2015/parl_sub_150212/>

Ohly A., 'European Fundamental Rights and Intellectual Property' in Ohly A. and Pila J. (eds), *The Europeanization of Intellectual Property Law* (OUP 2013) 145

Oliar D., 'Making Sense of the Intellectual Property Clause: Promotion of Progress as a Limitation on Congress's Intellectual Property Power' [2006] Georgetown Law Journal 1771

Olson D.S., 'A Legitimate Interest in Promoting the Progress of Science: Constitutional Constraints on Copyright Laws' [2011] Vanderbilt Law Review 185

Oman R., 'The Copyright Clause: "A Charter For A Living People"' [1987] University of Baltimore Law Review 99

Orofino M., 'L'intervento regolamentare dell'AGCOM in materia di diritto d'autore: profili di criticità formale e sostanziale' in Pizzetti F. (ed), *Il caso del diritto d'autore* (Giappichelli 2013) 123

Ottolia A., 'Proprietà intellettuale e trattamento dei dati personali: riflessioni su privacy "per il sistema" e "nel sistema"' [2010] AIDA 319

Pallaro P., 'La privacy nel settore delle telecomunicazioni: la direttiva comunitaria n. 97/66' [1998] Rivista diritto europeo 541

Pardolesi R., 'Dalla riservatezza alla protezione dei dati personali: una storia di evoluzione e discontinuità' in Pardolesi R. (ed), *Diritto alla riservatezza e circolazione dei dati personali* (Giuffrè 2003)

Pardolesi R. (ed), *Diritto alla riservatezza e circolazione dei dati personali* (Giuffrè 2003)

Pascuzzi G. and Giovanella F., 'Dal diritto alla riservatezza alla computer privacy' in Pascuzzi G. (ed), *Il diritto dell'era digitale* (Il Mulino 2016) 43

Pasetti G., 'Il garante per la protezione dei dati personali' in Monducci J. and Sartor G. (eds), *Il codice in materia di protezione dei dati personali* (Cedam 2004) 513

Pasquino T., *Servizi telematici e criteri di responsabilità* (Giuffrè 2003)

Patry W.F., *The Fair Use Privilege in Copyright Law* (2nd edn, BNA Books 1995)

Patry W.F., *Patry on Fair Use* (West Publishing 2010)

Patterson L.R., 'Understanding the Copyright Clause' [2000] Journal of the Copyright Society of USA 365

Patterson L.R. and Birch S.F., 'A Unified Theory of Copyright' [2009] Houston Law Review 215

Patti S., 'Il consenso dell'interessato al trattamento dei dati personali' [1999] Riv. dir. Civile, part II 455

Peguera M., 'The DMCA Safe Harbors and Their European Counterparts: A Comparative Analysis of Some Common Problems' [2009] Columbia Journal of Law & the Arts 481

Perrin S., Black H., Flaherty D.H. and Rankin T.M., *The Personal Information Protection and Electronic Documents Act: An Annotated Guide* (Irwin Law 2001)

Pino G., *Diritti e interpretazione. Il ragionamento giuridico nello Stato costituzionale* (Il Mulino 2010)

Pino G., 'Conflitto e bilanciamento tra diritti fondamentali. Una mappa dei problemi' [2016] Etica & Politica/Ethics & Politics 1

Posner R.A., *Reflections on Judging* (Harvard University Press 2013)

Pound R., 'A Theory of Social Interests' [1943] Harvard Law Review 1

Power M., *The Law of Privacy* (LexisNexis 2013)

Privacy Protection Study Commission, Personal Privacy In An Information Society, 1977 <www.ncjrs.gov/pdffiles1/Digitization/49602 NCJRS.pdf>

Prosperetti E., 'The Peppermint "Jam": Peer-to-peer Goes to Court in Italy' [2007] Entertainment Law Review 280

Prosser W.L., 'Privacy' [1960] California Law Review 383

Pyun G., 'The 2008 Pro-IP Act: The Inadequacy of the Property Paradigm in Criminal Intellectual Property Law and Its Effect on Prosecutorial Boundaries' [2009] DePaul Journal of Art, Technology & Intellectual Property Law 355

Queally J., '"Fake" Reform: Little to Celebrate as USA Freedom Act Passes House', *commondreams.org* (14 May 2015) <www.common dreams.org/news/2015/05/14/fake-reform-little-celebrate-usa-freedom-act-passes-house>

Rappaport K.L., 'In the Wake of Reno v. ACLU: The Continued Struggle in Western Constitutional Democracies with Internet Censorship and Freedom of Speech Online' [1998] American University International Law Review 765

Raucci M., 'Congress Wants to Give the RIAA Control of Your IPod: How the INDUCE Act Chills Innovation and Abrogates *Sony*' [2005] John Marshall Review of Intellectual Property Law 534

Raynolds K., 'One Verizon, Two Verizon, Three Verizon, More? – A Comment: RIAA v. Verizon and How the DMCA Subpoena Power

Became Powerless' [2005] 23 Cardozo Arts & Entertainment Law Journal 343

Regan P.M., *Legislating Privacy* (University of North Carolina Press 1995)

Reimann M. and Zimmermann R. (eds), *The Oxford Handbook of Comparative Law* (OUP 2006)

Reinbothe J., 'The EU Enforcement Directive 2004/48/EC as a Tool for Copyright Enforcement' in Stamatoudi I.A., *Copyright Enforcement and the Internet* (Kluwer 2010) 3

Reinbothe J. and von Lewinski S., *The WIPO Treaties on Copyright. A Commentary on the WCT, the WPPT, and the BTAP* (OUP 2015)

Rescigno P., 'Personalità (diritti della)', *Enciclopedia Giuridica Treccani*, vol. XXIII (1990)

Resta G., 'Anonimato, responsabilità e identificazione: prospettive di diritto comparato' [2014] Dir. Inf. 171

Resta G., 'Il diritto alla protezione dei dati personali' in Cardarelli F., Sica S. and Zeno-Zencovich V. (eds), *Il codice dei dati personali: temi e problemi* (Giuffrè 2004) 11

Resta G., 'Identità personale e identità digitale' [2007] Dir. informazione e informatica 522

Resta G., 'Personnalité, Persönlichkeit, Personality. Comparative Perspectives on the Protection of Identity in Private Law' [2014] European Journal of Comparative Law & Governance 215

Ricci S. and Vaciago G., 'Sistemi peer to peer: rilevanza penale delle condotte in violazione dei diritti d'autore e diritti connessi' [2008] Dir. Internet 280

Riccio G.M., *La responsabilità civile degli Internet providers* (Giappichelli 2002)

Riccio G.M., 'La responsabilità degli Internet providers nel d.lgs. n. 70/03' [2003] Danno e Resp. 1157

Rice C.M., 'Meet John Doe: It Is Time For Federal Civil Procedure to Recognize John Doe Parties' [1996] University of Pittsburgh Law Review 883

Ricketson S., *The Berne Convention of the Protection of Literary and Artistic Works: 1886–1986* (Longman 1987)

Ricketson S. and Ginsburg J., *The Berne Convention for the Protection of Literary and Artistic Works: 1886–1986* (OUP 2006)

Ricolfi M., 'Osservazioni del Centro NEXA for Internet & Society sullo schema di regolamento in materia di tutela del diritto d'autore sulle reti di comunicazione elettronica di cui all'allegato A) alla delibera n. 398/11/cons del 6 luglio 2011' (2011) <http://nexa.polito.it/nexafiles/Nexa_consultazione_398-11.pdf>

Ricolfi M. and others, 'Osservazioni del Centro NEXA for Internet & Società sulle proposte di intervento di cui all'allegato b) alla delibera n. 668/10/cons del 17 dicembre 2010 "Lineamenti di provvedimento concernente l'esercizio delle competenze dell'autorità nell'attività di tutela del diritto d'autore sulle reti di comunicazione elettronica"' (2011) <http://nexa.polito.it/nexafiles/Nexa-Consultazione%20AG COM%20definitivo-marzo2011.pdf>

Rodotà S., *Elaboratori elettronici e controllo sociale* (Il Mulino 1973)

Rodotà S., 'Persona, riservatezza, identità. Prime note sistematiche sulla protezione dei dati personali' [1997] Riv. critica diritto privato 599

Rodotà S., *Repertorio di fine secolo* (Laterza 1999)

Rodotà S., 'Diritto, scienza, tecnologia: modelli e scelte di regolamentazione' [2004] Riv. critica dir. privato 368

Rodotà S., 'Tra diritti fondamentali ed elasticità della normativa: il nuovo codice sulla privacy' [2004] Europa e Dir. Privato 1

Roffe P. and Seuba X. (eds), *The ACTA and the Plurilateral Enforcement Agenda: Genesis and Aftermath* (CUP 2014)

Rosati E., '2015: The Year of Blocking Injunctions?' [2015] Journal of Intellectual Property Law & Practice 147

Rotenberg M., 'In Support of a Data Protection Board in the United States' [1991] Government Information Quarterly 79

Ryan T.J., 'Infringement.com: RIAA v. Napster and the War Against Online Music Piracy' [2002] Arizona Law Review 495

Sacco R., 'Legal Formants: A Dynamic Approach to Comparative Law (Installment I of II) [1991] American Journal of Comparative Law 1

Sacco R., 'Legal Formants: A Dynamic Approach to Comparative Law (Installment II of II) [1991] American Journal of Comparative Law 343

Sag M., 'Copyright Trolling, An Empirical Study' [2015] Iowa Law Review 1105

Sammarco P., 'Alla ricerca del giusto equilibrio da parte della Corte di Giustizia UE nel confronto tra diritti fondamentali nei casi di impiego di sistemi tecnici di filtraggio' [2012] Diritto dell'informazione e dell'informatica 297

Sanders R., 'Will Professor Nimmer's Change of Heart on File-sharing Matter?' [2013] Vanderbilt Journal of Entertainment and Technology Law 857

Saperstein L., 'Copyrights, Criminal Sanctions and Economic Rents: Applying the Rent Seeking Model to the Criminal Law Formulation Process' [1997] Journal of Criminal Law and Criminology 1470

Sarti D., 'Privacy e proprietà intellettuale: la Corte di giustizia in mezzo al guado' [2008] AIDA 435

Sartor G., 'The Right to Be Forgotten: Balancing Interests in the Flux of Time' [2015] International Journal of Law and Information Technology 72

Sartor G., 'The Right to Be Forgotten in the Draft Data Protection Regulation' [2015] International Data Privacy Law 64

Scaccia G., 'Il bilanciamento degli interessi come tecnica di controllo costituzionale' [1998] Giurisprudenza Costituzionale 3953

Scaccia G., 'Il bilanciamento degli interessi in materia di proprietà intellettuale' [2005] AIDA – Annali Italiani Diritto D'Autore 198

Scagliarini S., 'La Corte di Giustizia bilancia diritto alla vita privata e lotta alla criminalità: alcuni pro e alcuni contra' [2014] Dir. Info e info 873

Scassa T., 'Recalibrating Copyright Law? A Comment on the Supreme Court of Canada's Decision in CCH Canadian Ltd. v. Law Society of Upper Canada' [2004] Canadian Journal of Law and Technology 89

Scassa T. and Deturbide M., *Electronic Commerce and Internet Law in Canada* (2nd edn, CCH 2012)

Schauer F., 'The Exceptional First Amendment' in Ignatieff M. (ed), *American Exceptionalism and Human Rights* (Princeton University Press 2005) 29

Schlesinger M., 'Legal Issues in Peer-to-peer File-sharing, Focusing on the Right to Make Available' in Alain Strowel (ed), *Peer-to-peer File-sharing and Secondary Liability in Copyright Law* (Edward Elgar Publishing 2009) 43

Schlink B., 'Proportionality (1)' in Michel Rosenfeld and András Sajó (eds), *The Oxford Handbook of Comparative Constitutional Law* (OUP 2012) 725

Schultz J.M., 'The False Origins of the Induce Act' [2005] Northern Kentucky Law Review 527

Schwartz P.M., 'The EU–US Privacy Collision: A Turn to Institutions and Procedures' [2013] Harvard Law Review 1966

Schwartz P.M. and Solove D.J., 'Reconciling Personal Information in the United States and European Union' [2014] California Law Review 877

Scorza G., 'Il conflitto tra copyright e privacy nelle reti Peer to Peer: il caso Peppermint – Profili di diritto interno' [2007] Dir. Internet 465

Seltzer L.E., *Exemptions and Fair Use in Copyright: the Exclusive Rights Tensions in the 1976 Copyright Act* (Harvard University Press 1978)

Sganga C., 'EU Copyright Law Between Property and Fundamental Rights: A Proposal to Connect the Dots' in Caso R. and Giovanella F. (eds), *Balancing Copyright Law in the Digital Age. Comparative Perspectives* (Springer 2015) 1

Shayesteh S.A., 'High-Speed Chase on the Information Superhighway: The Evolution of Criminal Liability for Internet Piracy' [1999] Loyola of Los Angeles Law Review 183

Sica S., 'Sicurezza e riservatezza nelle telecomunicazioni: il d.lgs. n. 171/98 nel "sistema" della protezione dei dati personali' [1998] Dir. informazione e informatica 776

Sieckmann J., 'Balancing, Optimisation, and Alexy's "Weight Formula"' in Jan-Reinard Sieckmann (ed), *Legal Reasoning: the Methods of Balancing* (Franz Steiner Verlag 2010) 101

Singer M.A., 'The Failure of the PRO-IP Act in a Consumer-Empowered Era of Information Production' [2009] Suffolk University Law Review 185

Sirotti Gaudenzi A., 'Violazione della proprietà intellettuale: non è ammesso il provvedimento di discovery in caso di peer to peer' [2008] Giur. it. 1742

Sirotti Gaudenzi A. (ed), *Proprietà intellettuale e diritto della concorrenza. La tutela dei diritti di privativa*, vol 2 (Utet 2010)

Sirotti Gaudenzi A., *Il nuovo diritto d'autore* (1st edn, Maggioli 2012)

Smith Ekstrand V., 'Unmasking Jane and John Doe: Online Anonymity and the First Amendment' [2003] Communication Law & Policy 405

Solove D.J., 'A Taxonomy of Privacy' [2006] University of Pennsylvania Law Review 477

Solove D.J., *Understanding Privacy* (Harvard University Press 2008)

Solove D.J., 'Privacy Self-Management and the Consent Dilemma' [2013] Harvard Law Review 1880

Solove D.J., 'Surveillance Law in Dire Need of Reform: The Promise of the LEADS Act' (17 March 2015) *linkedin.com* <www.linkedin.com/pulse/surveillance-law-dire-need-reform-promise-leads-act-daniel-solove>

Solove D.J. and Rotenberg M., *Information Privacy Law* (Aspen Publishers 2003)

Solove D.J. and Schwartz P.M., *Privacy, Information, and Technology* (Aspen Publishers 2009)

Solove D.J. and Schwartz P.M., *Information Privacy Law* (5th edn, Aspen Publishers 2015)

Soma J.T. and Rynerson S.D., *Privacy Law in a Nutshell* (1st edn, West Publishing 2008)

Sovern J., 'Opting In, Opting Out, or No Options At All: The Fight for Control of Personal Information' [1999] Washington Law Review 1033

Spedicato G., 'Postille in tema di responsabilità extracontrattuale del provider alla luce del recente Decreto Legislativo n. 70/2003' [2003] Ciberspazio e diritto 155

Spedicato G., '*Online Exhaustion and the Boundaries of Interpretation*' in Caso R. and Giovanella F. (eds), *Balancing Copyright Law in the Digital Age. Comparative Perspectives* (Springer 2015) 27

Spina A., 'Risk Regulation of Big Data: Has the Time Arrived for a Paradigm Shift in EU Data Protection Law?' [2014] European Journal of Risk Regulation 248

Stamatoudi I.A., 'Data Protection, Secrecy of Communications and Copyright: Conflicts and Convergences – The Example of Promusicae v. Telefonica' in Stamatoudi I.A., *Copyright Enforcement and the Internet* (Kluwer 2010) 199

Stamatoudi I.A., 'The Enforcement Directive' in Stamatoudi I.A. and Torremans P. (eds), *EU Copyright Law* (Edward Elgar Publishing 2014) 528

Staten M.E. and Cate F.H., 'The Impact of Opt-in Privacy Rules on Retail Credit Markets: A Case Study of MBNA' [2003] Duke Law Journal 745

Stazi A., 'Il regolamento di cui alla delibera n. 680/13/CONS dell'AGCcom per la tutela del diritto d'autore in rete' [2014] Riv. Dir. Industriale 142

Steinmetz R. and Wehrle K., *Peer-to-peer Systems and Applications* (Springer Verlag 2005)

Stone Sweet A., *The Judicial Construction of Europe* (OUP 2004)

Stone Sweet A. and Mathews J., 'Proportionality Balancing and Global Constitutionalism' [2008] Columbia Journal of Transnational Law 72

Strowel A., 'Introduction: Peer-to-peer File-sharing and Secondary Liability in Copyright Law' in Strowel A. (ed), *Peer-to-peer File-sharing and Secondary Liability in Copyright Law* (Edward Elgar Publishing 2009)

Sullivan K.M. and Gunther G., *Constitutional Law* (16th edn, Aspen Publishing 2007)

Sullivan K.M. and Gunther G., *First Amendment Law* (3rd edn, Foundation Press 2007)

Synodinou E., 'Intermediaries' Liability for Online Copyright Infringement in the EU: Evolutions and Confusions' [2015] Computer Law & Security Review 57

Tabatabai F., 'A Tale of Two Countries: Canada's Response to Peer-to-Peer Crisis and What It Means for the United States' [2005] 73 Fordham Law Review 2321

Taekama D., 'Journalist Group and Civil Liberties Association Start Constitutional Challenge to Anti-terrorism Bill C-51', *The Toronto Star* (21 July 2015) <www.thestar.com/news/gta/2015/07/21/journalist-group-and-civil-liberties-association-start-constitutional-challenge-to-anti-terrorism-bill-c-51.html>

Terracina D., *La tutela penale del diritto d'autore e dei diritti connessi* (Giappichelli 2006)

Terracina D., 'Lucro e profitto nella giurisprudenza della Corte di Cassazione in materia di violazione del diritto d'autore e dei diritti connessi' [2007] Dir. Internet 259

Tien L., 'Senate Intelligence Committee Advances Terrible "C–y–b–e–r– s–e–c–u–r–i–t–y–" B–i–l–l– Surveillance Bill in Secret Session', *eff.org* (19 March 2015) <www.eff.org/deeplinks/2015/03/senate-intelligence-committee-advances-terrible-cybersecurity-bill-surveillance>

Tolone A., 'La disciplina degli obblighi di conservazione dei dati telematici da parte dei providers' [2008] Riv. informazione e informatica 856

Toren P.J., *Intellectual Property and Computer Crimes* (Law Journal Press 2014)

Tribe L.H., *American Constitutional Law* (Foundation Press 1978)

Trotta A., 'Il traffico telefonico fra la tutela del diritto d'autore e quella della privacy' [2008] Dir. Industriale 76

Tunick M., *Balancing Privacy and Free Speech. Unwanted Attention in the Age of Social Media* (Routledge 2015)

U.S. Copyright Office, 'Summary of The Digital Millennium Copyright Act of 1998', 1998 <www.copyright.gov/legislation/dmca.pdf>

U.S. Department of Health, Education & Welfare, Secretary's Advisory Committee On Automated Personal Data Systems, 'Records, Computers, and The Rights of Citizens' (1973) <www.justice.gov/opcl/docs/rec-com-rights.pdf>

U.S. National Commission on Terrorist Attacks Upon the United States, 'The 9/11 Commission Report' (2004) <http://govinfo.library.unt.edu/911/report/911Report.pdf>

Ubertazzi L.C. (ed), *Il regolamento Agcom sul diritto d'autore* (Giappichelli 2014)

Ubertazzi L.C., 'Proprietà intellettuale e privacy' [2014] AIDA 435

Ubertazzi L.C., *Commentario breve alle leggi su proprietà intellettuale e concorrenza* (Cedam 2016)

Vaver D., *Copyright Law* (Irwin Law 2000)

Vaver D., *Intellectual Property Law. Copyright, Patent, Trademark* (2nd edn, Irwin Law 2011)

Verbiest T., Spindler G., Riccio G.M., Van der Perre A. and others, 'Study on the Liability of Internet Intermediaries' (2007) <http://ec.europa.eu/internal_market/e-commerce/docs/study/liability/final_report_en.pdf>

Vespaziani A., *Interpretazioni del bilanciamento dei diritti fondamentali* (Cedam 2002)

Vijayan J., 'Protests Against SOPA, PIPA Go Viral. Google, Wikipedia, Reddit, BoingBoing Plan Unprecedented INTERNET "Strike" Wednesday' *Networkedworld.com* (17 January 2012) <http://www.network world.com/article/2184877/data-center/protests-against-sopa–pipa-go-viral.html>

von Lewinski S., *International Copyright Law and Policy* (OUP 2008)

Walker J. and Sossin L., *Civil Litigation* (Irwin Publishing 2010)

Walter M. and Gobel D., 'Enforcement Directive' in Walter M. and Von Lewinski S. (eds), *European Copyright Law* (OUP 2010) 1993

Walter M. and Von Lewinski S., 'Information Society Directive' in Walter M. and Von Lewinski S. (eds), *European Copyright Law* (OUP 2010) 921

Walterscheid E.C., 'To Promote the Progress of Science and Useful Arts: The Background and Origin of the Intellectual Property Clause of the United States Constitution' [1994] Journal of Intellectual Property Law 1

Walterscheid E.C., *The Nature of the Intellectual Property Clause: A Study in Historical Perspective* (William S Hein & Co 2002)

Walterscheid E.C., 'Musings on the Copyright Power: A Critique of Eldred v. Ashcroft' [2004] Albany Law Journal of Science & Technology 309

Warren S.D. and Brandeis L., 'The Right to Privacy' [1890] 4 Harvard Law Review 193

Weiner R., 'Never Heard of the Privacy and Civil Liberties Oversight Board? You Should', *Washingtonpost.com* (10 June 2013) <www.washingtonpost.com/blogs/the-fix/wp/2013/06/10/never-heard-of-the-privacy-and-civil-liberties-oversight-board-you-should/>

Weiss M.A. and Archick K., 'U.S.-EU Data Privacy: From Safe Harbor to Privacy Shield', Congressional Research Service, 2016 <www.fas.org/sgp/crs/misc/R44257.pdf>

Westin A.F., *Privacy and Freedom* (Atheneum 1967)

White House Report, 'Consumer Data Privacy In a Networked World: A Framework for Protecting Privacy and Promoting Innovation in the Global Digital Economy' [2013] Journal of Privacy and Confidentiality 95 <http://repository.cmu.edu/jpc/vol4/iss2/5/>

Whitman J.Q., 'The Two Western Cultures of Privacy: Dignity versus Liberty' [2004] Yale Law Journal 1153

Wigmore J.H., *Evidence in Trials at Common Law*, vol 8 (Wolters Kluwer 1961)

Wildpaner C., *The U.S. Digital Millennium Copyright Act. A Challenge for Fair Use in the Digital Age* (Medien und Recht 2004)

Wilkins R.G., 'Defining the "Reasonable Expectation of Privacy": An Emerging Tripartite Analysis' [1987] Vanderbilt Law Review 1077

Wilkinson M.A., 'Battleground Between New and Old Orders: Control Conflicts Between Copyright and Personal Data Protection' in Gendreau Y. (ed), *An Emerging Intellectual Property Paradigm: Perspectives from Canada* (Edward Elgar Publishing 2008) 227

Wimmer K., 'Updating the Electronic Communications Privacy Act: An Essential Legislative Goal for Media Companies and the Public They Serve', mediainstitute.org (March 2015) <www.mediainstitute.org/PDFs/Policy%20Views%206%20LEADS%2031815.pdf>

Wright D. and De Hert P. (eds), *Privacy Impact Assessment* (Springer 2012)

Wu T., 'When Code Isn't Law' [2003] Virginia Law Review 679

Yu M.A., Lehrer R. and Roland W., 'Intellectual Property Crimes' [2008] American Criminal Law Review 665

Zeno-Zencovich V., 'Personalità (diritti della)', *Digesto discipline privatistiche, Sezione civile*, vol. XIII (1995), 430

Zeno-Zencovich V., 'La pretesa estensione alla telematica del regime della stampa: note critiche' [1998] Dir. Informazione e informatica 15

Zittrain J., 'A History of Online Gatekeeping' [2006] Harvard Journal of Law & Technology 253 <https://dash.harvard.edu/handle/1/4455491>

Zucca L., 'Conflicts of Fundamental Rights as Constitutional Dilemmas' in Brems E. (ed), *Conflicts Between Fundamental Rights* (Intersentia 2008) 19

Zuckerman A., *Zuckerman on Civil Procedure* (1st edn, Sweet & Maxwell 2006)

Zweigert K. and Kötz H., *An Introduction to Comparative Law* (3rd edn, OUP 1998)

Index